Teaching About
RELIGION
in the SOCIAL STUDIES
CLASSROOM

Edited by Charles C. Haynes

NCSS
BULLETIN 117

National Council for the Social Studies

8555 Sixteenth Street · Suite 500 · Silver Spring, Maryland 20910

NCSS BOARD OF DIRECTORS, 2018-2019

ISBN: 978-0-87986-113-1

© Copyright 2019 National Council for the Social Studies. All rights reserved.
Printed in the United States of America · First printing, February 2019

5 4 3 2 1

Table of Contents

PART III Approaches to Teaching about Religious Traditions

PART IV Appendices

Why Religious Literacy Matters

CHARLES C. HAYNES

To understand the urgent need for religious literacy, we need look no further than the daily headlines. At the core of the world's most dangerous conflicts are deep and seemingly intractable religious and ethnic divisions. Close to three fourths of the world's population now live in countries with high restrictions on religious freedom.[7] Even in the United States, home to the world's boldest experiment in religious freedom, religious differences and religious illiteracy contribute to bitter culture wars, growing Islamophobia, and resurgent anti-Semitism.

The lesson of world events and domestic division is simple, but profound: ignorance and fear breed hate and violence. Religious literacy matters because peaceful co-existence and religious freedom matter. Absent religious literacy, people are unprepared to live with one another across deep differences—and unlikely to respect the rights of others to practice a religion they do not understand. No arrangement in religious freedom in a religiously diverse society can long endure without religious literacy.

It is unfortunate and dangerous that many public schools are unprepared to take religion seriously a time when schools most need to teach about religions and beliefs. This is due, in large measure, to the historic failure to get religion right in public education. In the 19th century, a form of generalized Protestantism—the de-facto established religion of early America—dominated the ethos and practices of schools. As demographics changed, nativist fears shaped educational policy. Religion exited the curriculum (to prevent Catholicism from taking hold) but remained in daily prayers and Bible reading "without comment" consistent with the will of the Protestant majority.

By the time the U.S. Supreme Court finally struck down as unconstitutional state-sponsored religious practices in the 1960s, much of the curriculum rarely mentioned religion. Vestiges of the bygone Protestant era were retained in some schools,

particularly in the South, where one religion continued to be imposed through teacher-led prayer and other practices. Many other schools, out of confusion over Supreme Court rulings or fear of controversy, attempted to ban the expression or discussion of religion altogether. In these religion-free zones, students were often unconstitutionally prevented from expressing their faith during the school day.

THE NEW CONSENSUS

The tide began to turn in the 1980s. Litigation, including lawsuits over the absence of religion in textbooks, led to a national re-thinking of the role of religion in public schools. In the late 1980s, I joined with Oliver Thomas, then of the Baptist Joint Committee for Religious Liberty, to convene a broad coalition of 17 education, civil liberties and religious groups to seek common ground on religious studies in the curriculum and student religious expression in public schools.

Our initial consensus document—the first of nine that would be published over the next two decades— offered a shared vision of how to teach about religion in the public school curriculum under the First Amendment to the U.S. Constitution. For the first time in U.S. history, groups ranging from the National Association of Evangelicals to Americans United for Separation of Church and State joined with NCSS, teacher's unions, the National

School Boards Association and many others to offer guidance on how to address religion in the classroom. The agreement read in part:

> Because religion plays a significant role in history and society, study about religion is essential to understanding both the nation and the world. Omission of facts about religion can give students the false impression that the religious life of humankind is insignificant or unimportant. Failure to understand even the basic symbols, practices and concepts of the various religions makes much of history, literature, art, and contemporary life unintelligible.

This first agreement on religion in the curriculum was followed by a series of additional common ground documents, including "A Teacher's Guide to Religion in Public Schools," "Public Schools and Religious Communities," and "The Bible and Public Schools" among others. The widest distribution of the early guidelines came in 2000 when the U.S. Department of Education during the Clinton administration disseminated a packet of four of these guidelines to every public school in the country.

The consensus reached in the common ground documents continues to give public school educators a constitutional safe harbor for getting religion right. If implemented, schools are able to go beyond the failed policies and practices that either imposed religion or banished religion and create what could be called a First Amendment public school—a school that neither inculcates nor inhibits religion, but treats religions and beliefs with fairness and respect.

A First Amendment school recognizes that the academic study of religion is not only constitutional; it is an essential part of a good education. In such a school, teachers teach about religions and beliefs objectively or neutrally. The aim is to educate students about a variety of religious and non-religious traditions, not to indoctrinate them for or against any religion or belief. Teachers are careful to neither inculcate nor denigrate religion, while recognizing the right of students to express personal religious or non-religious views in class or as part of a written assignment or activity as long as the speech is relevant to the discussion and meets the academic requirements.

THE CURRENT CHALLENGE

Study about religions and beliefs in public schools has come a long way since the first consensus statements were disseminated almost thirty years ago. State social studies standards, for example, are now fairly generous to study about religion, in stark contrast to the virtual silence about religion in state curriculum frameworks of the 1980s. As a result, many history textbooks have expanded treatment of religions beyond the bare mention of religion typical of earlier editions.

Despite this progress, many policy makers and administrators continue to avoid religion out of fear of controversy, animus created by the culture wars, indifference to the need for religious literacy, or all of the above. As a consequence, textbook treatment of religion remains largely superficial— and far too many teachers remain reluctant to take religion seriously in the study of history, economics, government and other subjects where religious concepts, practices and issues need to be addressed in some depth.

Of course, it does not help the cause of religious literacy that religion in public schools continues to spark controversy and litigation. Although court battles over religious studies in public schools are rare, a few bad stories have a chilling effect on administrators and teachers across the country. Conflicts in Florida and Texas over the treatment of Islam in textbooks, a fight several years ago about the portrayal of Hinduism in California textbooks, and sporadic legal battles over Bible electives reinforce the fears that many risk-adverse educators have about tackling religion in the classroom.

To get beyond the reluctance and fear, public education must begin to take religion seriously in the curriculum. This will require significant reforms in pre-service and in-service teacher education to ensure that social studies teachers have both adequate preparation and reliable academic resources to teach about religions and beliefs in ways that are constitutionally and educationally sound.

While we advocate for these reforms, the essays collected in these pages–written by some of the nation's leading scholars and teachers in the field– can serve as a First Amendment roadmap for social studies teachers committed to enriching study about religions and beliefs.

Religious literacy is a critical mission for public schools because religious literacy is a critical mission for citizenship in a pluralistic democracy. Can we prevent hate, discrimination and violence by educating for religious literacy and religious liberty? We must.

NOTES

1. See the Pew Research Center report, "Trends in Global Restrictions on Religion," June 13, 2016, at http://www.pewforum.org/2016/06/23/trends-in-global-restrictions-on-religion/

PART I

The First Amendment and Education about Religion in Schools

CHAPTER ONE

Teaching about Religion in Public Schools

BENJAMIN MARCUS

Religion is a third rail in public schools. Legal battles about religion and education shock educators around the country who are fearful of provoking new lawsuits. Teachers' anxieties are understandable: issues related to religion and education account for more than two-thirds of the Establishment Clause cases brought before the Supreme Court of the United States.[1] Widespread misinformation about key legal rulings strengthens a culture of fear and avoidance. According to a major survey conducted in 2010 by the Pew Research Center, sixty-seven percent of Americans say incorrectly that the law prohibits public school teachers from reading the Bible as literature, and fifty-one percent of Americans say inaccurately that the Supreme Court has barred public schools from offering world religions courses.[2] Many educators lack the training to dispel the general public's legal illiteracy about religious literacy education because teaching institutions do not provide reliable information about the First Amendment or quality instruction in religious studies.

This book acknowledges educators' fears while affirming that religious literacy education can empower students to take informed action as guardians of our First Amendment rights. Religious literacy education is both constitutional and necessary for preparing young citizens to engage with an increasingly diverse country and globalized world. Teachers who follow the proper legal framework, informed by the theories and methods of religious studies, can protect themselves from legal challenges by parents or other members of the community. This chapter reviews key Supreme Court cases in order to sketch the boundaries of religious literacy education before suggesting a specific pedagogical framework for teaching about religion in the public school classroom.

Public schools cannot prepare students for college, careers, or civic life without teaching about religion. As Harvard scholar Diane L. Moore eloquently states in her book *Overcoming Religious Illiteracy*,

> Religious beliefs, expressions, and worldviews have inspired the full spectrum of human agency in artistic, philosophical, ethical, political, scientific, and economic arenas.[3]

Teachers who remove religion from any area of social studies make it impossible to understand the complex interplay of forces that shape our world. Students who cannot describe religion's influence on all aspects of life are ill-prepared for college-level courses, which require both content knowledge about religion and the critical thinking skills necessary to parse the elements of culture. Young professionals entering the workforce need to understand the role of religion in private and public life if they are to work with—and potentially within—religious communities to improve society as leaders in government, business, non-profits, education, and more. And as citizens of a religiously diverse democracy, young Americans must learn about religion in order to develop a stronger commitment to religious liberty, a cornerstone of our democracy. Religious literacy might not alone end religious bigotry or violence, but it can reduce discrimination and develop a stronger commitment to protect the rights of minorities.[4] Despite all of the benefits of religious literacy education, many teachers still hesitate to talk about religion in the classroom without clear legal guidelines.

Put simply: teachers may constitutionally teach about religion in public schools from an academic perspective, but they may not teach religion from a devotional perspective.[5] Moore writes, "First and foremost, scholars highlight the difference between the devotional expression of particular religious belief as normative, and the non-sectarian study of religion that presumes the religious legitimacy of diverse normative claims."[6] Teachers cannot legally "teach religion" in the way that a religious leader might in Sunday school with the children of parishioners. They may not advance or inhibit religion or non-religion. Nor may teachers ask students to accept, reject, or enact specific religious beliefs or behaviors.

Teachers can more fully differentiate between the academic and devotional approaches—teaching religion versus teaching about religion—by following the guidance found in *A Teacher's Guide to Religion in the Public Schools*, quoted below. A coalition of seventeen religious and educational organizations including the National Council for the Social Studies endorsed a version of the following statement, which the Department of Education distributed to all public schools in the nation in 2000:

- The school's approach to religion is academic, not devotional.

- The school strives for student awareness of religions, but does not press for student acceptance of any religion.

- The school sponsors study about religion, not the practice of religion.

- The school may expose students to a diversity of religious views, but may not impose any particular view.

- The school educates about all religions; it does not promote or denigrate religion.

- The school informs students about various beliefs; it does not seek to make students conform to any particular belief.[7]

These consensus guidelines outline some of the norms of religious studies, an interdisciplinary field that analyzes the variety of religious identities within and between religions without making a theological, evaluative claim about orthodoxy or orthopraxy. Teachers who utilize a religious studies approach in the classroom will remain within the legal boundaries set by Supreme Court jurisprudence over the last seventy years.

Public school educators need a basic understanding of Supreme Court jurisprudence in the 20th century to recognize how and why the religious studies and legal frameworks reinforce one another. Teachers' legal education should emphasize 20th century jurisprudence because in the 1920s, the Supreme Court began to apply portions of the Bill of Rights to the states, not just the federal government, through a process called "incorporation." By the 1940s the Court began to hear its first cases about the First Amendment—specifically, the establishment and free exercise of religion—in public schools.[8] The Supreme Court's landmark decisions in *McCollum v. Board of Education* (1948) and *Zorach v. Clauson* (1952) were among the first to affirm that public schools may not "teach religion" from a devotional, sectarian perspective. In fact, public schools may not allow guest speakers to teach religion on school grounds during normal school hours, even if the speakers are not paid or employed by the school. In *McCollum*, the Court struck down a religious education program in Illinois because devotional instruction took place on public school grounds during regular school hours. Justice Black wrote in the majority opinion in *McCollum* that the release time program on school grounds resulted in the use of "tax-supported property for religious instruction and the close cooperation between school authorities and the religious council in promoting religious education."[9] However, four short years later in *Zorach*, the Court ruled that schools could release students during normal school hours to attend sectarian religious education or services, as long as students left school property for those programs. *Zorach* and *McCollum* affirmed a key point: programs designed to teach religion from a devotional perspective belong in the home and community, not the public school.

Engel v. Vitale (1962) and *Abington Township School District v. Schempp* (1963) extended *McCollum* and *Zorach* by affirming that public schools may not endorse or teach religion through "nondenominational" devotional instruction, no matter how brief. In *Engel* and then again in *Abington*, the Court ruled that educators may not design and implement religious exercises to begin each school day, even if the school allows students to opt out of those exercises.[10] In *Engel*, the Court found that the State Board of Regents of New York violated the Establishment Clause of the First Amendment by adopting a nondenominational prayer for students and teachers to recite at the beginning of each school day. Soon after, the Court found in *Abington* that a local public school district in Pennsylvania violated the Establishment Clause by mandating that schools begin each day by reading ten Bible verses without comment. In both cases, the Court found that the schools' optional exercises attempted to promote devotional religious instruction and establish an official religion. In the words of Justice Black, writing for the majority in *Engel*, "When the power, prestige, and financial support of government is placed behind a particular religious belief, the indirect coercive pressure upon religious minorities to conform to prevailing officially approved religion is plain."[11] Public schools have a duty to safeguard the rights of all, including religious minorities, by leaving devotional instruction to parents and religious communities.

After the *Abington* and *Engel* decisions in the 1960s, political forces on the right and left generated and perpetuated a myth that the Supreme Court banished all religion from public schools. In reality, the Court's decisions consistently upheld the importance of students' religious free exercise while prohibiting the "establishment" of religion in the classroom.[12] Students may still exercise their right to religious liberty through un-coerced individual or group prayer, student-led religious clubs, garb, and other forms of religious expression that do not disrupt the learning environment. Teachers and administrators, on the other hand, act as agents of the state who must inculcate democratic values, and as such they may not favor one religion over others, or favor religion over non-religion.[13] Teachers should not force students to advocate for certain expressions of orthodoxy and orthopraxy (i.e. "correct" beliefs and practices within a religion), nor

should they ask students to evaluate the ultimate validity of various religious expressions. Teachers must adhere to an academic, not devotional, approach to instruction. To return to the distinction made by Dr. Charles Haynes and his colleagues, public schools may teach about religion, but they may not teach religion.

The Supreme Court has explicitly affirmed both the constitutionality and importance of teaching about religion, but the justices have declined to provide a substantive pedagogical framework. In the *Abington* case in 1963, for example, Justice Clark and the majority rejected school-sponsored devotional Bible readings (i.e. teaching religion), but Clark wrote in favor of religious literacy education (i.e. teaching about religion):

> It might well be said that one's education is not complete without a study of comparative religion or the history of religion and its relationship to the advancement of civilization. It certainly may be said that the Bible is worthy of study for its literary and historical qualities. Nothing we have said here indicates that such study of the Bible or of religion, when presented objectively as part of a secular program of education, may not be effected consistently with the First Amendment.[14]

While Clark furnished clear and compelling support for religious literacy education, he provided little specific pedagogical guidance for teachers. The Court has outlined legal boundaries for teaching about religion, but it has not commented on the specific foundational knowledge about religion that students should acquire or the measurable skills related to religious literacy that teachers should assess.

Fifty years after the *Abington* decision, do religious studies scholars still recommend Bible-as-literature courses or comparative religion courses? Not all scholars agree on an answer to this question, despite general consensus about the need for religious literacy education. After presenting one popular but highly contested traditions-based perspective as represented by the work of Stephen Prothero, a professor at Boston University and well-known scholar of religious literacy education, this chapter advocates for a six-point framework for teaching about religion that integrates the study of religion across social studies courses.[15] The proposed six-point framework—a response to Prothero's simplified depiction of religious norms and worldviews—leverages the disciplinary concepts and skills of religious studies to ensure that public school teachers develop curricula that are constitutionally sound, academically sophisticated, and consistent with the study of religion, not devotional expression.

Prothero takes Justice Clark's lead and strongly advocates for stand-alone world religions and Bible-as-literature courses. He does a great service by advocating for religious literacy as a core civic competency, and he convincingly argues that religious illiteracy not only fuels prejudice and misunderstanding but also weakens Americans' religiosity.[16] However, Prothero's prescription of a specific traditions-based approach to teaching about religion, which heavily emphasizes scriptural narrative and doctrine, can inhibit a student's ability to investigate the complexity of religious identity and the full extent of the relationship between religion and other aspects of life, including politics, economics, and culture.[17]

Prothero's traditions-based, doctrinally focused pedagogy is evident in *God Is Not One: The Eight Rival Religions that Run the World*. In this book, he describes the doctrines and narratives of Islam, Christianity, Confucianism, Hinduism, Buddhism, Yoruba, Judaism, and Daoism—with an extra chapter on atheism. Prothero rightly rejects the idea that all of these religions contain the same essential teachings, but he argues instead that students should study each religion using a distinct interpretive lens—including "submission" for Islam and "salvation" for Christianity.[18] Though this approach pays attention to the real differences between religions and requires an honest engagement with disagreements about issues of ultimate concern, this type of a traditions-based approach can reinforce the idea that religions are internally uniform.

Many religious studies scholars advocate for an even more rigorous investigation of difference not only between but also within religions. Utilizing a traditions-based model that considers different religions (e.g. Christianity, Islam, Buddhism) as discrete, monolithic categories can erase critical differences within religious communities.[19] For example, Prothero himself cites a study by eminent sociologist Robert Wuthnow, which demonstrates that liberal Protestants and Catholics are more similar in some ways than liberal and conservative Protestants.[20] Public school teachers should ask students to describe religious identity or expression and to compare and contrast religious expressions within a religious community, between religious communities, and between religious and non-religious communities. Students who study the many ways individuals and communities experience religion in their own lives will not only gain a more nuanced understanding of religion but will also cultivate a stronger commitment to work with and protect the rights of religious groups—a hallmark of constitutional, civic education.

The remainder of this chapter presents a constitutionally-sound six-point framework for planning academic, non-devotional lessons about religion that encourage students to engage with the full diversity of individual and communal religious identities and expressions. Teachers can utilize this framework when integrating the study of religion across the curriculum or when developing stand-alone religion courses that avoid the over simplification of some traditions-based models. Points one through three come from *Guidelines for Teaching about Religion in K-12 Public Schools in the United States* published by the American Academy of Religion, the world's largest association of religious studies scholars.[21] The first three assertions about a religious studies perspective provide a foundation for learning about religion across time and place. Points four through six will provide a framework for describing and analyzing different expressions of religious identity. Each of the six points satisfies, reinforces, and builds upon one or more key requirements of the legal guidelines for teaching about religion.

1 **"Religions are not internally homogenous but diverse."[22]** Whereas it might be obvious that students should learn about differences between religions, some teachers might not consider the importance of creating lessons for students to explore diversity within a single religion. Not all members of a religious group share the same beliefs or practices, and the public school has no legal right to advocate for a normative vision of what members of a religious group should think or how they should behave. Students should compare and contrast the ways that individuals within a religious community express their religious identities. For example, students might not only learn that Christianity contains multiple branches (including Catholic, Protestant, and Orthodox) and denominations (e.g. Roman Catholic, Baptist, and Russian Orthodox), but also that a diversity of expressions exists within any given denomination. A teacher might develop a lesson that asks students to describe differences in funerary rituals among Roman Catholics in the United States, Mexico, and Kenya. Such a lesson exposes students to various beliefs and practices while leaving room for religious communities to cultivate specific ways of thinking or acting through devotional instruction. Public school lessons about religions' internal diversity will challenge common stereotypes and prejudices by deconstructing crude generalizations.

2 **"Religions are dynamic and changing as opposed to static and fixed."[23]** In other words, religions change over time. Students should learn about religion in historical context in order to dispel the misconception that religious beliefs, practices, and communities remain absolutely uniform in different eras. For example, teachers may be tempted to explain contemporary relations between Sunni and Shia Muslims in the Middle East by investigating the split between these two groups thirteen hundred years ago. While history lessons are critical, students must also understand that they cannot project 7th century debates about communal leadership after the death of the Prophet Muhammad onto 21st century post-colonial power dynamics and geo-political concerns. Lessons about religious dynamism will destabilize narratives about inherent, intractable conflict between religious groups by exposing a history of change. Teaching about the dynamism of religion also assures that educators expose students to multiple views, per the legal guidelines for teaching about religion, instead of inadvertently imposing one particular view through an overly simplified presentation of a religion.

3 **Religions "are embedded in cultures and not isolated from them."[24]** Religion does not exist in a separate, private sphere unaffected by public life. Individuals and communities interpret and reinterpret religion according to cultural context; these same groups interpret and reinterpret culture according to religion. The components of culture—including politics, economics, geography, and social norms—all affect and are affected by religion. For example, late 19th century Native American religious expressions, including the Ghost Dance movement of the Lakota Sioux, influenced and were influenced by political and social forces related to the settlement of white Americans across the West. Students would be unable to explain the Ghost Dance movement and its effects without historical and cultural context. Lessons that enable students to identify the relationship between religion and culture in a given time period and location will more accurately represent the role of religion in American public life. Such lessons will avoid promoting non-religion, or at least pervasive secularism, over religion—a key requirement of the legal framework for teaching about religion.

While the first three points provide a foundation for learning about religion across time and place, the next three points provide a legally sound framework for describing and analyzing religious identity in a way that, per the legal guidelines, informs students about various identities but does not seek to conform students to any particular practice or expression. This 3B Framework teaches students to recognize that individuals and communities construct religious identity not only through their beliefs but also through their behaviors and experiences of belonging.[25] "Faith" and "belief"—which are often used as synonyms of "religion"—only comprise one aspect of religious identity. In fact, for some religious people, behaviors and experiences of belonging to a community or communities shape religious identity more than belief.[26] While religious belief might in some cases produce behavior (Model 1), research from sociology and psychology demonstrates that individuals' behaviors and experiences of belonging to religious community may affect belief (Model 2). Lessons about religion in the public school should encourage students to analyze others' religious identities in order to understand the relative importance of each of the three B's for an individual and community. In Model 3, for example, Person A values belief above all else, while Person B constructs her religious identity according to her experience of belonging.

Models of Different Relationships between the Three B's

MODEL 1

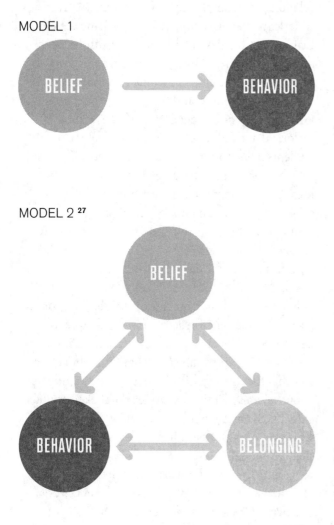

MODEL 2 [27]

MODEL 3

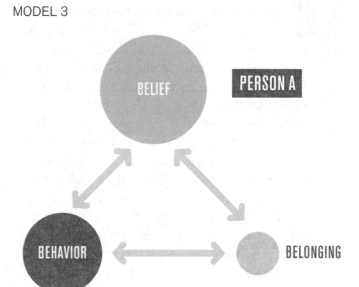

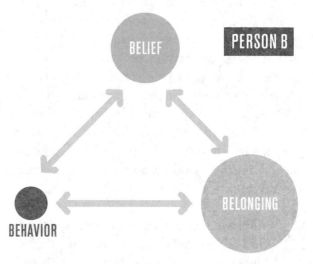

If religious literacy education trains students to understand the "language" of religion, then the 3B Framework is a linguistic exercise that begins by examining the "grammar" of religious identity (i.e. beliefs, behaviors, and experiences of belonging) before it tackles the distinction between "vocabulary" words across religions. Put another way, a traditions-based approach to teaching about religion excels at helping students memorize distinct religious vocabularies; taking a step beyond the traditions-based approach, the 3B Framework asks students to analyze the "grammar" that undergirds religion in order to "linguistically" compare and contrast the construction of religious identity for religious individuals and communities, whatever their vocabularies. For example, students might learn that "dialects" of two different religions (e.g. Theravada within Buddhism and Orthodoxy within Judaism) may employ "grammatical structures" (e.g. a religious identity centered on behavior, not belief) that more closely resemble one another than "dialects" of the same religion (e.g. Reform and Orthodox Judaism). This is a constitutionally admissible descriptive exercise, not an illegal prescriptive exercise that tells students what to believe or how to behave. Teachers must develop a keen familiarity with the fullest definitions of belief, behavior, and belonging if they are to guide students through this "linguistic" analysis.[28] Belief, behavior, and belonging are defined in points four through six of our six-point framework.

4 Religious beliefs affect behaviors and the construction of communities of belonging.

Teachers should remind students that beliefs manifest in a variety of ways, including theology, doctrine, sacred narratives, and holy texts, as well as the social values and ethics that guide daily life. In a classroom, for example, a teacher might ask students to examine multiple Islamic perspectives on justice, conducting a constitutional lesson that makes students aware of multiple beliefs but does not press for acceptance of any one belief. Primary source material might include passages about justice, in theory and in practice, in the Qur'an and Hadith, traditional commentary about justice in scriptural texts, and legal rulings by Islamic jurists. Students should also consider how beliefs and values in the "mundane" sphere of politics and society affect and are affected by beliefs and values drawn from religious tradition. A teacher might encourage students to compare and contrast the beliefs of Muslims in different social, political, and economic contexts, including the United States, the United Kingdom, Saudi Arabia, and Indonesia.

5 Habitual behaviors of religious individuals—within a place of worship as well as in the home and workplace—affect their beliefs and experience of belonging to a religious community.

Behaviors include holy rites and rituals as well as habits and practices associated with daily life outside of a strictly sacred setting. To explore religious behavior in a contemporary social studies course, students might study different Buddhist rites and rituals connected with the interaction between Buddhist monks, nuns, and laypeople in Thailand and Burma during the 20th and 21st centuries. A teacher might encourage students to compare and contrast the ways Thai and Burmese monks and nuns solicit alms from laypeople, and the lay practice of giving gifts to the sangha. Students might also examine how these practices forge a sense of community among Buddhists and create or reinforce a belief in the impermanence of material goods. Teachers should also encourage students to consider how Thai and Burmese habitual practices in daily life—those that dictate how people of different social rank greet one another, for example—might affect religious rites and rituals connected with the interaction between religious and laypeople. In this example, a teacher exposes students to multiple Buddhist practices without unconstitutionally promoting or denigrating religious behaviors, and without inappropriately asking students to physically perform Buddhist practices through participatory classroom exercises.

6 The experience of belonging to a religious community—which intersects with other types of communities—affects a person's behaviors and beliefs.

Belonging refers to a community of co-religionists, complete with a social structure, which extends through time and geographic space. Critically, belonging also refers to racial, ethnic, familial, class, gender, sexual, and other identities that may affect and be affected by an individual or community's religious identity. In a 20th century history course, teachers might choose to devote class time to study Jewish responses to the Holocaust. Students might analyze how religious communities in Europe, the United States, and the Middle East experienced and interpreted the Holocaust differently based on their nations of origin and proximity to Hitler's Germany. Students might also describe how Jews forged bonds despite geographic distance, including through a shared consciousness of the long history of oppression and diaspora, and the post-war creation of the state of Israel. Teachers might encourage students to pay particular attention to the intersection of religious

		A: SACRED	B: MUNDANE
●	1: BELIEF	theologies, doctrines, sacred narratives, and holy texts	social values and ethics
●	2: BEHAVIOR	holy rites and rituals	habits and daily practices
●	3: BELONGING	trans-historical, trans-national community of co-religionists complete with a social structure	racial, ethnic, familial, gender, sexual, and other identities

communities with national and racial identities that create a sense of belonging—for example, by contrasting the experience of white Ashkenazi Jews and Middle Eastern or North African Mizrahi Jews in the 21st century. This lesson exemplifies how teachers can inform students about multiple communities without forcing students to conform to any one community.

Note that each component of religious identity described above includes both a "sacred" and "mundane" element (see Model 4). This connects with the three premises about religion published by the American Academy of Religion. Since religion is embedded in culture, the components of religious identity affect and are affected by aspects of life that students might not recognize as religious per se. The definitions and examples provided reflect the interconnectedness of religion and culture, and the implications this has for internal diversity and change over time. Model 5 depicts how religious communities interpret and reinterpret a received religious tradition—which includes elements of belief, behavior, and belonging—based on their direct experience of the world around them, including social, economic, and political life. Through this process of interpretation and reinterpretation as mediated by people's embodied experience of specific times and places, religious expressions change over time and vary across cultures.

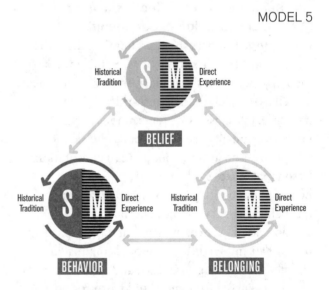

By combining the three premises about religion articulated by the AAR with the 3B Framework, teachers can develop lessons about religion for the public school social studies classroom that abide by the requirements of the legal framework for teaching about religion. The six-point approach derives from a religious studies perspective, not a devotional one. Teachers should be careful not to promote or denigrate the credibility of religious perspectives—including those that might contradict some of the key premises that undergird religious studies. For example, a specific religious community may consciously describe its beliefs and behaviors as unchanging and eternal. Teachers should not actively seek to undermine this religious system or evaluate its validity, but rather should encourage students to identify how and analyze why that community might conceive of itself in a particular way. The three premises cited in this chapter about religion and the 3Bs are meant to help identify and describe patterns that students might observe when they study religion in a social studies course, a valid practice according to the guidelines distributed by the Department of Education. The six-point framework does not claim to represent ultimate truth about what is "right" and "wrong" in a religious sense, but rather functions as a lens to study religion from an academic perspective.

Students with a strong working proficiency in the religious studies framework will be better prepared to excel in college-level courses in social studies disciplines, to engage professionally with religious and non-religious others, and to take informed action to safeguard fundamental religious and civil liberties through civic participation. Students will gain the skills necessary to continue learning outside the classroom through formal study about religion and informal conversations with people outside their own religious communities. Teachers can help students learn to ask open-ended questions that can identify those aspects of religion and religious identity most important for other people, and students can then participate in meaningful dialogue about issues of profound importance instead of surface level conversations about topics assumed to be—but not actually—important for themselves and their interlocutors. Perhaps most important in a religiously diverse nation experiencing a surge in religion-related hate crimes, the study of religion from a constitutional, academic perspective can decrease students' negative attitudes and prejudices toward the religious and non-religious other without affecting students' own religiosity.[29] Thus, social studies teachers who adhere to a legal framework for studying religion will ultimately reinforce the foundational principles that undergird our constitution, including the incalculable value of our "first freedom"—religious liberty.

NOTES

1. John Jr. Witte and Joel A. Nichols, *Religion and the American Constitutional Experiment*, Third Edition (Boulder: Westview Press, 2011), 191.

2. Pew Forum on Religion & Public Life, "U.S. Religious Knowledge Survey" (Washington: Pew Research Center, 2010), 33, http://www.pewforum.org/files/2010/09/religious-knowledge-full-report.pdf.

3. Diane L. Moore, *Overcoming Religious Illiteracy: A Cultural Studies Approach to the Study of Religion in Secondary Education* (New York: Palgrave MacMillan, 2007), 28.

4. *Ibid.*, 33. See also Emile Lester and Patrick S. Roberts, *Learning About World Religions in Public Schools: The Impact on Student Attitudes and Community Acceptance in Modesto, Calif.* (Nashville: First Amendment Center, 2006).

5. Charles C. Haynes *et al.*, *The First Amendment in Schools: A Guide from the First Amendment Center* (Alexandria: Association for Supervision and Curriculum Development, 2003), 52.

6. Diane L. Moore, "Diminishing Religious Literacy: Methodological Assumptions and Analytical Frameworks for Promoting the Public Understanding of Religion," in *Religious Literacy in Policy and Practice*, ed. Adam Dinham and Matthew Francis (Chicago: Policy Press, 2016), 27.

7. Charles C. Haynes, "A Teacher's Guide to Religion in the Public Schools" (Nashville: First Amendment Center, 2008), 3. Distributed to all public schools in a slightly different version in "Religion in the Public School Curriculum: Questions and Answers" (Nashville: First Amendment Center, 1988). The Teacher's Guide is reproduced in Appendix 1 of this book. The guidelines are based on those published by the Public Education Religion Studies Center at Wright State University.

8. For more on incorporation, see Witte and Nichols, *Religion and the American Constitutional Experiment*, 122-127.

9. *McCollum v. Board of Education*, 333 U.S. 203, 209 (1948).

10. See Stephen V. Monsma and J. Christopher Soper, *The Challenge of Pluralism: Church and State in Five Democracies*, Second Edition (New York: Rowman and Littlefield Publishers, 2009), 29.

11. *Engel v. Vitale*, 370 U.S. 421, 431 (1962).

12. Witte and Nichols, *Religion and the American Constitutional Experiment*, 198-199.

13. Instead of reviewing the full scope of First Amendment jurisprudence on religion in public education—including cases about free exercise and the right of religious groups to gain equal access to "facilities, forums, and even funds" provided by public schools—this chapter focuses on those cases relevant to religious literacy education. *Ibid.*, 192, 199.

14. *School District of Abington Township v. Schempp*, 374 U.S. 203, 225 (1963).

15. This six-point framework was first discussed in Benjamin Marcus, "Six Guidelines for Teaching About Religion," *Education Week*, April 4, 2016, sec. Global Learning, http://blogs.edweek.org/edweek/global_learning/2016/04/six_guidelines_for_teaching_about_religion.html.

16. Prothero claims that widespread religious illiteracy in the United States stems from Americans' "ironic" efforts to strengthen religion: missionaries in the early 19th century favored emotionally-driven religious revival over doctrine in their attempts to Christianize the country, replacing theology

with morality; Protestants set aside doctrinal differences to present a united front against Catholics in the mid to late-19th century, thereby forgetting distinctions between denominations; and Protestants, Catholics, and Jews—and later other religious groups—formed new coalitions to fight the rising tide of secularism in the 20th and 21st centuries, including through "nondenominational" prayers in public schools. As religious Americans built new and larger coalitions, they increasingly minimized doctrinal difference in favor of inter-communal bonds. See Stephen Prothero and Lauren R. Kerby, "The Irony of Religious Illiteracy in the USA," in *Religious Literacy in Policy and Practice*, ed. Matthew Francis and Adam Dinham (Chicago: Policy Press, 2016), 55-62.

17. For Prothero's approach, see Stephen Prothero, *Religious Literacy: What Every American Needs to Know—And Doesn't* (New York: HarperOne, 2007), 17-18. For an alternative approach, see Moore, *Overcoming Religious Illiteracy: A Cultural Studies Approach to the Study of Religion in Secondary Education*, 56-57.

18. See Stephen Prothero, *God Is Not One: The Eight Rival Religions That Run the World* (New York: HarperOne, 2011).

19. See Thomas A. Lewis, *Why Philosophy Matters for the Study of Religion—and Vice Versa* (New York: Oxford University Press, 2015), 119-143.

20. Prothero and Kerby, "The Irony of Religious Illiteracy in the USA," 62.

21. These premises also appear in Moore, "Diminishing Religious Literacy: Methodological Assumptions and Analytical Frameworks for Promoting the Public Understanding of Religion."

22. Diane L. Moore, "Guidelines for Teaching about Religion in K-12 Public Schools in the United States" (American Academy of Religion in the Schools Taskforce, April 2010), 12, http://aarweb.org/Publications/Online_Publications/Curriculum_Guidelines/ AARK-12CurriculumGuidelines.pdf. The Guidelines are reproduced in Appendix 2 of this book.

23. *Ibid.*, 13.

24. *Ibid.*, 14.

25. Benjamin Marcus, "Religious Literacy in American Education," in *The Oxford Handbook of Religion and American Education*, ed. Michael D. Waggoner and Nathan C. Walker (Oxford: Oxford University Press, 2018).

26. See, for example, Vassilis Saroglou, "Believing, Bonding, Behaving, and Belonging: The Big Four Religious Dimensions and Cultural Variation," *Journal of Cross-Cultural Psychology* 42, no. 8 (November 2011): 1320-40.

27. Adapted from Jonathan Haidt, *The Righteous Mind: Why Good People Are Divided by Politics and Religion* (New York: Vintage Books, 2013).

28. "Religious Literacy in American Education."

29. See the promising research conducted by Lester and Roberts in Modesto, CA. Lester and Roberts, *Learning About World Religions in Public Schools: The Impact on Student Attitudes and Community Acceptance in Modesto, Calif.*

CHAPTER TWO

A Tale of Two States: Teaching about Religion in Texas and California

EMILE LESTER

News from the nation's two most populous states made 2014 the worst of times and the best of times for religion in public schools. The bad news came out of Texas where the State Board of Education (SBOE), and publishers sought to construct textbooks that made students' knowledge about American history a casualty of our culture wars. The good news was made by the California State Legislature, which voted to celebrate a valuable experiment in teaching about religion in the state's Central Valley. Texas's experience serves as a warning about the perils of trying to use the school system to teach religion for political ends. California's example serves as a model for what schools can accomplish when the swords of partisanship are sheathed.

MESSING WITH HISTORY IN TEXAS

During 2009 -2010, the Texas State Board of Education (SBOE) consistently chose to contradict the curriculum advice of a panel of classroom teachers and academic historians carefully assembled by the Texas Educational Agency. Board member Don McLeroy, a dentist with no specialized academic training in history, played an instrumental role in the construction of social studies standards. The Board relied on guidance from several historians who assert that the U.S. was founded as and continues to be a Judeo-Christian nation, including David Barton whose 2012 book, *The Jefferson Lies*, had so many errors that its publisher pulled it from the market. The resulting Texas Essential Knowledge and Skills (TEKS) standards for U.S. Government courses are rife with dubious assertions. They mandate that students be able to "identify the individuals whose principles of laws and government institutions informed the American founding documents, including those of Moses," and "identify major intellectual, philosophical, political, and religious traditions that informed the American founding, including Judeo-Christian (especially biblical law)."[1]

Publishers submitted the first set of social studies textbooks written in response to the new social studies standards in 2014. Texas is the largest market for textbooks besides California, which has specific social studies requirements not shared by other states. This purchasing power gives publishers a strong incentive to conform their treatment of American history to the standards the Board of Education adopted. What makes it into Texas textbooks has a significant chance of influencing what students learn about American history and religion in public schools around the country.

The Texas Freedom Network (TFN), a civil liberties organization founded in 1995 whose governing board has included clergy members from various faiths and denominations, hired me to review seven textbooks proposed for use in U.S. Government 12th grade courses. My review found that while several publishers had the courage to place the truth above politics and profit, most decided to appease the State Board of Education. In particular, the treatment of religion and the American founding by five of the textbooks included inaccurate, unbalanced, and even demonstrably false statements.[2]

The most egregious errors concerned claims about the influence of Moses and Mosaic law on the Founders and the Constitution. The text of one publisher (Perfection Learning) that I reviewed had a list of historical figures who influenced the Founders. Moses, mentioned first, is credited with the idea that "a nation needs a written code of behavior."[3] The Pearson text I reviewed told students that "Moses helped establish a legal system, including the Ten Commandments, to govern his people. Similarly, the founders of the United States wrote the Constitution and established a system of laws to govern Americans."[4] The text conveniently does not tell students that John Adams in an 1825 letter to Thomas Jefferson disputed that the Ten Commandments influenced our legal system, and that no Founder affirmed their influence. Other influential figures on the Perfection Learning list, including William Blackstone and Charles de Montesquieu, receive numerous citations in *The Federalist Papers*; Moses is not mentioned once.

The Pearson U.S. Government 12th grade textbook I reviewed told students that "The roots of democratic government in today's world" can be traced to "Biblical figures such as Moses and Solomon."[5] Yet Exodus makes no mention of Moses holding a referendum when he orders the Levites to slaughter 3,000 heretical Israelites after returning from Mt. Sinai. Solomon was a monarch who took power in a coup d'état, and whose most notable policy was for a massive public works project (the temple in Jerusalem) made possible by heavy taxation and forced labor. Moses and Solomon are leaders of profound importance for the Western tradition, but describing them as forerunners of democracy is akin to describing Ronald Reagan as a Communist.

Other publishers also accepted the invitation of the State Board of Education to construct textbooks that reflected the Board's views on the American history of religious freedom. The TEKS standards required textbooks to "compare and contrast" the wording of the First Amendment's religion clauses with the phrase "separation of church and state." As if on cue, the McGraw-Hill text that I reviewed told students: "Thomas Jefferson once referred to the establishment clause as a 'wall of separation between church and state.' That phrase is not used in the Constitution, however."[6]

Jefferson was not a member of Congress during the drafting of the First Amendment, and his famous "wall" metaphor is from an 1802 letter. Yet suggesting that he and his metaphor have nothing to do with the First Amendment is like arguing that because Martin Luther King, Jr. was not a Congressman he had nothing to do with the 1964 Civil Rights Act. Jefferson may not have drafted the First Amendment, but he had immense influence on James Madison, the Amendment's principal architect. Madison was as staunch an advocate of church-state separation as Jefferson or today's separationists, as, for instance, his objection to government funding for military chaplains reflects.

Despite the light the Texas Freedom Network shed on these evident sins of omission and commission, the denouement to the battle over religion and American history in Texas textbooks was depressing. McGraw-Hill did amend its treatment of the history of separation of church and state to make it more balanced, but the problematic material about the influence of the Bible on the Founders remained essentially unaltered.

The State Board of Education's conservative majority demonstrated an unwillingness to engage with testimony from myself and other expert witnesses contradicting the accuracy of their standards and textbook passages based on them. Don McLeroy did lose his seat in 2010 in a Republican primary, but school board elections in Texas are typically low-turnout affairs where highly mobilized partisans have an out-sized influence. This arrangement gives many Board of Education members a greater political incentive to cater to extremists than to do the right thing for students.

The incentives facing textbook companies about the controversial passages on religion were equally perverse. The Texas Freedom Network did have considerable success in persuading textbooks to eliminate racially offensive cartoons about affirmative action, and language denying climate change in social studies texts. Scientific illiteracy and racial insensitivity are charges that publishers are eager to avoid.

By contrast, although it is impossible to determine with certainty why publishers retained demonstrably false claims about religion, it is likely that they were wary that alterations would trigger accusations that they were hostile to religion. Indeed, in November 2014, State Board of Education chairwoman Barbara Cargill accused the Texas Freedom Network of attempting to "discourage publishers from correctly writing about religion and its influence on our Founding Fathers" in a public call to action to members of the Concerned Women for America issued just days before the final Board of Education vote on textbook approval.[7]

It is unlikely that Ms. Cargill actually read the Texas Freedom Network's reviews. After all, the first sentence of its review of U.S. Government textbooks explains that "a full understanding of the historical roots and principles of the United States government is impossible without an understanding of religion's influence on our Founders."[8] The tragedy of Texas textbooks, the report contends, was that they constituted a "missed opportunity." The review proceeded to explain that no story of our nation's origins could be complete without mentioning that the evangelical Great Awakening inspired a questioning of established authority crucial to the American Revolution, or that the evangelical Baptist Roger Williams was moved to defend religious freedom because he wished to protect the pure garden of religion from the invasive wilderness of politics. The true story of religion in American history, the report concluded, was rich enough that the misguided embellishment the Board of Education and publishers engaged in to advance religion was utterly unnecessary.

To counter the partisan appropriation of religion in public schools like that in Texas effectively, organizations like the Texas Freedom Network must couple their criticisms with an explanation of what types of approaches to teaching about religion are legitimate. However, they must do this for reasons other than that it is good politics.

Instead, they ought to do so because, despite increased attention to religion in recent years, public schools still do not teach enough about religion. Warren Nord's survey of social studies texts, for instance, found a pattern of inadequate treatment of religion, including one U.S. history text that devoted significantly more discussion to the role of railroads in 19th-century America than it did to the role of religion in the 20th century.[9] Too often, history texts portray conservative forms of Christianity in an unflattering light by dwelling on its role in the 1925 Scopes anti-evolution trial, and not much else.

If critics of the Texas standards could point to an existing model that addressed the deficits in teaching about religion while avoiding the problems with the Texas approach, this would benefit their cause and, more importantly, the welfare of our nation's students. Fortunately, such a model does exist in at least one public school district in California.

RESPECTING RELIGION IN MODESTO

In 2001, the school district of Modesto, California, made the virtually unheard of decision to require that all high school students take a world religions course. In August 2014, California Assembly Concurrent Resolution 154 applauded the course for its effect in preventing bullying based on religion, and recommended its adoption statewide.

Modesto's course discusses the major tenets and practices of six different religions, and examines the impact of religion upon the morality of its adherents. Unlike Texas, the course was careful to avoid using religion as a weapon of political partisanship. In constructing its standards, the Texas SBOE dismissed a diverse panel of experts, and relied heavily on controversial political activists. Not only were the Board's majority and advisers uniformly Christian, but they represent a religiously and politically conservative version of Christianity. Since half of Texas's residents do not describe themselves as born-again, this version of Christianity is far from universally shared. Modesto initially required that all teachers attend a discussion with professors of religion at California State University Stanislaus prior to teaching the course to acquire expertise on the religions they would teach. The district also assembled an advisory board of religious leaders including Islamic, Sikh, Jewish, Protestant, Catholic, and Greek Orthodox clerics to review the course prior to its implementation.

The course begins with a two-week discussion of the tradition of religious liberty in the United States highlighting the contributions of heroes of conscience like the founder of Rhode Island and one of the first Baptist churches in America, Roger Williams. That course teaches that freedom of conscience is a reciprocal that students must extend to others if they themselves expect to benefit from it. Consistent with its commitment to objective, academic study and respect for religious diversity, the course devotes equal time to the six major world religions discussed, and examines them in the order of their appearance in history.

What information the Modesto course chooses not to concentrate on is perhaps as significant as the information it does convey to students. The course does not examine the differences between denominations within religious traditions. More crucially, its approach to religion is descriptive rather than comparative to ensure neutrality and avoid controversy. The course examines each religion's historical development and major contemporary beliefs and practices, but students are not encouraged to interpret religious texts based on historical context. The course does not, though, encourage students to evaluate the truth of the religions or religious texts they are taught about.

The disparate results of these approaches could not have been more glaring. The Texas State Board of Education hearings on the standards and textbooks became a battle in the culture wars in which the recommendations of scholars and classroom teachers were ignored. Conservative activists verbally wrangled with progressives, religious and racial minorities raised legitimate concerns about being misrepresented or ignored, and board members directed barbs at each other. While cacophony prevailed in Texas, concordance reigned in Modesto. The course has not been the subject of a single lawsuit. Although parents have the right to

opt their children out of the course, administrators estimate that an infinitesimal one out of a thousand students do so.

This is all the more remarkable because of Modesto's makeup. Sikh gurudwaras, synagogues, mosques, and Hindu temples dotting the local landscape are a testament to a robust array of religious diversity. Yet Modesto lies in the Central Valley known as the California Bible Belt for the strong presence of evangelical Christianity. Five evangelical megachurches serve a population of a little less than 200,000. And since Modesto is a bedroom community for San Francisco, progressivism is well-represented. Modesto's experience proves that diverse demographics need not mean a divisive destiny.

The effects of the course upon students were equally impressive. A survey I conducted with Patrick Roberts of Virginia Tech of over 300 students taking Modesto's course revealed statistically significant evidence that students left the course more knowledgeable about and respectful of other religions.[10]

HAVING FAITH IN FAITH

That Modesto has promoted the purpose of education by refusing to politicize religion while the Texas Board of Education has stubbornly persisted in misrepresenting the role of religion in U.S. history would not have surprised Thomas Jefferson. In his Notes on the State of Virginia, Jefferson wrote of the results of government manipulation of religion that "constraint . . . may fix him obstinately in his errors, but will not cure them. Reason and free enquiry are the only effectual agents against error."[11]

Jefferson and Madison understood that separation was the true friend of religion, and government interference its enemy. American history has largely borne out their prediction that religion would flourish if all people were free to practice their religion. Rates of religious adherence and attendance in the U.S. are much higher than in Western European countries with traditions of established churches. Jefferson's and Madison's wisdom was also evident in Modesto. Five of twenty-three students I interviewed told me the course strengthened their faith; none said their faith was weakened.

Of all the ignorance of American history displayed by the Texas State Board of Education, perhaps the most poignant is the failure to pay attention to the fruits of faith in religious freedom. The example that America has set to the rest of the world is that religious faith is powerful enough to stand on its own. It does not need the state to engage in coercion on its behalf. The majority of the Texas State Board of Education have been eager to loudly proclaim they are on God's side, but their actions reflect a lack of faith in the power of faith itself.

NOTES

1. *Texas Essential Knowledge and Skills for Social Studies*, Subchapter C. High School, §113.44. United States Government (One-Half Credit), Beginning with School Year 2011-2012. http://ritter.tea.state.tx.us/rules/tac/chapter113/ch113c.html

2. Emile Lester, "A Triumph of Ideology Over Ideas: A Review of Proposed Textbooks for High School U.S. Government in Texas," September 2014. http://tfn.org/cms/assets/uploads/2015/11/FINAL_Lester_GOV.pdf

3. See Lester, "A Triumph…," 5.

4. Lester, "A Triumph…," 8.

5. Lester, "A Triumph…," 31.

6. Lester, "A Triumph…," 9.

7. http://concernedwomen.org/the-texas-state-board-of-education-needs-to-hear-from-you-today/

8. Lester, "A Triumph…," 3.

9. Warren Nord, *Does God Make a Difference?* (Oxford: Oxford University, 2010), 56.

10. The report is available for download at http://www.religiousfreedomcenter.org/wp-content/uploads/2014/08/FirstForum_ModestoWorldReligions.pdf. For further discussion of Modesto's approach to world religions, see Emile Lester, *Teaching about Religions* (Ann Arbor: University of Michigan Press, 2011).

11. Thomas Jefferson, 1993. *The Life and Selected Writings of Thomas Jefferson* (New York: Random House, 1993), 255.

CHAPTER THREE

Whose Truth Should Students Hear? The Debate Over Guest Speakers On Religion

LINDA K. WERTHEIMER

For the first time in her 27-year teaching career, Kelly Miliziano was under public attack. Strangers were sending her hundreds of emails, often laced with profanity, questioning how she could have let a terrorist speak to world history classes at Steinbrenner High School, just outside of Tampa, Florida. Worse, people had left her vile voice mails.

In one of the most disturbing voice mails, a female caller had said: "You are the scum of the earth, and you do not represent women or any women in the United States, and you've never been in a Muslim stronghold… or you would not bring those filthy, stinky people into our schools to indoctrinate our little children."[1]

Miliziano kept that voice mail and two of the other most abhorrent messages on her cell phone as evidence of the ignorance and hate she witnessed during the 2011-12 school year. Miliziano, the chair of the world history department at Steinbrenner, had invited a Muslim to give a talk about Islam. The guest speaker, Hassan Shibly, was both an imam and the executive director of the Florida chapter of the Council on American Islamic Relations (CAIR).

The uproar over Shibly's visit to Steinbrenner, publicized on a national blog, newspapers, and on television, raised questions Hillsborough County School Board members believed they could not ignore. Should schools develop specific guidelines for guest speakers on religion and if so, what should those guidelines be? Should schools allow guest speakers on religion at all?

What Shibly, then just 25, said to students was never really at issue. Opponents to his visit said they objected mostly because Shibly worked for

CAIR.[2] CAIR as a national organization had been in the news many times because of battles with the U.S. Department of Justice over its depiction of the association. The Justice Department named CAIR as an unindicted co-conspirator in a trial of a Texas-based charity accused of funneling millions of donated money to Hamas, listed as a terrorist group by the U.S. government. The government shut down the charity, but CAIR was never convicted of anything.[3] Shibly, as a representative of CAIR, brought that baggage with him as a speaker at a public school. CAIR in Florida and elsewhere serves as an advocacy group for American Muslims. Shibly, also a lawyer, represents Muslims in civil rights cases and in his role as a CAIR leader, works to help dispel stereotypes of Muslims.[4]

For years, Steinbrenner's history department had invited guest speakers, including Muslim clergy, a Buddhist monk, and a rabbi, to enhance lessons on world religions. Miliziano picked Shibly because a local imam recommended the charismatic young lawyer and fellow imam as a great speaker.[5] On November 29, 2011, he gave seven presentations to students from the high school's world history classes and its elective world religions course. In the view of teachers and students, Shibly gave a human face to Islam in a school that had barely a handful of Muslim students. Sprinkling in personal anecdotes, he gave a PowerPoint presentation on the basics of Islam. When asked about his long beard, he explained that he kept it at fist length to pay homage to a custom set by Muhammad.[6]

The controversy began from two different sources, a concerned father of a Steinbrenner student and Pamela Geller, the author of the blog "Atlas Shrugs," and a book about what she calls the "Islamization of America." Shibly's organization had posted news of his visit to Steinbrenner on the CAIR Florida website. Geller then created a December 4, 2011 post headlined, "Child Abuse: Hamas-Linked CAIR Poisoning Minds of High School Students."[7] The Steinbrenner father read that post, became even more worried and had a heated conversation with Miliziano and an administrator. He questioned whether the teacher truly knew enough about Shibly and CAIR before the speaker was chosen. The parent believed the school should only bring in guests with unblemished integrity when the topic was religion. The teacher and her administrator thought Shibly had been a fine choice.[8]

Speakers at four school board meetings between January and April 2012 urged the board to adopt strict guidelines to keep CAIR and other organizations like it away from school children. Previously, teachers just had to let principals know someone was coming. On April 10, 2012, the school board approved a one-page statement about the use of guest speakers in schools. The guidelines said that teachers should "carefully consider whether a guest speaker has the appropriate experience or credentials to promote a knowledgeable discussion, which helps students learn about the topic."

The school board did not, as one board member and some CAIR opponents had hoped, explicitly ban speakers from advocacy groups. Rather, the guidelines said speakers should be used to educate and to inform the students, and teachers could seek recommendations for speakers from the school district. Teachers were now required to work with guest speakers to establish an outline for the presentation and to ensure it aligned with curriculum requirements. Teachers, as always, had to notify the principal that a guest speaker would be on campus.[9]

The new guidelines also added a note about the use of guest speakers on religious topics and quoted from *A Teacher's Guide to Religion in the Public Schools*, published by the First Amendment Center. The passage, which recommends using local professors, advises educators to find a speaker who has the academic background necessary to lead an objective, relevant discussion about the religion. It doesn't rule out religious leaders, but cautions that some clergy may have difficulty teaching about faith objectively. The guide also adds that educators should make sure the guest speaker understands the First Amendment guidelines for teaching about religion in public schools.[10]

Candy Olson, the Hillsborough County School Board chair during the controversy, said the main outcome was a reminder to teachers to be careful about whom they invite. She was not sure inviting only academics would prevent issues. "Just because you're a scholar doesn't mean you don't have a point of view," she said. She wanted teachers to keep having guests in the classroom because she believed speakers made the learning real.[11]

A 2010 report, *Guidelines for Teaching About Religion in K-12 Public Schools in the United States*, mirrors the First Amendment Center's recommendations but is a little stricter. The guidelines were produced by a task force of the American Academy of Religion, comprised of roughly 10,000 religion scholars. The report discourages schools from inviting religious leaders or practitioners into the classroom. It instead urges teachers to invite religious studies scholars who can better represent the diversity within one faith or to use films or personal written narratives to offer at least two different representations of one religion. It specifically cited the PBS Frontline video, "The Muslims", as an example of showing diversity within a religious tradition.[12]

One approach may not work for every school system given how much regions of the country vary. In Modesto, California, considered California's Bible Belt, the school system's policy is simple: No guest speakers on religion. Since 2000, the school system has required all high school students to take a world religions course before graduation. The course, given in the ninth grade, covers a minimum of six religions. The course's authors designed it using advice from the First Amendment Center and their own belief that bringing in outside speakers on religion was too risky. As part of training for the course, Modesto's teachers learned how to talk about religion in front of their students without stepping over that fragile line separating church and state. Modesto has never had a controversy because of its religion course.

In Wellesley, Mass., a Boston suburb, sixth-grade social studies classes have invited guest speakers on religion for years. Wellesley Middle School, since 2000, has focused only on world religions during the second half of the school year in sixth grade social studies. Students spend four weeks learning about Judaism, Christianity, and Islam, and three weeks on Hinduism. They go on field trips to a mosque and a Jewish temple and, sometimes, to a Hindu mandir. One mosque field trip went awry in 2010 when a handful of boys joined a line of worshippers at a mosque member's invitation. The school system has since reemphasized the importance of students observing rather than participating in any religious ritual on field trips. The teachers also use guest speakers, including parents, clergy, and religion scholars. The school does not have written guidelines for guest speakers, but has best practices for its teachers, says Adam Blumer, the middle school's social studies chair.[13]

Wellesley's best practices could work as a template for other schools:

1. Teachers must let the social studies supervisor know who is coming and whether they come from a particular organization.

2. Prepare speakers by giving them background about the course, letting them know what students have learned, and what the teacher hopes students will learn from the talk.

3. Remind speakers that the course, like their talk, should be about a religion rather than promoting one religion as better than others. In other words, heed First Amendment Center guidelines about

how to handle religion in public schools. Teach, don't preach.

4. Coach speakers to note when they are saying something that's unique to the way they practice their religion versus what may be universal for Jews, Muslims, or Christians. Coach them, too, to state that they are expressing their personal opinion when it's applicable.

5. During the talk, listen for anything that might be confusing or contradictory to information you've taught. Step in to clarify on the spot if you feel you need to do so, but also give leeway to presenters to share their perspective.

Besides remaining vigilant during a guest speaker's visit, teachers also should coach students to become active and respectful listeners. Follow the lead of several teachers I interviewed around the country, and advise students that a given speaker is only presenting one perspective of his or her faith and cannot possibly represent all Muslims or Jews, for example, given the diversity within religions. Educators, too, should debrief students after a guest speaker visits. Ask students what they learned but also whether they had any qualms because of the talk. Students at Steinbrenner saw nothing wrong with Shibly's speech. But a Muslim boy would complain later that same school year about another guest speaker, an Eastern Catholic from Lebanon who made comments about Muslims' ill treatment of women and talked about how girls were forced to marry at nine. The Muslim teen saw the speaker's comments as offensive and as promoting a stereotype. Miliziano had prepped the class by saying she brought in this speaker to show that the Middle East had many religions, not just Islam. She agreed with her student's concern that the speaker had overgeneralized. She followed up with the full class and emphasized that the man's comments about Muslims were his own perspective. She also spoke to the guest speaker about the concerns. The student remained unsatisfied. He believed all teachers should stick with more neutral speakers, the same issue raised by the uproar over Shibly's visit.[14]

Educators also should teach students how to ask questions of speakers and of each other about religion. Modesto teacher Sherry McIntyre, while she does not use guest speakers, has students of many religions in her world religion classes. She tells students they need to remember religion is a touchy, personal subject. "The wrong way to ask a question is, 'Well, that's really stupid, why do people believe that?' A better way to word it would be, 'Wow, that's really interesting,'" McIntyre says.[15] While Modesto shuns guest speakers, teachers have allowed students upon request to speak about their faith practices. Sikh and Buddhist students have explained to their world religions classes why they wear particular clothing or items. Modesto teachers, though, do not invite parents as speakers.

Blumer in Wellesley sees nothing wrong with having parents visit classrooms to describe their family's religious practices. "They should say, 'This is what I do,'" he says. "That's a good complexity for our kids to hear."[16]

In the San Francisco Bay area, one group thinks it has a solution that could prevent controversy: trained speakers on religion. Since 1993, ING, or the Islamic Networks Group, has provided guest speakers on religion to public schools and businesses. The non-profit organization was started by two lay people, both American Muslims motivated by concerns over growing misconceptions about Islam.

In public schools, the organization's speakers most often give a talk called "Getting to Know American Muslims and Their Faith." Most speakers are lay people, though a few are academics teaching in religious institutions. The program does not use religious leaders. Every speaker, who is a volunteer, must get 85 percent or more correct on two written tests, including one that quizzes them about their own religion. To get ING's approval, the speaker also must take an all-day training using the First Amendment Center's guide for teachers, according to Marcia Beauchamp, ING's chief operating officer. When ING speakers set foot in a public school, they, just like teachers, must wear the First Amendment hat.[17] Beauchamp said the big difference between ING and CAIR is that CAIR is an advocacy group that participates in political activities. ING is not, and its speakers also must stick to a prescribed script.

In February 2014, Miliziano once again invited Hassan Shibly to speak about Islam at Steinbrenner. At first the school's principal said yes, and then changed her mind. She was unwilling to create an opportunity for such backlash again. Miliziano was disappointed. So was Shibly, who saw it as giving into anti-Islam bigots. Since 2012, he has spoken at other public schools in the area. No one has complained.[18]

This chapter is partly excerpted from the author's book, *Faith Ed: Teaching about Religion in an Age of Intolerance*. The book examines how schools are teaching about the world's religions, often in the face of controversy over lessons on Islam, and offers guidelines that schools can use to promote religious literacy among students. It was published in 2015 by Beacon Press, Boston (http://www.beacon.org).

NOTES

1. Recording of voice mail, played by Kelly Miliziano during February 24, 2014 interview with author.

2. Conclusion made from listening to school board meeting hearings, available at the Hillsborough County School Board website http://sdhcwebcasts.com/index.html.

3. Neil MacFarquhar, "Muslim Groups Oppose a List of 'Co-Conspirators'," *The New York Times*, August 16, 2007, and previous articles about the Holy Land Foundation's court case.

4. Hassan Shibly, in-person interview with author, February 26, 2014.

5. Kelly Miliziano, multiple interviews with author, February 2014.

6. Account of Shibly's visit based on in-person interviews with Steinbrenner High School students, Hassan Shibly, and teachers in Tampa, February 24-27, 2014.

7. Pamela Geller, "Child-Abuse: Hamas-linked CAIR Poisoning Minds of High School Students," Atlas Shrugs blog, http://www.pamelageller.com, December 4, 2011.

8. The father who made the original complaint to Steinbrenner, in-person interview with author, February 26, 2014, and accounts of the conversation by Kelly King, Steinbrenner's principal and former assistant principal, and Miliziano. The father spoke on condition of anonymity. He did not want his daughter to be identified through him.

9. Copy of new speaker guidelines, provided to author by Hillsborough County School system.

10. Charles C. Haynes, author, and Natilee Dunning, editor, *A Teacher's Guide to Religion in the Public Schools* (Nashville, TN: First Amendment Center, 2008), 4. This guide is reproduced in Appendix 1 of this book.

11. Candy Olson, former chair of Hillsborough County School Board, in-person interview with author, February 25, 2014.

12. The AAR Religion in the Schools Task Force, Diane L. Moore, Chair, *Guidelines for Teaching About Religion in K-12 Public Schools in the United States*, American Academy of Religion, 2010. The report is reproduced in Appendix 2 of this book.

13. Adam Blumer, telephone interview with author, February 27, 2015.

14. Al Nafea, in-person interview with author, February 27, 2014.

15. Sherry McIntyre, in-person interview with author, October 1, 2013.

16. Blumer interview.

17. Marcia Beauchamp, telephone interview with author, February 25, 2015.

18. Follow-up information on Hassan Shibly and Steinbrenner stems from February 2014 interviews with Shibly, Miliziano and Kelly King.

CHAPTER FOUR

The Bullying of Religious Minorities in Schools: Consequences and Solutions

AMEENA JANDALI AND HENRY MILLSTEIN

Bullying is a prevalent and growing problem in American schools, impacting students of all ages and backgrounds. Bullying is defined as "unwanted, aggressive behavior among school-aged children that involves a real or perceived power imbalance. The behavior is repeated, or has the potential to be repeated, over time."[1] Students are bullied for diverse reasons, including physical appearance, such as being overweight; the way they dress; or unchangeable factors, such as gender, sexual orientation, race, ethnicity, or religion.

TYPES OF BULLYING

The different types of bullying include:

1. PHYSICAL BULLYING. This consists of engaging physically with another student to harm her/him, including pushing, hitting, kicking, tripping, taking or breaking their belongings, or stealing her or his money.

2. VERBAL BULLYING. This involves the use of words or gestures to harm or shame another student by taunting, teasing, name-calling, insulting, ridiculing, making inappropriate sexual comments or acts of sexual harassment, or threatening physical harm. This is the most common type of bullying.

3. INDIRECT OR RELATIONAL BULLYING. This form of bullying isolates another student from the group by ignoring, excluding, embarrassing publicly, gossiping, spreading rumors or telling lies about him or her, making sexual innuendos or gestures, or getting others to hurt him or her.

4. CYBER BULLYING. Cyber bullies threaten, harass, humiliate, embarrass, or otherwise target a fellow student using the Internet, interactive and digital technologies, or mobile phones. Some examples of cyber bullying include:

- Sending hurtful, rude, or mean text messages to others.

- Spreading rumors, lies, or inappropriate photos about others by e-mail or on social networks.

- Creating websites, videos, or social media profiles that embarrass, humiliate, or make fun of others.

FREQUENCY OF BULLYING

While different studies show varying rates of bullying, the National Center for Education Statistics reports that almost one out of every four students (22%) report being bullied during the school year.[2] A 2011 study by the National Education Association and Johns Hopkins University found that 41% of school staff witnessed bullying frequently, while 45% of teachers said that a student had reported bullying incidents to them within the past month.[3] One of the challenges of school bullying is that it is generally not reported. According to a 2010 study by Regional Education Laboratory (REL) Northeast and Islands, survey data show that only 36 percent of bullying victims reported their experience to a teacher or another adult at their school while 64 percent of students did not.[4] This may be due to the fear of recrimination from peers that may only serve to increase the bullying.

IMPACT OF BULLYING

Bullying impacts all involved parties, including not only the perpetrator and victim but also the students witnessing it. Bullying threatens a sense of security and well-being for all students. In the worst cases, it can cause physical injury and even lead to suicide. More commonly, bullied students can suffer from a number of behavioral and emotional problems, including a higher risk for depression, anxiety, sleep difficulties, and poor school adjustment than students who are not bullied.[5] Additionally, bullying increases school absenteeism and even school violence. According to a study in the *Journal of Adolescence*, bullying is linked to "antisocial behavior, low prosocial behavior, school failure, and substance abuse" for the bully and "psychosomatic complaints, school absenteeism, low self-esteem, anxiety, loneliness, and depression" for the victim.[6] Youth who bully others are at increased risk for substance use, academic problems, and violence later in adolescence and adulthood.[7]

STUDENTS AT RISK OF BEING BULLIED

While there are numerous reasons that students are bullied and anybody can be a victim of bullying, some students are more likely to be bullied than others. They may include youth with the following characteristics among others:

- Students who are perceived to be weak, have low self-esteem, or lack confidence.

- Students perceived as "different" from their peers, such as those who are overweight, new to a school, shy or quiet, or do not dress "cool."

- Students who have few friends or who are unpopular.

- Students belonging to an ethnic or religious minority.

BULLYING OF SOUTH ASIAN, HINDU, SIKH, ARAB, AND MUSLIM STUDENTS

Since 9/11, and particularly in recent years, South Asian, Hindu, Sikh, Arab, and Muslim students have been specifically targeted for bullying. This is due to a number of factors, including the fact that they are ethnically, racially, and religiously distinct and may have names and traditions and speak languages that are viewed as foreign or strange. According to a survey of 335 Hindu American middle and high school students in late 2015, "one out of three respondents said they had been bullied for their religious beliefs, while about half of the total sample size indicated feelings of awkwardness or social isolation because of their religious identity. About one in four respondents said they had been bullied within the past year, with about a third saying those who bullied them were 'making fun of Hindu traditions.'"[8]

The situation for Sikh students is equally troubling. According to 2012 and 2013 surveys, over 50% of Sikh children experienced school bullying with significantly higher numbers (67%) for turbaned Sikh children, as illustrated by this example: "I was in California like seven, six years ago. It was me and my brother–we had jooras [uncut hair tied in a topknot]... Just us two were Sikh ... For two years we got bullied, came home crying every day. Mom got tired of it. She went to school. They didn't do anything about it. Teachers were racist out there ... I was in 5th grade, and my dad took us to a barber shop, and he was like, 'It's today.' My mom was crying, my dad was crying. It was the day we just [took our patka] off, and we cut our hair. We went back to school and we still got bullied. And we had to move out to Indiana, just because of the bullies [in California]. I mean, we got bullies out here too."[9]

For Muslim students, religious, cultural, and ethnic differences are compounded by the ongoing association with terrorism and violence. In fact, bullying generally spikes after world events relating to conflict and terrorism. For example, after the death of Osama bin Laden, one study found that the prevalence of bullying against Muslim students rose. One participant in the study reported that she was repeatedly called a "terrorist" and asked if she was sad that her so-called "leader" had died. The study reports that other Muslim students had similar experiences after the death of Saddam Hussein.[10] The prospect of bullying after a terrorist attack causes increased anxiety for Muslim students and a fear of coming to school after an attack or event involving Muslims.[11] Common slurs that have long been used against Muslim students include "terrorist," "camel jockey," and "rag head."

The rise of ISIS and ISIS-related terror attacks in the United States and abroad, and resultant non-stop media coverage about them, combined with virulent anti-Muslim rhetoric by political figures, has greatly increased fear and bigotry against Muslims. Even prior to the Paris and San Bernardino attacks in late 2015 this resulted in a spike in reports of bullying of Muslim students. A 2017 survey by CAIR reported that 53% of Muslim students in California—one of the most liberal and diverse areas in the country— report that students at school are made fun of, verbally insulted or abused for being Muslim; this is twice the rate at which students in the U.S. overall report having been bullied. Fifty-seven percent of respondents reported seeing offensive online posts by peers; 26% reported cyberbullying; 19% reported physical harm or harrassment; and 36% of hijab-wearing girls reported having their hijab offensively touched or pulled.[12]

Verbal harassment associating Muslim students with terrorists or terrorism generally spikes after a terror attack. Following the 2015 San Bernardino attacks in Long Beach, a California student was asked "Are you part of the 9/11 or are you ISIS?" "Did you ever kill anyone?" "Are you going to bomb this place?"[13] In another incident in California in 2015, "Rasmia Shuman remembers when the schoolyard conversation among her ninth-grade peers in Redwood City turned to the Islamic State, the extremist group commonly known as ISIS. 'I kind of knew it would go bad because I was the only Muslim in the group,' said Rasmia, a 15-year-old sophomore at Summit Charter School. As the talk escalated, a classmate pointed at Rasmia, who wears the traditional Muslim head scarf or hijab, and simply said, 'You're ISIS.' Then he walked away. The verbal attack was a gut punch to the soft-spoken teen, but across California, such harassment is not uncommon for students who share her religion."[14]

The impact of this bullying and the anxiety it produces can be profound, yet students are often afraid to tell parents or other adults for fear of repercussions, increased harassment, or ostracism.

This is particularly true with young victims, who are often unsure or ambivalent about their identity. Bullying, especially if ongoing, results in a sense of shame for the victim and, as previously mentioned, can have long-term consequences, including an increased risk of depression, anxiety, sleep difficulties, and poor school adjustment.[15]

CLASSROOM DISCUSSIONS AND BULLYING

Verbal bullying of at-risk students also follows current event discussions in which the class discusses events relating to Muslim extremists or terrorists. For example, a Muslim student in New York reported being asked "Why are all Muslims terrorists?" after learning about Boko Haram massacres. She felt helpless to defend herself because she felt that "About 90 percent of the kids in my class feel that way."[16] Despite textbook publishers' greater attention in recent years to accuracy in portraying Islam and other non-Western religions, many teachers continue to use biased or unbalanced materials when teaching about Islam, 9/11, or terrorism. Students often report feeling targeted or marginalized during classroom discussions about Islam and Muslims, where they are called upon to be "experts" or viewed as the "other" in discussions about terrorism.

Classroom resources or discussions about the religion of at-risk students can be humiliating, create a sense of shame, and even lead to bullying. According to the 2015 survey, "More than three out of five Hindu students said that their schools focused on caste and Hinduism, including claims about the religion and Indian social practice that have been long debunked. About one in eight respondents said their teachers made sarcastic remarks about Hinduism in front of class. About one out of every four respondents surveyed said she/ he was put on the spot or singled out by a teacher when the section on Hinduism was discussed."[17] Muslim students have also complained of teacher bias in teaching about the religion, extremism/ terrorism, or related topics. The following incident reflects a trend reported by Muslim students across the country who complain of both the use of biased teaching materials and teacher prejudice. In late 2015, "A high school teacher in Richmond, Texas, sent all his students home with a new study guide he had created, with the title, 'Islam/Radical Islam (Did You Know).' In the study guide, which had not been approved by the school, the economics teacher presented fictional statements as if they were facts, including, '38% of Muslims believe people that leave the faith should be executed.' The teacher also wrote up instructions for what to do 'if taken hostage by radical Islamists.'"[18]

TEACHER BIAS

In addition to the use of biased teaching materials, another concern is bias by a teacher, administrator, or staff member. This may be subtle or subconscious bias, such as mispronouncing a student's name on the first day of school which, even if not deliberate, can set the stage for the rest of the year. Muslim students also complain about teachers' general interactions with the students, including failure to respond to their complaints of bullying, or making inappropriate or derogatory comments, such as a teacher in Florida who called a 14-year-old Muslim high school student a "rag-head Taliban" in March, 2015[19] or a teacher in Texas who told a Muslim student that "we all think you are a terrorist."[20] Bias or derision by a teacher can in turn lead to bullying by students as in the case of a teacher who told a Muslim student, "'I can't wait until Trump is elected. He's going to deport all you Muslims. Muslims shouldn't be given visas. They'll probably take away your visa and deport you. You're going to be the next terrorist, I bet.' On the bus ride home, one student's classmates mimicked his teacher's anti-Muslim comments, taunting him about the fact that his visa would be revoked because he is a Muslim, calling him a 'terrorist,' and accusing him of planning to blow up the bus."[21] This and other incidents by the same teacher are the basis for an October 28, 2016 letter of complaint and request for investigation from the ACLU to the U.S. Department of Justice Civil Rights Division.[22] According to the 2017 CAIR report, 38% of Muslim students experienced discrimination by teachers or school administrators.[23]

Students who experience teacher bias may feel afraid or embarrassed to report the problem to an adult, even their parents, for fear that they will react by calling and admonishing the teacher or staff member, which could make matters worse. Students are left with few or no options to address or even discuss an issue that is making their life miserable.

ADDRESSING THE PROBLEM
BULLYING PREVENTION

While bullying is a pervasive problem, there are steps that schools and educators can take which greatly reduce and prevent bullying. The first step is to recognize that bullying exists in one's school or classroom. The second step is to implement a zero-tolerance policy for bullying, with clear and strictly enforced consequences as soon as bullying occurs. If the bullying continues, there should be mediation involving all parties, including the parents, who should help address this issue with their children.

There are also a number of steps which schools can take to proactively prevent or reduce bullying. They include the following:

- Determine the extent of the problem by surveying school staff, students, and parents to assess the frequency of bullying. This will help guide and inform prevention efforts and increase the likelihood of their success.

- Familiarize school staff with school and district policies on bullying. Since the successful implementation of any new policy depends on the buy-in of all involved, it is important to engage and solicit the input of school staff first and ensure that they take ownership of and are committed to the policy so that it is effective.

- Based on the policy, develop a school-wide code of conduct, which clearly defines unacceptable behavior and its consequences. If needed, increase adult supervision in hallways, the cafeteria, stairwells, and locker rooms, where bullying often takes place.

- Promote school-wide programs and activities that encourage tolerance and diversity and help to create a safe space for all students to learn and grow. These can include:

  ▶ School-wide anti-bullying posters, including those created by the students.

- School-wide assemblies or classroom discussions with anti-bullying experts who address the issue of bullying to raise awareness and provide solutions.

- Guest speakers in classrooms or assemblies to address common stereotypes and misconceptions about marginalized groups to reduce bias.

- Classroom discussions, in which students relate and discuss their own experience with discrimination or bullying to help create empathy and then brainstorm possible solutions.

- Encourage students to initiate and implement a bullying prevention program.

- Programs through the PTA which target parents by informing them of the school's anti-bullying policies and programs and getting them on board.

■ Exhibit sensitivity in classroom discussions about little-known faiths or culture, the war on terror, or any other conflict concerning people of Muslim-majority regions, especially during a time of crisis. This will help reduce the potential for bullying.

■ Work with bullies directly to:

- Make it clear that their behavior is unacceptable and needs to stop immediately or there will be consequences.

- Follow through with consequences such as taking away privileges, informing parents, and more aggressive punishments if the behavior continues.

- Help them to recognize how their behavior is making the victim feel and to reflect on why they are behaving like this.

- Encourage them to perform an act of kindness, to feel better about themselves and to gain self-confidence. Bullies often lack self-esteem or self-confidence.

- Engage their parents in these efforts and work together to reduce negative behaviors. Also include parents in mediation efforts between students with long-term conflicts.

■ Most kids are neither a bully nor a victim, but are often a witness to bullying. How bystanders respond to bullying impacts whether or not bullying is tolerated. Encourage witnesses to bullying to help stop bullying by:

- Alerting an adult that bullying is about to occur or has already occurred.

- Showing support for the victim rather than the bully or requesting others to also support the victim by being upstanders, i.e., standing up for the person being bullied.

- Not repeating gossip even if it is true, as it can hurt others and lead to harassment and bullying.

■ If students are being bullied, help them to stop bullying by:

- Encouraging them to report bullying to an adult whenever it occurs.

- Providing tools to push back against bullying such as walking away.[24]

ADDRESSING TEACHER BIAS

It is important for teachers and staff to acknowledge and address their own personal views about any group or issues which might compromise their academic responsibility to be objective and neutral in their teaching and interaction with all students. Misconceptions, stereotypes, and bias should be addressed through proactive efforts such as staff sensitivity trainings for teachers and faculty as well as continuous follow-up with teachers and staff. When teaching about less-known religions or discussing current events, teachers should make special efforts to ensure that these discussions are balanced and show sensitivity to the feelings of students who are associated with the topic being discussed. Teachers or staff members who exhibit bias towards any student or who make inappropriate comments about a student's religion or practices should be dealt with in a manner consonant with their misconduct.

No student should suffer from bullying, bias, or discrimination; it must be a school's top priority that this behavior should not occur and that it should be swiftly addressed when it does. Only then will our schools be places of safety, growth and learning for all American students.

NOTES

1. Stopbullying.gov.

2. "Student Reports of Bullying and Cyber-Bullying: Results From the 2013 School Crime Supplement to the National Crime Victimization Survey," National Center for Education Statistics (April, 2015), 5. http://nces.ed.gov/pubs2015/2015056.pdf

3. Michaela Gulemetova, Darrel Drury, and Catherine P. Bradshaw, "National Education Association Bullying Study," Colleagues 6:2 (2011). http://scholarworks.gvsu.edu/cgi/viewcontent.cgi?article=1160&context=colleagues

4. A. Petrosino, S. Guckenburg, J., DeVoe, and T. Hanson, "What Characteristics of Bullying, Bullying Victims, and Schools are Associated with Increased Reporting of Bullying to School Officials?" (Issues & Answers Report, REL 2010–No. 092) (Washington, DC: U.S. Department of Education, Institute of Education Sciences, National Center for Education Evaluation and Regional Assistance, Regional Educational Laboratory Northeast and Islands, 2010). Retrieved from http://ies.ed.gov/ncee/edlabs

5. "Understand Bullying Fact Sheet." CDC National Center for Injury Prevention and Control Division of Violence Prevention. http://www.cdc.gov/violenceprevention/pdf/bullying_factsheet.pdf

6. Rebecca Bondü, Tobias Rothmund, and Mario Gollwitzer, "Mutual Long-Term Effects Of School Bullying, Victimization, and Justice Sensitivity In Adolescents," Journal Of Adolescence 48 (2016): 62-72.

7. Centers for Disease Control and Prevention. "Understanding Bullying Fact Sheet." https://www.cdc.gov/violenceprevention/pdf/bullying_factsheet.pdf

8. Murali Balaji, Raman Khanna, Aditi Dinakar, Harsh Voruganti,and Kavita Pallod, "Classroom Subjected Bullying and Bias Against Hindu Students in American Schools," Hindu American Foundation. Executive Summary. http://www.hafsite.org/sites/default/files/HAFN_16_008-BullyingReport_ExecutiveSummary.pdf

9. The Sikh Coalition, "'Go Home, Terrorist'": A Report on the Bullying of Sikh American School Children," March 1, 2014. https://www.sikhcoalition.org/resources/go-home-terrorist-a-report-on-the-bullying-of-sikh-american-school-children/

10. David R. Dupper, Shandra Forrest-Bank, and Autumn Lowry-Carusillo, "Experiences Of Religious Minorities In Public School Settings: Findings From Focus Groups Involving Muslim, Jewish, Catholic, And Unitarian Universalist Youths." Children & Schools 37, 1 (2015): 37-45 9p. CINAHL Plus with Full Text.

11. Donna St. George, "During a School Year of Terrorist Attacks, Muslim Students Report Bullying." The Washington Post, June 14, 2016. https://www.washingtonpost.com/local/education/during-a-school-year-of-terrorist-attacks-muslim-students-report-bullying/2016/06/14/1b066a44-3220-11e6-8758-d58e76e11b12_story.html

12. Council on American-Islamic Relations, Unshakable: The Bullying of Muslim Students and the Unwavering Movement to Eradicate It. October, 2017. 14-15. https://ca.cair.com/sfba/wp-content/uploads/sites/10/2018/04/2017_CAIR-CA_School_Bullying_Report.pdf?x93160

13. Kristin Rizga, "This Is What It's Like to Be a Muslim Schoolkid in America Right Now," Mother Jones, December 15, 2015. http://www.motherjones.com/politics/2015/12/muslim-kids-bullying-schools-teachers-islamophobia

14. Jill Tucker, "Study finds Majority of Muslims Have Faced Bullying at School," San Francisco Chronicle, October 30, 2015. http://www.sfchronicle.com/education/article/With-education-and-humor-taking-aim-at-bullying-6601785.php

15. "Understand Bullying Fact Sheet," CDC National Center for Injury Prevention and Control Division of Violence Prevention. http://www.cdc.gov/violenceprevention/pdf/bullying_factsheet.pdf

16. "Extreme Prejudice," Teaching Tolerance, Fall 2015. http://www.tolerance.org/magazine/number-51-fall-2015/feature/extreme-prejudice

17. Murali Balaji, Raman Khanna, Aditi Dinakar, Harsh Voruganti, and Kavita Pallod, "Classroom Subjected Bullying and Bias Against Hindu Students in American Schools." Hindu American Foundation. Executive Summary. http://www.hafsite.org/sites/default/files/HAFN_16_008-BullyingReport_ExecutiveSummary.pdf

18. Rachel Bertsche, "Teacher Under Fire for Anti-Muslim Lesson," Yahoo News, April 9, 2015. http://news.yahoo.com/teacher-under-fire-for-anti-muslim-lesson-115945553072.html?nf=1

19. Ann Henson Feltgen, "Weston Teacher Faces Discipline over Alleged Slur of Muslim Student," Miami Herald, March 2, 2015. http://www.miamiherald.com/news/local/community/broward/article11924603.html

20. Dean Obeidallah, "Anti-Muslim School Bullying: Sometimes, It's Even the Teachers Doing It," The Daily Beast, May 17, 2016. http://www.thedailybeast.com/articles/2016/05/18/anti-muslim-school-bullying-sometimes-it-s-even-the-teachers-doing-it.html

21. Heather L. Weaver, "Teacher to Muslim Refugee Student: You're a Terrorist, and I Can't Wait Until Donald Trump Deports All You Muslims," ACLU. https://medium.com/aclu/teacher-to-muslim-refugee-student-i-cant-wait-until-donald-trump-deports-all-you-muslims-365ee45a2282#.wm5v1vuwn

22. "Noor Complaint to the Department of Justice Requesting an Investigation Pursuant to Title IV." October 28, 2016. https://www.aclu.org/legal-document/noor-complaint-department-justice-requesting-investigation-pursuant-title-iv

23. Council on American-Islamic Relations, Unshakable: The Bullying of Muslim Students and the Unwavering Movement to Eradicate It. October, 2017. 14-15. https://ca.cair.com/sfba/wp-content/uploads/sites/10/2018/04/2017_CAIR-CA_School_Bullying_Report.pdf?x93160

24. Adapted from Islamic Center of Greater Cincinnati's Muslim Mothers Against Violence (MMAV) and Islamic Networks Group (ING) Bullying Prevention Guide. https://ing.org/bullying-prevention-guide/

CHAPTER FIVE

Diversity Over Uniformity: Teachers, Religious Garb, and Public Schools

NATHAN C. WALKER

In January 2013, Christine Flowers, a lawyer and newspaper columnist for the *Philadelphia Inquirer*, called for a legal ban on the burqa—the long, outer garment that some Muslim women wear outdoors to cover their entire body from head to feet. Flowers began her argument by speaking fondly of the nuns who wore habits when she attended a private Catholic school as a child. Then she expressed concerns that Muslim garb is a threat to the public welfare. She was reacting to an incident where a woman dressed in a burqa had kidnapped a child from a West Philadelphia elementary school. Flowers concluded that this particular religious clothing was a "public safety hazard" and therefore should be uniformly banned by the state.

Flowers failed to mention that throughout the United States, the month of December sees an increasing number of crimes committed by people wearing Santa Claus costumes: these criminals steal and vandalize property, and even kidnap and abuse children. Given this perennial problem, should the state ban fake beards, red coats, and fluffy hats in the name of security?

Should legislators ban masks that cyclists wear in the winter months, or generally ban all heavy coats, scarves, medical masks, or Halloween costumes? Or, most relevant to Flowers' upbringing, what about thieves and bank robbers who dress as Catholic nuns? (Hollywood loves that storyline.) If these are all safety hazards, why not also ban Santa costumes, masks of any kind, and nuns' habits?

These proposals are absurd because the state and its citizens are sophisticated enough to differentiate between criminal behavior and the clothing that criminals wear.

Clothing does not steal—people do.

Why then has it proven difficult for civic leaders to achieve the same differentiation process with the religious garb worn by religious people? The most obvious answer is that it is not about the garb. It is about how legal systems that seek to promote uniformity over diversity reflect the invidiously discriminatory practices of those in power, whether those authorities are conscious of it or not.

GLOBAL RESTRICTIONS ON RELIGIOUS GARB

Throughout the world, nation states have learned the hard way: increased regulation of religion results in greater social hostilities.From 2010 to 2011, 96 countries issued legal restrictions on religion, resulting in a wide range of social and political tensions, even violence. In the wake of a record number of refugees entering Europe, the global trend of government restrictions on religion has surged.[1]

For instance, France has seen an extraordinary amount of violence and political unrest as a result of the 2004 law that prevented citizens, in particular teachers and students, from wearing religious symbols and garb in public places. This political unrest was exacerbated in 2008, when the European Court of Human Rights (ECHR) unanimously affirmed France's decision to expel two twelve-year-old Muslim girls for refusing to remove their hijabs during physical education class. The following year, the ECHR upheld the French government's dismissal of Muslim and Sikh students for wearing religious garb. These *laïcité* (secular) laws target Arabs, but are not enforced for Catholic nuns who wear the habit or for Protestants who wear crosses that are smaller than three inches. This blatantly discriminatory legal practice fuels inter-religious hostility and religious-based violence. Other countries have learned from these social patterns.

By 2009, half of Germany's *Länders* (states) made it illegal for Muslim women to wear headscarves when working in the public sector, specifically in public schools. As a consequence, there was an increase in hostilities among public school students and for the public at large. In order to quell this unrest, school officials chose to not enforce the ban. In 2015, Germany's Supreme Court found these bans to be unconstitutional.

A similar change occurred in Turkey. In 2008, the European Court of Human Rights affirmed the Turkish law that prevented a Muslim medical student from entering a university campus if she wore a hijab. After several years of protests and religious-based conflicts, in 2012 the Prime Minister lifted the ban on headscarves in public institutions. This decision to deregulate resulted in a decrease in religious-based hostilities.

That has not been the case in Russia, however. In 2013, the Russian Supreme Court upheld the decision to prohibit three Muslim students from wearing headscarves in public secondary schools. The rationale was that students' appearance should "conform with business style and be of secular character." This ruling came after the school administration prohibited their parents from conducting the state-mandated education at home. The administration ruled that secular schools cannot be replaced by religious ones; therefore, today, garb-wearing students in Russia are not only compelled to attend public schools but are required to leave their religious dress at the schoolhouse gate.

REGULATING RELIGIOUS GARB IN THE UNITED STATES

The contemporary bans on religious dress in France, Germany, Turkey, and Russia are strikingly similar to the nineteenth-century laws in the United States that were intended to prevent Catholic nuns from teaching in Protestant-dominated public schools.

The 124-year-old debate over public school teachers' religious garb in the United States originated when, in 1894, the Pennsylvania Supreme Court ruled in favor of Catholic nuns who were dismissed for wearing habits while teaching at a public school (*Hyson v. Gallitzin*). The state's high court held that religious dress did not disqualify a teacher from employment. The court went on to issue these fateful words, setting this 120-year-old saga into motion: "The legislature may, by statute, enact that all teachers shall wear in the schoolroom a particular style of dress." In contemporary legal terms, the court explained that the legislature could create a "general/neutral" dress code that applied to all teachers. They did not.

Rather, the Pennsylvania General Assembly responded by enacting the first religious garb statute in the United States—a statute that was neither general nor neutral. The Assembly prohibited public school teachers from wearing "any dress, mark, emblem, or insignia indicating … that such teacher is a member or adherent of any religious order, sect or denomination." The statute provided criminal penalties for any public school administrator who failed to suspend or terminate the offending teacher after notice of a violation.

In 1909, a bonnet-wearing Mennonite (Protestant Christian) teacher challenged the garb statute, but this time the Pennsylvania Supreme Court upheld the ban (*Commonwealth v. Herr*). Pennsylvania's anti-garb statute remains in effect today, disproportionately affecting Muslims and Sikhs.

By the end of World War II, Pennsylvania was one of 22 states to ban religious garb worn by public school teachers. From 1894 to 2005, courts in eight states issued negative rulings on public school teachers wearing religious garb (Iowa, Indiana, Missouri, Nebraska, New Mexico, New York, Oregon, Pennsylvania); meanwhile, the courts of seven states issued positive rulings (Connecticut, Illinois, Kentucky, Minnesota, Mississippi, North Dakota, Ohio). Cases that ruled in favor of the religious-garb-wearing teachers found that there was no evidence of religious instruction or proselytization. The other set of cases were not narrowly focused on the garb question; they involved public school districts acquiring private schools that continued to operate as religious schools or cases where religious institutions were receiving taxpayer funds. In these cases, the teachers' wearing of religious garb was done in the context of public funds being used to administer a private religious school. Put simply, these sets of cases were about the schools, not the teachers.

The courts were, however, united from 1973 to 1986, when they uniformly issued negative rulings against a diversity of people wearing religious garb. These cases were brought forward by people from different religions, including Catholic and Sikh teachers, Pawnee and Jewish students, and Catholic attorneys who were also priests, as well as Jewish and Sikh military personnel.

For instance, in 1986, the U.S. Supreme Court upheld the military's decision to prevent an Orthodox Jew and ordained rabbi from wearing a yarmulke while on duty and when wearing an Air Force uniform (*Goldman v. Weinberger*). On the heels of this case, the Third Circuit upheld the dismissal of a hijab-wearing Muslim woman from her position as a teacher at a Philadelphia high school. A few months later Congress included a religious apparel accommodation clause in the 1987 defense authorization bill signed into law by President Ronald Reagan. This accommodation was limited to military personnel and did not address public school teachers directly; however, it effectively ended the regulatory era of the 1970s and 1980s.

DEREGULATING RELIGION IN THE UNITED STATES
Since then, the United States has been in an age of deregulation in terms of private acts of devotion in public places. In 14 religious garb cases since 1986, lower courts throughout the country affirmed the right of public school teachers, students, school visitors, witnesses in court, and police to wear religious garb. The petitioners in these cases represented a variety of religious traditions: African Hebrew Israelite, Catholic, Muslim, Native American, non-denominational Christian, Sikh, and Rastafarian.

In 2003, for instance, a District Court for Western Pennsylvania overturned the decision to dismiss a teacher's aide for wearing a cross necklace, because the aide did not meet the statutory definition of a full-time teacher; therefore, Pennsylvania's historic anti-garb ban remained in effect. Even though the judge dismissed the case on a procedural matter, he issued a lengthy analysis of the garb law arguing the unconstitutionality of the ban. Today, there is no evidence of Pennsylvania school administrators implementing the law, given the many garb-wearing teachers employed in public schools.

In other areas of the country, public school teachers have lost cases in which they wore t-shirts that expressed proselytizing messages, demonstrating that the courts distinguish private acts of devotion done in public with religious garb (legally defined as "dress, mark, emblem or insignia") from teachers' speech used to convert or coerce students.

In 2010, the Oregon Legislative Assembly repealed its 87-year-old ban on teachers' religious garb. Oregon's anti-garb law was originally proposed by leaders of the Ku Klux Klan as a way to prevent Catholic nuns and priests teaching in public schools. This law was later used by the school district in 1986 (the same year of the U.S. Supreme Court's *Goldman* case) to terminate the employment of Janet Cooper, a white convert to Sikhism who wore a Sikh turban in an Oregon public school. She not only lost her job, but the state revoked her teaching license. It was not until 2010 that the Oregon legislature overturned its ban on religious garb.

Given the pervasive bans on religious garb around the world, this legislative action made international headlines. Particularly, it inspired lawmakers in Pennsylvania in 2012, 2013, and 2014 to introduce a bill that would repeal the 1896 law, which also originally targeted Catholic nuns. The bill has not yet come to the floor of the Pennsylvania General Assembly for a vote. In 2017, Nebraska swiftly repealed its anti-religious-garb law, after a Catholic nun was denied a position as a substitute teacher in a public school for wearing religious garb. As a result, in 2018, Pennsylvania is the last remaining state with a legal ban on public schoolteachers' religious garb.

The U.S. Supreme Court has not yet determined the constitutionality of teachers' wearing religious garb in the public schoolroom. If given the opportunity, it will likely overturn these bans, as it did in two recent decisions: in 2014, the unanimous high court held that the ban on religious garb by the Arkansas Department of Corrections was unconstitutional; and in 2015 the U.S. Supreme Court held, in an 8-to-1 decision, that Abercrombie & Fitch knowingly refused to hire Samantha Elauf because she was a Muslim, as the supervisor interpreted because she wore a hijab during the job interview. This case focused on the employer's burden to notify applicants and employees of dress policies, at which point the employee can request an exemption based on religious grounds. These recent cases reinforced the trend of the U.S. government, at federal, state and local levels, to accommodate religious expression in the workplace.

Meanwhile, the question of who is and who is not worthy of religious freedom continues to perplex local school officials in the United States and around the world.

A GLOBAL RESPONSIBILITY

At least 32 countries throughout the world currently prohibit some private acts of devotion in public places. This is indicative of the difficulty governments throughout the world are experiencing as they struggle to define when and where to grant religious freedom, to whom, and based on what rationale.

Attorneys like Christine Flowers argue that in a post-9/11 era the United States should ban all people from wearing the burqa. Certainly, public schools can require teachers to show their faces for security reasons but American Muslim women rarely cover their entire face and if they do, they do so when outside. Religious illiteracy about Islam often drives flagrant attempts at religious-based discrimination. Current attempts to ban religious garb are now under particular international scrutiny, for the United States has a long history of enacting invidiously discriminatory anti-garb laws against the "suspect" religious minority of the day. These

laws mirror contemporary trends to deny religious minorities basic human rights, such as the right to practice one's religion and the human right to work.

Global regulations on religious expression affect not only who is allowed to attend public schools, but also who is formally or informally permitted to teach in public school, run for and hold public office, and have equal access to employment. Throughout much of the world, religious people are currently experiencing discrimination in employment: they are not able to find jobs because of their religious dress, and are stigmatized and treated unjustly for wearing religious symbols on the job or for requesting days off for religious observance.

Study after study demonstrates that legal regulations on religious expression disproportionately harm women.

Study after study demonstrates that increased regulation of religion results in increases in social tensions.

Americans cannot ignore these lessons at home and abroad. As a religiously diverse country, the United States must abandon all invidiously discriminatory attempts to ban religious garb, in schools and in places of employment. In doing so, we model for the world community how to promote diversity over uniformity.

NOTE

1. For more information about how government regulation of religion results in greater social hostilities see Brian J. Grim, *Rising Restrictions on Religion* (Washington, DC: Pew Research Center, August 2011); Peter Henne, *Trends in Global Restrictions on Religion* (Washington, DC: Pew Research Center, June 23, 2016); Brian J. Grim, *Religious Hostilities Reach Six-Year High* (Washington, DC: Pew Research Center, January 2014); Robert P. George and M. Zuhdi Jasser, eds., *Annual Report of the U.S. Commission on International Religious Freedom* (Washington, DC: United States Congress, April 2016); Lyal S. Sunga and Nathan C. Walker, "Freedom of Religion or Belief and the Law: Current Dilemmas and Lessons Learned," Rome, Italy: International Development Law Organization (November 8, 2016); and Katayoun Kishi, *Global Restrictions on Religion Rise Modestly in 2015, Reversing Downward Trend: Government Harassment and Use of Force Against Religious Groups Surge as Record Number of Refugees Enter Europe* (Washington, DC: Pew Research Center, April 2017).

CHAPTER SIX

The Georgia 3Rs ("Rights, Responsibility, and Respect") Project

DAVID CALLAWAY AND KRISTEN FARRINGTON

2016 was a year marked by civil unrest, a divisive presidential election, and protests that for some brought comparisons to other difficult times in our nation's history, such as the late 1960s. Yet the election year and subsequent months should not be viewed as outliers in an otherwise peaceful and cooperative time but rather as the predictable progression of a country grappling with increased polarization, changing demographics, and decreased trust in the institutions meant to protect us. A large part of our current social climate can be attributed to a breakdown in civil dialogue not only among our elected officials but also in small towns and large cities across the United States. As our society becomes more pluralistic, representing the views of an ever more diverse set of traditions and perspectives, we must come to understand that civil dialogue and cooperation are not inherent in our approach towards the world.

The complexity of our current situation cannot be understated, as numerous national protests and increased civil unrest have demonstrated. While there are many factors that have led to our current socio-political climate, one of the major contributing issues is the dramatic change the U.S. religious landscape has undergone in recent years and the subsequent rise in religious intolerance as a response to what many feel is an unfamiliar and sometime hostile public atmosphere.

In 2015, the Pew Research Center's report, "America's Changing Religious Landscape," showed startling changes in the religious demographics of our country.[1] The report found that, despite many Americans seeing the United States as a "Christian nation," the number of self-identified Christians in the county has dropped dramatically in the last two decades. In 2014, mainline Protestants represented an all-time low of 14% of the U.S. population. Similar trends have also affected Evangelical Christians and Catholics, 25.4%, and 20.8% of the U.S. population respectively, who have also seen significant declines in membership. Conversely, those identifying as religious "nones" or as unaffiliated have dramatically increased to 22.8%

of the U.S. population. And non-Christian faiths, including Judaism, Islam, and Hinduism, among others, have also seen steady growth during this time.

This disconnect between how communities understand their religious and national identities and the demographic realities of the United States population have left leaders and citizens uninformed and unprepared. For many, the sense of loss is great—the communities they grew up and lived in have changed, perhaps forever, as part of this demographic shift. The mix of loss, grief, and fear, can be palpable for such individuals, and this, combined with a lack of education or knowledge about different religious traditions or ideologies, has been explosive. Such fear of difference has led to growing religious intolerance in America, as numerous studies have highlighted.

In 2015, The Hindu American Foundation released a report, "Bullying and Bias against Hindu Students in American Schools," after surveying 335 middle and high school students.[2] One in three Hindu American students reported that they have been bullied for their religious beliefs; and one in eight students said that their teachers made sarcastic remarks about Hinduism in front of the class. The Georgetown Bridge Initiative released a report in 2016, "When Islamophobia Turns Violent,"[3] that tracked Islamophobia during the presidential election season. The sobering information shows that in 2015 there were over 170 incidents of anti-Muslim violence and vandalism. More disturbing is that not only adults, but children, as young as 12, participated in or encouraged violence against Muslims. The FBI's Hate Crime Statistics investigation reported in 2015 that of the 1402 offenses based on religious bias that year, 52 percent were anti-Jewish and 22 percent anti-Islamic.[4] Finally, the Anti-Defamation League's "Audit of AntiSemitic Incidents," released in 2016, shows that the number of violent anti-Semitic assaults taking place in the US rose dramatically in 2015.[5] Over 940 anti-Semitic cases were reported to the ADL that year. Most disturbingly, the number of incidents on college campuses doubled as compared to 2014. These reports highlight the rise of religious intolerance in our country alongside its changing religious landscape.

Billions of individuals around the world adhere to a religious tradition, and the beliefs, behaviors, and belonging they derive from that tradition deeply shape their political, economic, and social decisions. As a society, we are failing to educate our citizens about the religious diversity that exists within our own schools, neighborhoods, and cities. Civic, education, and even religious leaders are only effective when they understand what influences and motivates those with whom they share their community. Thus, in this time of growing religious diversity, becoming truly informed citizens by gaining a basic understanding of the diverse religious traditions and non-religious worldviews should be a priority for all. It should not be forgotten that our country was founded on the idea that all people have the right to pursue their deepest convictions, and that we have the responsibility to protect that right even for those with whom we disagree. Education about religious traditions and an understanding of the founding principles of the First Amendment help others generate respect and decrease hostility towards all Americans.

Effectively educating the next generation of citizens and producing successful leaders in pluralistic communities requires long-term solutions—solutions that are firmly embedded in the fabric of our Constitution and our communities. The status-quo cannot continue; currently, our country is more concerned with what makes us different rather than how we can all live peacefully and respectably together in diverse communities. We need citizens who are religiously literate, who understand their First Amendment rights and responsibilities, and who have the skills of civil dialogue required to navigate the challenges of living in a pluralistic country. The Georgia Rights, Responsibilities, and Respect Project (the Georgia 3Rs Project) was created to be a catalyst for a First Amendment Schools movement in which teachers, administrators, and students work together to live with their deepest differences. First Amendment schools use the founding principles of the Constitution and a respect for the rights of all people to promote civility and understanding among their constituents. With this approach, the Georgia 3Rs project works toward an educational system that rejects violence, hatred, and fear in the face of difference, and instead provides the resources, skills, and knowledge to heal and promote healthy, peaceful communities.

THE GEORGIA 3RS PROJECT

In 2015, Charles Haynes, the Founding Director of the Religious Freedom Center of the Freedom Forum was approached by Rev. George Wirth on behalf of the Cousins Foundation, an Atlanta-based family charitable foundation, to help develop a project that would address the above concerns. As a nonpartisan, nonsectarian national initiative focused on educating the public about religious liberty principles of the First Amendment, the Religious Freedom Center leadership saw this as an excellent opportunity to create a model for school districts that could be replicated across the nation and make a significant and sustainable impact on the future.

During the next twelve months, Dr. Haynes and Rev. Wirth, alongside Nate Walker, executive director of the Religious Freedom Center, Brad Bryant, Vice

President at REACH Georgia, and Erin Hames, President at ReformEd, developed a three-year initiative designed to create demonstration models of religious literacy and religious liberty in two Georgia public school districts. After securing significant gifts from several Atlanta-based foundations and individual donors as well as a contribution from the Freedom Forum Institute, the groundbreaking Georgia Rights, Responsibility, and Respect Project was launched in October 2016.

The Georgia 3Rs Project builds on 25 years of experience acquired by Dr. Haynes and Oliver "Buzz" Thomas, a religious liberty attorney, who have worked with over 500 school districts nationwide to help them assess the effectiveness of their current policies and ensure that school officials and educators understand and apply First Amendment principles throughout the district. The current Georgia 3Rs Project was also inspired by 3Rs Projects in California, Utah, and Georgia that were initiated in the early 1990s to address First Amendment issues in local school districts. Thanks to the deep commitment and resilience of volunteers, these projects continue to have a significant impact on their local communities.

Lessons from these projects and the experiences of Dr. Haynes and Mr. Thomas have shaped the current Georgia 3Rs Project. The project is grounded in: (1) a constitutional commitment to religious liberty as an inalienable right guaranteed by the First Amendment; (2) the civic responsibility of citizens to guard that right for all others, including those with whom we disagree; and (3) the respect necessary for civil discourse across differences in religion and belief. The project's "3Rs" framework is derived from The Williamsburg Charter, a consensus document signed by 200 national leaders on June 22, 1988 commemorating the 200th anniversary of Virginia's call for a Bill of Rights. The project is also informed by the national consensus guidelines on the role of religion in public schools collected in *Finding Common Ground: A First Amendment Guide to Religion and Public Schools*.[6]

Framed by these constitutional principles and consensus documents, the Georgia 3Rs Project seeks to empower schools to teach about the academic study of religion and religious freedom and thus promote greater civil dialogue and civic participation in our communities. Religious freedom issues are not only well suited for promoting such cooperation and understanding, but also prepare our students to be global citizens and compete in a global economy. The role of religion in literature, art, music, society, governance, and more is indisputable, and students graduating from secondary schools must have a working knowledge of the world's religious traditions and their impact in order to be fully educated and prepared for their future endeavors.

Uniquely, this project provides a holistic approach by engaging and providing support for all key stakeholders (school board members, administrators, teachers, parents, students, religious and civic leaders, etc.) in the demonstration districts. The project is also building institutional partnerships with local universities which can provide expert content-level knowledge to district teachers and host courses developed and taught by the Religious Freedom Center to equip pre- and in-service educators with the knowledge and skills necessary to teach about religion and navigate religious freedom issues in the classroom. These courses use a blended learning model of education to combine online instruction, peer-group interactions, and conventional reading and writing assignments and required videoconferences. Educators and the public can take these classes to learn about the world's religions, the history of religious liberty in America, how the First Amendment applies to public schools, and, most importantly, how to use and pass on the information they gain to students, administrators, and their communities. In addition, the project has created over fifty hours of online and on-site professional development resources, the vast majority of which can be easily accessed by educators across the country from the Religious Freedom Center's website.

Civic engagement and civil discourse do not come naturally, and if the United States is to overcome the increasing trend of hatred and violence seen over the last couple of years, all members of a community must be fully educated about the realities of religious pluralism and the responsibility we have to protect the rights of others.

Civil organizations like the U.S. Department of Justice, educational organizations such as the NEA, and many religious groups have either released statements on their own or come together to speak out against the current lack and subsequent detriment of almost any academically focused approach to teaching about religion in our public schools.

Most education officials are well aware of the importance of religion and its impact in the classroom. The majority of state curricula include short to moderate units on religious traditions from around the world. Yet, most current and soon-to-be educators receive little or no training in the academic study of religion, biblical studies, world religions, literary criticism, archaeology, and other disciplines relevant to religious freedom and literacy. The resources developed by the project align to these curricular standards to ensure that educators receive core competencies in the religions they teach, transforming units that were previously fraught and uncomfortable into spaces for deep conversations that model how Americans can live and thrive in a diverse democracy.

Religious freedom and religious literacy challenges often present themselves in ways that do not connect directly to the curriculum. Because religions shape our deepest convictions, religious liberty issues can come in the form of student expression, religious clothing and apparel, religious holidays for students, religious symbols, waivers of participation, and waivers of immunization. Every day, educators across the country are dealing with these concerns without a complete understanding of what laws and codes of conduct apply. Most colleges of education are sending graduates into public school classrooms who have never been taught about religious freedom or how it and the First Amendment apply to public

schools, nor have they received training in the methodology and content of religious studies. The professional development and blended learning courses that the project has developed will fill these gaps in education guaranteeing that those who participate will be able to confidently approach in-classroom and extra-curricula religious liberty and religious literacy concerns as soon as they occur.

The Georgia 3Rs project is driven by five objectives: engage schools, prepare leaders, publish resources, create partnerships, and model for the nation the positive outcomes when educational, civic, and religious leaders work together to promote religious literacy and liberty in their public schools. Each piece is crucial to the success of the program and ensures that parents, educators, community leaders, and especially students are fully supported along the way to becoming communities that champion principles of rights, responsibility, and respect for all people.

ENGAGE SCHOOLS

To ensure that the project can serve as a model for Georgia and the nation, the Georgia 3Rs leadership team has established partnerships with two innovative districts that represent the wide range of Local Units of Administration (LUAs) found in urban, suburban, and rural communities across the state.

Superintendent J. Alvin Wilbanks of Gwinnett County Public Schools and Superintendent Steve J. Smith of Bleckley County Schools are extraordinary leaders of education in Georgia and understand the deep challenges their communities face as ever more diverse perspectives are represented in the public sphere. They are committed to this groundbreaking effort in the hopes that they will help create models of First Amendment school districts that can be replicated across Georgia and throughout the nation.

Gwinnett County Public Schools is Georgia's largest district with over 175,000 students and has a well-earned reputation as a leader of educational excellence in the state. Gwinnett serves both economically and ethnically diverse urban and suburban communities, allowing the project to demonstrate success across diverse school clusters led by a district administration that is capable of managing one of the largest education systems in the county.

Bleckley County Schools brings to the Georgia 3Rs Project another high-performing district but one that serves a small, rural population. With Bleckley, the project will be able to show how a small-scale but tight-knit community of civic, religious, and educational leaders can come together to enrich their children's education.

In implementing the project, the Georgia 3Rs team consults with the districts' school boards to ensure that current and future policies addressing the teaching of religious literacy and religious freedom are effective and consistent with the First Amendment principles of rights, responsibility, and respect.

The team is also working with community leaders and other key stakeholders within the district representing a wide range of perspectives to ensure that all parties have a voice in the process. These stakeholders are encouraged to offer insights as well as become involved in the initiative's implementation. Parents and guardians will be reached through PTAs and community organizations to advocate for an education that is comprehensive and prepares their children to be global citizens. The project also encourages local religious leaders to be helpful resources for teachers and administrators while respecting the right guaranteed by the First Amendment of all to practice their faith or lack thereof. Civic leaders are also brought in to advocate for an education that includes religious liberty and literacy to promote genuine constructive dialogue and community fellowship.

By reaching out and involving each of these groups, the project can adapt dynamically to the specific needs and concerns of an individual district, and community members actively see their leaders and representatives involved in the project's implementation. The initiative is therefore viewed not as an outside group imposing change but as the community itself coming together to better their lives and the education of their youth.

PREPARE LEADERS

It is not simply enough for school districts to develop and implement policies that encourage teachers to educate students about religious practice and freedom in their public schools. Every day, parents across the nation entrust their child's education to teachers and administrators who have too often received little or no training in the academic fields and disciplines relevant to religious freedom and literacy. Central to the Georgia 3Rs project is the objective of preparing these leaders to enter the classroom with relevant and accurate knowledge and the understanding to present that knowledge to students in keeping with the framework established by the First Amendment.

Distance education and curriculum development experts at the Religious Freedom Center (http://www.religiousfreedomcenter.org) have built a virtual campus to support courses and resources for teachers and administrators. The campus includes platforms for the online and onsite blended learning courses and professional development for educators at partner school districts. Using best-in-class primary and secondary sources, the courses combine textual, video, and audio resources created specifically for teachers. By creating these courses, the Religious Freedom Center has developed a suite of new academically rigorous, constitutionally sound materials that educators can immediately adapt for their classrooms. In addition, the Religious Freedom Center has has partnered with educational organizations such as the National Council for the Social Studies to offer summer institutes in Washington D.C. for educators across the country interested in teaching about religion and religious freedom across the curriculum.

The Religious Freedom Center also launched two graduate-level blended learning courses (in the fall of 2017): "First Amendment Approaches to Religion & Public Schools" and "Teaching about Religion in Public Schools" as well as two online-only courses: "Histories of Religious Liberty in America" and "Religions of the World." These semester-long courses have been offered to graduate and undergraduate students, pre-service and in-service teachers, and will hopefully be available to high school students interested in earning college credit through Georgia's dual-enrollment program in the near future. The aim of these innovative courses on religious literacy and religious liberty is to change the education landscape in Georgia and the nation. Thanks to the distance-learning model, students, educators, and scholars from around the country will be able to participate in the initiative regardless of where they live.

PUBLISH RESOURCES

Supporting educators must also include the development and distribution of First Amendment friendly resources teachers can use in their classrooms. The Georgia 3Rs project website (http://www.ga3rs.org) houses resources that provide teachers lesson plans and materials they can download and insert into their curricula as needed. For example, teachers are able to access "Living with our Deepest Differences," a series of lessons that introduce students to the history of religious freedom in America. "First Freedoms: A Documentary History of First Amendment Rights in America," is another excellent example of a textbook and discussion guide resource that explores all five of the freedoms guaranteed by the First Amendment. The project has also partnered with the Society of Biblical Literature to create lesson plans that specially educate about the Bible in a constitutionally friendly way. The project team continues to seek and identify potential partner organizations to create additional resources for teachers. All applicable resources, including lesson plans, are peer-reviewed to ensure they meet the high standards expected of academic study. Resources will also adhere to state education standards so that teachers can easily implement them without fear of devoting time to material that does not prepare students for assessments and future classes. Many resources are currently available and the team will continue to add First Amendment friendly classroom resources as they are developed.

CREATE PARTNERSHIPS

The Georgia 3Rs project is heavily focused on creating partnerships. Some of these have already been discussed above, such as those with the districts themselves, the universities and colleges who will offer pre- and in-service teacher training, and the academic organizations like the Society of Biblical Literature that are creating in-classroom resources. The Georgia 3Rs project has also partnered with Emory's Center for the Study of Law and Religion to offer districts guidance and legal advice as they implement the policies and lessons that have been developed. The project leadership is also closely working with other public and private universities in Georgia to ensure that experts across the fields of teacher education and religious studies are available as resources to partner districts. Teachers, administrators, and educational leaders will never have to be helpless if challenges or issues arise in the district around teaching religious liberty or literacy.

The broader communities themselves are also partners in the Georgia 3Rs project. Efforts that come from extra-community organizations can face substantial opposition when they are perceived to disregard community insight in favor of broad and generic policies. No initiative is immune to this resistance whether it comes from small policy groups or state legislatures and departments of education, as the contention around the Common Core State Standards has shown. With this in mind, the Georgia 3Rs project has cultivated these partnerships with sustainability and institutionalization as a primary goal. For any community initiative to be truly successful, the community that will benefit from it must not only invest time and effort to create a successful outcome but also must own the initiative itself. The partnerships detailed above will continue to support and enrich the district for years to come.

MODEL FOR THE NATION

With the decline of civil dialogue in our country and the need for our students to understand global issues to be successful in a worldwide economy, it is more important than ever for our education system to address religious freedom and religious literacy. The Religious Freedom Center is continually being contacted by groups in states from across the country and abroad who have recognized the same challenges and seek similar solutions. Georgia is a diverse state with forward looking leaders and the experience that the project gains in Georgia will be invaluable as other states adopt the same kind of project in the future.

The Georgia 3Rs team has already begun building the framework to take this model across the nation. The project team is in conversations with several universities around the country—in Utah and Kentucky—and has also built an extensive network of educators in Illinois, Maryland, and the District of Columbia who are interested in replicating religious literacy and religious liberty programs in their own districts. The Georgia 3Rs team continues to look for ways to support the work that is currently being done by the California 3Rs project and the Utah 3Rs project.

Follow the progress of the Georgia 3Rs project on its website (http://www.ga3rs.org). There are many ways for a teacher to get involved: enroll in one of its graduate/undergraduate blended learning on-line courses for educators; use its online professional development materials for in-service teachers, administrators, and community members; take advantage of its many First Amendment friendly materials in your classroom. Effective educators in the 21st century—working, living, and educating in a pluralistic society—must have the knowledge and skills to promote civil dialogue, religious freedom, and religious literacy in the classroom and beyond. The Religious Freedom Center, the First Amendment Schools movement, and initiatives like the Georgia 3Rs project offer important resources to support these goals.

NOTES

1. The report is accessible at http://www.pewforum.org/2015/05/12/americas-changing-religious-landscape/

2. The report is available at https://www.hafsite.org/resources/classroom-subjected

3. See http://bridge.georgetown.edu/report/when-islamophobia-turns-violent-the-2016-u-s-presidential-elections/

4. See https://ucr.fbi.gov/hate-crime/2015/topic-pages/victims_final

5. Accessible at https://www.adl.org/news/press-releases/adl-audit-anti-semitic-assaults-rise-dramatically-across-the-country-in-2015#.WJfx2LYrL_9

6. Charles C. Haynes and Oliver Thomas, *Finding Common Ground: A First Amendment Guide to Religion and Public Schools* (Nashville, Tenn.: First Amendment Center, 2007).

PART II

Creative Pedagogy for Study about Religions

Teaching Lived Religion through Literature: Classroom Strategies for Community-Based Learning

HENRY GOLDSCHMIDT

A half century after the U.S. Supreme Court's landmark decision in *Abington v. Schempp*, which banned school-led devotional Bible reading in American public schools while encouraging the academic study of religion, there is a broad consensus among scholars, educators, policy makers, and religious leaders that the study of religion must be a significant component of American public education. Of course, not all Americans are aware of this consensus—a 2010 survey found that 64% of us mistakenly believe it is unconstitutional for public schools to offer comparative religion courses.[1] And one could hardly say that the study of religion is thriving in our public schools.[2] Nevertheless, most educators agree that an adequate education must include some understanding of religion. Indeed, many have advocated the academic study of religion as a way to bridge the sometimes bitter divides among religious and secular Americans. The study of religious diversity, they argue, is essential to the functioning of our multicultural democracy.[3]

Yet despite this invaluable—and hard-won—consensus, a number of fundamental questions remain. What do American students need to know about religion? And how is it best taught? Though there are a wide range of approaches to the academic study of religion, most secondary school religious studies curricula are still structured by the "world religions" model of conceptualizing religious diversity that was dominant in American universities in the mid-twentieth century. And unfortunately, I would argue, this pedagogic model too often promotes a superficial form of religious literacy, rather than a serious engagement with religious diversity—substituting a decontextualized knowledge of dates and doctrines for an empathic understanding of religious lives. In this essay, I will draw on current scholarship in religious studies to argue instead for a focus on "lived religion" in secondary school religious studies curricula—for an approach to the academic study of religion grounded in the everyday life of our pluralistic society.

Following a brief discussion of these two pedagogic models, I will explore specific strategies for teaching about lived religion. Although my own work at the Interfaith Center of New York has focused on community-based, experiential forms of religious diversity education, I will focus here on the study of religion through literature, as exemplified in a discussion of James Baldwin's classic novel *Go Tell it on the Mountain*. For teachers who may not be comfortable with community-based education, the study of religion through literature (as well as film, and other media) allows students to engage with the depth and complexity of religious life without leaving the relative comfort of the classroom.

Whether in a full-year course or week-long unit, the vast majority of secondary school religious studies curricula are framed as discussions of "world religions." This pedagogic model tends to describe global religious diversity in terms of a fixed set of six or eight "major" traditions, each of which is defined by a fixed set of four or five characteristics: (1) its core doctrines or beliefs; (2) the life history of its founder, if any; (3) its geographic origin and diffusion; (4) its sacred texts, if any; and in some cases (5) its major holidays or ritual practices. Islam, for example, may be taught fairly easily through a discussion of the Five Pillars, an account of the life of Muhammad and rapid growth of his movement, a map and timeline to illustrate its global expansion from the Arabian Peninsula, a few brief selections from the Qur'an, and perhaps a discussion of the customs surrounding Ramadan. Similarly, Buddhism can be encapsulated in the Four Noble Truths and Eightfold Path, the life story of the historical Buddha, the diffusion of his teachings throughout East Asia, excerpts from a sutra or two, and perhaps a discussion of meditation. And so on for a number of other traditions, each of which is assumed to fit—or remade to fit—the conceptual template of a world religion.

This "dates and doctrines" approach to the study of religion may give students the answers to factual questions about a number of significant faith traditions, but it fails to prepare them for participation in the civic life of their religiously diverse society. By defining each religion in terms of a single, static body of doctrine, ritual, and text, the world religions model offers students little or no understanding of the far more flexible forms of popular belief, practice, and interpretation that make up of the fabric of religious life. The Ten Commandments stand in for the broad spectrum of Jewish faith, doubt, and identity; the Four Gospels for the countless ways that Christians work to bring them to life; the Five Pillars for the kaleidoscopic diversity of the world's 1.6 billion Muslims; the Eightfold Path for the personal journeys of immigrant and American-born Buddhists.[4]

Recognizing these limitations of the world religions model, many scholars of religion have shifted, in recent years, towards a focus on what is often called lived religion. The study of lived religion is grounded in everyday religious life, rather than canonical doctrines or texts. Scholars of lived religion explore how doctrines, rituals, and texts

may shape—and be shaped by—the practical concerns and political aspirations of historically specific, local communities. They often question the boundaries of established religions, as well as the definition of "religion" as such. And they pay close attention to the racial, ethnic, gendered, and doctrinal diversity within every single religious community. In short, the study of lived religion takes the analysis of religious diversity out of the rarified realm of doctrine and text, and places it instead within the give-and-take of a multicultural public sphere.[5]

This, I would argue, is the most appropriate model of religious diversity education for American secondary schools. Our students certainly do need to learn about the histories and beliefs of diverse religious traditions, but much more than that, they need to learn about the religious lives of their diverse neighbors. They need an academically grounded engagement with the social realities of contemporary faith communities. They need to know how their own experiences of American society may be radically different—and not so different at all—from the experiences of their peers living in different religious worlds. These are the fundamental goals of a lived religion pedagogy.

But beyond these broad principles, how do you do it? How do you incorporate discussions of everyday religious life into a secondary school social studies curriculum? There is no single right answer to this question.

With my colleagues at the Interfaith Center of New York, I have developed programs for both teachers and students structured around panel discussions with local religious leaders and site visits to local houses of worship—programs that introduce New Yorkers and others to religious diversity by introducing them to their diverse neighbors.[6] But many teachers are understandably reluctant to invite religious leaders to speak with their students, or take students to visit a house of worship. This is especially true in American public schools, where a community-based religious diversity program that goes awry can raise very serious First Amendment concerns.[7] I will therefore focus here on classroom strategies for teaching about lived religion, and, in particular, on the study of religion through literature. I hope to demonstrate the richness of this approach by showing what students may learn about Christianity in reading James Baldwin's classic novel *Go Tell It on the Mountain*.[8]

Baldwin's semi-autobiographical novel explores the conflicted personal and spiritual awakening of fourteen year-old John Grimes, as well as the lives of his family and other community members at an African-American Pentecostal church in Harlem in the 1930s. Set over the course of a single day—and a long prayer service—the novel uses extended flashbacks to trace the painful saga of the Grimes family, and the broader contours of African-American history in the early twentieth century. In this short essay, I cannot discuss the complex details of Baldwin's narrative, but suffice it to say that the story of the Grimes family is tied to a series of moving, detailed, ethnographically and psychologically nuanced portraits of African-American Christian life.

Classroom discussions of *Go Tell It on the Mountain* can help students engage with a number of major themes in many high school social studies curricula.[9] The novel's reflections on African-American life in Harlem and the rural South, for example, can give students of U.S. history an intimate, first-person understanding of the Great Migration. Its portrait of a deeply segregated New York, as seen through the eyes of an African-American family, raises enduring questions about race and the modern American city—questions that echo in today's Black Lives Matter movement. And the poignant story of young John Grimes speaks to the personal and political choices faced by many high school students, as they struggle to reconcile the emerging tensions between their religious faith and sexuality. In these and other ways, *Go Tell It on the Mountain* can help teachers and students explore a range of issues at the heart of American history and civic life.

But while social studies teachers have grown increasingly comfortable with the use of literature to deepen their students' understandings of historical events like the Great Migration, they are often reluctant to apply the same rich pedagogy in teaching about religious diversity. Rather than asking students to explore evocative narratives of religious faith and experience, they generally stick to the comfort and security of dates and doctrines, texts and founders. Novels set in contemporary faith communities can thus enrich the study of religion, by offering students a more fully human, empathic understanding of religious lives that are different from their own. I hope to show (not just tell) you what I mean through a brief discussion of *Go Tell It on the Mountain*.[10]

The narrative unfolds over the course of the Saturday evening Tarry Service at the Temple of the Fire Baptized, which is "not the biggest church in Harlem, nor yet the smallest" (p. 5). Baldwin describes the spirit-filled prayers of the saints, and how "Their singing caused [John] to believe in the presence of the Lord; indeed it was no longer a question of belief, because they made that presence real" (p. 7). He captures the swelling, syncopated rhythms of Pentecostal worship, describing how:

> While John watched, the Power struck someone . . . they cried out, a long wordless crying, and, arms out outstretched like wings, they began the Shout. . . . then the tambourines began again, and the voices rose again, and the music swept on again, like fire, or flood, or judgment. Then the church seemed to swell with the Power it held, and, like a planet rocking in space, the temple rocked with the Power of God. (pp. 7-8)

In addition to such vivid descriptions of religious practice, Baldwin explores the spiritual lives and experiences of the Grimes family—their personal faith, doubts, and aspirations. At the very moment of his conversion and rebirth as a Christian, for example, Baldwin describes how Gabriel Grimes (John's authoritarian adoptive father) hears his mother's voice "a-singing low and sweet, right there beside me," and:

I argue in this chapter that the study of literature and film can enrich the study of religion in American secondary schools, by offering students a more fully human, empathic understanding of religious lives that are different from their own. But how do teachers choose novels and films to support classroom teaching on diverse faith traditions? What should they look for in literary and cinematic representations of religion? There's no one right answer to these questions—as with resources for teaching on any subject, the answer depends on you, your students, and your school community. But I can suggest some general guidelines.

First, you should acquaint yourself with the wide range of texts and films available for students and young adult readers. A Google search for "Buddhism novel" or "Islam film," for example, can identify suitable educational websites that open a world of possibilities. For specific suggestions, see the lists of novels, dramatic films, and documentaries set in American religious communities (as well as other resources for teaching religious diversity) on the website of the Religious Worlds of New York summer institute for teachers, at http://religiousworldsnyc.org/resource-page/resources-teaching-american-religious-diversity. And for a broader view of the field, see the scholarly articles and reviews in the journal *Religion & Literature* and the *Journal of Religion and Film* (both of which are available online).

But how to choose from this embarrassment of riches? Perhaps above all, look for novels and films that offer portraits of individuals and communities living their faith in specific social contexts. Don't waste your time searching for a single novel or film that captures the full spectrum of diversity within a global religious tradition. There is no such thing. One of your jobs as a teacher is to situate a novel or film within that larger whole, tying its distinctive characters and local settings to their broader social and religious histories. Effective teaching with *Go Tell It on the Mountain*, for example, would probably require a little research on African-American church history, and perhaps the strategic use of a "world religions" textbook, in order to place the Grimes family within the larger Christian world.

Similarly, look for novels and films that illustrate specific themes or issues within a given religious tradition, or perhaps comparative themes that are relevant to a range of traditions. Don't waste your time searching for a single novel or film that sums up the theological heart of a faith. There is no such thing. I have argued that *Go Tell It on the Mountain*, for example, is an extraordinary resource for teaching aspects of Christianity, but no one text can tell your students everything they need to know about two thousand years of Christian thought and practice. Again, one of your jobs as a teacher of lived religion is to draw out the ties between part and whole—revealing the world in a proverbial grain of sand.

Look for novels and films that include vivid, experiential descriptions of religious life and ritual practice, while avoiding sensationalist or stereotypical images. The challenge, of course, is to make this distinction when evaluating a novel or film set in a faith community you are not familiar with. If you've never been to an African-American Pentecostal church, for example, or read any scholarship on the Pentecostal movement, how can you judge whether Baldwin's description of the Grimes family's church "rock[ing] with the Power of God" (see p. 55 of this chapter) is a vivid portrait or a clichéd stereotype? In most cases, you can rely on your own critical reading skills—if you can spot racial stereotypes in a dusty old textbook, you can likely spot religious ones in an unfamiliar novel or film. When in doubt, however, it can be extremely helpful to gauge reactions to a novel or film among members of the faith community it describes. Ask your friends and colleagues, or look for comments online, but be sure to keep in mind the internal diversity of the faith tradition in question—members of a relatively elite African Methodist Episcopal church, for example, might react negatively to an accurate, sympathetic description of Pentecostal rituals with which they are unfamiliar or uncomfortable.

Look for novels and films centered on fully human, idiosyncratic characters, wrestling in creative ways with their faith traditions. Contrary to a widespread secular stereotype of religiosity, very few people of faith "blindly" follow the dictates of their tradition. I'd be suspicious, therefore, of any novel or film centered on cardboard cut-out images of piety. Whenever possible, look for novels and films that present a range of perspectives within and around a given faith community. Try to highlight the tensions among these diverse perspectives, as I have done here by discussing conflicting views of conversion in *Go Tell It on the Mountain*. There are few things more important for students of religion to understand than the simple fact that every faith community is home to rational, thoughtful individuals, with a wide range of personal opinions about their tradition.

And finally, whatever novels or films you may use to enrich your teaching on religion, it is essential for students to understand that no media representation offers an objective, transparent window into religious life. One of your jobs as a teacher is to help students appreciate the many ways that an author or filmmaker's own perspective may shape their portrayal of the religious worlds they describe. Of course, this is true of documentary films, academic research, and ostensibly objective textbooks as well, but the role of an author's personal voice is particularly clear when teaching with literature and dramatic film. In some cases—perhaps especially in teaching a semi-autobiographical novel like *Go Tell It on the Mountain*—it may be helpful to tell your students about the author's own religious or secular background. Don't rest too comfortably on biographical details, however, as it is essential to acknowledge—and indeed, to celebrate—the remarkable feat of imagination involved in capturing religious experience on the page or screen. An understanding of this creative process can only deepen your students' engagement with the religious lives they encounter in literature and film.

When he heard this singing, which filled all the silent air, which swelled until it filled all the waiting earth, the heart within him broke, and yet began to rise, lifted of its burden; and his throat unlocked; and his tears came down as though the listening skies had opened. "Then I praised God [says Gabriel], Who had brought me out of Egypt and set my feet on solid rock." (p. 93)

This passage, and many others like it, offers readers an intimate, first-person understanding of Christianity that they cannot gain from a world religions textbook.

Beyond these rich portraits of Christian life, *Go Tell It on the Mountain* also offers an extended meditation on one of the central premises of the Christian tradition: the transformative power of conversion. This may not be a "core doctrine" of Christianity—world religions textbooks don't generally rank it alongside the Trinity and the Incarnation—but ever since the Apostle Paul's dramatic change of heart on the road to Damascus (according to the biblical book of Acts 9:3-18), mainstream Christian thought has generally assumed that sinful individuals can be transformed through the salvific work of Christ.[11] Indeed, this promise of personal transformation—a present day, this-worldly correlate of eternal salvation—has been particularly significant within American Evangelical Protestantism, both Black and White, since the Great Awakenings of the eighteenth and nineteenth centuries.

The devout older teenager Elisha gives voice to this tradition in *Go Tell It on the Mountain*, when he reassures John, "when the Lord saves you . . . He gives you a new mind and a new heart, and then you don't find no pleasure in the world, you get all your joy in walking and talking with Jesus every day" (p. 49). Baldwin explores this claim throughout the novel, but ultimately questions the Christian promise of transformation. He offers unsparing accounts of individual sin—more often than not on the part of the saints—and a scathing critique of our sinful society, wracked by the brutal legacy of slavery. The Grimes family looks to its faith for redemption from a broken world. But against this backdrop, Baldwin asks, can one really find in Christ "a new beginning, a blood-washed day" (93)?

At a pivotal moment in the narrative, John's mother Elizabeth poses this searching question to her future sister-in-law Florence: "'But don't you think,' she hesitantly asked, 'that the Lord can change a person's heart?'" Florence replies:

> I done heard it said often enough, but I got yet to see it. These [people] running around, talking about the Lord done changed their hearts—ain't nothing happened to them [people]. [12] They got the same old black hearts they was born with. I reckon the Lord done give them those hearts—and, honey, the Lord don't give out no second helpings, I'm here to tell you. (p. 182)

Elizabeth's question—at once social, psychological, and theological—is the kind of question secondary school students need to explore if they wish to understand the human realities of religious life, as opposed to the clear-cut claims of doctrine. Elisha answers yes, "when the Lord saves you . . . He gives you a new mind and a new heart." Florence answers no, "the Lord don't give out no second helpings." John himself isn't sure, and Baldwin's narrative moves ambivalently back and forth between these perspectives. While the world religions section of a widely used high school history textbook blithely asserts that, "Christians believe that faith in Jesus saves believers from God's penalty for sin," *Go Tell It on the Mountain* offers a series of subtle reflections on this claim though the moving story of John Grimes, his family, their church, and their society.[13]

James Baldwin may stand out in his literary genius, but *Go Tell It on the Mountain* is hardly the only source available for such a rich, engaging account of religious life. Secondary school teachers might teach aspects of Judaism—and particularly the internal diversity of the American Jewish community—through Chaim Potok's *The Chosen*.

They might teach aspects of Islam through Mohja Kahf's *The Girl in the Tangerine Scarf*, or aspects of Haitian Vodou through Edwige Danticat's *Breath, Eyes, Memory*. In addition to novels like these, they might look to dramatic films like Bernardo Bertolucci's "Little Buddha," Spike Lee's "Malcolm X," or Jonathan Wacks' "Powwow Highway." They might have students explore the mainstream of American religious life through documentary films like Danny Alpert's "The Calling" and Rashid Ghazi's "Fordson: Faith, Fasting, Football, and the American Dream," or have them explore the ragged edges of contemporary religious identities through films like Lucy Walker's "Devil's Playground" and Omar Majeed's "Taqwacore: The Birth of Punk Islam."[14] None of these books and films is a perfect source (whatever that may mean) for the study of the traditions and communities they chronicle. To use them effectively, teachers must help students understand that no media representation—very much including documentary film—offers a purely objective, transparent window into social life. But with this essential caveat in mind, the study of literature and film can enrich—or transform—the study of religion in American secondary schools, by introducing students to the textures and tensions of everyday life in specific, local religious communities.

The most daunting challenge, and the greatest reward, of such a pedagogy lies in this local specificity. A serious engagement with lived religion focuses our attention on the diversity within every faith tradition, and makes it impossible to speak of world religions in sweeping, universal terms. In teaching *Go Tell it on the Mountain*, for example, it is important for students to understand that the Christianity of an African-American Pentecostal church is different, in many ways, from the diverse Christianities practiced in other communities throughout the world. The Grimes family cannot stand in for the world's nearly 2.2 billion Christians. But the essential point is that no one can—not even the ancient founder of the tradition. The study of lived religion should help students understand that global religious traditions only come to life in the particular concerns and experiences of their adherents. As the influential historian Robert Orsi has put it:

The key questions [for the study of lived religion] concern what people do with religious idioms, how they use them, what they make of themselves and their worlds with them . . . . There is no religion apart from this, no religion that people have not taken up in their hands.[15]

The Grimes family may stand, in its historical specificity, for the process of "tak[ing] up" religion in one's hands—the project of world-making, community-building, and self-fashioning through faith. Far more than any dates or doctrines, this deeply human project is what students need to understand if they are to be active participants in the civic life of their religiously diverse society.

NOTES

1. Data drawn from the June 2010 U. S. Religious Knowledge Survey, by the Pew Forum on Religion and Public Life. See http://www.pewforum.org/2010/09/28/u-s-religious-knowledge-survey (accessed January 5, 2017).

2. For a critical analysis of the state of religious studies in American schools see Warren Nord, *Does God Make a Difference? Taking Religion Seriously in Our Schools and Universities* (New York: Oxford University Press, 2010), 41-99. One need not accept Nord's far-reaching critique of the secularization of American education to recognize the dispiriting portrait he paints of religious diversity education in our public schools.

3. For relatively recent discussions of the pedagogic and/or civic significance of religious diversity education in American secondary schools, see for example: Nord, *Does God Make a Difference?*; Emile Lester, *Teaching about Religions: A Democratic Approach for Public Schools* (Ann Arbor: U. of Michigan Press, 2011); Diane Moore, *Overcoming Religious Illiteracy: A Cultural Studies Approach to the Study of Religion in Secondary Education* (New York: Palgrave Macmillan, 2007); Warren Nord and Charles Haynes, *Taking Religion Seriously Across the Curriculum* (Alexandria and Nashville: The Association for Supervision and Curriculum Development and First Amendment Center, 1998); Charles Haynes and Oliver Thomas, writers and editors, *Finding Common Ground: A Guide to Religious Liberty in Public Schools* (Nashville: The First Amendment Center, 2001); and the American Academy of Religion's *Guidelines for Teaching About Religion in K-12 Public Schools in the United States* (AAR Religion in the Schools Task Force, 2010). The *Guidelines* of the American Academy of Religion are reproduced in Appendix 2 of this book.

4. For a more detailed critique of the world religions model in American secondary education (from which I have drawn some of the text of this essay) see Henry Goldschmidt, "From World Religions to Lived Religion: Towards a Pedagogy of Civic Engagement in Secondary School Religious Studies Curricula," in *Civility, Religious Pluralism, and Education*, Vincent Biondo and Andrew Fiala, eds., (New York: Routledge, 2014), 177-192. And for influential critiques of the world

religions model in academic religious studies see, for example, Tomoko Masuzawa, *The Invention of World Religions: Or, How European Universalism was Preserved in the Language of Pluralism* (Chicago: The U. of Chicago Press, 2005) and Jonathan Z. Smith, "A Matter of Class: Taxonomies of Religion," *Harvard Theological Review*, no. 89 (1996), 387-403.

5. This description of recent research in religious studies characterizes the work of a wide range of scholars, not all of whom use the term "lived religion." For research explicitly focused on lived religion see, for example, Robert Orsi, *The Madonna of 115th Street: Faith and Community in Italian Harlem, 1880-1950* (New Haven: Yale U. Press, 1985); Meredith McGuire, *Lived Religion: Faith and Practice in Everyday Life* (New York: Oxford U. Press, 2008); David Hall, ed., *Lived Religion in America: Toward a History of Practice* (Princeton: Princeton U. Press, 1997); and Nancy Ammerman, ed., *Everyday Religion: Observing Modern Religious Lives* (New York: Oxford U. Press, 2007). For programmatic statements about the importance of studying lived religion see Robert Orsi, "Everyday Miracles: The Study of Lived Religion," in David Hall's collection (just cited), 3-21; and Robert Orsi, "Is the Study of Lived Religion Irrelevant to the World We Live In?" *Journal for the Scientific Study of Religion*, Vol. 42, No. 2 (2003), 169-174.

6. For detailed discussions of two such programs, see Goldschmidt, "From World Religions to Lived Religion" (cited above in note #4), 185-190.

7. Take, for example, the heated controversy that developed after a social studies class from Wellesley Middle School visited the Islamic Society of Boston in May of 2010. For a detailed discussion see Linda K. Wertheimer, *Faith Ed: Teaching about Religion in an Age of Intolerance* (Boston: Beacon Press, 2015), 39-70. Given these and other concerns, a number of scholars and educators have, in fact, advised against the use of guest speakers and site visits in secondary school religious studies curricula. See, for example, the concerns articulated in the American Academy of Religion's Guidelines, 23-24 (cited above in note #3).

8. James Baldwin, *Go Tell It on the Mountain* (New York: Random House, 2005 [orig. pub. 1952]). Subsequent references to Baldwin appear in parentheses in the text.

9. I've specified high school curricula in this passage, as opposed to middle school or younger grades, because *Go Tell It on the Mountain* could be a tough book to teach for younger students. It includes evocative descriptions of sexuality, though no real sex scenes to speak of. And perhaps more challenging, Baldwin's characters often use the fraught term "nigger," in ways that are entirely appropriate to their historical and linguistic context, but require some critical sophistication on the part of contemporary readers.

10. For more detailed discussions of religious themes in *Go Tell It on the Mountain* than I can offer here, see Barbara Olson, "'Come-to-Jesus Stuff' in James Baldwin's *Go Tell It on the Mountain* and *The Amen Corner*," *African American Review*, Vol. 31, No. 2 (1997), and Miriam Sivan "Out of and Back to Africa: James Baldwin's *Go Tell It On The Mountain*," *Christianity and Literature*, Vol. 51, No. 1 (2001). For a broader discussion of Baldwin's religious thought, and his fraught relationship with African-American Christianity, see Clarence Hardy, *James Baldwin's God: Sex, Hope, and Crisis in Black Holiness Culture* (Knoxville: The U. of Tennessee Press, 2003).

11. There are, of course, important exceptions to this generalization, including some views of predestination in and around the Calvinist tradition.

12. I have substituted the term "people" where Baldwin has Florence use the fraught term "niggers." As noted above, in note 9, Baldwin's use of this term is entirely appropriate to the historical and linguistic context of Harlem in the 1930s, but I am reluctant to use it in my own context as an author and educator.

13. Quote from Jackson Spielvogel, *Glencoe World History, New York Edition* (New York: McGraw Hill/Glencoe, 2006), 216.

14. For more suggestions of novels, dramatic films, and documentaries set in diverse religious communities (as well as other resources for teaching American religious diversity), see the website of the Interfaith Center of New York's Religious Worlds of New York summer institute for teachers, at: http://religiousworldsnyc.org/resource-page/resources-teaching-american-religious-diversity (accessed January 5, 2017).

15. Orsi, "Is the Study of Lived Religion Irrelevant" (cited above in note #5), 172.

CHAPTER EIGHT

Turn and Talk about Faith: A Student Forum on the Study of Religion in Public Schools

MAYA MESH, AMANI Z. H. MOHAMED, AND CHLOE PITKOFF

EDITED BY HENRY GOLDSCHMIDT

INTRODUCTION

HENRY GOLDSCHMIDT

Educators and policy-makers often describe the study of religion as a pedagogic equivalent of broccoli—something that students ought to have, whether they like it or not, because we know it's good for them. The experts agree that a deeper understanding of religious diversity will help our students become well-rounded, thoughtful adults, as well as better neighbors and more effective citizens of their multicultural democracy. So break out the steamer—broccoli for all.

But what do our students think? Do they like broccoli too? And how do they like it cooked? Nearly every K-12 teacher who teaches about religious diversity, whether in a full-year course or a week-long unit, will tell you that the subject is intellectually exciting and personally engaging to most students. But these student voices have generally been absent (with some exceptions, of course) from the long-running policy debate about the study of religion in American public schools. We tend to hear from academics, educators, attorneys, and religious leaders, but not from students themselves. The essays collected here will help fill this important gap.

The three authors were students in New York City public schools when, along with nine of their peers, they all participated in the Interfaith Center of New York's 2015 Learning Together youth fellowship program (a program sponsored by the Open Society Foundations Youth Initiative). The fellowship program brought together a diverse group of young New Yorkers to discuss the role of religious diversity

in local schools, develop their writing and critical thinking skills, and write original op-ed essays. We were pleasantly surprised, at the end of the program, when half of our fellows chose to write essays about the academic study of religion. These young people all called—in a chorus of distinct but overlapping voices—for more thoughtful, engaging discussions of religious diversity in school. It turns out they really do like broccoli, but it could use some garlic or a spicy sauce.

The three essays collected here raise a number of important questions for educators. How, for example, do we strike a balance between academic rigor and personal engagement in teaching about religion? All three authors take religion very seriously as an academic subject, but two (Amani Mohamed, and especially Maya Mesh) also speak movingly about the personal concerns that inform their interest in the study of religion—concerns that aren't always welcome in public school classrooms. How do we find time to teach effectively about religion in an era of high-stakes standardized testing? All three authors (especially Chloe Pitkoff) call for in-depth discussions of religious diversity that go beyond the time allotted to the subject in most test-driven global history courses. And finally, how do we offer our students something richer than the "dates and doctrines" pedagogy of a typical world religions course, while respecting the constitutional principles that structure the study of religion in American public schools? All three authors embrace the important First Amendment limits on faith-based discussion of religion in public schools, but two (Chloe Pitkoff, and especially Amani Mohamed) point out the value of conversations that push against, or even transgress, those limits.

Of course, K-12 educators need not take these authors' advice in every detail, or embrace their broader visions of American religious diversity. But we absolutely do need to hear their voices and understand their concerns. Their perspectives, and those of other students, can enrich the study of religion in American public schools.

IT'S NOT A DINNER PARTY—LET'S TALK ABOUT RELIGION IN SCHOOL

MAYA MESH

I have always attended New York public schools, and in my middle school on the Upper West Side of Manhattan we had a unit on world religions in our Global Studies class. Being in New York City, I did not think twice about studying different religions in school. Everywhere you turn here it's something new—New York feels to me like the most diverse city in the world. Unfortunately for many people, they exist in a reality where they're only able to interact with others who are of their same race, religion, or ethnic group. New York City planners built and zoned the city in a way that allowed our neighborhoods to be very diverse.

However this diversity does not always lead to mutual understanding. New York City is 305 square miles with about 8.5 million people, and 1.1 million children who attend public school. New Yorkers are packed tight, and when we don't get along the results can be catastrophic. In December 2012, for example, a woman named Erika Menendez shoved an Indian Hindu immigrant named Sunando Sen to his death in front of a subway train. In May 2015 she pleaded guilty to manslaughter, and was sentenced to 24 years in prison. Too many incidents like this have occurred in New York since 9/11. In fact, Menendez told police she did it because she has hated Muslims and Hindus ever since the 2001 terror attacks.

Too often we tolerate other New Yorkers on a basic level by avoiding certain topics like religion. There's a saying that there are two things you should never talk about during a dinner party— politics and religion. Regrettably, that is also true in some schools. Students, and even teachers, feel uncomfortable talking about religion. Whenever the topic comes up they completely shut down. Many people have a hard time just talking and sympathizing with people from other religions. The failure is in not educating children and teenagers about religions; they become fearful of what they don't know. These fears can turn into hatred and violence, as in the attack on Sunando Sen. This is just one reason why the world religions unit of my Global Studies course was so important.

As part of the religion unit we had opportunities to visit a local mosque, church, synagogue, and Buddhist temple. Visiting the mosque was the most impactful for me. Walking up to the Islamic Cultural Center on 96th Street and 3rd Avenue, I felt extremely nervous. The building looked well kept, organized, and intimidating. Like most of my female classmates, I kept touching my headscarf to make sure it was still on, with no hair showing, out of fear that I might offend someone. I was extremely curious to see how Muslim prayers would be different from a church or synagogue service.

The service was very interesting, and I left the mosque with mixed feelings because they have traditions I wasn't accustomed to. As a Reform Jew, I had never experienced the separation of men and women in prayer. My synagogue has female rabbis, hence I never felt like being a woman in synagogue was a big deal. But while visiting the mosque I was 100% aware of my gender. There was a wall blocking my view of the imam, although there were speakers attached to the wall so we could hear him loud and clear. It was hot in the women's section, as most of the air conditioning went to the men downstairs. And I wasn't used to the headscarf. The imam was passionate about spreading the message of the Qur'an, in English and Arabic, and he related it to today's world issues. He talked about Noah's ark, and his sermon reminded me of a speech my rabbi had given in our congregation earlier that year. Overall, the service made me appreciate Islam on a whole new level.

Even though I considered myself a very open-minded person before visiting different houses of worship, I left school that day feeling more accepting of other traditions. This experience made me aware of how different and similar religions and people of different cultures can be. I was extremely grateful for the lessons I learned from the field trip. The way I see it, a year later the students in my class might not remember the Five Pillars of Islam, or the names of the sacred sites in Mecca, but we will remember our first visit to a mosque. Whether we remember the musky smell of the carpet, or the feeling of joy that came from participants in the service, we will all remember.

Experiences like these are key parts of learning. The goal of education is to prepare students to go out into the world, and if teachers want to develop a generation of adults who can thrive in our globalized and divergent world, they need to stop ignoring the lines that divide us. It's time to stop neglecting our colors, and support the different shades we all bear. There needs to be a required curriculum to teach about religion from an objective perspective, including field trips to various houses of worship. If not, many students will be blinded by their own ignorance.

Lack of religious understanding has also impacted my own life and personal relationships. Coming from two very different religious and cultural backgrounds, I was always under pressure to explain myself to others. My mother is a first-generation Catholic immigrant from Ecuador who came to this county when she was 17, and my father is a White American Jew. Growing up I always had to explain my religion to my mother's side of the family, and I was often pushed to convert to Catholicism. When I was younger my maternal grandmother always said I should be baptized, even though I was going to Hebrew school and she knew it would never happen. I often heard stereotypical comments about Jews from my Hispanic cousins, as well as suggestions that my Jewishness makes me less Ecuadorian. I was awfully hurt because this made me feel I was abandoning my mother and her family. Then on the Jewish side of the family, I felt uncomfortable when I heard negative comments about the Catholic Church, because I believe that all religions have their own problems.

I have heard hurtful comments about my religion that no child should ever have to experience, and this is happening to people all over New York, and throughout the United States. The only way to break the cycle of prejudice and hatred against different religions is to carefully teach the next generation. By providing a class where objective information is taught and students can learn about each other's traditions, we are more likely to have a more tolerant tomorrow.

NOT QUITE TALKING ABOUT RELIGION: HOW WE FOCUS ON FACTS AND BURY OUR HEADS IN THE SAND

AMANI Z. H. MOHAMED

Religion can be one of the most intimate aspects of a person's life. For many people, it is a code that guides them, and the most sacred thing in their lives. In diverse places like New York City, it is sometimes difficult to reconcile the fact that you are living with a number of people who have their own different truth that they believe is the actual truth of the universe. While this diversity is beneficial to learning and expanding kids' minds, it can also lead to conflict. So generally, in diverse public schools, discussion of religion is swept under the rug completely. New York City is very diverse, but our curricula and standardized tests don't reflect this. Now however, with New York schools adding two Muslim holidays to the academic calendar in 2015, the topic of religion in schools has come into focus once more. With this in mind, we must wonder why schools don't do a better job of teaching about religious diversity.

One common argument is that teaching about religion teeters dangerously close to violating the constitutional separation of church and state. The Supreme Court's decisions against school prayer and Bible reading in *Engel v. Vitale* and *Abington v. Schempp* are usually sourced as proof of this. But what the court found unconstitutional in 1962 and 1963 was not teaching about religion, as an academic subject, but the enforcement of organized prayer and scripture reading, led by teachers during school hours. In fact, the First Amendment Center's *Teacher's Guide to Religion in the Public Schools* not only affirms that teaching about religion is absolutely constitutional, but provides wonderful advice for how these discussions should go. They say, for example, that "The school's approach to religion [must be] academic, not devotional," and that "The school may expose students to a diversity of religious views, but may not impose any particular view."

With these guidelines in mind, I had a conversation with Vincenza Mannino, an Assistant Principal at the Brooklyn Studio Secondary School. As someone who works primarily with English Language Learners (who comprise roughly 40% of my high school's population), Ms. Mannino believes it is important that our curricula reflect our diversity. "I was coming from my Catholic school world," she said, "and coming into a public school I've learned to embrace all religions. I think it is important that we, in turn, do that for other students." She went on to point out that, "Sometimes students come from one-minded homes where they do not want to expand [their horizons]." Where better to learn about all of the

different people they see on the street than in their classrooms?

But how can you really embrace all religions if you're not teaching about them in any depth? When we do discuss religion in school, we generally learn tedious facts about a faith, and not the intricate beauty of its details. In a regular social studies class, we'd never experience a Jewish girl talking about the beauty of candle lighting at Shabbat dinner, or Muslim students talking about the fun of an Iftar dinner during Ramadan, with the lighting of lanterns, and the Eid prayers, and biscuits and candy. Without things like these, a class about religion is only getting the bare bones of the topic, and giving us nothing of substance.

It is all well and good to teach within the safest confines of the constitution, but religion is not math. It is not fixed, the same way under every condition. It is subjective, interpretive, and can differ completely from one person's narrative to another. Public schools should therefore find new ways for students to learn about their own histories at a more personal level. Students like myself, for example, with a mother who converted to Islam, may have trouble learning all about their heritage in the family setting. In this case, school can be a great place to learn about your own faith, but this might require something other than the strictly academic, constitutional approach of a social studies class.

For example, Nechama Kamelhar, Director of the Brooklyn office of the National Conference of Synagogue Youth, goes into public schools to lead afterschool programs (not during regular class time) that connect Jewish students to their heritage and culture. As a student at Brooklyn Studio, I attended these weekly meetings and found a safe and welcoming space to learn a great deal about Judaism. Ms. Kamelhar told me her work is important for two reasons: So Jewish students can learn about their own culture, and feel a part of something. And also so all students can learn about different cultures, and be less closed-minded—learning to humanize others, and learning that there are good people everywhere. These are important goals, but not every student can attend afterschool clubs to learn about other faiths, and not every religious group has the resources to send teachers, free of charge, into public schools. The strictly academic approach to teaching about religion may thus be a serious limitation. It might be standing in the way of important conversations about heritage and identity.

Religious illiteracy is a huge social and personal problem in New York City. Muslims are ceaselessly accused of being terrorists, blamed for 9/11, and blamed for ISIS, when they have nothing to do with it. Sikh boys and men are given the same treatment because they are ignorantly assumed to be Muslim. Jews are confronted with drawings of swastikas in Jewish neighborhoods and on public transit. We have a problem, and the public school system must help ensure that our new generations grow up with a sense of tolerance that will herald a brighter age. So let me turn to you, reader, and ask this question: Must we continue to pretend that religion is a strictly factual subject? Or can we finally accept that it's so much more, and find ways for students to understand the beauty, complexity, and real effects that different religions have on the lives of their believers?

TEACH THE WHY OF RELIGION, NOT JUST THE WHAT

CHLOE PITKOFF

In my sophomore year of high school, I took AP World History. We started the year learning about early humans, and made it all the way to current events. Throughout the year I noticed that since formal religion began, it has played a major role in how history takes its course around the world. Religion has been the cause of unity and peace among people, as well as conflict and war. Although we learned about the results and impacts of religion in class, we never learned what any of the world religions are actually about. Although I know there are many religions out there, I've only ever heard the five or six major ones mentioned in school. And even for these, I still have questions. What does it mean to be part of a particular religion? Why do we get certain holidays off from school, but not others? What do the religious practices stand for? What's the story behind it all? As I've looked deeper into this issue, I've found out why many of my questions have not been answered.

I attend a public arts school. Both the teachers and students are very accepting of all different kinds of people and how they choose to express themselves. The students are opinionated and interested in learning about the world around them, to incorporate into their art. It's a very diverse, inclusive community, with kids from all different religions and backgrounds. Despite this, there are laws limiting religion in public school, both learning and practice. These laws make religious education very tricky. In public school, the administration has to be aware of how many different religions kids practice. They also have to be aware that there are kids of no particular religion, and kids who are atheists. It seems that in order to avoid potentially insulting anyone in any way, the public school system chooses not to go too deep into the study of religion.

Another issue is the curriculum and the school system itself. In one school year, we had to cover the entire history of the world. This doesn't leave a lot of time to delve into topics, especially if they could lead to potential debate and dispute between students. Our learning today is all based on state tests we need to take at the end of the year. As my

English teacher, Mr. Bar Lev, commented: "So many of these classes culminate in an exam that requires such a wide variety of knowledge that they don't take the time to explore the why, they just explore the what." These tests are based on fact, not opinion or preference. Teachers don't go as deep into topics as they might like, because it's not going to be on the test. "They [teachers] are under pressure to simply cover the basic facts that pertain to an exam," said Bar Lev. And this isn't just in history class. In many of my classes, kids have asked questions that haven't been answered because teachers only have time to cover what is necessary for the tests. The only way religion could be taught in detail in public school would be in an afterschool club, or a world religions class, which unfortunately isn't offered at my school.

History isn't the only class where you can learn about religion. Much of English literature is influenced by religion also. In my freshman English class, my teacher would put a quote on the board every day for us to respond to. Quite often, these quotes were from the Old Testament and the New Testament. He wasn't forcing us to believe any of it. He just wanted to introduce us to well known literature in a way that would help us understand more of what we were reading. I noticed, however, that of all the quotes he had us interpret, none were taken from the Qur'an, from Hindu or Buddhist texts, or from any religious texts aside from the Bible. These other religious texts and stories haven't come up often in my other English classes either.

There are several reasons why this is the case. For one thing, most of the English classes I've taken focused only on American and British literature. (These were the required classes all students are placed in. Now in my senior year, I'm glad to be taking a World Literature elective.) Many of the books we read in American and British literature were quite old, some written several centuries ago, when England and the U. S. had mostly Christian authors. Also, teachers don't have a large selection of books to choose from. They have a bookroom, and usually have to teach what they can find in stock. Teachers use what they know best, what they grew up with, what they are interested in, and what they have the most to say about. Sticking with what you know is far easier and more efficient, and it's harder to get in trouble for saying something wrong.

Though there are barriers preventing serious religious education in public schools, there are some obvious reasons why teaching about religion is necessary. Many people think students won't be interested, but how do we know if we're interested or not when we aren't introduced to things, or don't even hear about things that might catch our attention? There is also the idea of continued parental education at school. Parents drop their kids off and expect similar values to be taught in school and home. They want their kids to learn about who they are and where they come from. In school, students hear less biased points of view than what they might hear at home, where only one religion may be practiced. Students need to learn and grow to become more educated in world affairs. We must be able to form educated decisions. Not only do we need to learn about things happening around the world, we need to learn about the students in our class every day. Religious education could potentially resolve religious bullying, as kids learn about the beliefs of their fellow classmates—as they learn the why, not just the what.

With this kind of education, students will stop stereotyping and grouping people with terrorist attacks or wars, and instead might take an interest in learning about people's personalities and backgrounds for themselves. So let's have more religious education in public schools. It might not happen right away, but maybe in a few years, for another kid sitting in the back of a world history class, all of my questions will be answered.

CHAPTER NINE

Navigating Media Sources to Study World Religions

CHRISTOPHER C. MURRAY, JR.

It is more important than ever for our students to explore the amazing tapestry of religious beliefs and customs that have made the United States the home of religious liberty. By bridging the gulf of illiteracy and ignorance of religions, teachers can play a vital role in advancing interreligious understanding, cultural awareness, and global collaboration.

Since entering the classroom in 2005, my goal as a high school social studies teacher has been to create lessons that equip my students to be well-prepared 21st-century citizens. With that in mind, I created a one-semester World Religions course in 2009 that would provide students with knowledge and understanding of the world's major religions, and show them how to navigate a variety of media sources to learn about these religions.

If our students only encounter world religions in a stagnant way through passages in textbooks about world history or world cultures, they will understand very little about those religions as lived religions that are a continuous source of meaning and purpose to billions of people. Every back-to-school night, I hear from a handful of parents who share with me their experiences in high school that left them bewildered about the superficiality of some social studies courses that required the memorization of a mass of details at the expense of depth of understanding. We need to provide students with a greater understanding of the practice of different religions, which means seeing them from the perspective of those who believe in those faiths. This is an essential component of the academic study of religions, and does not imply an attempt to convert students to a belief in those faiths (a parental concern with which social studies teachers who teach about religion are familiar). I have found that the use of the right films can enhance the objective

of teaching about lived religions in ways that engage and fascinate students. Films are also an effective means of diminishing the stereotypes that students might hold about religions that are different from their own.

There are many excellent guidelines available for teachers who want to introduce students to the academic study of religions in conformity with the obligation of public school teachers to teach about religion but not to teach religion. I use the six guidelines suggested by Ben Marcus of the Religious Freedom Center, which are described in more detail in Chapter 1 of this book.

1. Religions are internally diverse, not homogenous.

2. Religions are dynamic and changing, not static and fixed.

3. Religions are embedded in cultures, not isolated from them. Religions influence and are influenced by culture.

People construct their religious identities in different ways based on the value they assign to each of the three Bs:

4. Belief,

5. Behavior, and

6. Experiences of belonging.

In using the films and other media sources mentioned in this chapter, it is important to teach students how to be wise and informed consumers of information, and I try to embed this in all my lessons. The Alliance for a Media Literate America has pointed out that:

> Media literacy empowers people to be both critical thinkers and creative producers of an increasingly wide range of messages using image, language and sound. As communication technologies transform society, they impact our understanding of ourselves, our communities and our diverse cultures, making media literacy an essential life skill for the 21st Century. [1]

As students investigate world religions through films and other media, I encourage them to develop their analytical skills through reflective class discussions that improve their understanding of those religions and increase their ability to distinguish between stereotypes and accurate information about religions in the vast array of media messages that they encounter. I have found the following films and media resources to be very helpful in the process.

HINDUISM

AN AMERICAN BOY'S JOURNEY THROUGH THE 3 Bs.

"SANJAY SUPERTEAM": SANJAY PATEL, DIRECTOR. DISNEY, 2015.

In the summer of 2015, Sanjay Patel created Pixar's first ever film depicting a young Hindu boy performing his morning *puja* (prayer ceremony) with his father. "Sanjay Superteam" was nominated for an Oscar. This heartfelt story is about young Sanjay's difficulty grappling with his father's Hindu practices and living the average American childhood. By embodying the essentials of Hindu philosophy while sharing the intimate personal practices of a family *puja*, this film is a perfect way for a teacher to conclude a unit or lesson on Hinduism and promote an understanding of the three B's (belief, behavior, and belonging). Through "Sanjay Superteam," students are able to better understand that religions are more than a stagnant

set of beliefs and scriptures, but are ever changing and evolving with cultures and context. After watching the film, my students reflect on the core elements of Hindu philosophy that are still at the heart of Hindu practice. Too often, Hinduism is taught in our schools only as an ancient religion, which neglects the fact that Hinduism is the world's third largest religion with close to 1 billion followers. Thanks to this brave film by both Patel and Pixar, I am able to expose my students to important dimensions of the religion.

SIKHISM

THE MISUNDERSTOOD "OTHER" UNDERSTOOD

For me, one of the most important religious groups to teach my students about has been the Sikhs. A faith of 26-30 million followers, Sikhs have been a part of the American landscape for over 100 years; yet since 9/11, turban-wearing Sikhs have continued to be attacked and killed because of religious illiteracy and misguided hate. When I began to teach about Sikhs I found wonderful partners who have created their own high quality educational materials. Between the Kaur Foundation's Cultural Safari (https://www.culturalsafari.org), the site of the Sikh American Legal Defense Fund (http://saldef.org), and the youth-oriented Sikh Kid to Kid site (http://sikhkid2kid.com), I am able to enlighten my students about their Sikh classmates, and work to dispel misconceptions that students often don't explore on their own.

The Sikh community is near and dear to my heart. Stories have been shared with me of dark moments involving school bullying. Boys are bullied for wearing a *putka* (head covering) and many girls have to combat bullies who find issue with the Sikh belief about not cutting any of your hair. Unfortunately, each semester I find new articles of Sikhs being targeted and attacked throughout America. Sadly, this allows our classroom to explore the role that religious illiteracy plays in the country's current rise of hate crimes against Sikhs. In an attempt to introduce an element of fun into our exploration, I also share the comedic views of religious illiteracy with the Daily Show's segment of the Sikh Coalition, and present a YouTube video on how to tie a turban.

USEFUL MEDIA SITES FOR TEACHING ABOUT RELIGION

- **Pew Research Center**
  Statistics and data on religious identity in America. http://www.pewforum.org

- **Religious Freedom Center**
  Offers courses designed for teachers. http://www.religiousfreedomcenter.org

- **Harvard Pluralism Project**
  Background information on world religions. http://pluralism.org/

- **God in America (PBS)**
  Series of six episodes on the history of religion in America. http://www.pbs.org/godinamerica/view

- **Religious Literacy Online Course (Harvard University)**
  Examines how religions have functioned in both historic and contemporary contexts. https://www.edx.org/course/religious-literacy-traditions-scriptures-harvardx-hds-3221-1x

- **The Story of God (National Geographic)**
  A six-part series on world religion. http://channel.nationalgeographic.com/the-story-of-god-with-morgan-freeman

- **Religious Freedom Institute**
  Supports religious freedom as a fundamental human right. https://www.religiousfreedominstitute.org

- **World Religions (BBC basics)**
  http://www.bbc.co.uk/religion/religions

- **Hinduism (Hindu American Foundation)**
  Powerpoints and other information on the fundamental beliefs of Hinduism. https://www.hafsite.org

- **Sikhism. Sikh Kid to Kid**
  A student-friendly site offering information about Sikhs and their religious beliefs. http://sikhkid2kid.com

- **Unity Productions Foundation.** Award-winning films on Islam. https://www.upf.tv

---

In 2012, I had a high school Sikh boy and his mother come up and thank me for introducing my students to their religion. I was embarrassed by just how little I had actually done, but it left an impact on me. Each opportunity that I have to stand in front of my classroom, I have an obligation to all of the parents who live with the fear of sending their sons and daughters into a world that does not fully understand who they are.

BUDDHISM

IT'S ABOUT MORE THAN THE DALAI LAMA

"THE LITTLE BUDDHA": BERNARDO BERTOLUCCI, DIRECTOR. RECORDED PICTURE COMPANY, 1993.

No other religion I teach has the level of Hollywood support that Tibetan Buddhism does. What is exciting about using a great film like the Little Buddha is the amazing depiction of the life of Buddha. The challenge becomes explaining to my students just how small the school of Tibetan Buddhism really is in the world's fourth largest religion. I have found that while teaching Buddhism, it becomes very easy for teachers to overlook the diversity of the Buddhist world and simply teach about this complex religion as the religion of the Dalai Lama. Over the years, I have continuously shared this classic film with my students. I find myself pausing it often for my students to explore the scenes of the colorful practices of Tibetan Buddhism, while reminding them that the overwhelming majority of Buddhists from Sri Lanka, Thailand, Japan, or America do not share the same practices or rituals seen in this film. Additionally, we look at the role that modern politics and the Cold War have played in our understanding of our media's fascination with the Dalai Lama and the Tibetan people. It is an important lesson for students to be able to compare the views of Buddhism presented by the western media with the presentation of Islam, which we explore later in the semester.

Students need to be able to understand that the forces that shape the financial production of a Hollywood film, and that help newspapers and online blogs to sell, have an impact on how we view and treat religions of the world. Millions of Americans had a desire to learn more about the likable and charismatic Dalai Lama in the late 1980s and 1990s, which led to not one but two Hollywood films in 1997 alone about the life of the Dalai Lama. These films approach the religion of Buddhism through a specific lens focusing on a religious figure, who is known to most of the world for his teachings on peace and compassion. In contrast, in 2012 Hollywood produced not one but three films around the life of Osama bin Laden, who is best known for his radical views of Islam and his justification for the slaughter of thousands of innocent people on 9/11. If millions of Americans learn about two of the world's largest religions via film then it is imperative that our education system prepares students not only to learn how to navigate news on the Internet but also to be able to view our summer blockbusters critically. What sold at the box office in 1997 and what sold movie tickets in 2012 changed dramatically. Our students need to better understand the context of the time and space in which films are made, or else we will be left with an entire society judging the religions of roughly a third of the world through the American storytelling of the lives of only two men in history.

SHINTO

SPIRITED AWAY: MUCH MORE THAN YOUR FAVORITE MOVIE

"SPIRITED AWAY": HAYAO MIYAZAKI, DIRECTOR. DISNEY, 2001.

When I first began to construct lessons to expose students to the rich religious traditions of East Asia, I found that many of my students had already fallen madly in love with the 2001 Hayao Miyazaki film, "Spirited Away," which won the 2002 Academy Award for Best Animated Film. In class, my students watched this classic film again, now in the context of the study of world religions.

After watching the film as a class, we discuss six core principles of Shinto tradition and philosophy and how they are integrated into the film. Through the film, students have the opportunity to better understand how traditional religions, like Shinto, are embedded into a culture. Filmmaker Miyazaki sends a powerful message as he taps into the core ideologies of the belief system, reminding viewers of the values that ancient traditions share with the modern world. I remind myself that the original appeal of this film, when my students were children, had nothing to do with Shinto beliefs. Therefore, the goal of watching this film in class (for the first time for a number of students) is to help students identify the message of Miyazaki imploring Japan to remember the importance that nature has played, and continues to play, in their past, present, and future. It's important for students to understand that the power of a well-executed plot can reach a diverse audience. Through exploring Shinto philosophy after the film, students can begin connecting the role religion continues to play in shaping the behaviors and beliefs of a society. Like all the films I share in my class, we view interviews with the director explaining his vision and inspiration for making the film, in order to gain a sense of the role religion played in the development of the storyboard and original screenplays. My fear, as well as my reason for exploring these religions and connections to the modern world, stems from the current trend of the "none" (young people not identifying with religion) movement. In order to prevent the next generation from losing the ability to recognize the importance of religions and how they interconnect societies and ways of life, we need to continue to grow our religious literacy.

JUDAISM

FIDDLER ON THE ROOF: THE DIVERSITY OF JUDAISM, AND THE ROLE OF TRADITION

"FIDDLER ON THE ROOF": NORMAN JEWISON, DIRECTOR. MGM, 1971.

Teaching comparative religion in a 21st-century high school setting provides an opportunity to approach ancient ideas and themes with modern techniques and technology. Like many teachers, I find that my students respond well to a variety of electronic media, including film. When I first shared with a scholar of Judaism over lunch that I continue to show my students the film classic "Fiddler on the Roof" as part of my Judaism unit, the look on her face was one of complete dismay. Over the next twenty minutes, we had a meaningful dialogue that allowed me to understand the major pitfalls of using one film to explain a religion as old and diverse as Judaism Her concerns were grounded in the idea that I was exploring the religion of fourteen million Jews through the musical of one American Jew, Joseph Stein, which reminisces about the now destroyed Jewish *shtetls* of pre-Holocaust Eastern Europe.

I was able to empathize with her concerns and fears: a teacher with limited background knowledge of Judaism and its diversity might just pop "Fiddler" into his DVD player, and students would get their 3-day lesson on Judaism only from this limited portrait of the religion that Hollywood created in 1971 for an audience that had a great wealth of background knowledge into which to place this film. This meaningful conversation reminded me that for each piece of media to which I expose my students, I have to explore and examine the time and context of the story, and that a single film like "Fiddler on the Roof" by no means begins to represent the diverse world of ideas, customs, and practices that is modern Judaism. Our conversation made me much more mindful of how I use media in my class and how I need to craft lessons and reflections in a way to avoid stereotypes and explore the diversity of religious communities. My lesson for "Fiddler on the Roof" now encompasses a chronology of events in Jewish history and an in-depth look at the setting in the fictional village of Anatevka in Russia in 1905. We explore other Jewish communities that are not on display in the film, and understand the growing secular Jewish movements that were emerging among both German and American Jewish communities at the time of the mid-19th century through the PBS film "God in America."

Students must also understand the impact an event like the Holocaust had on the hearts and minds of the American Jewish audience who made this musical one of the most successful on Broadway. After my conversation with the scholar of Judaism, I briefly contemplated omitting the "Fiddler" film from my curriculum. In the end, I concluded that if I did my research and worked to create a place for this film in a much broader look at Judaism, it could continue to serve as a wonderful piece to show my students that would enable them to see that religions are diverse, dynamic, changing, and embedded into larger cultures. To finish the unit, and balance students' perspectives, we explore the Pew Forum's comprehensive analysis of Judaism in modern Israel, entitled "Israel's Religiously Divided Society," just to drive home how inaccurate and incomplete a stereotype can be when defining a group of people.[2]

TRADITIONAL RELIGION

THE COMMEMORATION OF THE DAY OF THE DEAD IN CATHOLIC MEXICO

"THE BOOK OF LIFE": JORGE R. GUTIÉRREZ, DIRECTOR. REEL FX CREATIVE STUDIOS, 2014.

A wonderful animation film that my students love to watch in class is Jorge Gutiérrez's breakout film, "Book of Life." In this film, my students go on a journey with Manolo Sanchez as he navigates his way through both the Land of the Remembered and the Land of the Forgotten. He hopes to return to the Land of the Living to save his one true love, Maria, and his town from the bandit king, Chakal. The Amerindians, like many indigenous people, had their customs and cultures marginalized and forgotten in the expansion of European power and the advent of missionaries. When summer turns to fall in my class and my students begin to grow excited about Halloween, I become excited about the opportunity to share with my students the customs and often forgotten holiday of Dias de los Muertos.

When Jorge Gutiérrez was growing up in Tijuana, Mexico, he was upset to see so many of his friends turning away from their traditional Day of the Dead celebrations for Halloween. When I share this film with my students, it exposes them to the important concept that religion is not just found in scriptures, but that it also influences festivals that are celebrated within communities and have their own traditional commemorations, rituals, and food. Remembering and commemorating the dead is a critical belief and practice that we see spanning the globe. Students understand that, even when a new missionary religion arrives in a community that ends up embracing it, this does not necessarily mean that the traditional festivals, practices, and beliefs are forgotten. Those beliefs are often so embedded into a community that there is a marriage of the old and the new religion. This allows my students to comprehend why one Jewish family Passover seder contains rice because of its Sephardic roots in Spain and North Africa, while the grandmother of the family, who traces her Jewish heritage through Poland, will have none of that. A film like "The Book of Life" is a wonderful way to expose students to the world of pluralism and the multicultural tapestry that will continue to grow in the 21st century.

FOR THE BIBLE TELLS ME SO: CONFRONTING BIBLICAL LITERALISM

"FOR THE BIBLE TELLS ME SO": DANIEL G. KARSLAKE, DIRECTOR. ATTICUS GROUP, 2007.

When it comes to tackling one of the most controversial topics in my class, I always turn to Daniel Karslake's film, "For the Bible Tells Me So," which was nominated for the Grand Jury Prize at the Sundance Film Festival in 2007.

In the film, Karslake explores two major questions; What does the Bible say about homosexuality? And how do the parents in a conservative Christian family react when they find out that their child is gay or lesbian?

This amazing film exposes my students to the scholarship that interprets Jewish and Christian scripture in the context and culture of its time. What I really enjoy about this film is the diversity of the experts and families whom Karslake features. This movie is created in a manner that allows for students to have a meaningful dialogue rather than fueling a debate and labeling those with opposing views. Too often my students see the question of ideology or religious identity as a zero sum game that can be won with a clever argument or an insulting comeback.

The issue of finding room for both LGBTQ rights and conservative Christian beliefs is going to be a critical challenge for 21st century America, and even though the LGBTQ community has seen great progress since the debut of "For the Bible Tells Me So" in 2007, the question of how conservative Christian America will find room for LGBTQ people remains.

While this may not be a topic that all schools are ready to address, it is a conversation that must be facilitated sooner rather than later. In my estimation, the job of a teacher is to create an environment where all students can freely discuss the issues that divide our world. It has become very clear that this topic, especially the rights of transgender people, is an issue that has been used to drive a wedge into our great American democracy and must be explored.

ISLAM

WHAT DO MUSLIMS REALLY THINK? AND WHAT DOES ISLAM REALLY SAY?

"AMERICAN MUSLIM FACT VS. FICTION": ALEX KRONEMER, DIRECTOR. UNITY PRODUCTIONS FOUNDATION, 2016.

"MUHAMMAD: LEGACY OF A PROPHET": OMAR AL-QATTAN AND MICHAEL SCHWARZ, DIRECTORS. UNITY PRODUCTIONS FOUNDATION, 2002.

"ALLAH MADE ME FUNNY": ANDREA KALIN, DIRECTOR. UNITY PRODUCTIONS FOUNDATION, 2008.

"PRINCE AMONG SLAVES": ANDREA KALIN AND BILL DUKE, DIRECTORS. UNITY PRODUCTIONS FOUNDATION, 2007.

"ENEMY OF THE REICH: THE NOOR INAYAT KHAN STORY": ROBERT H. GARDNER, DIRECTOR. UNITY PRODUCTIONS FOUNDATION, 2014.

For my last unit of world religions we explore Islam from its foundation to the rise of violent extremism and Islamophobia. At present, there is no hot-button topic more likely to put a political bullseye on the back of a teacher than teaching about Islam. When my students learn that roughly one out of four humans on Earth are Muslim, it becomes clear that understanding Islam is an essential 21st-century goal. Secondly, this is also a topic that politicians and the media are drawn to and feed off, so it is the obligation of the education system to present students with background information to better process the overwhelming information that is presented daily on Muslims and the Islamic world.

How does a teacher even approach such a politically charged topic? Leave it to the experts! Unity Productions Foundation (UPF) is the nonpartisan media company that has taken on the task of providing America with standard PBS films that address issues in Islam, and feature experts on Islam. To begin, I have students start in the present day with the short film, "American Muslim Fact v. Fiction," which uses data collected by Gallup to paint a more accurate snapshot of who the over 2 million Muslims in America represent. I tell my students that if they were to believe that we (the West) are at war with Islam, then we would have a major problem on our hands. So if we hope to avoid the desired state of all-out war that extremists on both sides yearn for, I must get my students to: (1) meet the "typical" Muslim; and (2) understand the basics of Islam. The more Americans meet and interact with Muslims, the more positive their views on Islam will be.

The West still has a great fear about the religion of Islam, so we watch "Muhammad: Legacy of a Prophet," which allows my students to hear from experts on Islam. The film comes with all of the tools that allow teachers to step out of the role of speaking for the world's second largest faith with a Virtual Hajj option, lesson plans, and a dialogue guide to use before and after showing the film.

The level of scholarship behind the UPF films and the stamp of approval of PBS makes the whole UPF catalogue classroom ready. These films remain the cornerstone of my teaching about Islam, and facilitate a meaningful dialogue about the fear of Islam that is common in the West. One of my favorites is "Inside Islam: What a Billion Muslims Really Think," which is a Gallup poll analysis by John Esposito and Dalia Mogahed that has a teaching guide and allows my students to learn about the perspectives of Muslims throughout the world.[3]

Three other favorites are "Allah Made Me Funny," "Prince Among Slaves," and "Enemy of the Reich." The first features the comedy of Mo Amer, Azhar Usman, and Preacher Moss, and continually makes my students laugh while confronting issues that Muslims face both here in America and overseas. The second, "Prince Among Slaves," allows me to address the crucial narrative of American history and economic success that was built on the backs of African slaves, many of whom were Muslims.

This true story enables students to understand that before the rise of the West, Africa and the Islamic world had well-established and functioning societies involved in global trade with peoples of all religions and cultures. Finally, a film that grows more relevant by the day, "Enemy of the Reich," shares another story about a Muslim woman who worked with the French Underground against the Nazis. As the loyalty of Muslims and refugees continue to be the topics of many media messages to which students are exposed, this film is a good point of departure for learning about the continuous work that Muslims do in ensuring the safety of America and Europe by both condemning acts of violence and thwarting terrorist plots. It is important for students to be aware of the heroism and and fate of Muslims like Noor Inayat Khan. For her actions to sabotage the Nazi regime, she died in Dachau in 1944, like the millions of others who were deemed to be inferior by the Nazi Party.

NOTES

1. The statement is accessible on the website of the Center for Media Literacy at http://www.medialit.org/reading-room/what-media-literacy-amlas-short-answer-and-longer-thought

2. http://www.pewforum.org/2016/03/08/israels-religiously-divided-society/

3. http://erb.unaoc.org/wp-content/uploads/2012/09/Who_Speaks_for_Islam_Teaching_Guide1.pdf

CHAPTER TEN

Educating for Global Citizenship in a World Where Religion Matters

KRISTEN FARRINGTON AND IAN JAMISON

Students born in the mid-1990s through the present, Generation Z, will never know the world as a place that isn't connected by the click of a mouse or the tap of a screen. They are already connecting with strangers around the world, often with little skill or supervision. Globalization and rapid technological change are making the world a smaller place. Globalization offers huge benefits for societies, but it may also lead to some of this century's greatest challenges, including prejudice, conflict, and extremist views that can arise when different faiths and cultures are thrown together.

Globalization presents enormous challenges for U.S. educators who are responsible for preparing young people with the skills and competencies to engage in a global society. The introduction to the C3 Framework acknowledges this challenge:

> Now more than ever, students need the intellectual power to recognize societal problems; ask good questions and develop robust investigations into them; consider possible solutions and consequences; separate evidence-based claims from parochial opinions; and communicate and act upon what they learn.[1]

Students need to develop these skills to be prepared for college, career, and success in this fast changing, shrinking world.

WHY RELIGION? WHY NOW?

One thing is clear: As educators, we need to help students understand the complexity of the world around us. In a recent speech, former UK Prime Minister Tony Blair stated,

> Whereas in the 20th Century people fought over communism and fascism—big political ideologies and ideas which caused world wars, all of that is gone with the passage of the 20th century, but what has replaced it in the early part of this century is a clash between cultures. Where there is ignorance, there is usually fear, and where there is fear there can often be conflict. Where there is knowledge, there is often understanding, and there can be peace.[2]

In the last few years we have seen this clash of cultures, and have watched in horror as the violent acts of religious extremists reached a new level of barbarity. Events in France, Belgium, Syria, Iraq, Nigeria, Turkey, and the U.S., as well as the continued violence in the Arab-Israeli conflict, have brought an intense media focus on the role that religion and religious beliefs have played in these events.

The Institute for Economics and Peace (IEP) released a study in October 2014 that provides a comprehensive understanding of how religion interacts with peace. One of the report's key findings is that: "religion is not the main cause of conflicts today." This is surprising in light of the religious rhetoric used by ISIS and Boko Haram and the media's hyper focus on the religious ideology of groups engaged in violence. IEP reports that, "surveying the state of 35 armed conflicts from 2013, religious elements did not play a role in 14, or 40 percent." IEP's Global Peace Index (GPI) suggests that corruption, political terror, gender and economic inequality, and political instability are the key factors in violence and conflict to a greater extent than religious beliefs. The IEP's Peace and Religion report confirms this assumption, and its research demonstrates that when religion does play a role in conflict, it is part of a more complex set of factors, including political ideology, opposition to government, lack of resources, clashes of identity, and others.[3]

Why then is religion singled out as the main cause of these conflicts? The Georgetown Bridge Initiative team, which has explored the history of Islamophobia in the West, points out that:

> ...over time, geopolitical events abroad—wars, conflicts over natural resources including land and oil, and domestic security threats posed by violent extremists—have defined a relationship and engendered Western narratives that portray Islam as the source of violence and despair.[4]

Belinda Espiritu reports in *Global Research* that:

> There is a current obsession in mainstream media and academic discourse pertaining to Islam and the West. This current obsession is tinged with negative signifiers, with the global media's predominantly negative portrayal of Islam and Muslims depicting Muslims generally as violent, fanatical, bigoted, or as extremists and terrorists.[5]

In June 2018, the Pew Research Center published a report on restrictions on religion, "Global Uptick in Government Restrictions on Religion in 2016." One of the key findings in the report is that there has been an increase in nationalist activities around the globe. The report found that "government actors—whether political parties or individual public officials—at times used nationalist, and often anti-immigrant or anti-minority, rhetoric to target religious groups in their countries in 2016." The research showed that around the world Christians, Muslims, and Jews were targeted by nationalist political parties, but "overall, Muslims were the most common target of harassment by national

political parties or officials in 2016, typically in the form of derogatory statements or adverse policies."[6]

The historical narrative and current reality of imbalanced news coverage on Islam have helped create a false narrative about Islam. Is it surprising that since 9/11 there has been an increase in anti-Islam hate crimes? The FBI reported a spike in religion-biased hate crimes against Muslims after 9/11 from 28 incidents in 2000 to 481 incidents reported in 2001. In 2015 there was another sharp increase in anti-Islamic hate crimes—the highest since 9/11, with 22.2 % of single-bias incidents motivated by religion.[7]

In the United States, many Americans felt that the U.S. Supreme Court's 5-4 decision on June 26, 2018 to uphold President Trump's travel ban in *Trump v. Hawaii* showed hostility towards Islam. This order restricted the entry of nationals from seven countries into the United States. In five of these countries, the majority of the population is Muslim. In her dissent, Justice Sotomayor wrote, "The United States of America is a nation built upon the promise of religious liberty. Our founders honored that core promise by embedding the principle of religious neutrality in the First Amendment. The Court's decision today fails to safeguard that fundamental principle."[8]

Combine these recent trends with very little education in public schools about Islam and few mechanisms in place to educate everyday citizens about Islam, and the result is that many Americans do not have a full understanding of this religious tradition. When looking at the complexity of religion's role in violent conflicts around the world, religion gets the disproportionate attention.

Another key finding in the IEP report is that religion can be the motivator or catalyst to bring about peace through ending conflict.[9] Again, with the intense media focus on violence and brutality, the fact that religion can be a force for good in the world is often overlooked. As our students learn about the complexity of current conflicts around the world and efforts towards peace, they need to have a basic understanding about religions of the world.

According to the Pew Research Center study released on April 2, 2015, "The Future of World Religions: Population Growth Projections, 2010-2050," religion continues to be important worldwide. In fact, as individual religious affiliation in the United States shrinks, it is quickly growing in other parts of the world. In 2010, it was estimated that 83.6% of 6.8 billion people affiliated themselves with a religious tradition. This number is expected to rise in 2050 to 86.8% percent of an estimated population of 9.3 billion people.[10] Despite the discomfort that many teachers, administrators, and parents have in teaching students about the religions of the world, the risk of ignoring religion is that our students won't be able to understand the beliefs and motivations of the vast majority of the world's population.

In a speech announcing the Office of Faith-Based Community Initiatives at the White House, former Secretary of State John Kerry expressed the following, "In fact, if I went back to college today, I think I would probably major in comparative religion because that's how integrated [religion] is in everything that we are working on and deciding and thinking about in life today."[11]

The reality is that billions of people around the world are motivated by religious convictions. These deep beliefs inform their decisions and behaviors in society and their attitudes about the world around them. American students will not be adequately prepared to be leaders in a globalized world if they do not have the basic knowledge about religious traditions and the skills to engage with people from different cultures and traditions.

MORE THAN THE BASIC TENETS

Teaching students the basic tenets and history of major religious traditions is crucial. For students to understand the Arab-Israeli conflict, they need to understand the historical context and the deep beliefs that motivate the decisions and actions of people living in the Middle East. However, teaching the basic tenets and history of a religion is only the first step to understanding a religious tradition. Most important is helping students to learn the "lived experience" of religious people. We know that Christians living in Jakarta, Rome, and Salt Lake City live their faith out in very different ways. We know that Muslims living in New York City, Tehran, and Manila will experience their day-to-day faith differently. Each faith tradition is complex and there is often a wide spectrum of belief and practice within a tradition.

The American Academy of Religion's *Guidelines for Teaching about Religion*, prepared by a Task Force chaired by Diane Moore of the Religious Literacy Project, Harvard University, suggests best practices and pedagogy when approaching the study of religion. One point that many Americans do not understand is that

> ...religions are internally diverse as opposed to uniform; religions evolve and change over time as opposed to being a historical and static; and religious influences are embedded in all dimensions of culture as opposed to the assumption that religions function in discrete, isolated, 'private' contexts.[12]

The Pew Research Center Report, *The World's Muslims: Unity and Diversity*, conducted face-to-face interviews with more than 38,000 Muslims in 39 countries. The study explored the complexity and diversity of belief found among 1.6 billion Muslims worldwide. The report found that "Muslims are united in their belief in God and the Prophet Muhammad and are bound together by religious practices such as fasting during the holy month of Ramadan and almsgiving to assist people in need. But they have widely differing views on many other aspects of their faith, including how important religion is to their lives, who counts as a Muslim, and what practices are acceptable in Islam." The report explores differences in religious commitment, generational differences, and gender differences. For example, in most of the 39 countries surveyed, they discovered that men are more likely than women to attend mosque—especially in Central Asia and South Asia. They believe that the cultural norms and context are a key component in this disparity. Researchers also discovered that there was no difference between men and women in terms of the frequency of prayers, giving alms, and participating in fasting.[13]

How do we help our students understand the "lived experience" of a religious tradition? How do we help them learn cultural norms that impact the practice of one's faith? One way is to provide students with opportunities to meet people from different faith traditions and encourage them to engage in dialogue about their beliefs, traditions, and experiences. For these conversations to be meaningful and significant, we also need to prepare the students with the skills they need to successfully engage with, and learn from, one another.

This set of soft skills—the skills of dialogue— form part of the communications skills that are recognized by the C3 Framework, the Common Core State Standards, and global education frameworks as key 21st Century skills.

WHAT IS DIALOGUE?

There are many terms used to describe what is going on when students are talking to each other in class. These include discussion, deliberation, debate, and dialogue. Very often in common parlance, these terms are used interchangeably, but it is important to be precise about the differences—particularly if we are going to concentrate on cultivating one of these areas. One key difference is best explained by the following comparison:

- In a *debate*, there is a winner and a loser. One person wins by presenting a better argument, and the other loses. A debate is profoundly competitive, and is about establishing difference.

- In a *dialogue*, there are two winners. I learn from you; you learn from me. We may compromise

PROMOTING DIALOGUE

The following suggestions are based on the experience of Generation Global in promoting dialogues between students from different cultures with different religious traditions.

CREATING A SAFE PLACE FOR DIALOGUE

Students are encouraged to develop the skills of dialogue and to learn to approach one another in a respectful way. Generation Global materials emphasize that it is important to note that "respect" does not mean "agree with." Young people need to have the skills to disagree appropriately, and to find other ways to express themselves than through conflict, if they are going to learn to successfully navigate diversity.

In order for dialogue to be successful, teachers need to help create a safe space where students feel comfortable speaking freely.

Here are some simple tips to help with creating this safe space:

1. **Ground rules**: Clear expectations of behavior should be communicated and agreed upon. Encourage students to create the ground rules together.

2. **Trust**: There needs to be a certain level of trust between the participants. Give students the opportunity to practice their dialogue skills around non-contentious issues at first. After trust has been established, introduce more controversial issues.

3. **Non-judgmental**: Give your students the opportunity to explore one another's points of view. Dialogue is a space where we can challenge one another's deeply held beliefs and values but in a positive way, saying "I'm uncomfortable with x, because of y," rather than saying "You're wrong!"

4. **Inclusivity**: Ensure that everyone takes part. It's important that everyone's voice is heard in dialogue (or at least that everyone has the opportunity to take part—choosing to "pass" is fine too). Many of our students are strong, confident speakers, but it is equally important to remember that some of our students lack confidence, have low self-esteem, and may be excluded by their peers for various reasons. Their voices are critical to genuine dialogue as well.

5. **Trusted Facilitation**: The facilitator of the dialogue needs to ensure a safe neutral space throughout the dialogue.

or agree to differ. A dialogue is profoundly reciprocal, and acknowledges similarity and difference equally.

Generation Global is a program of the Tony Blair Institute for Global Change. The Institute provides free classroom resources that teachers can use to introduce their students to a range of critical dialogue skills.[14] The aim of fostering dialogue is central to the Institute's work, whether staff are working with diplomats, university professors, classroom teachers, or students in classrooms around the world.

Generation Global is a free program that provides moderated spaces in which students worldwide who are between the ages of 12 and 17 can discuss challenging issues from a variety of perspectives, in a respectful, safe way through video conferences and online communication. Its lesson plans and activities help students learn the essential skills of dialogue. Teachers can easily integrate these activities into their curriculum. The goal is for students to hone the skills of dialogue in their own classroom, and then practice the skills with students who live in another part of the world. Students can practice the skills through facilitated video conferences or through the secure online community. The program provides opportunities for young people to take part in meaningful dialogue around issues of identity, beliefs, and values, and to engage directly with the more challenging issues that often underlie misunderstanding and prejudice.

Generation Global describes dialogue in this way:

FIVE KEY DIALOGUE SKILLS

There are five key skills that teachers can practice with their students in different ways throughout the school day. These skills help students engage with their classmates better; help students feel confident in exploring controversial issues in class; and give them the skills to engage with people who have different beliefs, values, and perspectives within a context of respect.

1. **Global Communication**: Are the students able to speak for themselves and not on behalf of others (using "I" instead of "we")? Are they able to give good descriptions, details, and explanations when speaking about their communities, cultures, beliefs, and values? Do they refrain from making statements about "us" and "them" or making unfair comments about people/groups not represented in the room?

2. **Active Listening**: Are the students able to show respectful and attentive body language when talking with others? Are they able to process what they hear and ask questions that clarify, challenge, and seek a deeper understanding? Are they able to focus on the "other" in the conversation without being distracted by the teacher, their peers, or others? Are they able to listen carefully, process, and reflect before speaking again in order to avoid spontaneous responses that might be poorly thought through?

3. **Critical Thinking**: Are students able to think analytically about what they are hearing? Are they able to balance open-minded listening with appropriate challenge? Can they distinguish personal opinion from broader statements, and recognize emotive approaches? Are they able to reconsider and reflect upon their own positions in the light of new information? Will they take time to think about what they have heard, and return to it after the dialogue is over?

4. **Responding**: Are the students able to ask questions that are open-ended and that seek meaning and significance? Can they show that they value the ideas, experiences, and beliefs of others even when they do not agree with them? Are they are able to respond empathetically to others? Are they able to challenge others in the dialogue in a way that is respectful and open?

5. **Reflecting**: Are the students able to identify the major influences on their lives, behavior, beliefs and thinking? Are they able to place themselves in the local, national, and global communities and reflect on how they contribute to these groups? Are they able to find differences as well as similarities between their own lives, values and beliefs and those of others? Are they able to explain how their learning through dialogue may impact their behavior or choices in the future?

"In an encounter with those who might have different opinions, values and beliefs to my own, dialogue is the process by which we come to a rich and authentic understanding of one another." The program gives students a range of opportunities to practice and hone their skills of dialogue, both through engaging activities in class, and through facilitated encounters with their global peers using technology. Its resources have been endorsed by the National Council for the Social Studies, and included on the UK Department for Education's "Educate against Hate" website.[15] Its work is highlighted in both the UNESCO Guide for policy-makers on preventing violent extremism through education[16] and the Brookings Institution report on measuring global citizenship education.[17]

The aim of the program is to build a generation of young people who are prepared to be global citizens; who are equipped to navigate the diversity that they will encounter; who think critically about the narratives that inform their understandings of the world; and who take responsibility for communicating effectively, while building collaboration with their global peers. Generation Global helps young people to be more open-minded in their attitudes to others, by providing a robust set of preparatory materials, as well as opportunities for direct encounter with other students from around the world.

The Generation Global online site (https://generation.global) provides an innovative and safe space for students worldwide to practice online dialogue, in a site that is designed from the ground up for only that purpose. The site limits access to participants in the global program. Students can take part in both open topics (dialogues around particular questions, open to all), or in team topics (where teachers from a number of schools commit to their students taking part in online dialogue over a set period. Questions are automatically released by the site, and students are automatically grouped up to dialogue together). The site is also an environment where it is easy for teachers to provide support for their students and monitor them in a non-intrusive way.

In the past nine years the program has worked with

more than 2,500 schools in more than 40 countries. Over 10,000 teachers have been trained in the dialogical pedagogy, and they in turn have taken more than 430,000 students through the program. The Generation Global team has connected students through facilitating over 3,000 video conferences, and more than 150,000 students have connected through the purpose-built online community. The combination of education and exposure is a profound way of learning—one that produces deep understanding and recognition of the other.

During the four years during which one of the authors (Kristen) worked with Generation Global, she had the opportunity to facilitate over 130 video conferences with students all over the world. One of her most profound experiences as facilitator was during a video conference with two schools—one in Pakistan and one in St. Louis, Missouri. The video conference took place a few months after the shooting of Michael Brown in Ferguson, Missouri. As images of both schools came on to the video conference, the visual difference was striking. She knew the students were nervous—probably wondering what, if anything they would have in common. There were many poignant moments in the video conference, but the most extraordinary moment was when students discussed the one thing they most wanted to change about their communities. Students from both countries talked about the violence their communities had experienced, and students in Pakistan and the U.S. agreed that education was the best way to make a lasting impact in their communities. Students spoke with passion about their commitment to being change-makers in their respective communities. The connection they made that day, and their deeper understanding of each other's communities was profound.

By organizing direct encounters between students from different cultures and religious traditions, Generation Global's video conferences allow students to put a human face on the "other." One participating teacher, Samantha ("Sam") Reynolds, who taught a unit on Hinduism in her World Religions course at Chantilly High School in Fairfax County, Virginia, organized video conferences between students in her class and students in two schools in New Delhi, India. She was assisted by the Generation Global technology team, who worked with her school's technology director to test everything in the weeks before the video conference to ensure that everything would go smoothly.[18]

Prior to the first video conference, Sam discussed her curricular goals with the Indian teachers, and found that they all shared similar objectives for their students, including improving their skills of civil discourse, increasing their understanding of different values and beliefs, and fostering their appreciation for religious and cultural diversity. In a single year, Sam's students engaged students in India, Pakistan, Lebanon, and Italy in ways that enabled them to learn about the world's major faiths. As her students stepped beyond their comfort zones, they were fascinated by being able to engage students from a very different culture, and, when they emerged from the video conferences, were eager to do it again.

During the video conferences, students share their values and beliefs and discuss common challenges. Students in a school in Utah and a school in India discussed the meaning of service projects that they undertook, and whether they participated in them because of their religious faith, or peer pressure, or for other reasons. In a video conference with students in Lebanon, there was a profound discussion about the meaning of compassion. Students explored whether compassion occurred because of nature or nurture, discussed the motivation underlying compassion, and considered whether it was universal.

During the video conferences, teachers try as much as possible to leave the discussion to the students, who are encouraged to speak directly with one another about issues that matter to them. After a video conference, students can ask additional questions and deepen connections through the secure online learning community, stay in touch, and plan joint projects for tackling issues of shared concern. They can discuss a wide range of topics, including major global issues such as the environment, wealth, and poverty. Social studies teachers have been able to integrate these discussions into geography, world history, government and other courses.

When the teachers discuss religion, they do so in ways that uphold First Amendment principles and guidelines. Their teaching is neutral toward religion—neutral among religions and neutral between religion and non-religion. The students, however, are free to express their views about religion, including their personal beliefs, as long as these are relevant to the discussion.

The experience of these dialogues has left an impact on many students. One of Sam's students, Aish Iyer, thought that the program was "one of the best experiences of my high school career," adding that it

> … gave me a safe place to explore my curiosity about other cultures, because I had my teachers and peers (all of whom were just as interested as I was), and because the people we spoke to were open minded and ready to discuss topics that aren't typical conversation starters. It made me realize that in the end, religion isn't as scary a topic as everyone makes it out to be. More importantly, it gave me hope for a more peaceful world—a world filled with peaceful discussion, be it with my peers or between governments.[19]

DIALOGUE AND PEACE BUILDING

Over the years, the anecdotal evidence has been clear: when students meet face to face, previously held stereotypes and prejudice are challenged and replaced by a new and deeper understanding of their peers, both on the other side of the world and in their own classrooms. Recent academic research undertaken by a team from the University of Exeter under the direction of Professor R. Wegerif confirms that participation in Generation Global is having this effect:

> This research study showed that being part of this program had a positive impact on students' open mindedness and attitudes to others; further, corpus linguistic analysis of students' reflections provides unequivocal evidence of the program producing a significant shift towards increased open-mindedness.[20]

Dialogue lays the groundwork for significant and authentic relationships between students where they recognize each other as individuals. This recognition is vital for peace building.

More than any other generation in human history, the students we educate today will live alongside, work with, and relate to, peers with the widest possible range of cultures, beliefs, values, and perspectives. As the world continues to shrink through globalization, cultures and values will continue to clash. It is imperative that we help students to understand the world around them and give them tools to build societies that welcome diversity rather than fearing it. We must encourage an open-minded approach to the other, rather than the cultivation of prejudice: an approach that includes rather than excludes. The skills students learn and practice today will be the foundation for peace for generations to come.

NOTES

1. National Council for the Social Studies (NCSS), *The College, Career, and Civic Life (C3) Framework for Social Studies State Standards: Guidance for Enhancing the Rigor of K-12 Civics, Economics, Geography, and History* (Silver Spring, MD: NCSS, 2013).

2. Tony Blair Faith Foundation, "Education is the Way to Plant the Seeds of Peace." [Video file] London, U.K.: Tony Blair Faith Foundation, 2014.

3. Institute for Economics and Peace, "Five Key Questions Answered on the Link Between Peace and Religion," October 2014. Retrieved from http://economicsandpeace.org/reports

4. Georgetown Bridge Initiative, "Islamophobia the Right Word for a Real Problem," September 8, 2016. Retrieved from http://bridge.georgetown.edu/islamophobia-the-right-word-for-a-real-problem

5. Belinda F. Espiritu, "Islamophobia and the 'Negative Media Portrayal of Muslims,'" February 29, 2016. Retrieved from http://www.globalresearch.ca/islamophobia-and-the-negative-media-portrayal-of-muslims/5440451

6. Katayoun Kishi, Primary Researcher, "Global Uptick in Government Restrictions on Religion in 2016", Pew Research Center, June 21, 2018. Retrieved from http://www.pewforum.org/2018/06/21/global-uptick-in-government-restrictions-on-religion-in-2016/

7. United States Department of Justice, Federal Bureau of Investigation, Uniform Crime Reporting Program, Hate Crime Statistics, 2015. Retrieved from https://ucr.fbi.gov/hate-crime/2015

8. *Trump, President of the United States v. Hawaii*, Decided June 26, 2018. https://www.supremecourt.gov/opinions/17pdf/17-965_h315.pdf

9. Institute for Economics and Peace, "Five Key Questions…," *op. cit.*

10. Conrad Hackett, "The Future of World Religions: Population Growth Projections, 2010-2050" (Pew Research Center Study, April 2, 2015). Retrieved from http://www.pewforum.org/2015/04/02/religious-projections-2010-2050

11. "Secretary John Kerry Speech Announcing the White House Faith-Based Community Initiatives" [Television series episode]. C-SPAN, August 7, 2013. Accessible at http://www.c-spanvideo.org/program/314438-1 (Kerry's quote can be heard at the 10 minute mark).

12. Diane L. Moore, Task Force Chair, American Academy of Religion *Guidelines for Teaching about Religion*. Retrieved from https://www.aarweb.org/sites/default/files/pdfs/Publications/epublications/AARK-12CurriculumGuidelines.pdf. The *Guidelines* are reproduced in Appendix 2 of this book.

13. Pew Research Center, "The World's Muslims: Unity and Diversity," August 9, 2012. Retrieved from http://www.pewforum.org/2012/08/09/the-worlds-muslims-unity-and-diversity-executive-summary

14. Tony Blair Institute for Global Change, "Essentials of Dialogue," October 2017. Retrieved from https://institute.global/insight/co-existence/essentials-dialogue.

15. See http://educateagainsthate.com

16. UNESCO, *Preventing Violent Extremism through Education: A Guide for Policy-Makers* (Paris, France: UNESCO, 2017). Retrieved from http://unesdoc.unesco.org/images/0024/002477/247764e.pdf

17. Kate Anderson and Jasodhara Bhattacharya, *Measuring Global Citizenship Education, A Collection of Practices and Tools* (Washington, DC: Brookings, 2017). Retrieved from https://www.brookings.edu/research/measuring-global-citizenship-education

18. Information on the classes of Ms. Reynolds, and other classes mentioned in this section has been obtained from Charles C. Haynes, "Educating for Peace and Understanding: Face to Faith in America's Schools," *Social Education* 77, no. 6 (November-December 2013), 307-309.

19. *Op. cit.,* 309.

20. Jonathan Doney and Rupert Wegerif, "Measuring Open-Mindedness" (London, U.K.: Tony Blair Institute for Global Change, 2017). Retrieved from https://institute.global/sites/default/files/inline-files/Measuring%20open-mindedness_29.06.17.pdf

PART III

Approaches to Teaching about Religious Traditions

Methodological Assumptions and Analytical Frameworks for Teaching About Religions

DIANE L. MOORE

Religions have functioned throughout human history to inspire and justify the full range of human agency from the heinous to the heroic. Their influences remain potent here in the 21st century in spite of modern predictions that religious influences would steadily decline in concert with the rise of secular democracies and advances in science. Understanding these complex religious influences is a critical dimension of understanding modern human affairs across the full spectrum of endeavors in local, national, and global arenas. This chapter on methods outlines a framework for understanding how religions function in human experience, and this framework provides the foundation for the Religious Literacy Project at Harvard Divinity School.

FOUNDATIONAL ASSUMPTIONS

1. There is a fundamental difference between the devotional expression of a religious worldview as normative and the study of religion, which recognizes the factual existence of diverse devotional assertions;

2. Religions are internally diverse;

3. Religions evolve and change;

4. Religious influences are embedded in all aspects of human experience;

5. All knowledge claims (including religious ones) are socially constructed and represent particular "situated" perspectives;

6. There is nothing inevitable about either violence or peace; both are manifest in three intersecting formulations: direct, structural, and cultural; and both are shaped by conscious and unconscious human agency where religious influences are always operative.

DEVELOPMENT OF ASSUMPTIONS

For a variety of reasons dating back to the Enlightenment (including Christian influenced theories of secularization that were reproduced through colonialism) there are many commonly held assumptions about religion in general and religious traditions in particular that represent fundamental misunderstandings. Scholars of religion are well aware of these assumptions and have articulated some basic facts about religions themselves and the study of religion that serve as useful foundations for inquiry.[1]

DIFFERENTIATING BETWEEN DEVOTIONAL EXPRESSION AND THE STUDY OF RELIGION

First and foremost, scholars highlight the difference between the *devotional expression* of particular religious beliefs as normative and the nonsectarian *study of religion* that presumes the religious legitimacy of diverse normative claims. The importance of this distinction is that it recognizes the validity of normative theological assertions without equating them with universal truths about the tradition itself.

Unfortunately, this distinction is often ignored in public discourse about religion. For example, there is a great deal of contemporary debate about the roles for women in Islam. In truth, there are a variety of theological interpretations of the tradition that lead to different, sometimes antithetical practices and assertions. Equally common is that differing communities will have similar practices but with diverse theological justifications.

It is appropriate for members of a particular community to assert the orthodoxy of their theological interpretations of the tradition, but it is important to recognize the difference between a theological assertion of normativity and the factual truth that multiple legitimate perspectives exist. The latter represents the nonsectarian study of religion. This is the approach promoted here and the one most appropriate to advance the public understanding of religion.

There are three other central assertions about religions themselves that religious studies scholars have outlined and that flow from the recognition of the distinction between devotional expression and the nonsectarian study of religion outlined above:

1. Religions are internally diverse as opposed to uniform;

2. Religions evolve and change over time as opposed to being ahistorical and static;

3. Religious influences are embedded in all dimensions of culture as opposed to the assumption that religions function in discrete, isolated, "private" contexts.

RELIGIONS ARE INTERNALLY DIVERSE

This assertion is a truism but requires explanation due to the ways that religious traditions and practices are frequently portrayed as uniform. Aside from the obvious formal differences within traditions represented by differing sects or expressions (e.g., Roman Catholic, Orthodox, Protestant for Christianity; Vaishnavism, Shaivism, Shaktism, for Hinduism, etc.) there are differences within sects or expressions because religious communities function in different social/political contexts. One example is the debate mentioned above regarding the roles of women in Islam. The following assertions are also commonly repeated: "Buddhists are nonviolent", "Christians oppose abortion", "Religion and science are incompatible", etc. All of these comments represent particular theological assertions as opposed to factual claims representing any given tradition itself.

RELIGIONS EVOLVE AND CHANGE

This is another truism but again requires explanation due to the common practice of representing religious traditions without social or historical context and solely (or primarily) through ritual expression and/or abstract beliefs. Religions exist in time and space and are constantly interpreted and reinterpreted by believers. For example, the Confucian concept of the "mandate from heaven" evolved within dynasties, geopolitical regions, and historical eras and continues to evolve today. Another example is that the practice of slavery has been both justified and vilified by all three monotheistic traditions in differing social and historical contexts. Finally, in a more specific example, the Southern Baptist convention in the United States passed resolutions in 1971 and 1974 supporting the moral legitimacy of abortion but later reversed those resolutions.[2]

RELIGIOUS INFLUENCES ARE EMBEDDED IN CULTURES

Religions are collections of ideas, practices, values, and stories that are all embedded in cultures and not separable from them. Just as religion cannot be understood in isolation from its cultural (including political) contexts, it is impossible to understand culture without considering its religious dimensions. In the same way that race, ethnicity, gender, sexuality, and socio-economic class are always factors in cultural interpretation and understanding, so too is religion.

Whether explicit or implicit, religious influences can virtually always be found when one asks "the religion question" of any given social or historical experience. For example, political theorists have recently highlighted the ways that different interpretations of secularism have been profoundly shaped by varied normative assumptions about

Christianity.[3] This is just one representation of a fundamental shift in political theory that is challenging the legitimacy of the longstanding assertion that religion both *can be* and *should be* restricted to a private sphere and separated from political influence.

Modernist claims predicting the steady decline of the transnational political influence of religion that were first formalized in the 17th century have been foundational to various modern political theories for centuries. In spite of the ongoing global influences of religions in political life throughout this time period, it was only in the aftermath of (1) the Iranian Revolution in 1979; (2) the fall of the Berlin wall in 1989 and the subsequent rise (in contrast to the widely predicted demise) of religion; and (3) the 9/11 and 7/7 terrorist attacks that political theorists in the West began to acknowledge the highly problematic ways that religions and religious influences have been marginalized and too simplistically rendered.

This shift is a welcome one and paves the way for multi- and cross-disciplinary collaborations with religious studies scholars across the full range of social science investigations in order to explore the complex and critically important roles that religions play in our contemporary world.

DEFINITION OF RELIGIOUS LITERACY

Given the above principles, the following definition of religious literacy has been adopted by the American Academy of Religion to help educators understand what is required for a basic understanding of religion and its roles in human experience.

> Religious literacy entails the ability to discern and analyze the fundamental intersections of religion and social/political/cultural life through multiple lenses. Specifically, a religiously literate person will possess (1) a basic understanding of the history, central texts (where applicable), beliefs, practices and contemporary manifestations of several of the world's religious traditions and expressions as they arose out of and continue to be shaped by particular social, historical and cultural

contexts; and (2) the ability to discern and explore the religious dimensions of political, social and cultural expressions across time and place.[4]

Critical to this definition is the importance of understanding religions and religious influences *in context* and as *inextricably woven into all dimensions of human experience*. Such an understanding requires both the basic understanding of religious traditions described above and an awareness of the complex (and often contradictory) ways in which religion influences human behavior and social structures. A religiously literate person will be equipped not only to recognize religious references, whether to texts, ideas, or practices, etc., but also to critically interrogate how they manifest in cultural and historical contexts.

CULTURAL STUDIES

The cultural studies approach to understanding religion assumes the basic elements of the study of religion outlined above and frames them within a postmodern worldview with the following specific characteristics.

First, the method is multi and inter-disciplinary and recognizes how political, economic, and cultural lenses are fundamentally entwined rather than discrete. For example, economic or political dimensions of human experience cannot be accurately understood without understanding the religious and other ideological influences that shape the cultural context out of which particular political or economic actions and motivations arise. This is the methodological framework related to the third tenet of religious studies above: that religions are embedded in culture and that "culture" is inclusive of political and economic influences.

Second, the method assumes that all knowledge claims are "situated" in that they arise out of particular social/historical contexts and therefore represent particular rather than universally applicable claims. This notion of "situatedness" is drawn from historian of science Donna Haraway's assertion that "situated knowledges" are more accurate than the "god-trick" of universal or objective claims that rest on the assumption that it is possible to "see everything from nowhere."[5] Contrary to popular opinion, the recognition that all knowledge claims are "situated" is not a manifestation of relativism whereby all interpretations are considered equally valid. Rather, "situated knowledges" offer the firmest ground upon which to make objective claims that are defined not by their detachment but rather by their specificity, transparency, and capacity for accountability.

Regarding the study of religion, this understanding of "situatedness" offers a tool to recognize that religious claims are no different than other forms of interpretation in that they arise out of particular contexts that represent particular assumptions as opposed to absolute, universal and ahistorical truths. (For example, claims such as "Islam is a religion of peace" and "Islam promotes terrorism" are equally problematic and need to be recognized as particular theological assertions as opposed to ultimate Truths.)

Third, this notion of situatedness applies to the texts and materials being investigated, the scholarly interpreters of those materials, and all inquirers regardless of station. The method recognizes that all forms of inquiry are interpretations filtered through particular lenses. By acknowledging this fact, an essential dimension of the inquiry itself is to identify those differing lenses and make transparent that which would otherwise be hidden.

Fourth, the method calls for an analysis of power and powerlessness related to the subject at hand. Which perspectives are politically and socially prominent and why? Which are marginalized or silenced and why? Regarding religion, why are some theological interpretations more prominent than others in relationship to specific issues in particular social/historical contexts? For example, what are the factors that led to the Taliban's rise to power in Afghanistan and why did their interpretation of the role of women in Islam, for example, gain social legitimacy over other competing claims within the tradition itself?

In another vein, what are the converging factors that lend social credibility and influence to some religious traditions over others and which dimensions of those traditions are interpreted as orthodox and which heretical and by whom? What were the conditions that allowed Muslims, Christians and Jews to live together in relative harmony in medieval Spain between 786 and 1492, and what are the religious influences that have contributed to shaping contemporary tensions in the Middle East and more globally regarding the "war on terror" and "the Arab Spring"?[6]

Fifth, this approach highlights what cultural anthropologists know well: that cultural norms are fluid and socially constructed even though they are often interpreted as representing uncontested absolute truths. This dynamic tension is powerfully demonstrated in social science theorist Johan Galtung's three-pronged typology of violence/ peace. This framework also provides an excellent foundation for discerning and representing the varied ideological influences of religions in human affairs.[7] What follows is an overview of his typology and examples of how it can be useful for highlighting the significance of religious influences in human experiences across time and place.

JOHAN GALTUNG: DIRECT, STRUCTURAL, AND CULTURAL FORMS OF VIOLENCE AND PEACE

Often referred to as the "Father of Peace Studies," Norwegian theorist Johan Galtung has developed a three-pronged typology of violence that represents how a confluence of *malleable* factors merge in particular cultural/historical moments to shape the conditions for the promotion of violence (and, by inference, peace) to function as normative.[8]

- **Direct Violence** represents behaviors that serve to threaten life itself and/or to diminish one's capacity to meet basic human needs. Examples include killing, maiming, bullying, sexual assault, and emotional manipulation.

- **Structural Violence** represents the systematic ways in which some groups are hindered from equal access to opportunities, goods, and services that enable the fulfillment of basic human needs. These can be formal as in legal structures that enforce marginalization (such as Apartheid in South Africa) or they could be culturally functional but without legal mandate (such as limited access to education or health care for marginalized groups).

■ **Cultural Violence** represents the existence of prevailing or prominent social norms that make direct and structural violence seem "natural" or "right" or at least acceptable. For example, the belief that Africans are primitive and intellectually inferior to Caucasians gave sanction to the African slave trade. Galtung's understanding of cultural violence helps explain how prominent beliefs can become so embedded in a given culture that they function as absolute and inevitable and are reproduced uncritically across generations.

These forms of violence are interrelated and mutually reinforcing. Galtung provides a representation of these intersecting forces in the following commentary on slavery:

> Africans are captured, forced across the Atlantic to work as slaves: millions are killed in the process—in Africa, on board, in the Americas. This massive direct violence over centuries seeps down and sediments as massive structural violence, with whites as the master topdogs and blacks as the slave underdogs, producing and reproducing massive cultural violence with racist ideas everywhere. After some time, direct violence is forgotten, slavery is forgotten, and only two labels show up, pale enough for college textbooks: "discrimination" for massive structural violence and "prejudice" for massive cultural violence. Sanitation of language: itself cultural violence.[9]

Galtung's typology provides a helpful vehicle to discern the complex roles that religions play in all three forms of violence as well as in their corresponding forms of peace. The formulations of cultural violence and cultural peace are especially helpful and relevant. *In all cultural contexts, diverse and often contradictory religious influences are always present.* Some will be explicit, but many will be implicit. Some influences will promote and/or represent socially normative beliefs while others will promote and/or represent marginalized convictions.

For example, in Galtung's illustration cited above, religions functioned to both support and to challenge the moral legitimacy of the transatlantic slave trade, and religions continue to function to support and to thwart structural and direct forms of contemporary racism. Similarly, religions currently function in particular ways to shape and support as well as to challenge prominent economic theories and their policy manifestations. In a final example, normative cultural assumptions about gender roles and sexuality in particular social-historical contexts are always shaped as well as contested by diverse religious voices and influences. One has to simply look for these voices and influences in any context and about any issue to find the ways that religions are embedded in all aspects of human agency and experience. For professionals, this framework can serve as a useful tool for analyzing the diverse and sometimes contradictory ways in which religions function in all cultural contexts.

NOTES

1. See the American Academy of Religion, *Guidelines for Teaching About Religion in K-12 Schools in the United States* (Atlanta: American Academy of Religion, 2010) https://www.aarweb.org/sites/default/files/pdfs/Publications/epublications/AARK-12CurriculumGuidelines.pdf The *Guidelines* are reproduced in Appendix 2 of this book.

2. For a full text compilation of all the Southern Baptist resolutions on abortion from 1971-2005, see http://www.johnstonsarchive.net/baptist/sbcabres.html

3. See Charles Taylor, *The Secular Age* (Cambridge: Harvard University Press, 2007); J. Bryan Hehir, "Why Religion? Why Now?" in Timothy Samuel Shah, Alfred Stepan, and Monica Duffy Toft, eds., *Rethinking Religion and World Affairs* (New York: Oxford University Press, 2012), 15-24; José Casanova, "Rethinking Public Religions" in Shah, et. al., eds., 5-35; and Elizabeth Shakman Hurd, "The Politics of Secularism" in Shah, et. al., eds., 36-54.

4. I articulated the definition in Diane L. Moore, "Overcoming Religious Illiteracy: A Cultural Studies Approach," *World History Connected*, November 2006. http://worldhistoryconnected.press.uiuc.edu/4.1/moore.html. It is incorporated in the definition articulated by the American Academy of Religion in its *Guidelines for Teaching About Religion in K-12 Schools in the United States* (Atlanta: American Academy of Religion, 2010) that are cited in note 1 above.

5. Donna Haraway, "Situated Knowledges: The Science Question in Feminism and the Privilege of Partial Perspective" in *Simians, Cyborgs, and Women: The Reinvention of Nature* (NY: Routledge, 1991), 191.

6. See Maria Rosa Menocal, *Ornament of the World: How Muslims, Christians, and Jews Created a Culture of Tolerance in Medieval Spain* (Boston: Little Brown, 2002).

7. Though Galtung's own representation of religion is problematic in that he falls victim to making universal claims about religion based on a specific interpretation of one tradition, the typology itself is extremely useful when a more sophisticated and complex understanding of religion is employed.

8. Johan Galtung, "Cultural Violence" in *Journal of Peace Research*, Vol. 27, No. 3 (Aug., 1990), 291-305.

9. Galtung, 295.

CHAPTER TWELVE

Teaching about the Bible in a Social Studies Context

MARK A. CHANCEY

The 2014 dustup in Mustang, Oklahoma over a public high school Bible course drew national attention because its implications seemed to extend far beyond that suburban community itself. The course was intended to serve as a pilot project for a national effort to raise the number of Bible courses to the thousands. School officials initially embraced the idea of offering it with enthusiasm, citing religious literacy as their goal.

The personality behind the project was the controversial Steve Green, president of the craft store chain Hobby Lobby, the corporate headquarters for which stands only a few miles from Mustang High School. Green had commissioned the creation of a Bible curriculum that would utilize the collection of Bible-related artifacts he had assembled, an expansive assortment that ranges from a cuneiform tablet bearing part of the Gilgamesh Epic to unpublished biblical manuscripts to Elvis Presley's Bible, complete with the star's handwritten notes. The curriculum had been created by academics associated with the Museum of the Bible, an organization that now showcases this collection in its 430,000 square foot museum just off the Mall in Washington, D.C..[1]

Ultimately, however, Mustang abandoned the proposed curriculum before it was even implemented, unsure of whether Museum of the Bible would provide legal coverage should the district be sued. Two hundred leaked pages of a draft version of the curriculum had drawn criticism from scholars (myself included) for presenting material in ways that strongly promoted certain religious viewpoints. Comments Green had made in a 2013 speech suggested a commitment to portray the Bible in a way amenable to his own evangelical Protestant views: "The book that we have"—the Bible—"is a reliable historical document, and we are going to point that out time and time again." Civil liberties watchdog groups had been poised to file a lawsuit if the course went forward.

After rejecting the Museum of the Bible curriculum, Mustang pledged to consider alternatives, though as of yet it has not chosen one. Green himself dropped plans to complete a public school curriculum, instead shifting gears to produce textbooks, teacher's guides, and tablet and smartphone apps marketed to home schoolers, private schools, and church and synagogue study groups. Despite their religious bent, those resources will likely eventually make their way into at least some public school classrooms.[2]

Had Mustang moved forward with the course, it would have been one of numerous school districts across the country offering Bible elective courses. No one knows for sure how many districts do so each year, but the number probably reaches at least into the low hundreds. Occasionally, as in Mustang, a course generates conflict. In January 2017, for example, the Freedom From Religion Foundation filed a case challenging a longstanding Bible course in Mercer County, West Virginia; at the end of 2018, this suit is still winding its way through the legal system.[3] Despite the potential for such conflicts, political efforts to promote Bible courses continue. Thus far in the twenty-first century, eight states (Arizona, Arkansas, Georgia, Kentucky, Oklahoma,

South Carolina, Tennessee, and Texas) have passed laws encouraging schools to offer courses, and nine others have debated doing so. Indeed, the 2016 national Republican Party Platform called on state legislatures to create Bible electives.[4]

Many people are surprised to learn that no such state law is actually required to make Bible courses legal, at least in principle. The U.S. Supreme Court has deemed teaching about the Bible not only permissible but also desirable. In its famous 1963 ruling *Abington Township School District v. Schempp*, which prohibited the then widespread practice of school-imposed daily Bible reading in the classroom, the Court noted:

> It might well be said that one's education is not complete without a study of comparative religion or the history of religion and its relationship to the advancement of civilization. It certainly may be said that the Bible is worthy of study for its literary and historic qualities. Nothing we have said here indicates that such study of the Bible or of religion, when presented objectively as part of a secular program of education, may not be effected consistently with the First Amendment.[5]

Thus, what determines whether instruction about the Bible and other facets of religion is constitutional in a public school setting is the extent to which it succeeds in maintaining objectivity and serving secular purposes.

Lower federal courts have issued various guidelines on how to meet those goals. The Freedom Forum's Religious Freedom Center admirably sums up general requirements regarding teaching about religion in its publication *A Teacher's Guide to Religion in the Public Schools*. Legality is achieved if:

- The school's approach to religion is academic, not devotional.

- The school strives for student awareness of religions, but does not press for student acceptance of any religion.

- The school sponsors study about religion, not the practice of religion.

- The school ... expose[s] students to a diversity of religious views, but [does] not impose any particular view.

- The school educates about all religions; it does not promote or denigrate religion.

- The school informs students about various beliefs; it does not seek to conform students to any particular belief.[6]

The First Amendment Center's publication, *The Bible and Public Schools: A First Amendment Guide*, advises that

> ... a course that includes study about the Bible and its influence will not educate students about religion generally. Just as there is more to history than American history, so there is more to religion than the Bible, Judaism, and Christianity. Public schools should also include study about other religious faiths in the core curriculum and offer electives in world religions.... Some school districts require that high schools offering a Bible elective also offer an elective in world religions. There is considerable merit in this approach.[7]

Specific guidance on teaching about the Bible in schools can be found in the Religious Freedom Center's *The Bible and Public Schools* and the Society of Biblical Literature's *Bible Electives in Public Schools: A Guide*.[8] Both highlight the importance of issues such as previous academic course work in biblical or religious studies on the part of the instructor; educating students about differences between Jewish, Roman Catholic, Eastern Orthodox, and Protestant Bibles; exposing students to translations of the Bible associated with different religious traditions; exhibiting sensitivity to the fact that different religious groups often read the same passages in very disparate ways (for example, Jews reject classical Christian readings of portions of the biblical book of Isaiah as predictions of Jesus); and maintaining awareness of the Bible's importance as a set of ancient historical sources without lapsing into a mode of presentation that uniformly depicts it as historically accurate, particularly in regard to miracle stories.

This last matter—the historical reliability of the Bible—lay at the heart of much of the controversy around the Museum of the Bible curriculum, which seemed to underscore that reliability at every turn. Of all the issues associated with teaching about the Bible, this one may be the most challenging to handle effectively, at least in many educational contexts. For some theologically conservative circles—especially within Christianity but to a lesser extent, within Judaism as well—belief in the Bible's historical accuracy is a fundamental pillar of faith. At the other end of the theological spectrum, some Jewish and Christian groups place little weight on historicity issues. Most communities and adherents of those traditions fall somewhere in between the two poles.

Biblical studies scholars, needless to say, are all over the map on such questions, whether they teach in secular or religious institutions. Though some affirm literalistic readings, many others draw very different conclusions. For the latter group, the question is not, for example, whether Moses actually parted the Red Sea (or, to render the Hebrew phrase more accurately, the Sea of Reeds) as per Exodus 14, but whether Moses ever existed and the Exodus of Hebrews from Egypt to the Promised Land ever happened at all. A social studies teacher presenting such material must thus walk a fine line that respects both diverse religious sensibilities (whether present in that particular group of students or not) and diverse scholarly opinions, despite, perhaps, a lack of familiarity with different religious perspectives or biblical scholarship.

A pedagogical strategy that would serve many teachers well in such situations would simply be to be upfront about the fact of diversity of interpretation, belief, and scholarship and point students to other questions: How does the story of the Red Sea illustrate other themes in the Book of Exodus? From a literary perspective, what points does the story seem to be making about Moses, God, the Hebrews, and the Egyptians? Why do

you think ancient Israelites found this story so powerful? What does it say about how Israelites understood themselves in relation to their God, powerful neighboring peoples like the Egyptians, and the land in which they dwelled? Why has this story resonated so strongly with Jews through the centuries, and what does affinity for this story say about Jewish identity? In what ways does the Pesach/Passover festival recall this story, and what purposes does recalling it serve? Why is the story a favorite of many Christians, as well? How did African-Americans appeal to this narrative for inspiration in their struggles against slavery and for civil rights? What are different ways that other communities and individuals might find meaning in this story, whether they regard it as an accurate historical account or not? How have painters, writers, musicians, cinematographers, and other artists interpreted the story?

Questions like these sidestep the morass of questions about whether a particular interpretation is "correct" and point instead toward issues that are at the heart of social studies, as outlined in the NCSS Curriculum Standards. They provide opportunities to explore and discuss the social transmission of beliefs and traditions; the expression of cultural values in literature and other media; the development of belief systems and religious faith over time; the identification of the cultural bases for celebrations, rituals, and ways of life; and how parties sometimes differ in their determination of the usefulness and degree of reliability of certain types of sources.

Precisely by highlighting differences among and between religious communities and other interpreters, these questions robustly advance the civic purpose of social studies. Students learn about religious diversity in their own communities, the nation as a whole, and global society. In doing so, they learn, as the standards put it, "to recognize and respect different points of view."[9] An approach that neither promotes nor disparages particular religious stances toward the Bible teaches students about the nature of the First Amendment freedoms of religious expression and from government establishment of religion.

Opportunities to teach about the Bible in ways that promote those goals occur in more than just Bible electives of the sort considered by Mustang. They are found in any World History class that considers the origins and development of Judaism and Christianity and in any United States History course that considers the roles of religion in politics, culture, and social change. Many educators have often avoided incorporating study of the Bible into their classes, and understandably so in light of the potential for controversy. But when done with social studies goals and First Amendment provisions in mind, academic, nonsectarian study of the Bible can do a lot of good for social and civic education.

NOTES

1. Museum of the Bible, http://museumofthebible.org; Joel Baden and Candida Moss, "Can Hobby Lobby Buy the Bible?" *The Atlantic*, Jan./Feb. 2016, http://www.theatlantic.com/magazine/archive/2016/01/can-hobby-lobby-buy-the-bible/419088/

2. Adelle M. Banks, "Hobby Lobby President's Bible Curriculum Shelved by Oklahoma School District," *Religion News Service*, Nov. 26, 2014, http://religionnews.com/2014/11/26/hobby-lobby-presidents-bible-curriculum-shelved-oklahoma-school-district/; Mark A. Chancey, *Can This Class Be Saved? The 'Hobby Lobby' Public School Bible Curriculum* (Austin: Texas Freedom Network Education Fund, 2014), http://tfn.org/issue/education; Carla Hinton, "Mustang Schools Still Plans [sic] Bible Class, But Not with Controversial Green Scholars' Curriculum," *The Oklahoman*, Dec. 12, 2014, http://newsok.com/mustang-schools-still-plans-bible-class-but-not-with-controversial-green-scholars-curriculum/article/5375150; Jerry A. Pattengale et al, eds., *Homeschool Curriculum, Volume 1: Genesis to Ruth Teacher's Guide* (Washington, D.C.: Museum of the Bible, 2016); "Education," Museum of the Bible, https://www.museumofthebible.org/curriculum

3. Ryan Quinn, "Mercer County Board, Superintendent Sued over Bible Courses," *Charleston Gazette-Mail*, Jan. 19, 2017, http://www.wvgazettemail.com/news-education/20170119/mercer-school-board-superintendent-sued-over-bible-classes

4. The Republican Platform 2016 (Republican National Convention, 2016), 33.

5. *Abington Township School District v. Schempp*, 374 U.S. 203 (1963) at 225.

6. *A Teacher's Guide to Religion in the Public Schools* (Nashville: First Amendment Center, 2008), http://www.religiousfreedomcenter.org/wp-content/uploads/2014/08/teachersguide.pdf. This guide is reproduced in Appendix 1 of this book.

7. Bible Literacy Project and First Amendment Center, *The Bible & Public Schools: A First Amendment Guide* (Nashville, TN: First Amendment Center, 1999), http://www.religiousfreedomcenter.org/wp-content/uploads/2014/08/bible_guide_graphics.pdf

8. *Bible Electives in Public Schools: A Guide* (Atlanta: Society of Biblical Literature), http://www.sbl-site.org/assets/pdfs/SchoolsGuide.pdf

9. National Council for the Social Studies, *National Curriculum Standards for Social Studies: A Framework for Teaching, Learning, and Assessment* (Silver Spring, Md.: National Council for the Social Studies, 2010), chapter 2, at http://www.socialstudies.org/standards/strands. See also Walter Feinberg and Richard A. Layton, *For the Civic Good: The Liberal Case for Teaching about Religion in the Public Schools* (Ann Arbor: University of Michigan Press, 2014).

CHAPTER THIRTEEN

Sacred Diversity: Teaching about Judaism in the Classroom

MICHAEL FRIEDMAN

Teaching about Judaism is an exercise in making choices. The immense diversity of thought and practice in Jewish life means that no single approach to the tradition can capture its breadth and depth. Should one focus, for instance, on unfolding the intricacies of Judaism's historical evolution or painting the contours of its contemporary shape? Does one emphasize the experience of American Jews, whom students are more likely to encounter, or do we make efforts to capture the experience of Israeli Jews as well? How does one help students to understand the wide-ranging approaches of Orthodox and Reform Judaism as parallel answers to the same question, rather than as embrace of tradition on the one hand and rejection on the other?

Inevitably, the choices we make as instructors about what to teach and how to teach it leave important content on the cutting room floor, and the picture our students construct is therefore necessarily incomplete. What we should therefore strive for is not exhaustive accuracy, but intentionality in the decisions we make. If my students walk away feeling that they know everything there is to know about Judaism, then I have surely failed. If, however, my students come away with a sense of the complexity inherent in Jewish identity, then they may indeed have an effective understanding of what it means to be a Jew in the modern world.

The tactic I have come to rely on in teaching about Judaism has been to present *halakhah*, or Jewish law, at the core of Jewish religious life, with the major branches of American Judaism relating to it in distinct ways. This approach equips students with an organizing concept that speaks to both antiquity and modernity and which helps to make sense of Jews' extraordinary diversity. In presenting Judaism this way, however, I have encountered two recurring challenges. The first has been an impression among some students that Judaism was frozen in time during the first century CE, such that the New Testament's image of the Pharisees comprises students' operative notion of what it means to be a Jew even today. This presentation unfortunately carries a tinge of anti-Semitic stereotypes about punctilious observance of Jewish law at the expense of common decency. To combat this, it is essential to present Judaism as a lived religion in an ongoing dialogue with the modern world. The second challenge offers the old canard that Judaism prizes practice over beliefs. To a degree, depicting Jewish life as revolving around halakhah is complicit with this perception, so it is critical for students to grapple with Judaism's rich theological and philosophical traditions as well, not least the symbiotic relationship between those strands of thought and the details of Jewish law and practice.

The pages that follow will attempt to accomplish these goals by outlining a unit which assumes the instructor will have one or two weeks to explore this material with students who have had minimal exposure to Judaism. I will begin by introducing the culture and texts of the early rabbis, followed by a snapshot of rabbinic Judaism in American religious life, and closing with attention to vital but difficult contemporary topics.

HISTORY AND TEXTUALITY

On the first day of the unit, I introduce my students to a Jewish notion of history that breaks with modern and ancient conceptions of the past by interpreting historical events in terms of an unfolding relationship between God and humankind. It is therefore helpful to begin by unpacking how this idea has functioned in the tradition. In 1982, the distinguished professor of Jewish history Yosef Hayim Yerushalmi composed a slight volume entitled *Zakhor: Jewish History and Jewish Memory*, which interrogated this Jewish notion of history:

> In general, the historiography of the Greeks was an expression of that splendid Hellenic curiosity to know and to explore which can still draw us close to them, or else it sought from the past moral examples or political insights. Beyond that, history had no truths to offer, and thus it had no place in Greek religion or philosophy. If Herodotus was the father of history, the fathers of meaning in history were the Jews. It was ancient Israel that first assigned a decisive significance to history and thus forged a new world-view whose essential premises were eventually appropriated by Christianity and Islam as well. "The heavens," in the words of the psalmist, might still "declare the glory of the Lord," but it was human history that revealed his will and purpose. This novel perception was not the result of philosophical speculation, but of the peculiar nature of Israelite faith. It emerged out of an intuitive and revolutionary understanding of God, and was refined through profoundly felt historical experiences. However it came about, in retrospect the consequences are manifest. Suddenly, as it were, the crucial encounter between man and the divine shifted away from the realm of nature and the cosmos to the plane of history, conceived now in terms of divine challenge and human response. The pagan conflict of the gods with the forces of chaos, or with one another, was replaced by a drama of a different and more poignant order: the paradoxical struggle between the divine will of an omnipotent Creator and the free will of his creature, man, in the course of history; a tense dialectic of obedience and rebellion.[1]

Yerushalmi's words offer a poignant depiction of Jewish sacred time, such that Jews understand historical events in terms of the divine will and are consequently engaged in an ongoing and inescapable relationship with that divine power. Against this backdrop, the opening lesson continues with an abbreviated narrative of Jewish history. Somewhat rapidly, I walk the students through a timeline of key biblical events (the expulsion from Eden, the binding of Isaac, the exodus from Egypt, the construction of the Temple, and the kingdoms of David and Solomon), post-exilic events (the conquering of the Northern Kingdom and destruction of the Temple and the later rebuilding of the Temple under Cyrus the Great), the Second Temple Period (the proliferation of sectarian groups such as the Sadducees, Pharisees, Essenes, and Sicarii, followed by the arrival of the Romans, the rebellion against Rome, the destruction of the Second Temple, and the Babylonian exile), and the proto-Rabbinic Period (the compilation of the *Mishnah* and the redaction of the Talmud).[2] During and after this presentation, one can readily draw students back to Yerushalmi's central point: What does each event mean for the Jews? If you were a Jew living in the sixth century BCE, what would you make of the destruction of the Temple? If you were a Jew living in the second century CE, how would you understand the rise of the rabbinic academies? The goal in this lesson is twofold: to help students reframe the Jewish understanding of history as an ongoing interplay between God and the Jews, and also to familiarize students with the beginnings of rabbinic Judaism. This is essential, for one can draw an (albeit tenuous) connection from this point to the rabbis of today. In keeping with the theme of difficult choices, it is decidedly not accurate to suggest that the rabbis of 500 CE are synonymous with the rabbis of today, nor is it fair to omit the efflorescence of medieval Jewry. However, in courses where one is limited to a handful of lessons on each religion, the "Jewish History in 60 Minutes" approach takes students from the Genesis account of "Let there be light," with which many are familiar, to the redaction of the Talmud, which is foreign to most but offers a through-line to contemporary Judaism.

Having equipped students with this timeline, I then take two days to spotlight rabbinic texts, offering a taste of rabbinic thought in doing so and introducing the critical notion of halakhah that then becomes the central heuristic for the remainder of the unit. For the first of these textual lessons, I familiarize my students with Judaism's commentarial tradition through the biblical story of the akeidah, or the binding of Isaac (*Genesis* 22), which introduces Jewish theology in its stark discussion of the covenantal bond between God and humanity. For homework, I ask students to read the chapter and to generate an exhaustive list of questions about anything from the reading that seems peculiar or strange or seems to be missing.[3] Then, during class, we read through *Genesis* 22 together verse by verse, and I ask them to offer up any questions they noted. To answer these, I draw on the classic commentary of Rashi, or Rabbi - of medieval France, whose analysis of the Torah has long been established as rabbinic commentary par excellence.[4] In my experience, Rashi answers the vast majority of students' questions. That students' questions tend to line up so neatly with Rashi's musings is an effective reminder of the text's timelessness, while unanswered questions furnish rich openings to explore the ongoing process of biblical interpretation.

After exploring biblical commentary, I turn my students' attentions to a later Talmudic discussion of *hashavat aveidah*, or the positive requirement in Jewish law to return lost objects to their owners. Before proceeding further, it is helpful to share with students some background regarding the document now known as the Talmud, which consists of multiple layers spanning hundreds of years of composition and redaction. The earlier of these layers is the Mishnah, which is a compilation of legal opinions and debates surrounding the halakhah found in the Hebrew Bible. Roughly speaking, this layer was compiled from after the fall of the Second Temple in 70 CE to 200 CE. The next and more voluminous layer is the *Gemara*, which features rabbinical analysis of the Mishnah and was compiled from the redaction of the Mishnah around 200 CE until 500 CE. Rabbis in Jerusalem and Babylon engaged separately in the production of

Gemara, and it is the Babylonian Talmud, or *Bavli*, which is considered authoritative today.[5] Altogether, the Bavli consists of sixty-two *tractates*, or volumes, and a course of study known as *daf yomi*, in which one studies a single page of Talmud each day, takes roughly seven and a half years to complete. The grand celebration of the completion of the daf yomi cycle is known as *siyum hashas*, the last of which took place at MetLife Stadium in New Jersey in 2012.[6]

With this context in mind, I then look with my students to the laws of returning lost objects. The Jewish outreach organization Ner LeElef (NLE) has produced a number of excellent teaching materials related to Talmudic texts. Among these is a reader on the laws of returning lost objects which opens with the question of what to do when one finds a Rolex at Times Square and proceeds to walk students through a range of relevant primary sources.[7] In a traditional Jewish study setting, students would learn such texts in *havrutah*, or pairs, and the same model can be followed in the classroom for this lesson. For this purpose, I would suggest that instructors choose particular cases and sources from the NLE resource sheet, as the document is rather extensive, and the NLE teacher's guide can be quite helpful in narrowing down one's choices. The ultimate goal, however, should be to familiarize students with the nature of Jewish legal thinking—its granular focus, its emphasis on sound reasoning, its back-and-forth across time and space—in addition to exposing the ethical implications of the laws and the theology which provides those laws with their underlying rationale.

From this first section of the Judaism unit, in which one focuses on history and textuality, students should emerge with an understanding of the Jewish notion of sacred time, the multi-layered and commentarial nature of biblical and rabbinic texts, the importance of religious law especially in its ethical dimensions, and the foundational significance of the relationship between God and humanity for the Jews. Next, the unit will skip forward to contemporary Jewish life. Instructors with additional time may choose to offer more of the intervening history, but the foregoing lessons provide the minimum groundwork necessary to shift from Jewish life as memorialized in antiquity and in text to the lived practice of Judaism today.[8]

AMERICAN JUDAISM IN PRACTICE

An effective window into contemporary Jewish life is ritual practice, and among the most fundamental of Jewish practices is the observance of *Shabbat*. To introduce students to Shabbat, I ask them to read excerpts from the fourth chapter of Lis Harris' *Holy Days: The World of a Hasidic Family*, which provides an intimate accounting of Sabbath celebrations in an observant home.[9] Biblically, Jews are commanded to remember (*Exodus* 20:8) and observe (*Deuteronomy* 5:12) the Sabbath day, and Harris' ethnography provides excellent fodder for a classroom discussion of why and how Jews do so. It is also worthwhile to dwell on the social and communal effects of keeping the Sabbath, captured powerfully in Ahad Ha-am's famous pronouncement that "More than the Jews have kept the Sabbath, the Sabbath has kept the Jews."[10]

Given the opportunity to devote a bit more time to this lesson, one can delve a bit deeper by analyzing the *melachot*, or the activities prohibited during Shabbat. An entertaining and useful resource for this purpose is the "Questions & Answers" section of Chabad.org.[11] One entry, for instance, asks if reading library books during Shabbat is acceptable: "Many libraries stamp their names on the edges of the pages of their books. Is opening or closing such a book considered erasing or writing, and therefore a violation of the Shabbat laws?"[12] As erasing and writing are both melachot, some rabbinic authorities have ruled that reading library books with stamped edges is indeed forbidden, while others have noted that "since the letters exist regardless of their visibility, and can appear and disappear with virtually no effort, opening and closing the book is not considered to be dynamic and is therefore permissible."[13] An intermediate position holds that one should nevertheless avoid library books if other books are available.[14] Having considered this case in detail, one can explore with students how attention to such matters might enhance one's spiritual life and/or one's sense of community. In the past, I have assigned different Q&A entries of this type to pairs

of students, who have presented them to the class for consideration. In general or in detail, studying the contemporary observance of Shabbat shifts the unit's focus from antiquity and textuality to the present, where the laws of the Torah and Talmud engage in unique, subtle, and sometimes startling ways with the innovations of modern society.

One must bear in mind, however, the extraordinary diversity of contemporary American Jewish life, such that there is no single way to observe Shabbat. To wit, American Jews are divided across several major "denominations": Reform, Conservative, and Orthodox Judaism, not to mention other movements such as Reconstructionism and Renewal. To familiarize my students with this state of affairs, I task them with reading the Pew Research Center's fascinating "A Portrait of Jewish Americans."[15] This study was hotly contested in the Jewish community, but it offers an ideal introduction to the diversity of American Jewish perspectives, from its demographic breakdown of Jewish denominational identity (35% Reform, 18% Conservative, 10% Orthodox, 6% Other, 30% No denomination) to its blunt query "What Does It Mean to Be Jewish?" (the most popular answer being "remembering the Holocaust" at 73%, while "observing Jewish law" came in second to last at 19%).[16] These data points and others provide countless opportunities for fruitful classroom discussion and one might simply ask students what they found to be of interest in the report, but they also provide a platform to discuss key distinctions across the major denominations of Reform, Conservative, and Orthodox Judaism.[17]

To this end, I provide my students with a bit of historical background. Beginning with Reform Judaism, I explain that Reform thrived in America, where it offered Jews a commitment to tradition that nevertheless accommodated the demands of modernity and acculturation: Ritual practices adopted a Protestant aesthetic (including the introduction of pews and organ music to worship services), but commitment to Jewish moral law was essential.[18] An outstanding primary source to analyze with one's students is the 1885 Pittsburgh Platform, Reform Judaism's first theological pronouncement, which suggests that "the modern discoveries of scientific researches in the domain of nature and history are not antagonistic to the doctrines of Judaism, the Bible reflecting the primitive ideas of its own age," that Jews "accept as binding only its [Judaism's] moral laws, and maintain only such ceremonies as elevate and sanctify our lives, but reject all such as are not adapted to the views and habits of modern civilization," and that Jews "expect neither a return to Palestine, nor a sacrificial worship under the sons of Aaron, nor the restoration of any of the laws concerning the Jewish state."[19] Such citations can help students to recognize Reform Judaism's self-conscious break with tradition for a more modern lifestyle.

Conservative Judaism's origins in America are attributed to a fracture over the "Pittsburgh Platform" itself, which led to the founding of Jewish Theological Seminary, the Conservative Movement's flagship rabbinical school, in the following year.[20] Ideologically, the Conservative Movement attempted to hew closer to halakhah, holding that ritual laws were binding though they could be adapted to new circumstances through scientific interpretive processes. A classic example of this approach is the 1950 decision of the Conservative movement's Committee on Jewish Law & Standards to permit the use of a motor vehicle on the Sabbath only "where a family resides beyond reasonable walking distance from the synagogue… for the purpose of synagogue attendance."[21] In this way, the Conservative Movement promoted flexibility within halakhah, but only where the purposes of the accommodation would fit with Judaism's broader goals. Historically, both Reform and Conservative Judaism were responses to the wave of political emancipation which confronted Jews across Europe in the 18th century. During this period of newfound political freedom, Jews were able to eschew historical isolation and seek recognition as citizens. Consequently, some Jews turned to the accommodationist stances of Reform and Conservative Judaism, while others embraced traditional behaviors under the rubric of Orthodoxy.[22] Today, Orthodox Judaism runs a spectrum from mainstream Orthodoxy, whose rabbinical school, the Rabbi Isaac Elchanan

Theological Seminary, was founded in 1897, to Ultra-Orthodox Judaism, which was revived on American soil in the wake of the Holocaust.[23] Orthodox Judaism holds itself to rigorous standards of commitment to halakhah, while Ultra-Orthodoxy generally combines this commitment with additional communal restrictions. However, even within Ultra-Orthodoxy, one finds a range of opinions as to the proper direction for Jewish life, from the guarded Satmar community to the well-known Chabad Lubavitch movement.[24]

One effective way to expose students to the differences between denominations is to pick a particular legal requirement and analyze it from each perspective in turn. I have found dietary laws related to the consumption of milk and meat useful for this purpose. The relevant biblical citation appears at *Exodus* 23:19, *Exodus* 34:26, and *Deuteronomy* 14:21: "You shall not boil a kid [young goat] in its mother's milk." In explanation, rabbinic authorities have offered a variety of responses. Among Reform rabbis, a popular opinion holds that the law is intended to teach "sensitivity to the pain of animals."[25] Conservative authorities raise similar ethical concerns but point to the Bible's three-fold repetition of the rule to emphasize that one should have separate cookware for milk and meat, that one should wait between eating meat and eating dairy, and that one "should not prepare or provide or sell milk/meat mixtures (or any non-kosher foods) to anyone else, even if not technically doing the cooking."[26] Orthodox authorities similarly emphasize this threefold interpretation but also require that the process of milking be supervised to "ensure that the source of the milk is from a kosher animal."[27] Finally, ultra-Orthodox authorities emphasize that the law regarding mixture of milk and meat is a "*chok*—a statute that we fulfill simply because it is the will of G-d, although we don't understand it" and suggest further that if an individual eating milk is joined at a table by someone eating meat products, the two may only eat together if they "set up a reminder to ensure that they will not share food from each other's plates," and that this reminder "may be an object placed on the table which is not usually there," such as a basketball.[28] By walking students through sources such as these, one can emphasize each movement's unique reaction to modernity through its specific approach to the minutiae of Jewish law and ritual: To what degree should one shift tradition to accommodate modern understandings and/or norms? If one does so, how can one ensure those accommodations are reasonable and acceptable? To the extent that such questions similarly afflict other religions, this can also be a rich topic for comparative discussions.

Suggested Readings

General Surveys

Robinson, George. *Essential Judaism: A Complete Guide to Beliefs, Customs & Rituals*. New York: Pocket Books, 2000.

Scheindlin, Raymond P. *A Short History of the Jewish People: From Legendary Times to Modern Statehood*. Oxford: Oxford University Press, 1998.

Rabbinic Texts

Holtz, Barry W., ed. *Back to the Sources: Reading the Classic Jewish Texts*. New York: Touchstone, 1992.

Rubenstein, Jeffrey L. *Talmud Stories: Narrative Art, Composition and Culture*. Baltimore: The Johns Hopkins University Press, 1999.

American Judaism

Diner, Hasia R. *The Jews of the United States: 1654 to 2000*. Berkeley: University of California Press, 2004.

Zola, Gary Phillip and Marc Dollinger, ed. *American Jewish History: A Primary Source Reader*. Lebanon NH: Brandeis University Press, 2014.

Contemporary Topics

Bergen, Doris L. *The Holocaust: A Concise History*. Lanham MD: Rowman & Littlefield Publishers, Inc., 2009.

Hartman, Tova. *Feminism Encounters Traditional Judaism: Resistance and Accommodation*. Lebanon NH: Brandeis University Press, 2007.

CLOSING CONSIDERATIONS

At this point in the unit, students have been introduced to a basic framework of Jewish history, the core religious texts of the Bible and Talmud, the critical role of halakhah, the significance of ritual, and the diversity of contemporary American Judaism. Given a bit more time, instructors might be interested in confronting the specter of the Holocaust or the complicated history of the Israeli state. Both topics are too expansive to be considered here, but resources are mentioned in the notes below.[29] For my part, since I aim to close units with attention to present-day debates, I focus in my Judaism unit on fascinating and recent work around expanding women's roles in Orthodox religious life. To this end, I introduce students to the work of JOFA, the Jewish Orthodox Feminist Alliance, which works to advance social change around gender issues in the Orthodox community within the framework of halakhah.[30] JOFA's primary areas of advocacy include ritual inclusion, the heart-rending issue of *agunot* (women trapped in marriages), and women in leadership roles.[31] Each of these topics is worthy of its own course, but the most accessible for students is likely the issue of women in leadership. Here, it can be noted that the Reform movement ordained its first female rabbi in 1972, while the Conservative movement did so in 1985. Among Orthodox Jews, however, women have thus far been denied rabbinic ordination. Today, however, a new movement known as Open Orthodoxy has pushed against this barrier by ordaining Orthodox women as *maharats*—or "leader[s] in Jewish law, spirituality, and education"— since 2009.[32] This development has generated blunt rejoinders from mainstream Orthodoxy's ruling body, the Rabbinic Council of America, and the topic in general has sparked a serious dispute over Orthodox identity.[33] For students, delving into this conversation can be an enlightening window into the ongoing and unresolved nature of Judaism's confrontation with the modern world. Ideally, these lessons will enable students to understand what it means to be a Jew today and how to parse complex questions of Jewish identity.

NOTES

1. Yosef Hayim Yerushalmi, *Zakhor: Jewish History and Jewish Memory* (Seattle: University of Washington Press, 1996), 7-8.

2. To make this lesson more student-centered, one could assign each event to a pair of students and ask the class to construct the timeline together.

3. For this purpose, I would recommend using a translation of the Hebrew Bible from a Jewish publishing house, such as the Jewish Publication Society, Koren Publishers, or Artscroll.

4. For a free and accessible version of Rashi's commentary, see "The Complete Tanach with Rashi's Commentary," Chabad. org, accessed June 15, 2017, http://www.chabad.org/library/bible_cdo/aid/63255/jewish/The-Bible-with-Rashi.htm

5. For a technical but comprehensive overview of the Talmud, see Adin Even-Israel Steinsaltz, *Reference Guide to the Talmud, Revised Edition*, ed. Joshua Schreier (Jerusalem: Koren Publishers, 2014).

6. Sharon Otterman, "Orthodox Jews Celebrate Cycle of Talmudic Study," *New York Times*, August 1, 2012, http://www. nytimes.com/2012/08/02/nyregion/nearly-90000-jews-celebrate-talmud-at-metlife-stadium.html

7. "Returning Lost Objects," NLE Resources, accessed June 15, 2017, http://nleresources.com/kiruv-and-chinuch/nle-gemara/hashavat-aveidah/#.WYY2P8aZPVp

8. For those interested in the political and social history of Jews in the medieval period, see Mark R. Cohen, *Under Crescent & Cross: The Jews in the Middle Ages* (Princeton: Princeton University Press, 2008). For those interested in the philosophical and theological history of Jews in the medieval period, see Colette Sirat, *A History of Jewish Philosophy in the Middle Ages* (Cambridge: Cambridge University Press, 1995).

9. Lis Harris, *Holy Days: The World of a Hasidic Family* (New York: Touchstone, 1985), 60-76.

10. Judith Shulevitz, "Remember the Sabbath," *Forward*, March 31, 2010, http://forward.com/opinion/126978/remember-the-sabbath/

11. "Questions & Answers," Chabad.org, accessed June 15, 2017, http://www.chabad.org/library/article_cdo/aid/5724/jewish/Questions-Answers.htm

12. Menachem Posner, "Can I Read Library Books on Shabbat?" Chabad.org, accessed June 15, 2017, http://www.chabad.org/library/article_cdo/aid/757573/jewish/Can-I-read-library-books-on-Shabbat.htm

13. *Ibid.*

14. *Ibid.*

15. "A Portrait of Jewish Americans," Pew Research Center, October 1, 2013, http://www.pewforum.org/2013/10/01/jewish-american-beliefs-attitudes-culture-survey/

16. For instance, see Marvin Schick, "The Problem with the Pew Study," *Tablet*, October 18, 2013, http://www.tabletmag.com/scroll/149510/the-problem-with-the-pew-study; Jack Wertheimer and Steven M. Cohen, "The Pew Survey Reanalyzed," *Mosaic*, November 2, 2014, https://mosaicmagazine.com/essay/2014/11/the-pew-survey-reanalyzed/; and J.J. Goldberg, "Pew Survey About Jewish America Got It All Wrong," *Forward*, October 13, 2013, http://forward.com/opinion/185461/pew-survey-about-jewish-america-got-it-all-wrong/

17. I should note that I have been criticized for not including Reconstructionist Judaism here, but I would reply that Reconstructionist Judaism's unique philosophy is overly confusing to students facing a week-long introductory unit. Given more time, however, it would make sense to explore this subject as a significant development in Jewish life and thought. For those interested in the subject, see Mordecai M. Kaplan, *Judaism as a Civilization: Toward a Reconstruction of American-Jewish Life* (Philadelphia: The Jewish Publication Society, 2010).

18. For the classic history of the Reform movement, see Michael A. Meyer, *Response to Modernity: A History of the Reform Movement in Judaism* (Detroit: Wayne State University Press, 1995).

19. "The Pittsburgh Platform – 1885," Central Conference of American Rabbis, October 27, 2004, https://ccarnet.org/rabbis-speak/platforms/declaration-principles/

20. Anecdotally, this split is also attributed to the "Trefa Banquet," an event celebrating the first graduates of the new Reform seminary, at which non-kosher food such as clams and soft-shell crabs were served.

21. Michael R. Cohen, *The Birth of Conservative Judaism: Solomon Schechter's Disciples and the Creation of An American Religious Movement* (New York: Columbia University Press, 2012), 140. The use of motor vehicles is otherwise not allowed during the Sabbath due to the presence of an internal combustion engine, which violates the prohibition against use of fire on Shabbat (*Exodus* 35:3).

22. For a fuller treatment of this narrative, see Leora Batnitzky, *How Judaism Became a Religion: An Introduction to Modern Jewish Thought* (Princeton University Press: Princeton, 2011).

23. For an authoritative study of Orthodoxy, see Jeffrey S. Gurock, *Orthodox Jews in America* (Bloomington: Indiana University Press, 2009).

24. For a fascinating article on the Satmar community, see Sam Roberts, "A Village With the Numbers, Not the Image, of the Poorest Place," *New York Times*, April 20, 2011, http://www.nytimes.com/2011/04/21/nyregion/kiryas-joel-a-village-with-the-numbers-not-the-image-of-the-poorest-place.html. For a recent biography of the Lubavitcher Rebbe, see Joseph Telushkin, *Rebbe: The Life and Teachings of Menachem M. Schneerson, the Most Influential Rabbi in Modern History* (New York: Harper Wave, 2016). For a thoughtful memoir from an individual who left a Hasidic community for secular life, see Shulem Deen, *All Who Go Do Not Return: A Memoir* (Minneapolis: Graywolf Press, 2015).

25. "The Civilized Diet: Interview with Rabbi Simeon Maslin," *Reform Judaism*, accessed June 15, 2017, http://www.reformjudaism.org/civilized-diet

26. "Kashrut: Connecting the Physical to the Spiritual," The United Synagogue of Conservative Judaism, accessed June 15, 2017, http://www.uscj.org/JewishLivingandLearning/Kashrut/default.aspx

27. "The Kosher Primer," Orthodox Union, accessed June 15, 2017, https://oukosher.org/the-kosher-primer/. Per this authority, the United States Department of Agriculture's regulations are sufficient for this purpose.

28. Aryeh Citron, "Meat & Milk," accessed June 15, 2017, http://www.chabad.org/library/article_cdo/aid/1149824/jewish/Meat-Milk.htm

29. For materials on the Holocaust, see the many teaching resources of the United States Holocaust Memorial Museum and the Holocaust & Human Rights Education Center. For those interested in the state of Israel, see Itamar Rabinovich, *The Lingering Conflict: Israel, The Arabs, and the Middle East 1948-2012* (Washington: The Brookings Institution, 2011) and Ari Shavit, *My Promised Land: The Triumph and Tragedy of Israel* (New York: Spiegel & Grau, 2013).

30. "Who We Are," Jewish Orthodox Feminist Alliance, accessed June 15, 2017, https://www.jofa.org/Who_We_Are/Mission

31. The issue of *agunot* typically centers on women trapped in marriages by husbands who refuse to grant a religious divorce. For more information, see Matthew Shaer, "The Orthodox Hit Squad," *GQ*, September 2, 2014, http://www.gq.com/story/epstein-orthodox-hit-squad. For a powerful film on the subject, see Ronit and Shlomi Elkabetz's *Gett: The Trial of Viviane Amsalem* (Arte France Cinema, 2014).

32. Sigal Samuel, "Feminism in Faith: Sara Hurwitz's Road to Becoming the First Publicly Ordained Orthodox Jewish Rabba," *Buzzfeed*, March 6, 2014, https://www.buzzfeed.com/sigalsamuel/feminism-in-faith-orthodox-judaism?utm_term=.nnB1jDjLB#.jcpG1P18Y

33. For one such response, see "2015 Resolution: RCA Policy Concerning Women Rabbis," Rabbinical Council of America, October 31, 2015, http://www.rabbis.org/news/article.cfm?id=105835. For an overarching discussion of the controversy, see David Zvi Kalman, "Preaching to the Choir," *Tablet*, November 6, 2015, http://www.tabletmag.com/scroll/194827/preaching-to-the-choir

CHAPTER FOURTEEN

Teaching about Christianity: A Worldwide Tradition

THE PLURALISM PROJECT AT HARVARD UNIVERSITY

Christianity is a worldwide religious tradition, a river of faith with many branches and with streams flowing on every continent. But its common source is one: the life, the teachings, the death, and the resurrection of Jesus. This man, whom Christians call the Christ, the Messiah or anointed one, was born in Roman-ruled Palestine about 2,000 years ago. He lived his life as a Jew in a region governed by the Roman authorities. Like many prophets before him, he spoke of the urgent need to turn to God and he taught a message of love and justice. His active ministry of teaching was, at most, about three years long. Still in his thirties, he was accused of being a kingly pretender and a disruptor of the public order and put to death. His followers affirmed that he was resurrected from the dead and that he appeared to them.

Jesus left no writings, nor did others write about him until some years after he died. Remarkably, however, the small group of disciples who stated that they had experienced his resurrection were inspired with an energy that would create communities of faith throughout the Mediterranean world and, eventually, throughout the whole world. It was in Antioch, now in Turkey, that they were first called "Christians," followers of the way of Christ. In the first three centuries, Christianity spread throughout the Greco-Roman world, which extended from the Iberian to the Indian coast. From the fifth to the seventh centuries, Christian outreach spread throughout northern Europe as well as into Asia and Africa. Syrian Christians even missionized in China during this time. In the tenth century, missionaries from Constantinople brought Christianity to Russia.

Today Christianity has three major streams, each possessing its own internal pluralism—the Catholic Communion, the Orthodox Christian Churches, and Protestant movements. Orthodox Christianity has two main branches, Eastern Orthodoxy and Oriental Orthodoxy, which parted ways in antiquity over beliefs about the nature of Christ. Some view Anglicanism, which followed the course of the British Empire, and the Pentecostalism sweeping the globe, as other major streams of the Christian tradition. But these broad categories hardly do

The Pluralism Project at Harvard University (http://pluralism.org) offers many resources for the academic study of world religions. The text of this chapter has been abridged and adapted from the Project's "Introduction to Christianity" and "Christianity in America."[†] The editorial staff of this book have added some teaching suggestions in sidebars, as well as two appendices that provide statistical information on world Christianity and U.S. Christianity from surveys by the Pew Research Center.

justice to the hundreds of particular churches and denominations that have come into being through the centuries and continue to be born today. In the early twenty-first century, Christianity has more adherents than any other religious tradition on earth. One third of the human race call themselves Christians. The Christian scriptures have been translated into a multitude of languages as the Gospel, and this "good news" of Christ's way has been communicated in cultures throughout the world. The great diversity of Christianity is one of its most striking characteristics.

---

† Reproduced by permission of the Pluralism Project at Harvard University. The full text of the Project's "Introduction to Christianity" can be accessed at http://pluralism.org/religions/christianity/introduction-to-christianity/ and the full text of "Christianity in America" is available at http://pluralism.org/religions/christianity/christianity-in-america/

Christianity has continued to grow and change in the twenty-first century, with the rapid multiplication of Christian churches in Africa, including many vibrant independent churches. In Latin America, four centuries of Roman Catholic dominance is now being challenged by the rapid growth of Pentecostalism. By the late twentieth century, the majority of the world's Christians lived in the southern hemisphere. While Christianity is growing most rapidly in Africa and Latin America, it is still the dominant religious tradition of Europe and North America. According to the Pew Forum on Religion and Public Life's Religious Landscape Survey, 78 percent of people in the United States identified themselves as Christians in 2007.

THE LIFE AND TEACHINGS OF JESUS

The story of Jesus, as Christians know and tell it, comes from that part of the Bible called the "New Testament." The first four books—Matthew, Mark, Luke, and John—are known as the "gospels," meaning "good news." They were likely written between about 70 and 100 CE, about two generations after the death of Jesus, and are based on stories of Jesus, told and retold by his followers. Matthew, Mark, and Luke are called the "synoptic" gospels, because they present a "common view" of Jesus through many common sayings, parables, and events. Both Matthew and Luke seem to have used Mark's gospel in writing their own accounts. John's gospel has a distinctive voice, focusing more on the divinity of Christ in the context of a cosmic worldview.

According to the traditions of Luke and Matthew, Jesus was born in Bethlehem in Judaea in the lineage of King David. Theirs is a story in which the ordinary and the miraculous intertwine. The mother of Jesus is said to be Mary, who conceived Jesus by the power of the Holy Spirit while she was still a young unmarried virgin; according to Matthew and Mark, her betrothed, Joseph, was a carpenter from Nazareth. Luke's story is familiar to Christians throughout the world: The couple traveled to Bethlehem to be counted in the census but were unable to find a room at an inn. Jesus was born that night, his first bed a manger filled with hay. Nearby shepherds with their flocks heard angels singing and hurried to see the newborn child. Matthew's story is different from that of Luke. In his account, wise men or astrologers saw the light of a star and came to Bethlehem from the East bringing gifts to honor the child. Mark and John omit the birth story altogether, Mark beginning his account with the baptism of Jesus, and John with the creation of the cosmos.

The gospels preserve little information about the childhood of Jesus, aside from Luke's story of him impressing teachers in the Jewish temple in Jerusalem at the age of twelve. Matthew, Mark, and Luke speak of the critical event of Jesus' baptism by John the Baptist. John's message was one of radical repentance and transformation. He looked to the new age, announcing that the Kingdom of God was near and baptizing people by the thousands in the River Jordan, as an initiation into the kingdom to come. It was a time of political turmoil and religious expectation; there were many Jewish movements that looked forward to a new age, the coming of the Kingdom of God and the long-promised Messiah, the "anointed one."

One of those baptized by John was Jesus of Nazareth. Jesus' baptism marked the beginning of his public ministry of preaching, teaching, and healing. According to Luke, Jesus was about 30 years old when he began his ministry. He was accompanied by a group of followers, some of them fishermen, who left their nets and their families, and some of them women, whose presence can be seen throughout the period of Jesus' ministry. Jesus attracted large crowds as he began to teach in Galilee. His message of repentance and turning to God was coupled with a message of God's generosity and forgiveness, God's love and justice.

The gospels describe Jesus as performing miracles: healing the sick, casting out the demons of mental illness from the tormented, and even bringing the dead back to life. They also portray a powerful teacher, whose parables made their point in surprising ways. Yes, one should love one's neighbor, but, who is the neighbor? In one parable, a man is robbed, beaten, and left on the road. Many pass him by without giving him help, including respected members of his own community. The one who stops to help him is a Samaritan, a person from Samaria considered a foreigner and an outsider. Jesus insists that the "great commandment" to love one's neighbor as oneself, a command found in Jewish scripture, crosses all ethnic and religious barriers.

In his ministry, Jesus crossed many social barriers as well, mingling with the tax collector, the adulterer, and the prostitute. He warned critics to remember their own imperfections before condemning others and invited those who were wholly without sin to cast the first stone of condemnation. The great commandment is not to judge one's neighbor, for judgment is God's alone, but to love one's neighbor.

Jesus taught that the expected Kingdom of God was close at hand. But it would not be an earthly political kingdom, rather a new reign of justice for the poor and liberation for the oppressed. Those who would be included first in the Kingdom were not the elites and the powerful, but the poor, the rejected, the outcasts. Jesus likened the coming of the Kingdom of God to the growth of a tiny mustard seed, growing from within to create a new reality. His disciples and many who heard him began to speak of Jesus as the long-awaited redeemer, the Messiah, who would make the Kingdom of God a reality. When the term "Messiah" was translated into Greek, the word used was *Christos*, the Christ.

The Gospel of John, in particular, attributes to Jesus a divine nature and emphasizes his close relationship to God the Father. In John, Jesus tells his disciples, "I am in the Father and the Father is in me." He boldly asserts, "I and the Father are one." Such claims would play an important role in the development of Christian theology. So, too, would references in New Testament documents not only to the Father and the Son but also to the Holy Spirit. Efforts to reconcile these references with monotheism would lead to the Christian doctrine of the Trinity, the belief that the one God consists of three distinct persons, Father, Son, and Holy Spirit.

Early Christian sources tell us that many of Jesus' followers believed that his crucifixion was a sacrifice for the sins of humanity and his resurrection was the sign that death had been overcome and eternal

life was available to all believers. Today, Christians continue to affirm that eternal life is available to those who repent of their sins and accept the gift of salvation through Christ. Jesus' followers spread what they saw as the "good news" of God's action in Jesus, and already by the mid-first century, groups of Christians could be found as far away as Asia Minor, Greece, and Italy. Early on, the movement began to draw non-Jews, heralding its future as a separate religion from Judaism. The best-known Christian missionary from the first century was Paul, a Jew who believed that non-Jews could be saved through faith in Christ. Paul established churches in various cities in Greece and Asia Minor, and his letters to various Christian communities constitute much of the New Testament.

Those who have followed the path of Christ through the centuries have understood his life, death, and resurrection as a profound affirmation of God's presence in the midst of humanity. The "Christ event," according to many Christians, cannot be understood in the context of the first century alone: It is as much a twenty-first century event, repeated and renewed daily in the lives of those who take this as the story of their own faith.

ORTHODOX CHRISTIAN CHURCHES

The Eastern family of churches, today called the Oriental Orthodox and Eastern Orthodox churches, go back to the very earliest days of Christianity. During the first four centuries of the Christian era, Christianity had spread not only into the Roman and Byzantine Empires, but also into the present-day Middle East, North Africa, and India. The most influential groups were united through a pentarchy that revered patriarchal sees in Antioch, Alexandria, Constantinople, Jerusalem and Rome. Theological disagreements over the nature of Christ led to the departure of Oriental Orthodox churches from this system in the fifth century. In the centuries that followed, the Latin-speaking churches led by Rome and the Greek-speaking churches of the East increasingly became estranged. Distinct worship customs, resistance to the bishop of Rome's claims of authority over the other bishops, and disputes over the nature of the Trinity led to the second major schism of 1054. The crisis grew until the

Pope of Rome and the Patriarch of Constantinople excommunicated each other. The institutions headed by each became known respectively as the (Roman) Catholic Church and the (Eastern) Orthodox Churches.

The distinctive theologies and liturgies of the Orthodox churches have continued into the twenty-first century. One particularly characteristic theological stance of the Christ event, for example, is the emphasis upon the incarnation of Christ as a means to raise human nature to the Divine. As Athanasius put it in the fourth century, "the Son of God became man so that man might become God." This emphasis on theosis, "becoming divine," stands in contrast to the heavy emphasis on human sinfulness present in much of the theology of the Western churches.

Today, the Eastern Orthodox churches constitute a family of related churches, including the Greek, Russian, Bulgarian, and Romanian churches, each with a rich history and distinctive liturgical forms. Oriental Orthodox churches include the Armenian Apostolic Church, the Coptic Church of Egypt, the Ethiopian Church, the Eritrean Church, the Church of St. Thomas in India, the Syriac Orthodox Church of Antioch, and the Jacobite Syrian Church.

THE ROMAN CATHOLIC CHURCH AND THE CATHOLIC COMMUNION

The early church spoke of its fellowship of believers as *catholic*, a word which means "universal." Today, many Christians still affirm "one holy, catholic, and apostolic church" in the Nicene Creed. However, the term Catholic with a capital "C" also applies in common parlance to the Churches within the Catholic Communion, centered in Rome. The Church of Rome is one of the oldest Christian communities, tracing its history to the apostles Peter and Paul in the first century. As it developed, it emphasized the central authority and primacy of the bishop of Rome, who became known as the Pope. By the eleventh century, the Catholic Church broke with the Byzantine Church of the East over issues of both authority and doctrine. Over the centuries, the Catholic Church and the Eastern Orthodox Church have made several attempts to restore union and to

heal the wounds of division between the Churches.

In the sixteenth century, an Augustinian friar Martin Luther (1483-1546), trying to address what he saw as problems within the church, ultimately broke with it entirely and launched the Protestant Reformation. At the Council of Trent (1545–1563), the Roman Catholic Church addressed some of the Protestants' critiques and introduced administrative reforms, while also affirming the visible, hierarchical, and structured authority of the Roman Catholic Church. This period of Catholic renewal reinvigorated the educational and missionary zeal of the church with the establishment of the Society of Jesus, also called the Jesuits, founded by Ignatius Loyola (1491-1556). Especially with the colonization and conversion of Latin America and with its missions to Asia and Africa, the Roman Catholic Church became a worldwide church.

Today, the Catholic Communion is centered at the Vatican in Rome, but its synods, councils of bishops, and local parishes carry on the life and work of the church on every continent. More than half of the world's Christians are Catholic. The Second Vatican Council (1962-65) considered seriously the new role of the church in the modern world. Among the many decisions of the Council was to abandon the predominantly Latin mass in favor of worship in the language and in the cultural forms of the local community. The Council declared clearly that the Catholic Church is not just the visible hierarchy centered in Rome, but "the whole people of God." The church should emphasize not only preaching and sacraments, but a vigorous mission to the poor and those in need. The many documents of the Second Vatican Council include *Nostra Aetate* (In Our Time), which addresses with a new openness the relation of the Catholic Church to other religious traditions.

THE PROTESTANT MOVEMENT

A number of reformers, including John Wycliffe (d.1384) and Jan Hus (c.1370-1415) challenged the doctrines and authority of the Church prior to the sixteenth-century Protestant Reformation. The Reformation itself was sparked by Martin Luther, a German monk whose studies of the Bible led him to attack the leadership of the Catholic Church in his day. First, Luther insisted that religious authority lay not primarily in church traditions, nor in the hierarchy of bishops and popes, but in the Bible alone. The teaching of the church and its leaders must be judged by the standard and teaching of the Bible, which, he argued, is the sole authoritative source of the Christian faith. Further, Luther insisted that the Bible and the worship life of the church be translated from Latin into the language of the people, so that all might hear and understand it.

The Protestant Reformation marked the beginning of what would become a new movement in the Christian tradition. Its leaders and forms were many, but the spirit of the Protestant tradition continued to emphasize the importance of personal faith, the gift of grace, and the authority of the Bible. In Germany, the Lutheran tradition built on Martin Luther's heritage. Lutheran national churches also developed in Sweden, Denmark, Norway, and Finland. The Lutheran churches of America today include descendants from all of these churches.

The "Reformed" churches have their roots in Switzerland, where Ulrich Zwingli launched a movement of church reform in Zurich in 1522. Soon thereafter, in Geneva, John Calvin, in some ways the most influential of the reformers, led a movement that helped found Reformed churches in the Netherlands, Hungary, England, and Scotland. The Presbyterian churches are also part of this Reformed tradition, and developed initially under the leadership of the sixteenth-century Scottish reformer, John Knox. Today's Baptists and Congregationalists trace their lineage back to the ideas of Zwingli and Calvin as well.

The more radical Anabaptists took issue with Zwingli and the reformers in Zurich over two issues: the establishment of a state church and infant baptism. They held that Christian faith is a conscious and voluntary commitment of the heart. Thus, they rejected the coercion of any state church and also rejected infant baptism in favor of the baptism of adult believers. The Anabaptists influenced the later formation of the Baptist churches and shaped the historic "peace churches,"

such as the Quakers and the Mennonites—all of which have been broadly influential in American Christianity.

The English Reformation began in the sixteenth century when King Henry VIII declared the independence of the Church of England from the authority of the Pope. Some Protestants in England went even further than Henry and called for a complete purification of the church. Later known as "Puritans," these radical dissenters in the Church of England set out for North America in the early 1600s. They envisioned establishing a Christian community, a "holy commonwealth" in the new world. In the 1700s, John Wesley (1703-1791), a priest of the Church of England, launched an energetic devotional reform movement, emphasizing the forgiveness and grace of a loving God. This movement eventually broke with the Church of England and became known as Methodism. Those who remained within the Church of England spread their version of Christianity as the British Empire encircled the world. After the Empire's dissolution, those churches banded together as the Worldwide Anglican Communion.

RELIGIOUS DIVERSITY IN THE UNITED STATES IN THE NINETEENTH AND EARLY TWENTIETH CENTURIES

The Protestant Reformation launched not a Protestant Church, but a Protestant movement—a dynamic movement of many churches, engaged in energetic and ongoing reformation, even today. Evangelicals played a key role in ongoing reformation efforts. Originally, the term "evangelical" was used to describe the 18th-19th century religious reform movements and denominations that resulted from the revivals that swept the North Atlantic Anglo-American world. These revivals were often led by figures like John Wesley, the itinerant English evangelist George Whitefield (1715-1770), and American preacher and theologian Jonathan Edwards (1703-1758), who played prominent roles in the First Great Awakening of the 1730s and 1740s. As a result of the Second Great Awakening of the late eighteenth century and the first part of the nineteenth century, Evangelicals dominated the American Protestant scene by the 1820s, and

THE DIVERSITY OF U.S. CHRISTIANITY: A STUDENT PROJECT

It has been said that "the United States in the twenty-first century is home to perhaps the most diverse and varied Christian population on earth." Immigrants to the United States have included Christians of European, African, Asian, and Latin American birth or descent. Native American Christians worship in a variety of churches. (See the Pluralism Project at Harvard University, "Race and Ethnicity," at http://pluralism.org/religions/christianity/issues-for-christians-in-america/race-and-ethnicity/.)

Students should select a Christian religious denomination to study. Some religious denominations are growing as they increase the numbers of their followers, and others are losing members. After consulting primary and secondary sources, including reliable online sources, students should evaluate why the selected church is gaining or losing members.

played a major role in reform movements such as abolitionism and Prohibition. During the nineteenth century there was a significant increase in the number of Baptist congregations and regional Baptist associations and societies in the United States. The Triennial Convention, which was created in 1814, became the first national Baptist denomination, although Southern Baptists broke with the Convention over the issue of slavery in 1845.

In the nineteenth century, new Christian groups emerged in the United States. The Church of Jesus Christ of Latter-day Saints was founded as a Christian restorationist movement whose history began with the affirmation by Joseph Smith (1805-1844) that he had received messages from an angel named Moroni that led him to discover and translate a text from golden plates left by an ancient American Christian civilization that became known as the Book of Mormon. The nineteenth century also witnessed the emergence of the Seventh Day Adventist Church and the Jehovah's Witnesses, who advocated beliefs based on distinctive interpretations of Biblical texts and the anticipation of the return of Christ.

Immigration transformed American Catholicism from a small church dominated by Maryland gentry at the opening of the national period into the largest single denomination in the United States by the time of the Civil War. Raw statistics tell one part of the story. From about 1820, when the migrations began, to about 1920, the Catholic population rose dramatically: 4,300,000 Irish by 1850; 1,650,000 Germans by 1880. About four million Italians arrived between 1880 and 1920, two million Poles between 1870 and 1920, one million French Canadians between 1880 and 1910. Slovaks, Czechs, Lithuanians, and other immigrants, as well as the Spanish Catholics of the old Southwest, transformed American Catholicism into a multi-national, multi-ethnic church in which twenty-eight different languages were spoken and many different kinds of devotional forms flourished. Moreover, many Eastern rite Catholics also began to immigrate to the United States in the 1870s, particularly Ukrainian and Carpathian Greek Catholics who worked in the mills and mines of the Northeast.

Orthodox Christianity was first established in North America in 1794 when Russian monks from Valaam Monastery founded a successful mission to native Aleut peoples on Kodiak Island in Alaska. Russian Orthodox influence remained substantial after the sale of Alaska to the United States in 1867. Other kinds of Eastern Orthodoxy came into America during the great migrations of the late nineteenth century. At that time, Ukrainians, Serbs, Bulgarians, Romanians, Albanians, Syrians, and additional Russians settled in the United States, all bringing with them ancient and distinctive national Christian traditions.

Separate black churches began to emerge in the 1760s, although they remained few in number until the demise of slavery a century later. For example, the African Baptist Church of Savannah was founded in 1788 and, by 1830, had over two thousand members, free and slave. A former slave and licensed Methodist preacher named Richard Allen, who had formed Philadelphia's Bethel Church in 1794, founded a distinct denomination called the African Methodist Episcopal Church (A.M.E.) in 1816. The A.M.E. Zion denomination was founded in New York in 1821, having seceded from a mixed-race church in which blacks could take communion only after all the whites had received it. Many of the independent black Baptist congregations and associations formed after the Civil War merged to form the National Baptist Convention in 1895. All these denominations became vital institutions in the African-American community, both in the rural South and, with black mass migration to industrial centers, in northern cities.

THE GLOBAL SPREAD OF CHRISTIANITY

The spread of Christian churches followed in the tracks of empire, trade, and colonization. At times, the churches and missionaries were involved or complicit in the exploitation and oppression of colonized people. It is also true, however, that missionaries were among the strongest critics of colonial excesses. Many were the first scholars to study the religious and cultural traditions of the peoples among whom they worked. Especially in Asia, missionaries were also the first to challenge the exclusivist teachings of the church, for they saw what they understood to be evidence of God's living presence in non-Christian faiths.

The order of Jesuits or the Society of Jesus, founded in the sixteenth century, was influential as a Catholic missionary order, sending Jesuits to such places as India, China and the Americas. Later, Protestant missionary societies were formed to link the Protestant churches of Europe, and later the United States, with the new churches established in Asia and Africa.

With the end of the colonial era, the mission churches began to develop strong voices and leadership of their own. Today, much of the dynamism and energy of the Christian churches worldwide is coming from the churches of Africa, Asia, and Latin America. The last few decades have seen a renewed emphasis on the authentic expression of the gospel in every culture and language. In the post-colonial era, churches in all parts of the world have moved away from European or American expressions of Christianity and have claimed their own culture, music, and arts in order to shape their own forms of Christian worship and community.

CHRISTIANITY AND RACIAL JUSTICE

In describing the civil rights issues of the 1960s, Martin Luther King, Jr. wrote, "Over the last five years, many religious bodies—Catholic, Protestant, and Jewish—have been in the vanguard of the civil rights struggle, and have sought desperately to make the ethical insights of our Judeo-Christian heritage relevant on the question of race. But the Church as a whole has been all too negligent on the question of civil rights. It has too often blessed a status quo that needed to be blasted and reassured a social order that needed to be reformed." (In *Where Do We Go From Here: Chaos or Community* (1967), quoted at http://pluralism.org/religions/christianity/issues-for-christians-in-america/race-and-ethnicity/)

Divide the class into groups and assign each group to research the official position of a religious denomination on the actions of the civil rights movement in the 1960s, and to examine the debates that took place among members of the selected denomination on the actions of the civil rights movement. What arguments based on religion were used by church members to support their positions, and what arguments were used by church officials to uphold their positions?

After students have shared their findings, each student should choose two denominations whose positions on the actions of the civil rights movement differed and write a research paper analyzing the reasons for their differing attitudes toward the actions of the civil rights movement.

As additional research projects, students could analyze the positions of different churches, and the debates among their members, on historical topics such as slavery, the dispossession of Native Americans, and prejudice against immigrants.

WOMEN'S MINISTRY IN THE CHURCH

Beginning in the mid-twentieth century, the question of whether women should be ordained as ministers became a widespread and intensively debated issue for many denominations in the United States.

In the 1950s and 1960s, the Presbyterian and Methodist churches began ordaining women as ministers of full status. The Lutheran churches followed in the 1970s, and the Episcopal Church admitted women to the priesthood in 1976.

The Roman Catholic Church, the Eastern Orthodox Church, and some theologically conservative Protestant groups (such as the Southern Baptist Convention) continued to be opposed to the ordination of women.

Assign groups of students to examine the policies of different churches toward the ordination of women. In examining the policies of denominations that do not accept the ordination of women, students should examine the points of view expressed by members of the denomination who are for women's ordination and the points of view of those who are against women's ordination, and identify how each side justifies its point of view by reference to religious beliefs, the scriptures, and the current role of women in the church today. In examining the decisions of denominations that chose to ordain women, students should examine the arguments that were presented in favor and against the ordination of women, show how each side justified its point of view by reference to religious beliefs and the scriptures, and evaluate the effect on the church of its decision to ordain women.

Today, many of these new cultural and ethnic expressions have come to America with the new immigration. As with first-generation immigrants in the past, these immigrants have maintained their own congregations—Hispanic, Korean, Samoan, Ethiopian, South Indian, or Chinese—and have brought an astounding new diversity to the face of American Christianity.

CHRISTIANITY AND SCIENTIFIC KNOWLEDGE

The growth of the scientific revolution that transformed assumptions about the natural world posed challenges to Christian theology. Charles Darwin countered the biblical story of creation with his theories about the development and evolution of species as published in *The Origin of Species* (1859) and *The Descent of Man* (1871). His work provoked a clash between religious beliefs and science as Christian conservatives challenged the concept of evolution. Christian fundamentalism, which became powerful in the early twentieth century, expressed strong opposition to Darwinist thought, and the Scopes Trial in 1925 was a watershed in fundamentalist efforts to prevent schools from teaching ideas that ran counter to the scriptures.

Christian thinkers of each succeeding generation have had to claim and articulate their faith anew in the light of a wider worldview, informed by the expansion of science. Does faith today occupy the shrinking area of mystery left over by the growing body of scientific knowledge? Or is faith an orientation to all of life that is not threatened by science but consonant with it?

Biblical scholarship has also posed challenges to faith in the modern era. The text of the Bible has been laid open to study by methods of critical and historical analysis. What is the Bible? How did this particular collection of writings come into being? To what extent should scriptural texts be studied and interpreted as products of particular historical contexts, with their own historical concerns? In the early twentieth century, Christian fundamentalism opposed many trends in modern biblical scholarship. Conservative Protestants have often been concerned with protecting the literal interpretation of the Bible from what they consider to be the undermining effects of much biblical scholarship. More liberal Christians, on the other hand, find that this biblical scholarship enhances their understanding of the Bible, and they do not believe that the theological and ethical importance of the Bible depends on its literal accuracy.

NEW CURRENTS

The second half of the twentieth century saw new currents of confluence, bringing together once again the divided streams that have characterized Christianity for nearly a thousand years. This trend is called the ecumenical movement, from the Greek term "oikoumene" which means "the whole inhabited earth." The most prominent expression of this ecumenical movement is the World Council of Churches (WCC), which was formed in 1948. Seventy years later, it is a fellowship of 350 Protestant and Orthodox churches committed to growing together in faith and working together on shared issues of justice, peace, education, and emergency relief. In the 1960s, the Second Vatican Council also made far reaching contributions to Christian ecumenism, opening the door to closer cooperation between the Roman Catholic and other Christian churches. Toward the end of the Second Vatican Council, the Pope and the Patriarch of Constantinople removed their one-thousand year old mutual excommunication and embraced.

The convergence of churches today is visible in many ways. National, regional, and local councils of churches throughout the world are another expression of the ecumenical movement. While old divisions are beginning to heal, new areas of tension and fission are opening in the Christian churches of the early twenty-first century. The interpretation of the Bible, the ordination of women, attitudes toward gays and lesbians, and the ethics of abortion and reproduction are all issues that have opened new fissures, not so much between but within denominations.

World Christianity

A Pew Research Center Survey in 2010 found that almost 32% of the world's population were Christian. The second most widely practiced religion was Islam (23.2%).

The information on world Christianity in this section is derived from the results of the survey by the Pew Research Center's Forum on Religion & Public Life at http://www. pewforum.org/2011/12/19/global-christianity-exec/. Percentages may not add to 100 due to rounding.

* Includes Bahai's, Jains, Sikhs, Shintoists, Taoists, followers of Tenrikyo, Wiccans, Zoroastrians, and many other faiths.

** Includes followers of African traditional religions, Chinese folk religions, Native American religions, and Australian aboriginal religions.

Pew Research Center's Forum on Religion & Public Life
Global Religious Landscape, December 2012

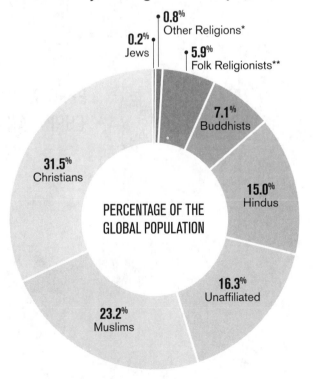

Size of Major Religious Groups, 2010

PERCENTAGE OF THE GLOBAL POPULATION

- 0.8% Other Religions*
- 0.2% Jews
- 5.9% Folk Religionists**
- 7.1% Buddhists
- 15.0% Hindus
- 16.3% Unaffiliated
- 23.2% Muslims
- 31.5% Christians

Among the world's Christians, the 2010 Pew survey found that about half were Catholics, while almost 37% were Protestant and 11.9% Orthodox.

Estimated Size of Christian Traditions (2010)

TRADITION	* ESTIMATED 2010 CHRISTIAN POPULATION	PERCENTAGE OF WORLD POPULATION	PERCENTAGE OF WORLD CHRISTIAN POPULATION
Catholic	1,094,610,000	15.9%	50.1%
Protestant	800,640,000	11.6%	36.7%
Orthodox	260,380,000	3.8%	11.9%
Other Christian	28,430,000	0.4%	1.3%
Total Christian	**2,184,060,000**	**31.7%**	**100%**

* Population estimates are rounded to the ten thousands. Percentages are calculated from unrounded numbers. Figures may not add exactly due to rounding.

Pew Research Center's Forum on Religion & Public Life
Global Christianity, December 2011

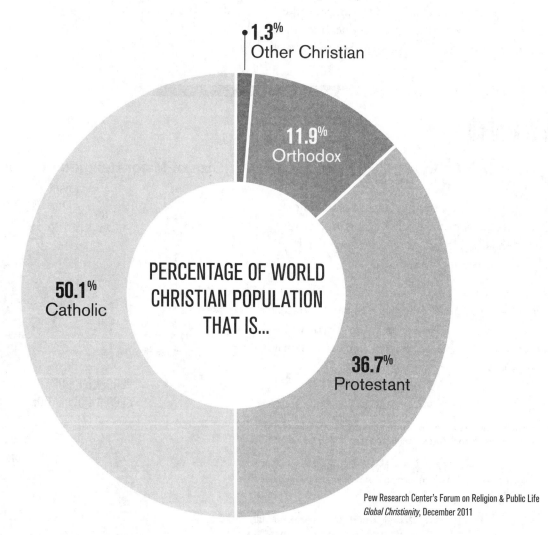

Major Christian Traditions (2010)

1.3% Other Christian

11.9% Orthodox

50.1% Catholic

PERCENTAGE OF WORLD CHRISTIAN POPULATION THAT IS...

36.7% Protestant

Pew Research Center's Forum on Religion & Public Life
Global Christianity, December 2011

During the 20th century, there was a major change in the worldwide distribution of Christians. Although in 1910, more than 90% of Christians lived in Europe and the Americas, by 2010 about 62.7% of Christians lived in Europe and the Americas, and 37.3% lived in other regions of the world. The United States was the country with the largest number of Christians.

Regional Distribution of Christians (1910 and 2010)

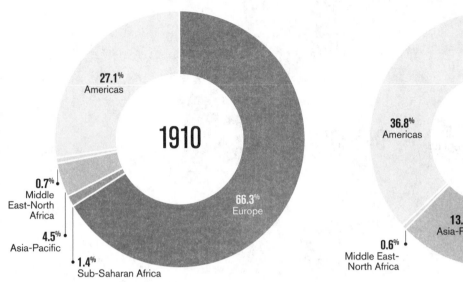

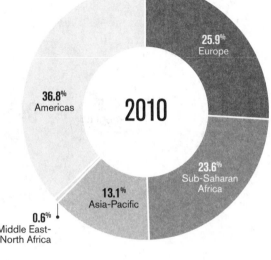

* Figures for 1910 are from a Pew Forum analysis of data from the Center for the Study of Global Christianity. Figures may not add exactly due to rounding.

Pew Research Center's Forum on Religion & Public Life
Global Christianity, December 2011

Ten Countries with the Largest Number of Christians (2010)

COUNTRY	* ESTIMATED 2010 CHRISTIAN POPULATION	PERCENTAGE OF POPULATION THAT IS CHRISTIAN	PERCENTAGE OF WORLD CHRISTIAN POPULATION
United States	246,780,000	79.5%	11.3%
Brazil	175,770,000	90.2%	8.0%
Mexico	107,780,000	95.0%	4.9%
Russia	105,220,000	73.6%	4.8%
Philippines	86,790,000	93.1%	4.0%
Nigeria	80,510,000	50.8%	3.7%
China	67,070,000	5.0%	3.1%
Dem. Rep. of the Congo	63,150,000	95.7%	2.9%
Germany	58,240,000	70.8%	2.7%
Ethiopia	52,580,000	63.4%	2.4%
Subtotal	1,043,880,000	40.4%	47.8%
Total Rest of World	1,140,180,000	24.2%	52.2%
WORLD TOTAL	2,184,060,000	31.7%	100%

* Population estimates are rounded to the ten thousands. Percentages are calculated from unrounded numbers. Figures may not add exactly due to rounding.

Pew Research Center's Forum on Religion & Public Life

Global Christianity, December 2011

Among the countries with the largest Christian populations, Brazil had the greatest number of Catholics, the United States the largest number of Protestants, and Russia the largest number of Orthodox Christians.

Regional Distribution of Catholics (2010)

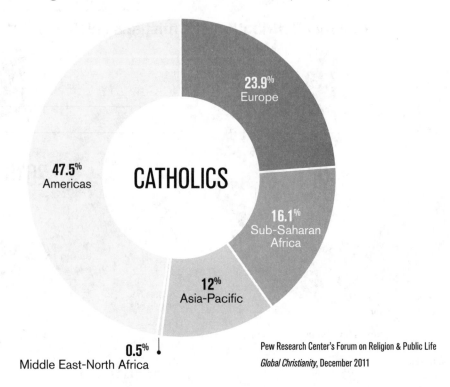

47.5% Americas

23.9% Europe

16.1% Sub-Saharan Africa

12% Asia-Pacific

0.5% Middle East-North Africa

CATHOLICS

Pew Research Center's Forum on Religion & Public Life
Global Christianity, December 2011

Ten Countries with the Largest Number of Catholics (2010)

COUNTRY	* ESTIMATED 2010 CATHOLIC POPULATION	PERCENTAGE OF POPULATION THAT IS CATHOLIC	PERCENTAGE OF WORLD CATHOLIC POPULATION
Brazil	133,660,000	68.6%	12.2%
Mexico	96,330,000	84.9%	8.8%
Philippines	75,940,000	81.4%	6.9%
United States	74,470,000	24.0%	6.8%
Italy	50,250,000	83.0%	4.6%
Colombia	38,100,000	82.3%	3.5%
France	37,930,000	60.4%	3.5%
Poland	35,290,000	92.2%	3.2%
Spain	34,670,000	75.2%	3.2%
Dem. Rep. of the Congo	31,180,000	47.3%	2.8%
Subtotal	607,830,000	58.9%	55.5%
Total Rest of World	486,780,000	8.3%	44.5%
WORLD TOTAL	1,094,610,000	15.9%	100%

* Population estimates are rounded to the ten thousands. Percentages are calculated from unrounded numbers. Figures may not add exactly due to rounding.

Pew Research Center's Forum on Religion & Public Life

Global Christianity, December 2011

Regional Distribution of Protestants (2010)

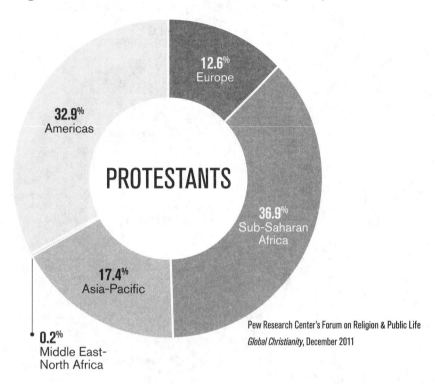

12.6% Europe

32.9% Americas

PROTESTANTS

36.9% Sub-Saharan Africa

17.4% Asia-Pacific

0.2% Middle East-North Africa

Pew Research Center's Forum on Religion & Public Life
Global Christianity, December 2011

Ten Countries with the Largest Number of Protestants (2010)

COUNTRY	* ESTIMATED 2010 PROTESTANT POPULATION	PERCENTAGE OF POPULATION THAT IS PROTESTANT	PERCENTAGE OF WORLD PROTESTANT POPULATION
United States	159,850,000	51.5%	20.0%
Nigeria	59,680,000	37.7%	7.5%
China	58,040,000	4.3%	7.2%
Brazil	40,500,000	20.8%	5.1%
South Africa	36,550,000	72.9%	4.6%
United Kingdom	33,820,000	54.5%	4.2%
Dem. Rep. of the Congo	31,700,000	48.1%	4.0%
Germany	28,640,000	34.8%	3.6%
Kenya	24,160,000	59.6%	3.0%
India	18,860,000	1.5%	2.4%
Subtotal	491,820,000	13.9%	61.4%
Total Rest of World	308,820,000	9.2%	38.6%
WORLD TOTAL	800,640,000	11.6%	100%

* Population estimates are rounded to the ten thousands. Percentages are calculated from unrounded numbers. Figures may not add exactly due to rounding.

Pew Research Center's Forum on Religion & Public Life

Global Christianity, December 2011

Regional Distribution of Orthodox Christians (2010)

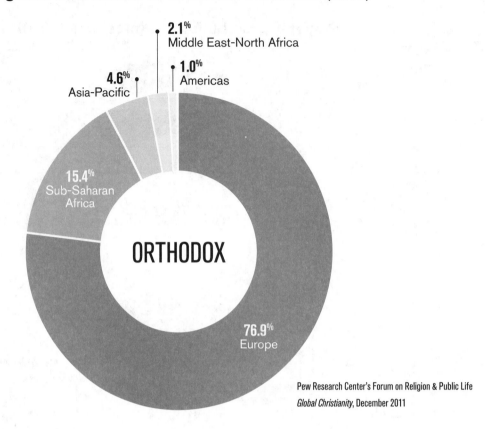

2.1% Middle East-North Africa

1.0% Americas

4.6% Asia-Pacific

15.4% Sub-Saharan Africa

ORTHODOX

76.9% Europe

Pew Research Center's Forum on Religion & Public Life
Global Christianity, December 2011

Ten Countries with the Largest Number of Orthodox Christians (2010)

COUNTRY	* ESTIMATED 2010 ORTHODOX POPULATION	PERCENTAGE OF POPULATION THAT IS ORTHODOX	PERCENTAGE OF WORLD ORTHODOX POPULATION
Russia	101,450,000	71.0%	39.0%
Ethiopia	36,060,000	43.5%	13.9%
Ukraine	34,850,000	76.7%	13.4%
Romania	18,750,000	87.3%	7.2%
Greece	10,030,000	88.3%	3.9%
Serbia	6,730,000	86.6%	2.6%
Bulgaria	6,220,000	83.0%	2.4%
Belarus	5,900,000	61.5%	2.3%
Egypt	3,860,000	4.8%	1.5%
Georgia	3,820,000	87.8%	1.5%
Subtotal	227,660,000	54.9%	87.4%
Total Rest of World	32,720,000	0.5%	12.6%
WORLD TOTAL	260,380,000	3.8%	100%

* Population estimates are rounded to the ten thousands. Percentages are calculated from unrounded numbers. Figures may not add exactly due to rounding.

Pew Research Center's Forum on Religion & Public Life

Global Christianity, December 2011

Christianity in the United States, 2007 and 2014

In the United States, according to a Pew Research Center survey in 2014, just over 70 percent of the population were Christian, but this proportion was smaller than that seven years earlier.

The information on religion in the United States presented here is taken from a survey by the Pew Research Center's Forum on Religion & Public Life whose results are presented at at http://www.pewforum.org/2015/05/12/americas-changing-religious-landscape/. Percentages may not add to 100 due to rounding.

Religious Affiliations of the U.S. Population, 2007 and 2014

	2007 SHARE	2014 SHARE	*CHANGE
Christians	78.4%	70.6%	-7.8%
Protestant	51.3%	46.5%	-4.8%
Evangelical	26.3%	25.4%	-0.9%
Mainline	18.1%	14.7%	-3.4%
Historically Black	6.9%	6.5%	–
Catholic	23.9%	20.8%	-3.1%
Orthodox Christian	0.6%	0.5%	–
Latter-day Saints	1.7%	1.6%	–
Jehovah's Witness	0.7%	0.8%	–
Other Christian	0.3%	0.4%	–
Non-Christian Faiths	4.7%	5.9%	+1.2%
Jewish	1.7%	1.9%	–
Muslim	0.4%	0.9%	+0.5%
Buddhist	0.7%	0.7%	–
Hindu	0.4%	0.7%	+0.3%
Other World Religions**	<0.3%	0.3%	–
Other Faiths**	1.2%	1.5%	+0.3%
Unaffiliated	16.1%	22.8%	+6.7%
Atheist	1.6%	3.1%	+1.5%
Agnostic	2.4%	4.0%	+1.6%
Nothing in Particular	12.1%	15.8%	+3.7%
Don't Know/Refused	0.8%	0.6%	-0.2%
TOTAL	100%	100%	–

*   The "change" column displays only statistically significant changes; blank cells indicate that the difference between 2007 and 2014 is within the margin of error.

** The "other world religions" category includes Sikhs, Bahai's, Taoists, Jains, and a variety of other world religions. The "other faiths" category includes Unitarians, New Age religions, Native American religions, and a number of other non-Christian faiths.

Source: 2014 Religious Landscape Study, conducted June 4–September 30, 2014 by the Pew Research Center's Forum on Religion & Public Life. Figures may not add to 100% and nested figures may not add to subtotals due to rounding.

The Pew Research Center survey of 2014 found significant differences in religious affiliation between generations. Although the majority of younger millennials stated that they are Christian, about 36 percent of this group of millenials declared themselves to be unaffiliated.

Generational Differences in Religious Affiliation in the United States, 2014

	SILENT GENERATION (BORN 1928–1945)	BABY BOOMERS (BORN 1946–1964)	GENERATION X (BORN 1965–1980)	OLDER MILLENNIALS (BORN 1981–1989)	YOUNGER MILLENNIALS (BORN 1990–1996)
Christians	85%	78%	70%	57%	56%
Protestant	57%	52%	45%	38%	36%
Evangelical	30%	28%	25%	22%	19%
Mainline	22%	17%	13%	10%	11%
Historically Black	5%	7%	7%	6%	6%
Catholic	24%	23%	21%	16%	16%
Other Christian Groups*	3%	3%	4%	3%	3%
Other Faiths	4%	5%	6%	8%	8%
Unaffiliated	11%	17%	23%	34%	36%
Don't Know/Refused	–	1%	1%	1%	1%
TOTAL	100%	100%	100%	100%	100%

* The "other Christian groups" category includes members of the Church of Jesus Christ of Latter-day Saints, Orthodox Christians, Jehovah's Witnesses, and a number of smaller Christian groups.

Source: 2014 Religious Landscape Study, conducted June 4–September 30, 2014 by the Pew Research Center's Forum on Religion & Public Life. Figures may not add to 100% and nested figures may not add to subtotals due to rounding.

Christianity in the United States showed an increase in racial and ethnic diversity between 2007 and 2014.

Increasing Racial and Ethnic Diversity Within U.S. Christianity, 2007–2014
Percent non-white, by Christian group

* The demographic characteristics of the 2014 Religious Landscape Study's overall sample were weighted to known parameters from the Census Bureau's 2012 American Community Survey (ACS), which helps to ensure that the demographic characteristics of the sample closely match those of the U.S. adult population.

Source: 2014 Religious Landscape Study, conducted June 4–September 30, 2014 by the Pew Research Center's Forum on Religion & Public Life. Whites include only those who are not Hispanic; the non-white category includes African Americans, Asian Americans, those of other races those of mixed race and Hispanics. Results recalculated to exclue nonresponse.

CHAPTER FIFTEEN

Teaching about Islam in Public Schools

SUSAN DOUGLASS

For at least three decades, teaching about religion has been an established part of teaching humanities and social studies in public schools. The K-12 curriculum includes content on the major religious traditions practiced in the United States and the world. Teaching about religion in U.S. and world history and geography generally reflects acceptance of the guidelines of the Religious Freedom Center of the Freedom Forum for teaching about religion.[1] Academic standards reflect this rare state of consensus, due in no small part to the efforts made by the First Amendment Center and Religious Freedom Center to disseminate these guidelines.

The study of state and national standards published in 2000 by the First Amendment Center determined that all states with content-specific standards in U.S. and world history mandated teaching about religion.[2] These mandates imply that any tests based on the standards could include items on religion. These standards range from mandates mentioning study of all religions, to elaborate mandates about specific aspects of human religious expression across time and space. Advanced Placement history, literature, and geography courses also include extensive content on religions. Most content on world religions appears between grades 5 and 12, but elementary grades feature diversity, holidays, food, and the civic framework of religious freedom embodied in the U.S. Constitution.

WHY TEACH ABOUT ISLAM?

The rise of Islamophobia since September 11, 2001 has caused some students and teachers, as well as activists in anti-Islamic organizations, to question why Islam—which they see as having no redeeming qualities—should be included in the curriculum at all. This stance ignores over 1400 years of history, imagining that Islam as a totality is the sum of what has happened since 9/11. This stance also ignores the legacy of misunderstanding about Islam in Western civilization since the middle ages, which continued through the colonial period into modern times, long before 9/11.[3]

It is important to note at the outset that Islam does not occur in the school curriculum in isolation. Teaching about Islam as a world religion and as a religion practiced by people in the United States occurs together with coverage of other traditions such as Hinduism, Buddhism, Judaism, and Christianity, in addition to content on traditions such as Greek and Roman mythology, and indigenous American and African religions. The guidelines require fair, accurate, and balanced treatment of all, in a manner that aids student acquisition of analytical thinking about art and literature, historical thinking skills, and media literacy.

Teaching about Islam makes sense for many reasons, despite the efforts of some to paint it as an exceptional case. There are about 1.5 billion Muslims in the world today—more than 20% of the human population—living in most of the world's countries, of which 65 are countries with a Muslim majority. For the past 1400 years, the history of Islam and Muslim societies has been deeply entwined with the history of Europe, Africa, Asia, and the world as a whole. World history does not make much sense without it. Even from a Western civilization perspective, Islam belongs to the Abrahamic tradition—that is, Judaism, Christianity, and Islam share a common scriptural heritage and hold a similar core of beliefs and worldview. To exclude any one of them or to dismiss Islam as merely derivative or some kind of heretical offshoot obscures understanding of all three. Islam was influenced by and influenced cultural traditions in science, technology, and the arts shared with Europe and other civilizations over a long period of time. The effects of these exchanges are apparent even today.

Religious illiteracy is not bliss in a diverse nation and a globalizing world.

CONSTRUCTIVE WAYS TO TEACH ABOUT ISLAM

The following suggestions for teaching about Islam reflect adherence to the First Amendment Center guidelines, and many are applicable to teaching about all world religions effectively.

THE GEOGRAPHIC AND CULTURAL/CIVILIZATIONAL SETTING

In the sequence of major world religions, Islam is often taught last, since its rise occurred in the seventh century of the Common Era. In world history courses, medieval to modern expressions of Christianity and Judaism should be covered in tandem with the history of Islam in Muslim societies, and should include their complex, lasting interactions, both positive and negative. Farther east, Buddhism and Hinduism spread and changed in tandem with the spread of both Islam and Christianity. On the Asian overland routes called the Silk Roads, as well as the maritime routes in the Indian Ocean, spiritual seekers, merchant communities, and missionaries of the major world religions mingled and exchanged ideas and goods. Therefore, taking an integrated approach to teaching about religion(s) is more revealing than the outdated but still prevalent practice of covering civilizations in isolation from one another, and religions as separate entities.

The region in which Islam arose—the Arabian Peninsula—includes the whole land mass from the Sinai Peninsula near Egypt to the Tigris-Euphrates Valley. It stretches as a bridge between Asia and Africa, and is geographically named Southwest Asia. Though much of it is desert, the Arabian Peninsula is part of a major zone of interaction in the eastern hemisphere. Through the caravan trade and shipping routes on the Red Sea and

Persian Gulf, it linked the Mediterranean Sea and Indian Ocean to land routes extending into Central Asia. The western end of the Silk Road is the eastern Mediterranean coast.[4] The fertile areas in the northern and southern parts of the Arabian Peninsula were important locations for agricultural innovation and trade throughout history. During the nineteenth century, a tendency developed to separate the Holy Land and the eastern Mediterranean coast (the Levant) from the rest of the peninsula. To the contrary, throughout history, the entire area has been in communication through trade, migration, conquest, and the spread of languages and ideas. Artificial separation inhibits understanding these connections. Judaism, Christianity, and Islam are rich in meaningful narratives about the desert, but they share powerful stories about life in urban communities and their roles in world affairs, such as empires near and far. Islam is not a religion of the desert, but one characterized more by urban environments, and its spread and cultural achievements are tied closely to the expansion of religiously and ethnically diverse cities.

TEACHING ABOUT COMMON BELIEFS IN THE ABRAHAMIC TRADITION

In describing the relationship between Islam, Christianity, and Judaism, the guidelines and academic standards require that the basic beliefs and practices of the world religions be described in an authentic manner. Some have expressed the idea that teaching about overlapping beliefs would be "confusing" to students, so they argue for leaving out important areas of overlap in beliefs and even shared principles. Under this scenario, Judaism emphasizes Abraham and Moses, Christianity Jesus and the Apostles, and Islam Muhammad. This approach to the three religions is neither accurate nor authentic. It simply does not correspond to what people believed and acted upon, nor does it accurately reflect the scriptures. For example, Abraham is highly revered in Islamic teachings from the Qur'an, commemorated in the Five Pillars. Prayer, fasting, pilgrimage, and obedience to God follow an Abrahamic model, and Muslims aspire to all prophets' adherence to faith and piety. One need not adhere to these beliefs in order to relate them by attribution through fair and balanced teaching about all religions. Wherever possible, it is most valuable to cite the actual primary sources on which they are based, which are readily accessible through search engines and prepared sources.[5]

Attempts to explain the overlap in beliefs among these three Abrahamic traditions often veer off into judgmental territory. Under such scenarios, which reflect the Orientalism of an earlier era, Muhammad is described as the "author" of the Qur'an who "incorporated" stories of earlier prophets into "his" scripture, in order to attract followers. According to the most basic Islamic beliefs and teachings held universally by Muslims, the Qur'an—the holy scripture of Islam—was revealed to Muhammad by God, the Creator, through the Angel Gabriel, over a period of 23 years. Muslims believe that the source of this revelation is the One God, and that the revelation is part of the continuous messages revealed to other prophets including Adam, Abraham, Noah, Moses, Solomon, David, and Jesus. In contrast, textbook statements that Muhammad was the author of the Qur'an immediately frame him as an imposter—echoing the medieval view of Muhammad. The belief that Muhammad was the author of the Qur'an, and not a prophet, should no longer have a place in contemporary textbooks in any form.

The First Amendment guidelines quite simply require teaching about religion to explain the history of stories told, because this is what believers historically acted upon. No more, no less, is required. Stating such facts is not "confusing," and is the only way to dispel stereotypes and replace ignorance with a sound knowledge base. Authentic teaching about religious beliefs should not be confused with proselytizing, either, as long as the text carefully avoids stating claims of truth as fact without attribution of the textual source or describing it as the teachings of a tradition. For example, it is a violation of the constitutional guidelines for teaching about religion to state that "The Qur'an, the holy scripture of Islam, was revealed to Muhammad by the Angel Gabriel." In contrast, it is compatible with the guidelines to state that "According to Islamic teachings, the source

of the holy scripture of Islam, called the Qur'an, is the messages received by Muhammad as revelation from God through the Angel Gabriel." There are many different and simpler formulations that could be used for different grade level texts, with the same accuracy.

INTRODUCING CONCEPTUAL VOCABULARY FOR RELIGIOUS TRADITIONS

For purposes of differentiation, some teaching guides attempt to create a graphic organizer headed by categories such as "founder," "book," and "creed." These categories do not apply to all world religions, and create confusion and misunderstanding, especially when used as study guides for multiple choice testing. Instead, a more flexible conceptual vocabulary will help students understand the unique characteristics of each tradition.

For example, Muslims consider Muhammad, who was born in about 532 CE/AD, to be a prophet, or "messenger of God." Because the basic teachings of Islam are believed to be continuous with earlier revelations since the time of Adam, Noah, Abraham, Moses, and Jesus, Muhammad is not considered to be the "founder" of Islam. Accordingly, Muslims do not consider Islam to be a "new" religion, but part of the Abrahamic tradition.

Hinduism is also often misrepresented in charts that seek to identify "founder," "book," and "creed," because it is such a diverse tradition with multiple sources, regional and temporal forms of expression and worship, and no centralized religious dogma. Reducing complex traditions to categories with one-word answers creates misunderstanding.

RELIGIOUS LEADERSHIP OVER TIME

One area often neglected in teaching about religions is the category of religious leadership. Each tradition's institutions, forms of authority, and communication to followers played essential historical roles that should not be subsumed under familiar but unsuitable categories. For example, the word "Church" refers to an institution that is unique to Christianity, and essential to understanding it, but it should not be universalized to other religions. The forms and institutions of religious leadership are unique to each tradition and played important roles in spreading and sustaining those traditions among ordinary people.

The basis of Islamic teachings is that the Prophet Muhammad received revelation and guidance from God, recorded in the Qur'an, the holy scripture of Islam and its first authoritative source. During his lifetime, Muhammad was an example of righteous behavior and a pattern to follow in carrying out the practices of the faith such as prayer, fasting, and charity, and he judged among his followers in matters of faith and practice of community life. His sayings and deeds were recorded during his lifetime by his followers, and make up a second authoritative source, the *Hadith* (recorded words and deeds). Muhammad had led the nascent community in his lifetime as a spiritual, political, and at times military leader. After his death, the legacy of the *Qur'an* and *sunnah* (his example, known through recorded *hadith*) lived on, though the revelation had ceased. This is true of both major branches of Islam, called Sunni and Shi'a. The major difference is that Shi'a Muslims believe that the legacy of Muhammad's teachings is carried most authoritatively through his family members and their descendants, who are heirs to his spiritual and worldly leadership. Conflicts between Sunni and Shi'a in Muslim history revolve around this original dispute over the legitimacy of leadership—either restricted to direct descendants of the Prophet Muhammad (the Shi'a belief), or chosen from among pious members of the Muslims of the wider community of Muhammad's companions (the Sunni belief).

Two institutions of leadership emerged after Muhammad's death: the *caliphate* (political successorship) and the *ulama'* (scholars of Islamic knowledge). These two should not be conflated or confused. The caliphate developed as a form of political leadership (and military in the sense of a commander in chief). The word caliph simply means "successor." The first four successors were companions of Muhammad who were his earliest followers, and in the case of Ali ibn Abi Talib, the fourth caliph, also a member of Muhammad's household. They did not take on his spiritual authority, though their legitimacy was based on their close connection to him and their knowledge (and in the case of Ali, being one of Muhammad's family members enabled him to carry that authority among Shi'a Muslims). After the deaths of the third and fourth caliphs amid civil strife, the Umayyad dynasty was established, viewed by many as usurpers of that legacy—especially among those who came to be called Shi'a, but also among Sunni who nevertheless acquiesced to Umayyad rule as preferable to continued conflict. Thereafter, the caliphate struggled with issues of legitimacy, and unitary rule fragmented even as Muslim society and culture continued to develop. This widened the breach that was initially a difference of opinion about leadership between Sunni and Shi'a, to a political rift. The Umayyads harshly persecuted the family of the Prophet in an effort to shore up their authority in the face of the Shi'a challenge. Basic beliefs, principles, and a shared legacy of theology, law, philosophy and science, continued to bind the two branches of Islam throughout history, even though sectarian strife has also punctuated that history, usually around struggles over political power. The Shi'a represent a significant minority at 15%-18% of Muslims, concentrated in certain regions and in the modern country of Iran.

Religious scholars—*ulama'*—were the second form of leadership crucial to authentic teaching about Islam. The role of the ulama' in Islamic history and society was crucial. Equating the ulama' to the Christian clergy is not appropriate, since the ulama' were not set apart by ordination by a religious authority, nor did they serve in a centralized, authoritative religious institution. The ulama', whose name comes from the Arabic word for "those bearing knowledge," were recognized by their peers for their broad training in a variety of disciplines. They were sometimes advisors and sometimes adversaries to the caliphs. Some served as judges in court systems. Their qualifications were broad knowledge and training in the Arabic language and religious disciplines, later including logic, and they were seekers of knowledge, transmitters of traditions and learning, teachers, and interpreters of Islamic sources. They offered guidance to rulers and ordinary people alike.

Over time, formal institutions and a system of legal thought called *shari'ah* developed. By the 9th and 10th centuries, the five major schools of Islamic law—four Sunni and one Shi`a—had become established as an intellectual and civic tradition, as well as a source of stability and diversity of opinion and practice in Muslim societies. These schools of law differed not in doctrines concerning belief, but in their application of the sources to some minor details of worship and especially in the area of action in the human social sphere. The ulama' outlasted the rise and fall of dynasties, invasions by foreign powers, and political fragmentation. Modern colonialism and nationalism have posed serious challenges to their institutions, training, and authority. Today, both formal and informal institutions of ulama' survive, and they are a part of ongoing intellectual ferment.

Whether teaching about Islam, Judaism, Buddhism or Hinduism, it is important to cover indigenous types of religious leadership and their traditions of law, or regulation of human affairs, in order to understand these intellectual traditions. Such persons were often influential in the spread and transformation of these traditions, and as mediators between political authorities and the common people.

THE VIEW FROM THE PALACE VS. THE "VIEW FROM THE EDGE"

The most common mode of teaching about civilizations has been through rulers, empires, and dynasties. Arts, scientific activity, and general prosperity are often named after dynastic periods, and "empire" is often deployed as shorthand for "civilization" in textbooks. This view of society from the palace misses the important perspective "from the edge" of society where the bulk of people lived and encountered one another in their diversity. Dynasties have been major patrons of arts and science, and their decisions are very important, but not the whole story.

Muslim society is a prime example of the limitations of the view from the palace. The spread of Islam and the development of its religious and intellectual life took place in the new and older cities. It is true that territory under Muslim rule expanded rapidly

in the first century after Muhammad. Conquest, however, was not the means by which Islam became the majority religion, nor did this change take place suddenly. Historian Richard Bulliet traced the spread of Islam in the first 400 years to the movement and migration of people into and among new and older cities of the Mediterranean and Central Asia.[6] Encounters among people of multiple religions shaped the language and the artistic, scientific, and religious traditions for which Islamic civilization is known. Among the first translators of Greek, Aramaic, Persian and other manuscripts into Arabic were Jewish and Christian secretaries and other intellectuals in the major cities. This mingling of Greek philosophical tradition with interreligious dialogue created the legacy of preserving the classical heritage and indelibly shaped Islamic thought. The view from the palace misses this most significant development.

Focusing on dynasties and empires misses the fact that the unitary state broke up within a hundred years, while Islam continued to spread in Africa, Asia, Europe, and around the Indian Ocean, and Muslim civilization continued to develop.

SHARI'AH ISLAMIC LAW

The most misunderstood aspect of Islamic thought and institutions is certainly Islamic law, or *shari'ah* in Arabic. The term shari'ah in Arabic means literally "the well-worn path to a watering place," with reference to the search for equitable and moderate ways of interpreting and understanding how to apply the Islamic sources to human needs. Shari'ah is not a legal canon, nor a single book or even a set of books. It is the diffuse result of a cumulative decision-making process by knowledgeable scholars in response to questions about how to adapt Islamic beliefs and values to real situations at different times and places.[7] The formulation of Shari'ah was not the project of a theocratic government to impose authoritarian rule. To the contrary, Shari'ah decisions often challenged ruling groups and policies.

Shari'ah developed in the spirit of transmitting knowledge after the revelation and prophethood had ended with Muhammad's death. The means for making a judgment about a potential course of action were careful weighing of the Islamic sources closest to the case by a person knowledgeable in Arabic, textual interpretation, and other religious disciplines. Shari'ah covers religious practice in detail, which is a large part of the Shari'ah, such as explaining how to carry out the five pillars of Islamic worship (testimony of faith, prayer, charitable giving, fasting, and pilgrimage). The sphere of human activity is the other arena covered in the Shari'ah. It governs interpersonal, interfamilial, inter-communal, and intra-communal affairs in the spirit of piety and mutual trust. Its scope includes personal status, regulation of family matters such as marriage contracts, divorce, and inheritance, and protection of the community from crime, as well as economic relations such as the fair conduct of trade, contracts, labor and even agreements between political entities.

Over time, the training and output of Muslim jurists became institutionalized, but so long as the sources have been available to knowledgeable, literate people, Muslim jurisprudence could and did change to meet new circumstances, and was always subject to vigorous critique. This process continues today. To demonize it as medieval, simplistic, and unchanging is to ignore important movements continuing to re-think and consider how Muslims live in the world today. Islamic law played an influential role in the history of legal systems, including the West, just as Islamic legal practices of commerce have been widely influential. Among Muslim intellectuals today, there is a great deal of ongoing deliberation to meet the challenges of modernity.

CULTURAL ACHIEVEMENTS

Not so long ago, technological and scientific achievements leading to modernity were only attributed to Europeans. When other civilizations began to be credited in textbooks and other teaching resources, individual inventions were usually mentioned in checklists of what "we" got from "them." A century of research in science and technology, however, has shown how interactions among people resulted in the spread of various inventions, and has made teaching about pathways

Teaching Resources

There are many text and online resources that provide background information and teaching materials on Islam and other world religions. Here is a small sampling.

- **WHFUA**
  http://worldhistoryforusall.sdsu.edu (See Panorama and Landscape lessons, Eras 5 and 6)

- **Our Shared Past in the Mediterranean**
  Teaching modules for world history at
  http://mediterraneansharedpast.org

- **Berkley Center for Religion, Peace and World Affairs**
  http://berkleycenter.georgetown.edu/resources#t1a has knowledge resources on the five major world religions and religious issues in the world today.

- **Rethinking the Region: New Approaches to 9-12 U.S. Curriculum on the Middle East and North Africa**
  info@teach-mena.org

- **Unity Productions Foundation**
  Documentary films and teaching resources at http://www.upf.tv/teachers/ include films on historical topics and those relevant to civic life today.

- **NEH/ALA Bridging Cultures Bookshelf**
  http://bridgingcultures.neh.gov/muslimjourneys
  The Bridging Cultures Bookshelf/Muslim Journeys is a project of the American Library Association and the National Endowment for the Humanities, which identified about 25 books and media and created a website with support materials for learning about Muslim societies and religion over time, including dozens of articles from the Oxford Islamic Studies Online on subjects such as Shari'ah, historical topics and the arts.

Mapping the Global Muslim Population

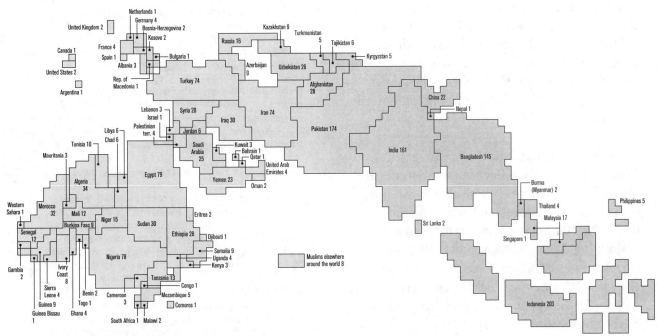

PEW RESEARCH CENTER ON RELIGION AND PUBLIC LIFE

by which knowledge traveled much more interesting and helpful in cultivating historical thinking skills than deciding which group to credit with a single invention. Instead of lists of multicultural "achievements," it is more fruitful to think of how human beings developed complex skill sets and inventions that accumulated over time to bring forth modern technologies. Teaching need not omit the stories of individual inventors and inventions, where known, but they can be shown as part of a whole. In teaching about the relationship between religion and science in human history, this approach avoids stereotypes about religion as opposed to science. In fact, religious scholars of many traditions were often the carriers of literacy in pre-modern societies. Through their work as translators and cultural intermediaries across time and place, they contributed to preserving and transmitting the written heritage in science, philosophy and other areas, which might have been lost without them. Examples of such scholars include Buddhist monks, Jewish, Christian and Hindu translators of Persian, Arabic, Greek and Sanskrit working in 8th century Abbasid Baghdad, and their counterparts in the Iberian Peninsula in the 12th century, who translated scientific, philosophical, religious, and literary works from Arabic into Latin.[8] Overuse

of the term "Islamic" for sciences and arts should not isolate these achievements of a geographically and religiously diverse Muslim civilization that was open to influences and whose members contributed to and diffused many influences. The sum total of such interactions, whether from "Islam," China, India, Africa or Europe, produced modern technologies over a long period. It would be impossible to credit every part of these, but instead our teaching should celebrate the human spirit of invention and collective learning by exploring the complex pathways by which ideas moved in time and space.[9]

GEOGRAPHIC DIVERSITY AND REACH OVER TIME
Constructive teaching about Islam and other world religions requires accurate coverage of their presence in the modern world. In the case of Islam, it is important to avoid the Middle East bias; half the world's Muslims live east of Pakistan, and only about 20% in the Middle East. Many textbooks fail to describe the geographic reach of the world religions from their origins to the modern period. The Pew Research Center for Religion and Public Life has compiled a rich set of data and interactive maps on the major contemporary religious traditions and their global reach and movement. It is important

that teaching about religion in the modern period should include a variety of maps. The typical map of modern nations and their political boundaries hides the ethnic, religious, and linguistic diversity of modern nations. Comparing the map of nations with maps showing regions where religious majorities and minorities live challenges students' categorical thinking.

The map on page 125 from the Pew Research Center on Religion and Public Life adjusts the size of each country to reflect the number of Muslims in the country. It is part of the study Mapping the Global Muslim Population at http://www.pewforum.org/2009/10/07/mapping-the-global-muslim-population/#map-distribution-of-muslim-population-by-country-and-territory, which includes an interactive map showing Muslim population by country.[10] The study can be downloaded as a pdf, along with studies on many aspects of world religions today.

A final point is that issues involving Islam and modernity are shared in common with all world religions, whose expressions, responses to modern conditions and contemporary forms of social life and governance are in flux, even as many people who consider themselves thoroughly modern are still committed to belief in and practice of their faith traditions.

NOTES

1. Charles C. Haynes and Oliver S. Thomas, *Finding Common Ground: A First Amendment Guide to Religion and Public Schools* (Nashville, TN : First Amendment Center, 2007).

2. Susan Douglass, *Teaching about Religion in National and State Social Studies Standards* (Nashville, TN: First Amendment Center; Fountain Valley, CA: Council on Islamic Education, 2000.)

3. Negative stereotypes of Islam have existed for centuries in the West. These include the beliefs that Islam is intolerant toward non-Muslims and that it is a religion that encourages violence. In the West, these stereotypes are often evident in public reactions to acts of terrorism committed by extremist groups that claim to speak in the name of Islam, even though their views and actions are rejected by the overwhelming majority of the world's Muslims. Unfortunately, the violent acts of these extremist groups receive more media publicity than statements by mainstream Muslims condemning this kind of violence, and it is not unusual to hear the claim in the West that Muslim communities and religious scholars worldwide have been reluctant to condemn extremism. In fact, there are many examples of condemnation of this kind of extremism and terrorism by mainstream Muslims and leading religious scholars throughout the Islamic world.

Islam does not have a centralized religious authority. In some cases, religious statements that are considered authoritative are issued by individual scholars who hold leading positions in important institutions of Islamic religious learning and who are acknowledged to have great influence in the Muslim world. In other cases, consensus statements are issued by conferences that have brought together large numbers of influential scholars.

There have been many such statements reaffirming the principle of religious tolerance in Muslim societies and condemning terrorism. For example, in March 2014, more than 250 Islamic scholars from throughout the world attended a Forum for Promoting Peace in Muslim Societies in Abu Dhabi. Noted Muslim scholar Abdullah bin Bayyah, as President of the Forum, issued a statement on behalf of the Forum against acts of extremism and crimes of terrorism, and affirming that "all forms of oppression and aggression against religious minorities are in direct contradiction to the values of our religion" (see https://georgetown.app.box.com/s/gtug0odush54onzyihlf1qrdwj36e8y7, p. 6). A conference held in Marrakesh, Morocco, in 2016 brought together more than 200 highly regarded Islamic scholars and intellectuals to discuss "the rights of religious minorities in predominantly Muslim societies." It issued a statement opposing "all forms of religious bigotry," which also affirmed that "it is unconscionable to employ religion for the purpose of aggressing upon the rights of religious minorities in Muslim countries." It condemned "brutal atrocities inflicted upon longstanding religious minorities" by extremist movements in several Muslim countries, and stated that "such heinous actions have absolutely no relation whatsoever to the noble religion of Islam." (See http://www.marrakeshdeclaration.org/marrakesh-declaration.html; the citation is on the first page).

Regarding terrorism, at a major conference in Amman, Jordan in 2006, 200 leading Muslim religious scholars from 50 different countries rejected "the illegitimate opinions of radical fundamentalists and terrorists" as contrary to true Islam. The scholars recognized the diversity of Islam and condemned attempts by extremist groups to declare other Muslims to be apostates. (See "the Amman message" at http://ammanmessage.com; the citation is on the first page.) In 2010, the renowned Pakistani Muslim scholar, Muhammad Tahir ul-Qadri, issued an influential fatwa (a pronouncement of religious law) condemning terrorism and suicide bombing, stating that "in the light of manifest Islamic injunctions, terrorism has absolutely no place." (See http://www.minhaj.org/english/tid/12902/Shaykh-ul-Islam-Dr-Tahir-ul-Qadri-speaks-at-Georgetown-University-in-Washington-DC.html)

One of the most common misinterpretations of Islam in the West relates to the concept of jihad, which is widely regarded by mainstream Muslims as denoting a defensive, not an aggressive war (the word "jihad," which means "striving," can also be used to refer to non-military endeavors). The statement issued by the Chair of the Forum for Promoting Peace in Muslim Societies, Abdullah bin Bayyah, on behalf of the Forum, pointed out that "jihad is not synonymous with fighting," and that "fighting and conflict for reasons other than self-defense and repelling aggression are not Islamic values" (see https://georgetown.app.box.com/s/gtug0odush54onzyihlf1qrdwj36e8y7, pp. 5, 7). In September 2014, 126 leading Muslim scholars signed an open letter addressed to the leader of ISIS, Abu Bakr al-Baghdadi, emphasizing that "it is forbidden in Islam to force people to convert" and that "jihad in Islam is defensive war." (See http://www.lettertobaghdadi.com/14/english-v14.pdf, p.1).

4. For a lesson plan, see *Our Shared Past in the Mediterranean*, Module 2, Lesson 2.3 at http://mediterraneansharedpast.org/items/show/14)

5. See, for example, The Islam Project at http://www.theislamproject.org, or Introduction to Islam, the background module of the Center for Contemporary Arab Studies at Georgetown University, at http://ccas.georgetown.edu/k14/resources.background

6. Richard W. Bulliet, *Conversion to Islam in the Medieval Period: An Essay in Quantitative History* (Cambridge, MA: Harvard University Press, 1979); Richard W. Bulliet, *Islam: The View from the Edge* (New York: Columbia University Press, 1994).

7. The Islamic scholar Asma Asfaruddin answers some common questions about Shari'ah law in "What Sharia Law Means: Five Questions Answered" at https://theconversation.com/what-sharia-law-means-five-questions-answered-79325

8. One of many accessible books on this topic is Jim Al-Khalili, *The House of Wisdom: How Arabic Science Saved Ancient Knowledge and Gave Us the Renaissance* (New York: Penguin, 2011). An interactive web page for student readings is the feature on contributions transmitted to Europe through Islamic Spain at http://islamicspain.tv/Arts-and-Science/The-Culture-of-Al-Andalus/index.html

9. See the article on this topic by Edmund Burke, III, "Islam at the Center: Technological Complexes and the Roots of Modernity," *Journal of World History*, 20, no. 2 (2009), pp. 165-186.

10. Pew Research Center, *Mapping the Global Muslim Population*, 2009 at http://www.pewforum.org/2009/10/07/mapping-the-global-muslim-population/

LESSON 1

Islamic Beliefs and Practices

MATERIALS
Student Handout

OBJECTIVES
Students will:

■ Describe the basic beliefs of Islam and list its two major authoritative sources.

■ List the Five Pillars of Islam and associate each one with its definition and basic practices.

■ Associate the Five Pillars with social and cultural practices that vary across geographic regions and over time.

PROCEDURE

1. Distribute and assign the Handout, "Basic Islamic Beliefs and Practices." (pp. 128–129) Use the study questions to review and develop understanding of the basic information on Islamic beliefs and practices.

2. After students have understood the basic practices called the Five Pillars of Islam, the next part of the lesson calls upon them to think about how such basic practices as belief in a common creed, daily prayer, annual charitable giving, and annual fasting and pilgrimage (real or aspired) affect the individual and the society, and how these practices impact the culture. Divide the class into five groups and assign each group to read, think, and report on the significance of one of the pillars.

3. Many religions in world history share similar basic elements of worship such as prayer, fasting, charity, and pilgrimage. Some adhere to a statement of creed, while others do not. Students should reflect on the individual and communal, spiritual and worldly effects and influences that these basic elements of worship have on the cultures of societies that practice them. How do these compare with your group's findings on Islam and the impact of its Five Pillars?

Basic Islamic Beliefs and Practices

The word *Islam* means "peace through submission to God." Muslim practice is defined by two authoritative sources: the *Qur'an* (Islamic holy scripture) and the *Sunnah*, or example set by Prophet Muhammad and transmitted through the *Hadith* (recorded words and deeds). Islam is a universal religion, meaning that anyone may accept its beliefs and become a Muslim, or follower of Islam. A Muslim is "one who seeks peace through submission to God." This means striving to reach a goal rather than achieving a fixed identity. "Seeking the face of God" is an expression often used to describe this lifetime goal.

These basic acts required of Muslims are called the Five Pillars. They are required of every Muslim who is of age, and of sound mind, body, and capability. Accepting Islam requires only that a person state the basic creed, "There is no god but God" and "Muhammad is the messenger of God." That is the first of the five basic acts or duties. The Five Pillars of Islam are:

1. *Shahadah*: to state belief in One God and the prophethood of Muhammad,

2. *Salah*: to pray five obligatory prayers each day,

3. *Siyam*: to fast from dawn to sunset during the month of Ramadan each year,

4. *Zakat*: to pay obligatory charity each year,

5. *Hajj*: to make the pilgrimage to Mecca once in a lifetime.

The following sections describe the pillars in detail.

Shahadah (the Islamic Creed)

The declaration of faith in Islam is a simple statement in Arabic that begins *Ashud anna* ("I witness that"), continues with the statement *La ilaha illa Allah* ("There is no god but God"), and ends with the affirmation *wa Muhammad rasul Allah* ("and Muhammad is the messenger of God"). Muslims interpret the first part as defining the role of the Muslim as a continuous striving throughout life that reaches into all aspects of personality and activity toward the self, the family and the community, and extends to the entire community of humankind and the natural environment. The second part affirms the existence of one God by negating the existence of any other creature that people might worship, or any partner with God. It underlines the Muslim's direct relationship with God as a witness and as a servant of God. No central authority nor privileged persons stand between God and the individual. The third part of the creed testifies that God sent prophets to humankind, as stated in the scriptures revealed before the Qur'an. Then, it affirms that Muhammad was a prophet, or messenger who received revelation (the Qur'an) and guidance from God. Among the earlier revelations mentioned in the Qur'an are the Torah (given to Moses), the Psalms (given to David) and the Evangelium (given to Jesus, who is recognized by Muslims as a prophet, though not as divine). This series of prophets and revelations includes—among others—Adam, Noah, Abraham, Isaac, Ishmael, Joseph, Moses, David, Solomon, Jesus, and Muhammad, according to the teachings of Islam that are universally accepted by Muslims. The Qur'an states that what was revealed to Muhammad confirmed the basic message of the earlier scriptures.

Salah (Muslims' Daily Prayer)

Salah refers to the five daily prayers that are the duty of every Muslim. Muslims perform the recitations and physical movements of salah as taught by their prophet Muhammad, according to Islamic sources. Each of the five prayers can be performed within a window of time: (1) between dawn and sunrise, (2) noon to mid-afternoon, (3) between mid-afternoon and just before sunset, (4) at sunset, and (5) after twilight until nighttime. Prayer time is determined by the sun's position, which Muslims today calculate by clock time, using charts that change with the longer and shorter days of each season. No matter what language they speak, all Muslims pray in the Arabic language. They can pray in any location, and they face Mecca during their prayers.

In the salah, Muslims recite specific words and selected verses from the Qur'an while standing, bowing, kneeling with the hands and forehead touching the ground, and sitting. Each cycle of movements is one rak'at, or unit of prayer, and each of the five prayers has between two and four units. At the end of the prayer, and throughout their lives, Muslims pray informally, asking for guidance and help in their own words.

Sawm (Fasting)

During one month each year, Muslims fast, meaning that they do not eat or drink anything between dawn and sunset. The fast begins at dawn on the first day of Ramadan, the tenth month of the Islamic lunar calendar. Fasting is a duty for adults, but many children participate voluntarily, for at least part of the day, or only a few days.

The fast begins with *sahoor* (a pre-dawn meal). While fasting, Muslims perform the dawn, noon and afternoon prayers, and go about their normal duties. At sunset, Muslims break their fast with a few dates and water, then pray, then eat *iftar* (a meal that breaks the fast). Iftar is usually eaten with family and friends, or at the *masjid* (mosque), which hosts meals donated by community members for all. After the evening prayer, many Muslims go to the masjid for congregational prayers that feature a reading of one thirtieth of the Qur'an each night. They complete the whole Qur'an by the end of the month.

Each individual experiences hunger and its discomforts, but in a few days, the body gets used to it. Muslims are supposed to fast in the spirit as well, and make extra efforts to avoid arguments, conflicts and bad words, thoughts, and deeds.

Zakat (Charity as a Duty)

Zakat is the annual giving of a percentage of a Muslim's wealth and possessions beyond basic needs. The word means "purification," meaning that a person is purified from greed by giving wealth to others. When Muslims have cash savings for a year, they give 2.5% of it as zakat. Zakat on other forms of wealth, such as land, natural resources, and livestock is calculated at different rates. Paying the zakat reminds Muslims of the duty to help those less fortunate, and that wealth is a gift entrusted to a person by God rather than a possession to be hoarded selfishly.

Muslims may make charitable donations to needy and deserving people and groups on their own, and each person is responsible for figuring out the amount owed. Of course, 2.5% is a minimum amount, and more may be given. Islamic traditional sources mention charity often, and quote many statements by the Prophet Muhammad about its importance.

Hajj (Journey to Mecca)

The basic act of worship in Islam is the pilgrimage (journey) to the city of Mecca during a certain time of year. The *hajj* rites symbolically reenact the trials and sacrifices of Prophet Abraham, his wife Hajar, and their son Ishmael over 4,000 years ago, including Abraham's willingness to sacrifice his son in response to God's command. The Qur'an teaches that it was received by Abraham in Mecca. Muslims must perform the hajj at least once in their lives, provided their health and finances permit. The hajj is performed annually by over 2,000,000 people during the twelfth month of the Islamic lunar calendar, Dhul-Hijjah. In commemoration of the trials of Abraham and his family, Muslims make a pilgrimage to the sacred city at least once in their lifetime.

Muslims from all over the world, including the United States, travel to Mecca (in today's Saudi Arabia). They remove their ordinary clothes and put on the simple dress of pilgrims—two seamless white sheets for men, and usually, white dresses and head covering for women. The pilgrims are dressed in the same simple clothes. No one can tell who is rich, famous, or powerful. White clothes are a symbol of purity, unity, and equality before God. The gathering of millions of pilgrims at Mecca is considered by Muslims to be a reminder of the gathering of all humans before God at the Judgment Day. It is a symbol of the Muslim *ummah* (the worldwide Muslim community), because pilgrims gather from all corners of the earth. It is a symbol of the past, because the pilgrims visit places where Abraham and his family are believed to have faced the challenge of their faith, and where Muhammad was born and preached. Pilgrims go around the *Ka'bah*, a stone cube structure that, according to Islamic teachings, was constructed by Abraham and Ishmael as a house dedicated to the worship of one God. Pilgrims call "*Labbayka Allahumma Labbayk*," which means "Here I am at your service, O God, here I am!" This echoes the call of Abraham in the Hebrew Bible, in answer to the call of God.

1. What is the most basic belief for Muslims?

2. What is the Islamic statement of belief called?

3. Identify and describe the prayers required of Muslims. How do Muslims prepare for prayer?

4. Who is required to pay the zakat, and who may receive it?

5. Which of the Five Pillars is linked to the lunar month of Ramadan? When, why, and how do Muslims fast?

6. What is the hajj, and how often must a Muslim perform it? What is the significance of clothing for the hajj?

7. What is the relationship of Abraham to the Fifth Pillar of Islam?

8. Extension: The Five Pillars are acts of worship required of Muslims. They do not represent the entire moral and ethical system of Islam, but they are intended to support moral behavior when practiced regularly. Discuss the relationship between such acts of worship and moral behavior by individuals and their communities. Research some of the moral and ethical principles in Islam.

LESSON 2

The Spread of Islam

MATERIALS

■ Student Handout on "The Spread of Islam."

■ Large wall map of the Eastern Hemisphere suitable for a bulletin board display

■ Multi-colored sticky note strips in six bright colors

OBJECTIVES

Students should be able to:

■ Relate the spread of Islam to historical events and processes of historical change.

■ Trace the spread of Islam chronologically and regionally.

■ Assess the importance of cultural and political factors in the spread of Islam.

STUDY QUESTIONS

1. In what important way was the conquest of territory by Muslims different from the spread of Islam?

2. How many centuries do historians think it took from the time Islam was introduced until it became the religion of the majority population in Egypt, Syria, Iraq, and Iran?

3. To which regions did Islam spread mainly as a result of trade and travel?

4. How might laws tolerating other religions have affected the spread of Islam among the population?

5. Locate the regions mentioned in the text on a map, and make labels showing the dates when (1) Islam was introduced there and (2) when it embraced a majority of the population. Compare your findings with other maps from different periods on the extent of Muslim territory.

ISLAM AS A GLOBAL RELIGION

Islam is often thought of as a religion centered on the Middle East, when in fact it is a global religion whose adherents make up about one fifth of humankind. Today, Muslims live in communities on every continent and in nearly every country. One way to understand the global presence of Islam is to know about the historical process by which Islam spread from its origins in the Arabian Peninsula during the past fourteen centuries. The most important aspect of the spread of Islam is that its initial spread from Arabia to the Mediterranean region was not rapid, despite its association with the rapid conquest of territory from about 630 CE to 750 CE. The early caliphs ruled as a minority over a very diverse religious landscape. Through social and economic interaction, migration, and urbanization, Islam spread among the people in the following centuries until Muslims became the majority in much of the Middle East and North Africa. This multi-generational process was the subject of an innovative study by Richard W. Bulliet in his book *Conversion to Islam in the Medieval Period,* which used literary sources such as biographical dictionaries, combined with demographic studies, to illuminate the conversion process in six areas of the Middle East and North Africa between the seventh and the thirteenth centuries. †

Beyond the Middle Eastern region, Islam spread to other important areas of the globe. In some of these, Muslims became a majority, and in others, Muslim communities were in the minority. These regions include Central Asia and the Indian subcontinent, as well as parts of China and Southeast Asia, where Muslims were present and significant from the early centuries of Islam even though in many areas they were not the majority, but coexisted side by side with other groups. From about 1000 CE, Islam established a presence in sub-Saharan West Africa, becoming concentrated in towns and cities around the Niger River. In East Africa, contact with Arabia was continuous before and after the rise of Islam, and spread through trade among the coastal city-states through the medieval period.

The early modern period witnessed the spread of Islam through the rise of various regional powers (Ottoman, Safavid, and Mughal), and the continuing expansion of trade. After the fifteenth century, the expansion of Islam in Southeastern Europe was facilitated by Ottoman military power, but the faith then spread gradually in areas under Ottoman rule or influence in the ensuing centuries. The period of European colonization in Asia and Africa, but also the Americas, opened a new phase in the spread of Islam alongside Christianity, from the sixteenth to the twentieth centuries, in which the main dynamic was the intensified means and pace of travel and communication by land and sea. The twentieth and twenty-first centuries continued with the acceleration of the migration of peoples from former European colonies to Europe and the Americas, and marked the growth of Muslim communities in the West. The forces of globalization and rapid transportation and communication will continue this trend, in which Muslims, like others, bring with them their culture and religion to new homes, and introduce it to others. As a result of migration and travel to and from Muslim regions of the world, Islam has become a global religion.

This lesson includes a handout for students on the spread of Islam between the seventh and early sixteenth centuries. Teachers can ask students to focus on selected periods and regions within that time range. The teaching suggestions can also be used in classes studying the spread of Islam in later periods than those in the handout.

PROCEDURE

1. Assign or read as a class the Student Handout on "The Spread of Islam." (See pp. 135–138.) Its study questions offer suggestions for comprehension and discussion activities. A key concept of the reading and research on the spread of Islam is the distinction between the historical process characterized by the rapid expansion of territory under Muslim rule and the gradual spread of Islam among the populations. Discuss previous ideas students may have about the spread of religions among populations, and about Islam in particular. Evaluate the historical evidence of rapid vs. gradual conversion processes.

---

† Richard W. Bulliet, *Conversion to Islam in the Medieval Period* (Cambridge, MA: Harvard University Press, 1979). Bulliet's book is the source for information on those areas in the accompanying student handout. This lesson and handout draw on information provided in the book about Iran (pp. 16-32), Iraq (pp. 80-91), Syria (pp. 104-113), Egypt and Tunisia (pp. 92-103), and the Iberian Peninsula (pp. 114-127).

Expansion of the Islamic World, 632–1500*

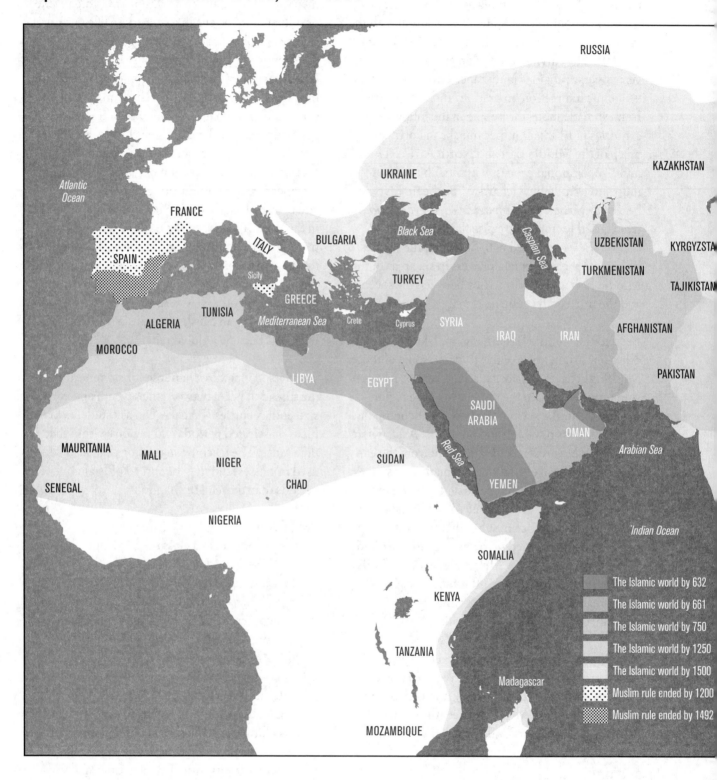

Legend:
- The Islamic world by 632
- The Islamic world by 661
- The Islamic world by 750
- The Islamic world by 1250
- The Islamic world by 1500
- Muslim rule ended by 1200
- Muslim rule ended by 1492

CHINA

NEPAL

BANGLADESH

NDIA

Bay of Bengal

South China
Sea

MALAYSIA

Sumatra

Java Sea

INDONESIA

Java

* Place names are modern not historic.
The map designates areas that were either under Islamic rule
or had significant Islamic influence.

2. Ask students to list the reasons why people might have changed from the religion they grew up with.††

▶ What are the conditions for converting from one faith to another (being exposed to different ideas, evaluating potential advantages and disadvantages of conversion, and so on)?

▶ What influences might play a role in a decision to convert (social, political, or economic)?

▶ Is it more challenging for individuals to join a faith when it appears to be a minority faith or when its members form the majority?

▶ How do poverty and persecution of members of the faith, or, conversely, the wealth and power of adherents affect an individual's choice about conversion?

▶ How might people across a wide geographic area learn about the beliefs of a faith?

▶ What role might spiritual leaders play? What other role models, such as traders, travelers, and teachers might influence people in converting?

3. Access a chronology of the spread of Islam and share it with students. (See https://georgetown.box.com/s/0j7lfz4nqi0tcdglrrvp5li6za14ljwv or http://www.religionfacts.com/islam/timeline for suitable chronologies). Preview the information the students will find in the chronology, and review the information in the student handout about the time periods it covers and the different geographical regions into which Islam spread. Reinforce for students the difference between the historical concepts of expanding Muslim-ruled territory and the spread of Islam among peoples in Africa, Asia and Europe.

†† One helpful resource on the spread of world religions is Jerry H. Bentley, *Old World Encounters: Cross-Cultural Contacts and Exchanges in Pre-Modern Times* (New York: Oxford University Press, 1993).

Select the period or periods of the chronology on which the students will focus. The student handout covers a wide time period, and teachers can select specific periods within it, or other periods mentioned earlier. World history is often taught within a global framework of eras, such as a division into Big Eras (e.g. http://worldhistoryforusall.sdsu.edu) Within that frame, teachers conventionally study the Classical Islamic Period (from the seventh to the tenth or twelfth century or so, trailing off with the Crusades, the Reconquista, and the Mongol Empire), and then invariably the period of Three Empires (Ottoman, Safavid, Mughal) from the fifteenth to the eighteenth century, followed by the period of European expansion and Imperialism, ending with World War I and World War II and the rise of independent nation states on the post-colonial pattern to today. This coverage is somewhat discontinuous, and there are also other periods in which the spread of Islam is worth examining.

▶ Discuss the major events listed in the selected historical periods. Students should pay particular attention to items on the chronology that represented advances as well as setbacks for the spread of Islam.

▶ Discuss how the events described in the chronology may have related to events taking place in other regions and societies.

▶ In middle schools in particular, teachers may find it useful to break up the chronology into parts that correspond to historical periods or geographic regions being studied in class, using the chronology in conjunction with individual units corresponding to textbook chapters or content standards. By doing so, students can focus on five or six items at a time. If the class is making a world history timeline on the wall or in a notebook, they can insert these items from the chronology into the larger timeline.

4. This is a bulletin board activity, correlating chronology to geography. Have the class review the chronology and divide them into six groups, each group taking one of six historical segments. Give each group a set of rectangular sticky-note strips, each set in a different bright color. Have students in each group identify the historical events in their section of the chronology that relate to the spread of both Islam and Muslim rule. Also identify any events that indicate the retreat of Islam or Muslim rule. Write brief summaries and dates of these events on the colored sticky-notes. At the end of the work period, have each group attach their strips to the classroom's wall map of the world at a location or locations appropriate to the event. (A physical map is preferable to a modern political map for this exercise.) The collection of strips on the map will show patterns in the sequence of the spread of Islam and Muslim rule from the seventh century to about 1500 CE. Make a map key on or next to the map using the six color sticky-notes.

5. Extension activity: Compare the map produced for the bulletin board activity with published maps on the spread of Islam. What agreement or disagreement do you find?

The Spread of Islam

A Slow Process

In the century after Muhammad's death, Muslims conquered territory "from the Atlantic to the borders of China." Many students reading this often wrongly imagine that this huge region instantly became "Islamic," meaning that most of the people living in those lands quickly became Muslims. To the contrary, the spread of Islam in these vast territories took centuries, and Muslims made up a small minority of the population for a long time. In other words, the expansion of territory under Muslim rule happened very rapidly, but the spread of Islam in those lands was a much slower process. There are several kinds of historical evidence of this gradual conversion process that we will examine in this lesson.

"Let There Be No Compulsion in Religion"

The Qur'an specifies, "Let there be no compulsion in religion" (2: 256). This verse states that no person can ever be forced to accept religion against his or her will. It tells Muslims that they cannot force people to convert to Islam. Muslims regard Muhammad as having set a precedent for this as the leader of the city of Medina, where the Muslims practiced tolerance towards those of other religions. They were signers of the Constitution of Medina and of treaties with the non-Muslim groups. According to tradition, Muhammad often discussed religious ideas with the Jews, Christians, and polytheists (believers in many gods), and he heard their questions about his teachings. The Qur'an records some of the questions that people put to Muhammad, and his replies. Muslim leaders after Muhammad were required to be tolerant, based on the authority of both the Qur'an (in this and many other verses), and the Sunnah, that is, the custom practiced by Muhammad or by early members of the Muslim community.

With some exceptions, Muslim leaders have adhered to this precedent over time. One major type of evidence for the historical tolerance by Muslim political leadership is the persistence throughout centuries of many religious minorities in the lands Muslims have ruled. Medieval Spain was one example of this historical tolerance: Christians and Jews lived and worshipped under Muslim rule and contributed to the society in many ways. The writings of well-known Jewish and Christian scholars, physicians, scientists, and artisans of that time still exist. After the expulsion of Jews and Muslims from Spain following the conquests of Ferdinand and Isabella, Jews settled in North Africa under Muslim rule, and then settled throughout the domains of the Ottoman Empire as it expanded. The Ottoman Empire also followed policies of tolerance toward Christian communities. In Lebanon, Syria, and Turkey, for example, Christian groups that pre-date the coming of Islam still exist, as do Coptic Christians in Egypt, after 1400 years of Muslim rule there.

Becoming Muslim

To accept Islam, a person only has to make the profession of faith (*shahada*) in front of two or more witnesses. Even after a person has accepted Islam, he or she may take a long time to learn and apply its practices, going through many different stages or levels of understanding and practice over time. As Islam spread among large populations, this process was multiplied.

Different individuals and social classes may have had different understandings of Islam at the same time. Also, many local variations and pre-Islamic customs remained, even after societies had majority Muslim populations for a long time. These differences have been a source of diversity among Muslim societies and regions.

Growth of Muslim Population

It is quite easy to map the large territory ruled by different Muslim political groups, or to illustrate the expansion of an empire. We can shade in areas of a map, and we can track the dates of Muslim rulers and dynasties from the time of Muhammad to the present day. It is more difficult, however, to understand why historians speak of a geographic area as a "Muslim region," "Muslim society," "Muslim civilization," or even "the Islamic world." At a minimum, such terms must mean that most of the people who lived in those places considered themselves to be Muslims—people who believed in the religion called Islam. By what point in time did the majority of people in those places accept Islam, and how rapid was its spread? What effect did the gradual or rapid spread of Islam have on language, customs, art, and politics? How did the fact that many people were converting to Islam relate to the development of Muslim culture and civilization? We know, of course, that substantial numbers of people in those regions continued to practice the faiths they had belonged to before Islam, including Jews, Christians, Zoroastrians, Buddhists, Hindus and others. The social contributions of people of these religions continued under Muslim rule. As these former majorities became minorities, how were they affected? How did the presence of a large region in which the majority of its inhabitants were Muslim affect adjoining regions where the majority accepted other faiths?

The Process of Conversion

In the decades after Muhammad's death, nearly all of the inhabitants of Arabia accepted Islam, except Christian and Jewish communities, which were allowed to continue practicing their faiths. As Muslim rule extended into regions beyond the Arabian tribal system, however, caliphs—the successors of the Prophet as leaders of the Muslim community—did not always encourage conversion to Islam among the populations of newly conquered areas.

Nevertheless, during the early caliphates (632–750) non-Arabs began to accept Islam. Conversion took place at first among the lowest classes of people. Men and women migrated to Muslim garrison cities to look for jobs and to offer their services to the ruling group. Learning about Islam in these centers, some converted and expanded the Muslim population. These migrants became associates, or *mawali*, of Arab tribes, a traditional method of integrating outsiders. Some migrant Arab and mawali converts founded families that later made important contributions in preserving and spreading Islamic knowledge. They became scholars of Islamic law, history, literature, and the sciences. In this way, Islam spread in spite of the policies of political rulers, not because of them.

During the years of the Umayyad Caliphate (Umayyad dynasty) from 661–750 CE, the overwhelming majority of non-Arab populations of the empire, which stretched from Morocco to Inner Eurasia, did not practice Islam. Toward the end of that time, the North African Berbers became the first major non-Arab group to accept the faith. Within a few centuries, Christianity disappeared almost completely in North Africa (today's Tunisia, Algeria, and Morocco), though Christian groups persisted in many other Muslim regions. Jews remained as a small minority, with many living in Muslim Spain. The spread of Islam among Iranians and other peoples of Persia was the second major movement, beginning about 720 CE. Both of these early groups of converts caused problems for the central government. In North Africa, Berbers set up an independent caliphate, breaking up the political unity of Islam. In Persia, a revolution arose that replaced the Umayyad with the Abbasid dynasty in 750.

There was a time lag between the conquest of territory by Muslim forces and the time when the majority of the population became Muslim. For example, Arab Muslim forces conquered Egypt in 642, but by 700 few Egyptians had become Muslims. By 900 CE, about fifty percent of the population was probably Muslim, and by 1200, more than 90 percent. In Syria, Islam spread even more slowly. There, the 50-percent mark was not reached until 1200, nearly six hundred years after the arrival of Islam. Iraq and Iran probably reached a Muslim majority by around 900 CE, like Egypt. In much of Spain and Portugal, Islam became established in the 500 years following the initial conquests of 711 CE, though it may never have become the majority faith. After Spanish Catholic armies completed the conquest of the Iberian Peninsula in 1492, many Muslims and Jews were either expelled from Spain or converted to Christianity.*

In Persia, Inner Eurasia, and India, Muslim law treated Zoroastrians, Buddhists, and Hindus just as it treated Jews and Christians. Muslim rulers offered adherents of these religions protection of life, property, and freedom of religious practice in exchange for the payment of a tax, as an alternative to military service. In Sind (northwestern India), the Buddhist population seems to have embraced Islam in the eighth and ninth centuries. Buddhism disappeared entirely in that region. Hinduism, however, declined there more slowly than Buddhism did.

All of the lands described above had Muslim rulers. After the decline of the unified Muslim empire—from about 750—Islam gradually spread to lands outside the boundaries of Muslim rule. After 1071, Anatolia (or Asia Minor), which makes up most of modern Turkey, came under the rule of Turkish animal-herding groups that had become Muslims. Islam spread gradually for centuries after that, and when the Ottoman Turkish empire enfolded much of southeastern Europe in the mid-fourteenth century, most Albanians and Bosnians, as well as some Bulgarians, became Muslims.

Continuing Spread

Beginning in 1192, other Muslim Turkish military groups conquered parts of India, including most of the north all the way to present-day Bangladesh, which borders the Bay of Bengal. The number of Muslims in India gradually increased from that time. The people of Bangladesh had been Buddhists, but beginning about 1300, they rapidly embraced Islam. Elsewhere in India, except for Punjab and Kashmir in the far northwest, Hinduism remained the religion of the majority.

---

* See Bulliet, *Conversion to Islam in the Medieval Period*, pp. 16-32, 80-127.

In reviewing the spread of Islam, it is essential for students to be aware of the crucial roles that were played by merchants, artisans, scholars, and lawyers who spread the religion in word and by example.

In South India and Sri Lanka, both merchants and Sufi preachers, that is, followers of mystical Islam, spread the faith. By 1300, traders and Sufis also introduced it to Southeast Asia. Over the next two centuries, Islam spread from Malaysia to the great archipelago that is today Indonesia. Entering a region where Buddhism, Hinduism, and local polytheist religions existed, Islam required several centuries to become well established.

In Inner Eurasia beginning in the eighth century, Islam gradually spread to the original homelands of the Turkic-speaking peoples until it became the main religion of nearly all of them. Islam also spread into Xinjiang, the western part of China, where it was tolerated by the Chinese empire. Islam entered southern China through seaports, such as Guanzhou, the city where the earliest mosque in China exists.

Africa

Before 1500, Islam spread widely in sub-Saharan Africa. Before 1000 CE, the first major town south of the Sahara to have a Muslim majority was Gao, a commercial center located on the Niger River in Mali. Over the centuries, many other rulers and parts of their populations followed this pattern. By 1040, groups in Senegal had become Muslims. From there, Islam spread to the region of today's Mali and Guinea. Muslims established the kingdom of Mali in the thirteenth century and the Songhai empire from 1465 to 1600. Farther east, Kanem-Bornu near Lake Chad became Muslim after 1100. In West Africa, like Turkestan, India, and Indonesia, traders and Sufis introduced Islam. When rulers accepted the faith, numerous Muslim scholars, lawyers, teachers, and artisans migrated into the region to help build Muslim administration and cultural life. African Muslim scholars became established in major towns like Timbuktu, where they taught and practiced Islamic law as judges. By 1500, Islam was established in West Africa in a wide east-west belt south of the Sahara. Local polytheistic religions remained strong, however, and Islam did not become the majority faith in this region until the nineteenth century.

In East Africa, traders spread Islam along the coast beginning at least by the tenth century. By the fourteenth century, the numerous commercial city-states along the coast from today's Somalia to Tanzania were predominantly Muslim. In the Sudan, south of Egypt, the population of Nubia gradually became Muslim during the fourteenth century, through immigration of Muslim Arab pastoral groups and because Christian rule became weak in that region.

Strong Governments and the Spread of Islam
By understanding that the expansion of Muslim rule was different from the spread of Islam, we can see an interesting trend. Ironically, Islam spread widely and rapidly among populations at times when Muslim rule was weak and not unified. When Muslim political regimes were decentralized, disunited, or completely absent, Islam as a religion often flourished and spread to non-Muslims. The influence of traders and Sufis, as well as Muslim scholars, lawyers, and artisans in the cities, aided the spread of Islam to new areas. On the other hand, the Ottoman Empire in southeastern Europe, or the Sultanate of Delhi, and the later Mughal Empire of India had little success in spreading Islam, though their rulers did gain territory. Non-Muslim populations seem to have viewed these powerful, tax-gathering Muslim rulers negatively, and so they resisted conversion to Islam. Those who did embrace Islam in such circumstances, if not for material gain, usually did so because of the efforts of merchants, teachers, and traveling Sufi preachers, who were not part of the government.

CHAPTER SIXTEEN

Navigating the Minefield of Teaching about Hinduism

MURALI BALAJI

The topic of religion in the public school curriculum has long been a touchy one, but over the past decade, it has taken center stage in curriculum battles across the country. However, teaching about religion is more important than ever as the country becomes rapidly more diverse and increasingly globally connected.

In trainings I've conducted across the country, one of the most common concerns teachers and curriculum specialists have expressed is how to introduce religion within courses of study, primarily because of their worry that classroom discussions could become theological in nature. That fear greatly underestimates the ability of educators to discuss religion from a historical and comparative lens, an approach that can significantly enrich their students' understanding of social and cultural histories. After all, understanding religion—and the development of diverse faith traditions—is a critical part of world history and geography, and is vital to a good social studies education.

THE CHALLENGE OF PEDAGOGY

One key challenge is defining good pedagogy when it comes to religion. To be sure, this is an obstacle even for experienced specialists in teaching about religion, due largely to the dilemma over what to include about particular religions and what to leave out. Additionally, even scholars of religion have differing opinions on what should be taught in schools. As a result, what a professor of religion may suggest to a curriculum specialist may not necessarily be appropriate for the grade level or even the content standards for a particular school district or state.

For example, the work I do as the director of education for the Hindu American Foundation (HAF) is premised upon the pedagogy of Hinduism.

Some of our academic advisors—religion professors at universities across the country—have urged us to embrace the "banyan tree" approach to teaching about the faith in schools. This approach, which views Hinduism as a collection of roots and branches that are intertwined and often indistinguishable from one another (like a banyan tree), enables a more comprehensive understanding of Hindu philosophy and even the diversity of practice that exists across the world. That ideal is a lot more difficult to put into practice because religion as a subject is often limited in scope within the K-12 curricula.

What are some of the key points to take into account? For starters, while excellent guidelines for teaching about religion exist,[1] exploration of content is not bound by a one size fits all approach. Religion can be explored both in a specific time period, and as a living tradition.

Secondly, there is the issue of parity. While it is unrealistic to give every major religion full parity within the curriculum and in instructional content, educators should strive to present key concepts that provide students with at least a basic understanding of each faith. In the next section, I'll discuss some of the issues educators have shared with me in incorporating cultural and religious sensibility into their pedagogy.

HINDUISM WITHIN A PUBLIC SCHOOL CONTEXT

Before we understand what makes Hinduism such a challenge to teach, it is worth actually explaining what the basics are. Hinduism is one of the oldest major faith traditions. With about 1 billion people, Hinduism is the world's third largest religion. While most of the world's Hindu population is located in the Indian subcontinent, Hinduism has spread globally over many centuries. Today, significant Hindu populations can be found in the Caribbean, southern Africa, Southeast Asia, and North America. Unlike many religions, Hinduism does not have a central set of laws or a governing institution. Some say that Hinduism today is a combination of many local traditions and beliefs, but most agree that it has evolved over thousands of years and adapted to social, cultural, and political changes in India and other parts of the world.

While highly decentralized and not dogmatic, much of Hindu practice worldwide is guided by the central concepts of *karma* (the consequences of one's actions),[2] *dharma* (righteous conduct), the paths of yoga, and liberation. More importantly, Hindu philosophy is viewed as guiding one towards liberation, and texts such as the *Bhagavad Gita* and *Ramayana* (both widely read among Hindus and non-Hindus alike) are seen as moral handbooks stressing the importance of *dharma*, or righteous conduct. While Hinduism has four major intellectual traditions and sects (Shaivism, Vaishnavism, Smartism, and Shaktism), many Hindus in practice draw from all four. The lack of dogmatism in Hinduism has also led to syncretic co-worship, as seen in the blending of Hinduism and Buddhism in countries like Nepal (and in earlier periods, Cambodia and Thailand), and with Jainism in parts of India. As in the case of any world religion, cultural norms and social context often play a critical role in how Hinduism is practiced. That is why many scholars often refer to Hinduism in the plural sense, given how many "Hinduisms" are practiced, and how they vary. The Hinduism in Indonesia, for example, is markedly different from the Hinduism in Gujarat, India, and the Hinduism practiced in Guyana is different from that in South Africa. The diversity of Hinduism is one reason why it is challenging to teach about it.

BALANCING ACCURACY, DIVERSITY AND RELIGIOUS SENSITIVITY

More than a few educators and textbook editors have told me that they struggle with weighing accuracy versus considerations of diversity and religious sensitivity. My response is: why should one be sacrificed for the other? Striving for factual accuracy and religious/cultural sensitivity in the classroom is not an either/or proposition; in fact, they go hand-in-hand when we look at best practices in pedagogy.

It isn't easy, and Mark Fowler at Tanenbaum does an excellent job of highlighting how educators can at least shape their classroom content from the eyes of a practitioner.[3] Fowler notes that adapting inclusive materials requires making sure that they are contextualized. In other words, educators and curriculum specialists should ask themselves whether a textbook provides enough context about a particular religion. More importantly, do depictions take into consideration the sensitivities of a practitioner? This is a critical point, because some historians would argue that creating instructional content that is sensitive towards practitioners would somehow dilute historical study. To me, some of the best historical textbooks are the ones that highlight the philosophies of religions but make clear distinctions between these philosophies and the social, cultural, and political practices that developed among followers of each religion.

We also need to be mindful that proactive and informed pedagogy can be a great deterrent to bullying in classrooms, particularly of students who adhere to minority traditions. As Khyati Joshi notes, educators' lack of awareness about how to teach about religious minority traditions such as Hinduism, Islam, and Sikhism, contributes to students' feelings of alienation, marginalization, and being discriminated against.[4]

To be sure, religious sensitivity involves a degree of reflexivity. How does a teacher use her/his experience with a particular religious tradition to inform classroom instruction? A summer trip to India, for example, might provide a teacher added context about Dharmic traditions such as Hinduism,

Buddhism, and Jainism, at least from an experiential perspective. However, one summer trip does not make a person an expert. Even being a practitioner of the faith does not qualify a person to make sweeping generalizations. Whenever I present in front of social studies teachers, I always make the point that I am not an expert on Hinduism. I also tell teachers that in classrooms with Hindu students (or active Hindu parents), such expertise shouldn't be presumed either. One's experience should never be used as a means of universalizing—or homogenizing—a religion's practice.

Let me go through a few examples from my training. Last year, a teacher came up to me before a session and said, "I think I know everything I need to know about Hinduism, but I'm curious to hear what you have to say." She told me she went to a Hindu temple in her community and had a lot of Indian friends. After the session, she rushed up to me and said, "I take back everything I told you before." Much of what she thought she knew about Hinduism stemmed from her belief that India (a diverse country) and Hinduism (the world's third-largest religion) were synonymous. That's one reason why, when teachers say they have a lot of Indian students in their classroom, I tell them not to assume their religious affiliation. Many Indians are not Hindus and many Hindus are not of Indian descent, making cultural and religious conflation deeply problematic.

Another issue that comes up quite often is the complex Indian social class system known commonly as caste. One of the common misconceptions in textbooks and in pedagogy is the idea that caste is somehow central to Hinduism, or that only Hindus practice caste. In fact, the *Rig Veda*, one of the oldest Hindu texts, states: *Ajyesthaso akanishthaso ete sambhrataro vahaduhu saubhagaya* (No one is superior, none inferior. All are brothers marching forward to prosperity.) Although discussions of the caste system often refer to the Untouchables, no Hindu scriptures, particularly the *Vedas*, mention untouchability. As the idea of caste became an entrenched element in social stratification across South Asia, communities of Muslims, Sikhs, Buddhists, and Christians in different parts of the Indian subcontinent all

organized around caste identities, and have even had intercaste conflicts among themselves.[5] It's important for educators to be able to nuance sensitive topics and also explain them in context, particularly if most students believe that caste and Hinduism are inextricably connected to one another. For educators in areas where there is a sizable South Asian community, subjects such as caste can draw angry responses from parents, who see it as either taboo or something that shouldn't be discussed in classrooms.

To understand the caste system, it is important to distinguish between *varnas* and *jatis*, two terms that are easily confused. *Varnas* refer to social classes that are based on talents, capabilities, and temperaments; the Brahmins are the priest and teacher class; Kshatriyas are the warrior class; Vaisyas are the merchant class; and Sudras are the laborer class. This system of social hierarchies was never intended by the Hindu scriptures to be rigid and hereditary; for example, two of Hinduism's most prominent Vedic sages, Valmiki and Vyasa, were Brahmins who were not born into Brahmin families.

Jatis refer to communities defined by occupation, and can loosely be compared to medieval European trade guilds. Over time, thousands of *jatis* developed in India, each with its own religious and social practices, and bound by numerous conventions governing their interactions and perceived hierarchies. One convention was endogamy (marriages took place within the *jati*). The rules within each *jati* were not tied to scriptures so much as they were traditions and norms that were passed down from one generation to another, and slowly became associated with birthright. If anything, the understanding of caste by Europeans emerged from observing the daily practices within *jatis*. (The word "caste" is derived from the Portuguese word "casta," which the Portuguese used to describe the Indian social stratification system when they arrived in India.) The British utilized and thus further formalized the concept of caste in India with the introduction of the census in the 19th century as a way of tracking the different groups in the colonial subcontinent. Although the connection between *varna* and *jati* had long been in existence, it had generally been more regional and loosely defined until the British refined and formalized the system. This codification led to a more intractable social hierarchy and was made to better facilitate social and political control of India and its people.

In this case, an educator has a unique opportunity to highlight the development of the caste system in India as a social practice (outside of Hindu scriptures) while explaining its disconnect with actual Hindu philosophy. This can be done as a means of underscoring how social practices diverge from religious ideals, or how social practices gain religious sanction over time as a means of entrenching power and privilege. Moreover, by de-linking the notion of caste (which actually evolved over many thousands of years and wasn't formalized in India until the British census of 1850) from Hindu theology, educators can guide their students to more critically examine how the notion of caste became hierarchical and discriminatory in India and other countries in South Asia. In this sense, a nuanced explanation of topics such as caste embodies the best means of combining accuracy, religious sensitivity, and nuance into one's pedagogy.

Lastly, religious sensitivity can help to facilitate a more empowered pedagogical approach. Given how politicized the climate in teaching about religion can be, educators can talk about how religious practice and interpretation are not applicable to all adherents. Too often, textbook depictions and curriculum standards force teachers to essentialize or universalize religious practice. But what if a teacher is more sensitive to diverse religions and strives for accuracy by teaching about a particular religion from a multi-dimensional lens? One example I got from a teacher recently was how he invited three Muslim speakers of different cultural backgrounds and sects to share their experiences as practitioners. He said that the students responded well because it allowed them to see that religion is lived through individual practice, and appreciating that diversity became critical to an accurate understanding of diverse faiths.

When we think about religious sensitivity as a facilitator for better pedagogy, it significantly reduces the need to "walk on eggshells" when teaching about religion. It also alleviates the need to try to "over teach" commonalities among faith traditions. After all, an important—and often undervalued—aspect of teaching about religion is appreciating diversity and difference among (and within) religions. This is something we as educators need to do a better job of explaining, especially since students—regardless of how diverse or homogeneous their communities—will inevitably interact with someone of a different religious tradition. What they learn in school is critical in shaping their perception of those who do not share their cultural or religious tradition.

In this sense, world religion survey courses are important to understanding the global religious and cultural landscape, but the idea of world religions in one's backyard is just as important to consider in curriculum development. The less we exoticize or Otherize diverse religions and the more we equitably integrate them into our pedagogical approaches, the more we can provide academically and experientially enriching learning environments for our students. After all, as I used to tell my students, "We must know the world we live in." The politics of teaching about religion in the classroom and in the curriculum cannot be an excuse to insulate our students from the diversity of the world they will encounter.

Here are some important takeaways to consider when seeking to improve accuracy, embrace religious sensitivity, and highlight diversity:

- The experience of one is not the experience of all.

- Bringing marginalized/misunderstood religions into a curriculum is parity, not promotion.

- Classroom speakers representing religious organizations or a local community should be encouraged to speak from their perspective, not a universal one.

- Find primary sources that can help explain religious scriptures in better detail.

- It's not the best practice to put your students of diverse faiths on the spot to explain or defend their religion.

- Practitioner-scholars at local colleges and universities can provided an added value in understanding a religious tradition from both the academic and lay experiential perspective.

- Get a sense of the diversity within your own community. Visit houses of worship and appreciate the differences in their approach. That will empower your pedagogy.

LESSON PLAN: TEACHING ABOUT INDIA'S CASTE SYSTEM

The following lesson plan was developed by the Hindu American Foundation to help teachers explain the differences between Hinduism and Indian social practice while providing context for the discussion. This lesson plan—reviewed by academics, teachers, and community members—reflects an attempt to converge religious sensitivity, accuracy and proactive pedagogy. It helps teachers better understand the caste system by using the novel *Divergent* by Veronica Roth. In the book, Roth describes a society divided by five factions fighting over a post-apocalyptic Chicago. The lesson plan can help explain how a society idealizes roles based on talents (varnas), but how those ideals become complicated by social norms and divisions based on one's occupation (jatis).

It is easy to get varnas and jatis confused, but the idea is that societies develop often in contradiction to their highest ideals. This can help explain the development of the caste system, particularly the fusing of varnas and jatis, over many centuries.

FIVE-STEP LESSON PLAN TEMPLATE

VISION SETTING

TOPIC: THE CASTE SYSTEM

KEY POINTS: What highlights do you want to point out?
- Caste is a complicated concept that comes up often in the context of Hinduism and India
- To understand the system and its evolution, we must understand the terms *varna* and *jati*
- Social hierarchies are not sanctioned by the Vedas (the most ancient scripture in Hinduism)
- The system was never intended to become rigid and birth-based

KEY VOCABULARY

Varna: a social class described in the Vedas based on one's talents

Jati: a social group associated with an occupation

Brahmin: the priest and teacher class

Kshatriya: the warrior class

Vaisya: the merchant class

Sudra: the laborer class

Caste: the formal term for social categories and hierarchy in the Indian subcontinent. Derived from the Portuguese term *casta*.

Untouchables: also known as Dalits or Harijans; a group that has occupied the lowest rungs of the social ladder in the Indian subcontinent

Continued on next page

DETERMINING METHODS

1. OPENING
A hook that will engage the students.

MATERIALS: The novel *Divergent*, by Veronica Roth

Tell the students that today, you'll be describing ways that societies can be set up. Pull out a copy of the novel *Divergent* by Veronica Roth, and ask how many of the students are familiar with it. If comfortable, ask one of the students to summarize how the society in the novel is set up. Alternatively, read the following description.

In this dystopian novel, set in futuristic Chicago, society is based on factions. Most members of the society are divided into the factions Abnegation, Erudite, Dauntless, Amity, and Candor. The book describes each faction:

"I choose to turn away from my reflection, to rely not on myself but on my brothers and sisters, to project always outward until I disappear."	**Abnegation** *(the faction that values the needs of others above the needs of oneself.)* Their propensity for selflessness made them the most incorruptible, hence suiting them to rule.
"Knowledge is the only logical solution to the problem of conflict. Therefore, we propose that in order to eliminate conflict, we must eliminate the disconnect among those with differences by correcting the lack of understanding that arises from ignorance with knowledge."	**Erudite** *(the faction that puts the quest for knowledge above all else)*. Their passion for knowledge has made them great researchers and scientists.
"We believe in ordinary acts of bravery, in the courage that drives one person to stand up for another.... We believe in shouting for those who can only whisper, in defending those who cannot defend themselves."	**Dauntless** *(the faction that values courage)*. Their quest to be fearless has equipped them to be security for the society.
"Give freely, trusting that you will be given what you need.... Do not be angry. The opinions of others cannot damage you.... The wrong is past. You must let it rest where it lies.... You must no longer think cruel thoughts. Cruel thoughts lead to cruel words, and hurt you as much as they hurt their target."	**Amity** *(the faction that values peace and harmony above all else)*. Their love of peace has led them to be excellent care takers.
"Truth makes us transparent. Truth makes us strong. Truth makes us inextricable."	**Candor** *(the faction for those who value truth)*. The honesty in Candor leads them to be leaders of law.

At the age of 16, a personality test is administered to help each member of the community pick the faction in which they would like to lead the rest of their life. Those who do not make it past the initiating tests of their chosen faction become the factionless, and do menial labor for the rest of their lives, while the other factions provide them with food and other necessities.

Pose the following questions to the students: is this a valid way to set up a society? What are its benefits? What are its drawbacks?

Continued on next page

2. INTRODUCTION TO NEW MATERIAL

MATERIALS: The Hindu American Foundation Caste System PowerPoint.*

Tell the students you will now be focusing on a real society, and how it was set up, and how it changed over time.

3. GUIDED PRACTICE: DISCUSSION QUESTIONS

After reviewing varnas, pose the following question: What do you think are the merits and drawbacks of setting up a society in this fashion?

After reviewing jatis, pose the following question: What do you think are the merits and drawbacks of society being based on this system?

After the section on the evolution of caste: Ask any of the students if they see any parallels between the change of the caste system over time, and the change in the faction system. The harmony of the faction system ended as the Erudite reached for more power than was inherent in the checks and balances system of the factions.

4. INDEPENDENT PRACTICE

Define the following terms: *Varna*

Jati

Caste

Draw a diagram illustrating the connections between Brahmins, Kshatriyas, Vaisyas, and Sudras. Label each component with its function.

Write a paragraph explaining how the varna and jati system evolved over time and became conflated.

Choose a graphic organizer of your choice, and illustrate the differences and similarities between the social systems in Ancient India and the novel *Divergent* as they were initially conceived.

5. CLOSING

In closing, point out the parallels between the societal system in *Divergent* and the varna system, and how both systems changed over time to stop representing the ideal with which they were created.

* This refers to HAF's Hinduism 101 resource presentation on caste, which can be found at https://www.hafsite.org/resources/hinduism101/big-questions/social-issues

Questions to Consider

▶ **With an increasingly diverse student population, educators must become aware of the diversity within faith communities. How would you deal with the concerns of community members who say their particular view of their faith is not being represented in content?**

Suggestion: Sit down with them and ask what their views are. Be sure to mention that teaching about religions requires surveying the religious landscape and does not involve in-depth theological presentations. Be open to hearing them out, but make sure you are able to explain why highlighting the diversity within faith traditions can be complex in a middle or high school setting.

▶ **Some of the toughest cases of religious sensitivity and accuracy come after a textbook adoption, when the new content is completely different from the old. Sometimes, this is for the better. Other times, it's not. How do you deal with discrepancies in the way a particular religion is covered?**

Suggestion: Resolve these discrepancies by researching information from an authoritative educational source on that religion. This chapter and book list some excellent resources that can provide concise and accurate information about religious traditions.

▶ **While religion and culture do overlap, cultural norms cannot be conflated with religious philosophy. How would you deal with practitioners of the same faith who come from different cultural backgrounds, and whose culture influences their religious understanding?**

Suggestion: Try to make the distinction between culture and religion by noting that there are different perspectives within the same faith. The same faith can be practiced differently in different countries that have different cultures.

RECOMMENDED READING AND WEB SITES
GENERAL

A Teacher's Guide to Teaching About Religion in the Schools. This overview of do's and don'ts for teachers provides a framework for how to approach teaching about religion.
http://www.religiousfreedomcenter.org/wp-content/uploads/2014/08/teachersguide.pdf

HAF Hinduism 101 Materials. The Hindu American Foundation's Hinduism 101 provides teachers with updated multimedia resources to teach about Hinduism, as well as a list of recommended readings for students of all age groups.
http://www.hafsite.org/Hinduism-101-Materials-for-Educators

Religions in my Neighborhood. Tanenbaum's handbook provides teachers with tools on how to teach about diverse religious groups in a sensitive and culturally competent manner.
https://tanenbaum.org/programs/education/curricula_for_educators/religions-in-my-neighborhood/

ELEMENTARY SCHOOL
FILMS/MULTIMEDIA

"Sanjay's Super Team." Disney-Pixar, 2015. Academy Award nominated short film about a boy's relationship with Hindu deities in the form of superheroes

BOOKS

Finders Keepers? A True Story, Vol. 1 by Robert Arnett. Columbus, GA: Atman Press, 2003. Illustrated children's book on the real-life implications of dharma. Appropriate for grades 1-5.

The Diwali Gift by Shweta Chopra and Shuchi Mehta. Belmont, CA: 3 Curious Monkeys, 2015. Book highlighting the personal meaning of Diwali for those who celebrate the holiday. Appropriate for grades 1-5.

It's Time for Holi by Amita Roy Shah. Indianapolis: Dog Ear Press, 2011. Book that explains the meaning of the Hindu festival of colors. Appropriate for grades 1-5.

Padmini is Powerful by Amy Maranville. Cambridge, MA: Bharat Babies, 2016. A book that introduces young readers to Hindu gods such as Ganesha, Lakshmi, and Parvati through the eyes of a young girl. Appropriate for grades 1-5.

MIDDLE SCHOOL
FILMS/MULTIMEDIA

"Learn about Hinduism and Karma/Have a Little Faith." This segment, featured on Rainn Wilson's Soul Pancake channel, gives students an introduction to Hinduism through a practitioner lens.
https://www.youtube.com/watch?v=v-NzVlwyZso

"What is Yoga?" Hindu Students Association. This animated video highlights the four paths towards liberation.
https://www.youtube.com/watch?v=gNcx8H7pcMg

BOOKS

Katha Sagar: An Ocean of Hindu Wisdom for Every Age by Sarah Conover. Boston, MA: Skinner House Books, 2016. This book shares the moral lessons from Hindu stories in a way suitable for public schools.

Ramayana: Divine Loophole by Sanjay Patel. San Francisco, CA: Chronicle Books, 2010. This book, drawn by the Academy Award-nominated animator, is an engaging look at the Hindu epic.

HIGH SCHOOL
FILMS/MULTIMEDIA

"Hinduism at the University of Southern California." A short video that gives students a sense of how Hinduism is practiced by Indian graduate students at USC.
https://www.youtube.com/watch?v=rDigZyrnLOw

"Hinduism 101: Practitioner Perspectives Featuring Dr. DC Rao." A short video led by a Vedanta scholar who explains the basic paths of Hinduism.
https://www.youtube.com/watch?v=pJklC_qWT64

"Introduction to Hinduism" (Oprah's Belief Series). Narrated by USC's dean of religious life Varun Soni, this short introduction to Hinduism is a good fit for high school classes with limited time to teach about the religion.
http://www.oprah.com/belief/Introduction-to-Hinduism

BOOKS

The Life of Pi by Yann Martel. Edinburgh, U.K: Canongate Books, 2002. A fiction piece that highlights a young Hindu boy's spiritual journey under adverse circumstances. The book inspired the 2012 movie.

American Veda by Phil Goldberg. New York: Harmony Books, 2010. An engaging book on the spread of Hinduism and Hindu philosophy in the West.

NOTES

1. See the First Amendment Center's *Teachers Guide to Religion in the Public Schools*, which is Appendix A in this book and is accessible at http://www.religiousfreedomcenter.org/wp-content/uploads/2014/08/teachersguide.pdf

2. The karma of an individual's actions, positive or negative, may be experienced immediately, later in their present life, or possibly in a future life or lives. It is important to remember that an individual's karma is based on their thoughts, words, and actions and the choices they make.

3. See my article "Tanenbaum's Seven Principles Can Be a Guiding Force for Pluralism" at http://www.huffingtonpost.com/murali-balaji/tanenbaums-seven-principl_b_5549207.html

4. Khyati Joshi, "Because I Had a Turban," *Teaching Tolerance*, 32 (Fall 2007), 46-49.

5. See Sumit Guha, *Beyond Caste* (Boston: Brill Academic Publishers, 2013).

CHAPTER SEVENTEEN

Teaching about Sikhism

PRITPAL KAUR AHLUWALIA AND JOHN CAMARDELLA

Sikhism is one of the world's major religions. There are approximately 27 million Sikhs worldwide, 76% of whom live in Punjab, a region of northern India that is divided between India and Pakistan. Eighty-three percent of all Sikhs live in India itself. Some of the largest Sikh populations outside the Indian subcontinent reside in the United Kingdom and Canada, where there are an estimated 500,000 Sikhs in each country. The World Religion Database at Boston University estimates there are about 280,000 Sikhs in the United States. Large Sikh populations can also be found in Malaysia and East Africa, and Sikh communities are growing in Australia, Thailand, and Italy.

Religion and religious identity are not monolithic, and the American Academy of Religion states that all religions are, "internally diverse, culturally embedded, and change over time."[1] For this lesson, we have adopted the 3B framework described in Chapter 1 of this book to help students learn how religious identity is formed and understood. Each of the three components—belief, behavior, and belonging—informs the other two in varying degrees across communities of the same religion. Students should understand that individuals and communities value these religious components differently.

To teach Sikhism through the 3B framework, we recommend a lesson that focuses on the introductory section below, followed by a set of comprehension questions and possible answers on which students can be assessed. The lesson is aimed at high school students between the 10th and 12th grades, but can be adapted for earlier grades.

INTRODUCTION TO SIKHISM[2]
WHAT IS SIKHISM?

Sikhism is a word used to refer to the religious tradition of the Sikhs, an estimated 27 million people worldwide. Sikhs however identify more with the concept of *dharam* (*dharam* means the righteous path of living and is associated with the classical Sanskrit noun *dharma* from the ancient, classical language of India). The word holds multiple meanings in various Indic traditions, but for Sikhs it refers to a sense of duty or living in the right way. The Sikh religious tradition is therefore often described as the "Sikh *dharam*." (The glossary on page 152 includes this and other definitions.)

The word "Sikh" means learner and "Guru" means teacher. The word Sikh originates from *shishya* in Sanskrit, meaning "disciple." In modern Punjabi (the language most associated with Sikhs, whose tradition emerged in northern India), *sikhna* means "to learn" and *sikhya* means "teaching" or "something which is learnt." Sikhs therefore also refer to their tradition as "Sikhi" or the "path of learning."

The word Guru holds great significance for Sikhs. Sikhs are guided in their learning by the Guru's wisdom or understanding, and aspire to live by the Guru's teachings. A popular understanding of the word Guru is one through whom spiritual darkness (*gu*) is dispelled by spiritual light (*ru*), an enlightener.

For Sikhs, the word "Guru" refers to Guru Nanak, the founder of the Sikh dharam and his nine human successors. The word "Guru" is also the title given to the Guru Granth Sahib, the volume of sacred scripture that is respected as the eternal guiding voice and living spirit of the Gurus, and which is literally revered as the body and physical presence of the human Gurus themselves. Sikhs believe that through its teachings, the Guru Granth Sahib has the ability to transform and enlighten them.

Thirdly there is also the notion of "Guru Panth"– the Guru dwelling in the body of disciples dedicated to the Guru's path. This means that because the spirit of the Guru is also present within the community of practicing Sikhs, collectively they can come to decisions concerning matters affecting their community with guidance and authority. Another use of the word Guru is when it occurs in scripture. In this sense it is often interpreted to mean the Eternal, Formless Guru, understood as God.

THE GENESIS OF THE SIKH DHARAM IN PUNJAB

The Punjab lies in the north-west of India, divided between present-day India and Pakistan. The Sikh dharam has had a close relationship with the land and culture of Punjab, since it was the birthplace of Guru Nanak, its founding Guru, and was the base for some of the subsequent Gurus.

Punjab has been a home to Vedic culture and modern day Hinduism since 2000 BCE. As Punjab was a "gateway" over land from the west into India, it also gave rise to many invasions and Muslim settlers. The earliest Muslim settlers were Arabs, who came in the 7th century CE. In 1526, Babur, a Muslim descendant of the Mongol Genghis Khan, invaded India and founded the Mughal empire. The rise and fall of the Mughal dynasty ran almost in parallel with the duration of the ten Sikh Guruships. Islamic thought, culture, and governance came to pervade daily life as the Hindu majority was ruled by Muslims, and a number of Hindus converted to Islam. The Mughal Emperor Akbar who reigned from 1556-1605, showed an openness to India's broad religious traditions, and it was under his rule that the Sikh community took shape under the early Sikh Gurus. However, Akbar's successors, Emperors Jehangir (1605-1627) and Aurangzeb (1658-1707), introduced an era of great oppression against Sikhs.

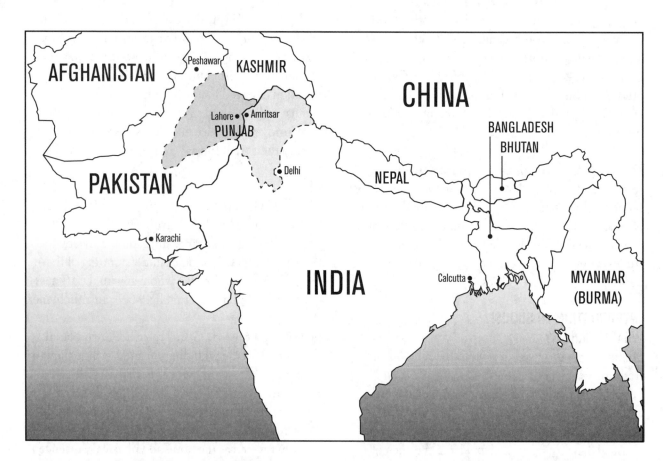

The Punjab, divided between India and Pakistan.

GURU NANAK

Guru Nanak was born in 1469 in present-day Pakistan, into a Hindu family in the town of Nankana Sahib. He worked in Sultanpur in his late twenties, and tradition recounts how, when he was bathing in the river Bein, he disappeared for three days, was mystically transported to God's presence, and there sipped the nectar of Naam–God's Name. Through this he received a revelation of the Truth and became conscious of a mission to awaken others. When he emerged from the river, he described God in the following words, which became the central message for Sikh belief and teachings and the opening verse of the Guru Granth Sahib:

God is One — all is His creation,

Eternal Truth by Name,

the Supreme Creator,

free from fear, free from vengeance,

image of the Timeless Being,

beyond the cycle of births and deaths,

realized through the Guru's divine grace.

Thus meditate on Him (God).

God was True before the dawn of time,

true throughout the ages.

True now,

and says Nanak, forever True.

Guru Nanak's message was a call against "falsehood" and the "famine of truth." His verses reflected the political and social circumstances of the Punjab during his time. They spoke out against the lack of compassion he witnessed during the brutal invasion of Emperor Babur (who reigned from 1526-1530); they spoke out against women being treated as inferior to men and urged that women be cherished as divine equals; they spoke out against the elite priestly classes and the caste system, stating that God could be reached by anyone; and they spoke out against empty rituals which promised to bring people closer to God.

Guru Nanak also proclaimed that "there is no Hindu; there is no Muslim," suggesting that he was living in a time of insincerity and hypocrisy when people were not being "true" to their faith. Without inner substance, outward identity or labels were meaningless. Sikhs believe that in God's eyes, it is not one's label, but what one has made of life, spiritually and morally, that counts.

Guru Nanak set off on four long journeys to encourage people to walk the path of Truth. In a period of over twenty-four years, he went Eastwards, visiting cities sacred to the Hindus such as Hardwar, Ayodhya, Benares, and Bihar. He then went Southwards to Sri Lanka, returning via Gujarat and Rajasthan, and later journeyed Northwards into the Himalayas as far as Tibet. He then went Westwards towards the Middle East, to Mecca and Medina, the sacred cities of Islam, returning through Iran, Iraq, Uzbekistan, and Afghanistan.

There are many historical accounts associated with these journeys, which Guru Nanak made with his childhood friends, a Muslim musician named Bhai Mardana and a Hindu named Bhai Bala. With each interaction there was a call for integrity and truth, by teaching through practical example, with humility and a love for humanity.

After his years of traveling, Guru Nanak returned to settle in the Punjab with his family in Kartarpur (literally meaning the town of God, the Creator). Guru Nanak discarded the robes of a wandering holy man and put on those of an everyday householder, establishing that spirituality should be cultivated in everyday life. Kartarpur became a *dharamsaal*–a place from where to learn and practice *dharam*, or righteous living. Guru Nanak's threefold motto was *Naam japo, kirat karo, wand ke chakko*–remember God through prayer and repeat God's Name (Naam), work honestly, and share with others. These were the building blocks for Sikh life and the beginnings of a Sikh community.

Guru Nanak's life teachings had attracted both Hindu and Muslim followers. It is a Sikh belief that, when Guru Nanak departed from the world in 1539, Hindus and Muslims wanted to conduct a funeral according to their respective customs. In the end they found only flowers under the shroud covering the body and divided the shroud in two. The Hindus cremated their half of the shroud, and the Muslims buried the other half. Both memorial sites are in close proximity to one another in Kartarpur, a short distance from what has become the border that divides India from Pakistan.

The attitude of Sikhs towards others stems from the teaching of Ik Oankar (the message that there is only One God the Creator). Sikhs believe that every human being, regardless of which path they follow, must be treated equally because God is present within them. Many paths have been created by God to reach Him and they must all be respected as equally valid. Sikhs do not actively proselytize but remember the sentiment behind Guru Nanak's teachings to Hindus and Muslims: if you are a Hindu be a good Hindu; if you are a Muslim be a good Muslim. If people practice their religion truthfully and with integrity, the outward label is not significant.

The philosophy behind the attitudes of Sikhs to other faiths is further illustrated in teachings from subsequent Gurus. The foundation stone of the Harmandir Sahib (the Golden Temple) in Amritsar, was laid by a Muslim Saint at the invitation of the fifth Guru (Guru Arjan). It was also designed with four entrances, indicating that Sikhs welcome people from all walks of life. The tradition of Langar—free vegetarian food distributed from all Gurudwaras (Sikh places of worship)—is one of serving all people without discrimination. A verse by Guru Gobind Singh teaches the need for Sikhs to "recognize the entire human race as one large family." As such, Sikhs find that they have a strong foundation for understanding and respecting other traditions.

Glossary of Sikh Terms

Amrit: holy water (lit. nectar of immortality).

Bhai: Used as a term of respect (lit. brother).

Chaur sahib: A fan waved over the Guru Granth Sahib to signify eminence and respect.

Dastaar: turban.

Dharam: righteous path of living.

Dharamsaal: place of worship.

Gurmukhi: the name of the script in which the Guru Granth Sahib is written (literally, from the mouth of the Guru).

Guru: an enlightened teacher. The term can refer to the ten human Gurus, the Guru Granth Sahib (the eternal sacred scripture), or, in a scriptural usage, the True Guru, sometimes interpreted to be God.

Guru Granth Sahib: the sacred scripture of the Sikhs revered as the living, eternal Guru.

Gurudwara: Sikh place of worship, the home of the Guru Granth Sahib.

Harmandir Sahib: popularly known as the Golden Temple, the first Sikh Gurudwara built by three of the Gurus themselves in Amritsar, Punjab, India.

Ji: a term of respect added at the end of a name.

Kakaar: One of the five articles of faith for the Khalsa, beginning with the letter K.

Kanga: a small wooden comb.

Kara: a steel bracelet.

Kashera: undergarment (shorts).

Kes: uncut hair.

Kirpan: small sword.

Khalsa: refers to the community of initiated Sikhs (pl.) or a member of this community (sing.)

Mughal Empire: the Muslim dynasty from Central Asia that ruled the Indian subcontinent during the times of the Gurus.

Naam: God's Name.

Panth: the collective community of Sikhs.

Punjab: An area in Northern India that has been partitioned since 1947 between India and Pakistan.

Punjabi: the language spoken in Punjab.

Sikh: a learner.

Vaisakhi: a spring festival commemorated in remembrance of the creation of the Khalsa.

Sikh Historical Timeline

1469	Guru Nanak is born.
1539	Guru Angad becomes the second Guru.
1552	Guru Amar Das becomes the third Guru.
1574	Guru Ram Das becomes the fourth Guru.
1581	Guru Arjan Dev becomes the fifth Guru.
1604	First installation of the scripture in Harmandir Sahib (Golden Temple), Amritsar, Punjab.
1606	Guru Arjan gives his life under Mughal oppression. Guru Hargobind becomes the sixth Guru.
1644	Guru Har Rai becomes the seventh Guru.
1661	Guru Har Krishan becomes the eighth Guru.
1664	Guru Tegh Bahadur becomes the ninth Guru.
1675	Guru Tegh Bahadur gives his life under Mughal oppression. Gobind Rai (later Gobind Singh) becomes the tenth Guru.
1699	Guru Gobind Singh creates the Khalsa.
1708	The line of human Gurus ends with the passing of Guru Gobind Singh. The sacred scripture, Guru Granth Sahib, becomes the perpetual and eternal Guru.
1708-1716	Leadership of Banda Singh Bahadur, who established Sikh rule in the Punjab.
1746-1767	Oppression of Sikhs by Mughal and Afghan rulers; Sikhs form an armed resistance.
1783	Sikh army under Baghel Singh enters Delhi, and then withdraws under an agreement with the Mughal Emperor.
1799-1839	Reign of Maharaja Ranjit Singh, who establishes the Sikh Empire based in Punjab.
1845-6	First Anglo-Sikh war.
1848-9	Second Anglo-Sikh war.
1849	British annexation of Punjab.
1907	First Gurudwara in Canada.
1912	First Gurudwara in USA.

TEN GURUS

The ten Sikh Guruships spanned from 1469-1708. One way that Sikhs picture the Guruships is as light. The Gurus embodied God's Divine light or message, which was passed from Guru to Guru. Sikhs believe that God's light is also latent within all human beings and the Guru teaches Sikhs how to kindle this light and connect with God.

After Guru Nanak, each successive Guru was a former disciple selected on the basis of merit. Each Guru indicated their successor themselves before they passed on. In the later Guruships, the lineage progressed in a family, but the model of selection based on merit prevailed. Some became Gurus at an early age, some later, serving as a reminder to Sikhs that true wisdom is not bound by age. The Gurus were based in different towns and regions within and beyond the Punjab, living family lives among people rather than in isolation. The Gurus, their sons, and their families provided male role models for the community, but the Gurus also advocated for equality between men and women. Their wives, mothers, daughters, and sisters played crucial roles throughout the Guruships. When Guru Amar Das (the third Guru) appointed and trained 146 devotees to travel to various parts of India to share Sikh teachings and unify the Sikh community, 52 of them were women. Women continue to lead and take an active role in Sikh congregations worldwide today.

GURU GRANTH SAHIB

During their own lifetimes, the Gurus compiled their compositions together with those of revered Saints from Hindu and Muslim traditions into a unique interfaith scripture. A special phonetic script was also devised by the second Guru, called *Gurmukhi* (literally meaning from the mouth of the Guru) which was very close to the alphabet of Punjabi—the commonly spoken language in Northern India.

The Gurus encouraged literacy, and the phonetic script meant that the scripture could be read and accessed by the masses, regardless of what language the particular composition was written in. The compositions were also meticulously organized according to musical genre or *raag*, each being expressive of a certain mood or state of mind. The singing of these verses (*Kirtan*) forms an essential part of Sikh worship. A special numbering system also ensured that no additions or changes could be made to the "authenticated" text. The *Guru Granth Sahib* is 1430 pages (referred to as Ang or limbs of the Guru). Each corresponding page of every copy is identical.

In 1604, Guru Arjan ceremoniously enthroned the first compilation of the sacred scripture in the Harmandir Sahib (Golden Temple) in Amritsar, Punjab, India. It was placed under a canopy and "robed" in beautiful fabrics, while an attendant waved a *chaur sahib* (often translated as a fan or fly whisk) over it, as was done for emperors and empresses to signify their royalty and eminence. Traditional accounts describe how Guru Arjan bowed in front of the sacred scripture in reverence. The Guru also slept on the floor from that day forth as a sign of humility and as an indication that the scripture was being accorded the status of a Guru, even during the times of the human Gurus.

CREATION OF THE KHALSA

During the time of Guru Tegh Bahadur (the ninth Guru), widespread religious oppression under the Mughal Emperor Aurangzeb escalated. A group of Hindu Pandits from Kashmir approached the Guru for help. Learning of their plight, the Guru stood up to the Mughal authorities and made the supreme sacrifice. He willingly offered his life to spare the Hindu Pandits, even though he was the leader of a different religion. He resisted conversion and was subsequently beheaded in 1675 in Delhi, where the Gurudwara Sis Ganj Sahib now stands. Sikhs recall the Guru's sacrifice as a lesson to uphold the freedom and dignity of all people to practice their respective faiths without fear of persecution.

The public execution of a respected and loved figure created shock and fear in the population. When the Guru's son, the young Gobind Rai (who became Guru Gobind Singh, the tenth Guru) came to learn of this, he decided he would create a community of Sikhs who were fearless and courageous in the face of adversity. The Sikh way of life started by Guru

Nanak had been nurtured for 230 years by nine successive human Gurus. In 1699, it was given its final form by Guru Gobind Singh who created the Khalsa on Vaisakhi day (a spring festival).

The Khalsa is the community of initiated Sikhs. The initiation ceremony involves instilling God's Name (Naam) within devotees through holy water (Amrit – literally meaning the "nectar of immortality"). Initiation continues today and is administered by five initiated practicing Sikhs in the presence of the Guru Granth Sahib.

The creation of the Khalsa in 1699 on Vaisakhi is important to Sikhs because it was then that Sikhs were given their distinct outward identity. They were also blessed with the names of Singh (meaning Lion, for men) and Kaur (meaning Princess, for women) signifying that they were all equals in a casteless fraternity. Guru Gobind Singh uplifted the politically downtrodden. He created an army of Saint-Soldiers who would not be afraid to stand up against oppression. Even though Sikhs do not live in the same political climate today, they still honor the notion that they have a responsibility to stand up against injustice.

The Khalsa were blessed with five gifts from the Guru to keep constantly on their person. These are called the five Kakaars and Dastaar. The following section explains these articles of faith, which are cherished by initiated Sikhs.[3] Some of these are also maintained by non-initiated Sikhs.

KES

Associated values: wisdom, saintliness, sovereignty, and endurance

Kes is uncut hair. This practice is also observed by many Sikhs who have not been formally initiated. Throughout history and across cultures, hair has been associated with wisdom and spirituality. For Sikhs the uncut hair affirms an acceptance of God's will as Creator, and the cherishing of a God-given gift. In Sikh history, during times of intense religious persecution, the kes became a powerful marker of Sikh identity, commitment, loyalty and endurance.

Suggested answers are in italics.

1. Look at the translation of the opening verse of the Guru Granth Sahib. What is the key Sikh belief about God as described by Guru Nanak? *The notion of One God, the Creator.*

2. How do Sikhs understand the word "Guru"? *Teacher, guide, enlightener (from spiritual darkness to spiritual light).*

3. Why do Sikhs describe their sacred scripture as the Guru Granth Sahib? *They consider the scripture to be a living, eternal Guru, not just a scripture.*

4. Belonging to the Khalsa inspires certain behaviors. Choose one of the five *kakaars* or the *dastaar* and explain how you think it inspires action in the individual wearing it. Suggested answers are presented on pages 154–156.

5. How does the Khalsa identity instill a sense of belonging? *It instills a sense of outward identity and casteless fraternity.*

KANGA

Associated values: clarity, order, introspection, and detachment

The kanga is a small wooden comb which is used twice daily to comb and keep the hair tidy. The process of detangling the hair is seen as encouraging people to remove tangles from their lives, promoting clarity, introspection, order and detachment.

KIRPAN

Associated values: blessings, benevolence, dignity, and courage

The kirpan is associated with the words kirpa (blessings and benevolence) and aan (honor and dignity). The kirpan is a curved blade, kept in a sheath which is secured in a gatra (cloth sash). Crossing over one's heart, this sash holds the kirpan in place. The gatra regulates the wearing of the kirpan, securing it in qualities such as mercy and compassion. The kirpan upholds noble values and is a constant reminder of one's duty to defend the weak and oppressed. The kirpan is categorically

not to be used for aggression, and the right to carry the kirpan by an initiated Sikh carries with it the unflinching responsibility of never misusing it. The kirpan is also used to bless food, thus extending its association with blessings and benevolence.

KARA

Associated values: allegiance, self-awareness, and ethical conduct

The kara is an iron or steel wristlet worn on the right arm. It is commonly worn by those born into the Sikh dharam, as well as by initiated Sikhs. The kara signifies a Sikh's allegiance, bond, and commitment to the Guru; it is a visible reminder that the Guru has taken the arm of a Sikh to carry him or her through life. It also serves as a constant reminder to be noble and ethical in one's thoughts and actions.

KASHERA

Associated values: self-restraint, self-respect, and respecting others

The kashera is a specially designed undergarment, which closes securely with a drawstring and is changed and washed each day. By wearing the kashera a Sikh is taking an honorable vow of respect towards the opposite sex. Fidelity to one's spouse is

Photographic representation showing the Five Kakaars (Ks) of an Initiated Sikh

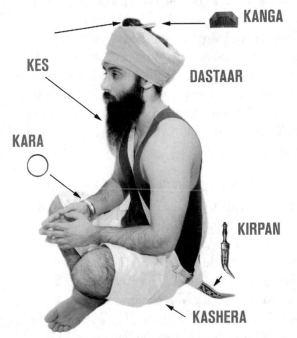

Image courtesy of Guru Nanak Nishkam Sewak Jatha.

sacred and Sikhs are prohibited from engaging in sexual relations outside wedlock. The kashera thus encourages a culture of self-restraint, self-respect and respect for others.

DASTAAR
Associated values: divinity, holiness, sovereignty, wisdom, and accomplishment

The dastaar or turban, is an integral part of Sikh identity, in addition to the five kakaars. It is worn by Sikh males, and some females. It covers, protects and crowns the head—the center of wisdom. The dastaar safeguards the uncut hair of a Sikh, which is tied in a topknot underneath. It is not put on or taken off like a hat or cap, but tied anew daily. To ask for it to be removed inconsiderately in public is demeaning and disrespectful to the wearer. In cultures the world over, the turban has signified divinity, holiness, sovereignty, wisdom and accomplishment—all qualities that are embedded in the wearing of the Sikh turban.

When a young boy transitions from wearing a patka (a cloth which is tied to cover the topknot), to a dastaar, a ceremony called the dastaar-bandi takes place, in which a respected member of the community or family will tie the dastaar on him in the presence of the Guru Granth Sahib.

AUTHORITY VESTED IN GURU GRANTH AND GURU PANTH

Through the creation of the Khalsa in 1699, Guru Gobind Singh established Guru Panth, or the "Guru's community"—indicating that the presence of the Guru would still dwell amongst the community of practicing disciples. He also declared that after him, spiritual authority would rest in the Guru Granth Sahib, the sacred scripture (from 1708-forever).

WHO IS A SIKH? A LIVELY DEBATE

There is an active debate in the Sikh community over the questions "who is a Sikh?" and "who constitutes the Panth?" This debate is similar to those that are taking place within the communities of other world religions. The 3B Framework mentioned earlier in this chapter, which focuses on belief, behavior, and belonging, offers a useful context for understanding this debate.

In the view of many Sikhs, having a belief in one God, the ten Gurus, and the Guru Granth Sahib makes a person a Sikh. Some members of the community question whether one can be a considered a member of the Panth without having undertaken the initiation that was mentioned above in the description of the Khalsa. This is a significant question because the number of Sikhs who are or have been initiated is currently a minority within the larger community. Some Sikhs acknowledge that they do not belong to the Khalsa, but see initiation as an ideal to which to aspire at some point in their lives. Others believe that initiation is essential as an entry point, because they hope that belonging to the Khalsa will inspire the necessary beliefs and behaviors. Some other Sikhs express the viewpoint that some initiates can outwardly belong to the Khalsa, but inwardly remain far from being a Sikh by demonstrating poor behavior or by not living up to the teachings of the Gurus in everyday life. From their perspective, behavior that conforms to Sikh beliefs is an essential criterion for determining whether a person is a Sikh.

As in many other religious traditions, a sense of identity and a feeling of belonging to the community play a very important role. For many, being born into a Sikh family and knowing about Sikh beliefs and the Sikh heritage is central to their sense of belonging. For others, having a family connection to the Punjab, or to the Punjabi language and culture, is the basis of their Sikh identity.

These issues all sustain lively debates within the Sikh community. Ultimately, however, Gurudwaras are welcoming to all and inclusive in nature. Sikhs believe that each individual's journey is unique and that we are all learners on the path toward leading a truthful life.

NOTES

1. American Academy of Religion, *Guidelines for Teaching About Religion in K-12 Schools in the United States* (Atlanta: American Academy of Religion, 2010), i. These Guidelines are reproduced in Appendix 2 of this book.

2. This section includes adaptations from Gopinder Kaur et. al., *Edexcel AS Religious Studies: Student Book* (mixed media product: United Kingdom, Edexcel, 2008).

3. Adapted from the Guru Nanak Nishkam Sewak Jatha pamphlet, "The Five Kakaars and Dastaar."

CHAPTER EIGHTEEN

Lists and Lives: Teaching about Buddhism in the Classroom

MICHAEL FRIEDMAN

One persistent stereotype about Buddhism holds that Buddhism is a philosophy rather than a religion. Much of the approach to teaching about Buddhism described below intends to combat this misperception and to demonstrate how Buddhism provides a complex and variegated religious worldview for its diverse adherents. Historiographically, this misrepresentation is the legacy of European scholars' early encounter with Buddhism, as described in Tomoko Masuzawa's *The Invention of World Religions*.

In her masterful study, Masuzawa unravels these scholars' participation in the "textual construction" of a Buddhism which saw "the rich and various manifestations of actual Buddhism observed throughout modern Asian nations…as so many derivative forms and latter-day innovations and corruptions."[1] According to this narrative, the doctrinal teachings of the historical Buddha, to which European scholars had primary access, came to be understood as the "pure" message of the Buddha's wisdom, whereas the lived manifestations of Buddhism across Asia had fallen prey to "a history not of development but of deterioration."[2] This interpretation of Buddhism was bequeathed to later generations through the "Buddhism as philosophy" canard which rears its head today in classroom debates that ask, "Is Buddhism a Religion or a Philosophy?"[3] As such, one critical task for educators is to disabuse students of this notion by presenting Buddhism in its great complexity and variety.

In the remarks which follow, I will lay out my approach to teaching about Buddhism on the assumption that the instructor will have one or two weeks to explore this material with students who have had minimal exposure to the tradition. I will begin by laying out a few images and concepts from Buddhist thought which govern my approach, followed by a run-through of my typical curriculum, and closing with additional possibilities for classroom discussion based on topics of contemporary interest.

THREE JEWELS AND SIX REALMS

The content of my lessons is divided across the Three Jewels, a Buddhist typology also known as the Three Refuges or the Triple Gem. These are the *Buddha*, or Siddhartha Gautama; the *Dharma*, or the Buddha's teachings; and the *Sangha*, or the Buddhist community. Though this approach relies heavily on texts in its exploration of the Buddha and the Dharma, it nevertheless draws on a traditional Buddhist organizational schema in doing so, and it further presents the Sangha, or the lived experience of Buddhism, as its culmination.

In terms of the general Buddhist worldview, I contextualize this discussion of the Three Jewels around images of the *bhavacakra*, or the wheel of existence. The bhavacakra is helpful in that it not only introduces students to key Buddhist ideas—the three poisons, the six realms of being, the twelve links of dependent origination, and so on—but its striking imagery also provides students with mental Velcro for a worldview typically unlike their own. I introduce the bhavacakra at the outset of the unit and return to it when touching on various aspects of the Buddha's life and teachings, as noted below.

In describing the bhavacakra itself, I walk students through its iconography, beginning with the six realms, which depict the six planes of existence where sentient beings can be reborn in the cycle of reincarnation, or samsara. These include the three positive realms—of humans, demigods, and gods—and the three negative realms—of animals, hungry ghosts, and beings in hell. In laying out this framework, it is essential to emphasize that existence in all realms is temporary, such that beings continually transmigrate from one realm to another, driven by their karma. To help students understand that hell and heaven, in Buddhist cosmology, are waystations rather than destinations in the unending cycle of reincarnation, I simply reiterate that even gods die and are reborn. Aside from the six realms, I also highlight the three animals at the hub of the wheel—the rooster, the snake, and the pig—which signify the emotional afflictions of greed, hatred, and ignorance, respectively. Letting students know that much of Buddhism is concerned with transforming these afflictions into their opposites— greed into generosity, hatred into compassion, and ignorance into wisdom—can help orient their understanding of the tradition's overall goals.[4]

BUDDHA AND DHARMA

A natural extension of discussing the six realms is contextualizing the Buddha's last rebirth as the culmination of many lifetimes. A traditional outline for teaching the Buddha's life is the Twelve Acts, which begin with the Buddha's descent from the Tushita Heaven (Act One) into his mother's womb (Act Two) before being born as Siddhartha Gautama (Act Three). Siddhartha's pleasurable life in the palace then spans Acts Four and Five, which move into his eventual renunciation (Act Six) and mastery of austerities (Act Seven) before he planted himself at the base of the Bodhi tree (Act Eight) and overcame Mara, the demonic master of death and desire (Act Nine). The Buddha's full enlightenment (Act Ten) then precedes his teaching (Act Eleven), which continues for many years before the Buddha's eventual *mahaparinirvana*, which refers to the final death of one who has attained enlightenment (Act Twelve).[5] Referring back to the bhavacakra, noteworthy here is the manner in which the Buddha's life in the palace in Acts Four and Five can signify the heavenly realms, whereas the Buddha's asceticism in the forest in Acts Six and Seven can represent the hell realms. Furthermore, this juxtaposition reveals the Buddha's central insight regarding the Middle Way: Excessive pleasures blind us to our suffering, whereas excessive sufferings divert us from spiritual

efforts. Consequently, a human rebirth constitutes a rare and precious opportunity, in which one is balanced between suffering and pleasure such that enlightenment becomes a genuine possibility.

As for the mechanics of this lesson, I rely heavily on artwork, both classical and contemporary. While displaying one or more images for each of the Acts, I ask students to explain what is happening in each moment. From here, one can explore broader trends in the development of religious literature, such as the significance of fantastical elements in the extraordinary circumstances surrounding the Buddha's birth, or the politics at play in Buddhist absorption of Hindu imagery.

Having discussed the Buddha's life, I turn next to the second of the Three Jewels, or the Dharma, spending two or three days exploring the Four Noble Truths and the role of meditation in particular. In teaching the Four Noble Truths, I draw on the image of the Buddha as a physician, in which the First Noble Truth of suffering serves as the patient's complaint, the Second Noble Truth of craving offers a diagnosis, the Third Noble Truth of nirvana suggests a prognosis, and the Fourth Noble Truth of the Eightfold Path presents the prescription.

Broadly speaking, my emphasis in teaching the Four Noble Truths is to help students see beyond the truth of suffering as nihilistic or the truth of nirvana as other-worldly, in order to experience the richness and beauty of Buddhist thought. Accordingly, after offering this initial image of the Buddha as physician, I delve into each of the Noble Truths through more detailed teachings on each topic. Thus, for the First Noble Truth of suffering, we consider the three main types of suffering: (1) the suffering of aging and death, (2) the suffering of change, and (3) the suffering of conditions. Students can usually recognize the first type of suffering in their own lives, but the Buddha's insight regarding the suffering of change is subtle. The suffering of change is informed by the Second Noble Truth of craving (more below) and argues that when you want something, you either never get it (in which case, you suffer), or you do get it; if you do get it, it either fails to meet expectations (in which case, you suffer), or

An image of the bhavacakra (wheel of existence).

for existence, and (3) craving for non-existence. The first of these tends toward the obvious, but attachment to existence and non-existence can be somewhat more slippery. I have had success with my students in using modern fitness trends to illustrate the desire for a beautiful and healthy body, whereas I have used the explosion of interest in mindfulness to demonstrate craving for transcendent experiences.[6]

Far more difficult to parse than the truth of suffering or the truth of craving is the Third Noble Truth, or nirvana.[7] My advice here is largely pragmatic, to turn back to the image of the bhavacakra and the three poisons at its hub: the rooster for greed, the pig for ignorance, and the snake for hatred. As mentioned above, one psychologized explanation of nirvana suggests that the goal of Buddhist practice is to transform these poisons into their opposites: Greed becomes generosity, ignorance becomes wisdom, and hatred becomes compassion. Simply put, a life defined by greed, ignorance, and hatred is characterized by suffering, whereas a life defined by generosity, wisdom, and compassion is characterized by freedom from suffering, or nirvana. Students tend to grasp this explanation readily, though it runs the drawback of being evasive, in that a classical explanation would depict nirvana as nameless and unconditioned through metaphors and parables which point toward nirvana but say nothing directly about it. Here, however, each instructor must make their own determinations in balancing clarity and accuracy.

it does meet expectations, which makes its eventual disappearance all the more painful. Discussing the suffering of change therefore lends itself readily to an exploration of consumerism and materialism in contemporary society, so I often ask students how they feel if their parents will not get them a cell phone, or if they have one, how they feel when their screen cracks, or when a new model comes out. The third type of suffering, the suffering of conditions, is the most subtle and refers to the base level of suffering from which we can never escape but which we almost always ignore. Here, I point out those students who are shifting uncomfortably in their seats or scratching an itch to draw attention to this suffering as the "background noise" of our lives.

The Second Noble Truth of craving can likewise be examined by turning to a traditional typology as follows: (1) craving for sensual pleasures, (2) craving

As for the Fourth Noble Truth of the Eightfold Path (which denotes Right View, Right Aspiration, Right Speech, Right Conduct, Right Livelihood, Right Effort, Right Mindfulness, and Right Meditation), I attempt to help students see how the various steps of the path are mutually reinforcing. For instance, attempting to be more mindful can make one more aware of the impact of one's speech, rendering

Right Speech more likely, while more carefully guarding one's speech provides an increasingly solid foundation for Right Meditation, which thereby offers positive gains for one's mindfulness. I tend not to go into great depth with the various steps but choose instead to focus on Right Meditation in particular. Tech-savvy instructors might enjoy working with popular meditation podcasts or smartphone apps such as Calm or Headspace, but I have primarily used readings and recordings from Jack Kornfield's *Meditation for Beginners* alongside a viewing of the documentary *The Dhamma Brothers*.[8] Kornfield, one of the pioneers of vipassana, or insight, meditation in the West, methodically introduces a range of Buddhist meditative practices in this volume, and students usually enjoy doing a brief meditation in class, which can be used as a prompt for discussion or journaling. Watching *The Dhamma Brothers* then adds some detail to this picture, as the film documents a vipassana meditation program which was implemented at a maximum security prison in Alabama. The striking footage creates openings to discuss any number of topics from the mechanics of meditation to the Westernization of Buddhism.[9] One especially profound aspect of the film is its depiction of meditation as freeing practitioners from patterns of behavior and furnishing a newfound ability to make choices about how to act, rather than running on autopilot in stressful situations.

SANGHA, THEN AND NOW

Unfortunately, focusing on the life of the Buddha and his teachings tends to reaffirm a "textual construction" of Buddhism, so it is crucial to supplement these topics with consideration of lived Buddhism. A lovely text for this purpose is Donald Swearer's *The Buddhist World of Southeast Asia*. The first paragraph reads as follows:

> All too often a textbook picture of Theravada Buddhism bears little resemblance to the actual practice of Buddhism in Southeast Asia. The lived traditions of Myanmar, Thailand, Laos, Cambodia, and Sri Lanka seem to distort and sometimes subvert the cardinal teachings of nibbana [nirvana], the Four Noble Truths, or the Noble Eightfold Path familiar to the Western student of Buddhism. The observer enters a Theravada Buddhist culture to discover that ordination into the monastic order (sangha) may be motivated more by cultural convention or a young man's sense of social obligation to his parents rather the pursuit of transforming wisdom….[10]

Swearer's remarks help to collapse the neat picture of Buddhism constructed thus far and to reveal Buddhism in practice as multifaceted and dynamic. Broadly speaking, lived Buddhism is spread across three schools known as the Three Vehicles. In the quote above, Swearer is speaking of the oldest iteration, known as Theravada, or "The Way of the Elders," which is predominant in Southeast Asia. The other vehicles include Mahayana Buddhism, or "The Great Vehicle," and Vajrayana Buddhism, or "The Diamond Vehicle." Mahayana Buddhism boasts the greatest number of adherents and is principally found in East Asia, while Vajrayana Buddhism stems from Tibet and offers the most radical approach to Buddhist teachings. It is worth noting that the Three Vehicles are not understood hierarchically, but rather as corresponding to different personality types; and while this schema elides important differences, it nevertheless helps students see the broad patterns and understand key distinctions.

For each of the Three Vehicles, I emphasize a specific practice or teaching in order to push my students toward depth in their study of Buddhism. For Theravada, therefore, I spotlight the "forest monks" of Thailand, in particular their contemporary rite of tree ordination, in which ecologically-minded monks ordain trees as members of the Sangha in order to protect them from loggers.[11] This practice raises awareness around the use of ritual in ordinations, as well as Buddhism's engagement with modernity, and it helps to combat and complicate erstwhile images of monks as solitary meditators.

I then introduce Mahayana Buddhism by way of Thich Nhat Hanh's *The Heart of Understanding*, which comprises Hanh's commentary on the

Buddha's "Heart Sutra" and which presents, in concise and clear language, fundamental Mahayana insights regarding the nature of reality. Much of the volume centers on the critical notion of sunyata, or emptiness:

> Emptiness is the ground of everything. Thanks to emptiness, everything is possible. That is a declaration made by Nagarjuna, the Buddhist philosopher of the second century. Emptiness is quite an optimistic concept. If I am not empty, I cannot be here. And if you are not empty, you cannot be there. Because you are there, I can be here. This is the true meaning of emptiness. Form does not have a separate existence. [The enlightened being] Avalokita wants us to understand this point. If we are not empty, we become a block of matter. We cannot breathe, we cannot think. To be empty means to be alive, to breathe in and to breathe out. We cannot be alive if we are not empty. Emptiness is impermanence, it is change. We should not complain about impermanence, because without impermanence nothing is possible.[12]

In other words, Self and Other cannot ultimately be separate because we are constantly informed and shaped by our experiences of the world around us. Simply put, one cannot describe the self without reference to one's relationships or encounters with others, and these shift and change in every moment. This argument then leads to a fundamental reordering of one's ethical obligations, for if we are mistaken to think of ourselves as discrete and isolated beings, then the instincts we have to protect and care for our own person should apply to all others with equal force. No longer concerned with their own suffering and enlightenment, Mahayana Buddhists are therefore driven by compassion toward the *bodhisattva* ideal, in which one vows to be reborn continuously until all beings have been released from suffering. The bodhisattva ideal represents a seismic shift in Buddhist thought, opening the possibility for practitioners to beseech such enlightened beings for compassionate assistance.[13] One of the most well-known examples of Mahayana Buddhism is that of Japanese Zen,

Suggested Readings

General Surveys
Gethin, Rupert. *The Foundations of Buddhism.* New York: Oxford University Press, 1998.

Mitchell, Donald W. *Buddhism: Introducing the Buddhist Experience.* New York: Oxford University Press, 2002.

Primary Sources
Rhys Davids, C.A.F. and K.R. Norman, tr. *Poems of Early Buddhist Nuns (Therigatha).* Oxford: The Pali Text Society, 1989.

Santideva. *The Way of the Bodhisattva.* Translated by the Padmakara Translation Group. Boston: Shambhala Publications, 2006.

The Buddha
Khoroche, Peter, tr. *Once the Buddha Was a Monkey: Arya Sura's Jatakamala.* Chicago: The University of Chicago Press, 2006.

Chogyel, Tenzin. *The Life of the Buddha.* Translated by Kurtis R. Schaeffer. New York: Penguin Books, 2015.

The Dharma
Wimala, Bhante Y. *Lessons of the Lotus: Practical Spiritual Teachings of a Traveling Buddhist Monk.* New York: Bantam Books, 1997.

Gyamtso, Khenpo Tsultrim. *Progressive Stages of Meditation on Emptiness.* Edited by Shenpen Hookham. Auckland: Zhyisil Chokyi Ghatsal Publications, 2001.

The Sangha
Fields, Rick. *How the Swans Came to the Lake: A Narrative History of Buddhism in America.* Boston: Shambhala Publications, 1992.

Nishimura, Eshin and Giei Sato. *Unsui: A Diary of Zen Monastic Life.* Edited by Bardwell L. Smith. Honolulu: University of Hawaii Press, 1983.

Tibetan Buddhism
Childs, Geoff. *Tibetan Diary: From Birth to Death and Beyond in a Himalayan Valley of Nepal.* Berkeley: University of California Press, 2004.

van Schaik, Sam. *Tibet: A History.* New Haven: Yale University Press, 2013.

which seeks to foster awareness of our inner Buddha-nature (according to which, we are already enlightened but have merely forgotten), through sudden bursts of insight generated by koans, or paradoxes requiring meditation.[14] These koans are rich fodder for classroom discussions about the use of poetry and artwork in Buddhist contexts.

In closing with Vajrayana Buddhism, I emphasize the intensity of Tibetan Buddhism, in which practitioners are understood to be so driven by their compassion that they seek to become bodhisattvas as quickly as possible in order to aid and teach other sentient beings. Consequently, Vajrayana deploys the logic of emptiness and nonduality through powerful rituals which help practitioners overcome mundane ways of thinking by subverting negative tendencies for karmic benefits. For instance, in the meditative practice of *tonglen*, or giving-and-taking, a practitioner absorbs others' sufferings while transmitting one's own joys to those in need.[15] However, students may be more familiar with rituals concerning sand mandalas, in which advanced practitioners visualize and construct a sacred cosmos that is then destroyed in a powerful teaching on impermanence. The emphasis in both practices is on use of potent techniques to move one towards enlightenment as quickly as possible.

CLOSING CONSIDERATIONS

Finally, my unit closes with attention to one of several contemporary issues regarding Buddhism in the modern era. For classes interested in religion and violence, I focus on Buddhist extremism against Muslims in Myanmar.[16] For students interested in international relations, I highlight the debate over Tibetan sovereignty.[17] Most commonly, however, I receive requests to explore the role of gender and sexuality in Buddhism, which provides for a rich investigation of traditional Buddhist attitudes over and against the present-day campaign to revive the ordination of Buddhist nuns.[18] In each case, one can ask students to engage in powerful acts of empathy and understanding in applying their knowledge of the Buddhist worldview, the Three Jewels, and the Three Vehicles to an issue which confronts contemporary Buddhists.

NOTES

1. Tomoko Maszawa, *The Invention of World Religions: Or, How European Universalism Was Preserved in the Language of Pluralism* (Chicago: The University of Chicago Press, 2005), 126.

2. Masuzawa, 128.

3. To varying degrees, some Buddhist modernists have embraced this presentation of Buddhism as philosophical rather than religious in order to bolster its popularity. For one example, see: Dzogchen Ponlop, *Rebel Buddha: A Guide to a Revolution of Mind* (Boston: Shambala Publications, 2010).

4. With introductory students, I omit discussion of the bhavacakra's outer ring, which represents the twelve links of dependent origination. These provide Buddhism's metaphysical explanation for causality, which is unnecessarily complex in courses geared toward religious literacy. For more background, see: Geshe Sonam Rinchen, *How Karma Works: The Twelve Links of Dependent Arising*, trans. Ruth Sonam (Ithaca: Snow Lion Publications, 2006).

5. There are many details worth filling in here. For a classic account of the Buddha's life, see: Ashvaghosa, *Life of the Buddha*, trans. Patrick Olivelle (New York: New York University Press, 2008).

6. Chogyam Trungpa, a Tibetan teacher critical to spreading Buddhism in the West, warned of the dangers of such "spiritual materialism" in his *Cutting Through Spiritual Materialism*, ed. John Baker and Marvin Casper (Boston: Shambhala Publications, 2002).

7. For an excellent though technical volume on this subject, see: Steven Collins, *Nirvana: Concept, Imagery, and Narrative* (Cambridge: Cambridge University Press, 2010).

8. Jack Kornfield, *Meditation for Beginners* (Boulder: Sounds True, 2008). Jenny Phillips, Andrew Kukura, and Anne Marie Stein, *The Dhamma Brothers: East Meets West in the Deep South* (Concord: Freedom Behind Bars Productions, 2008).

9. For lengthier writing assignments, I have also used a companion volume of written materials: Jenny Phillips, *Letters from the Dhamma Brothers* (Onalaska: Pariyatti Press, 2008).

10. Donald K. Swearer, *The Buddhist World of Southeast Asia* (Albany: State University of New York Press, 2010), 1.

11. For more detail on tree ordination, see: Susan M. Darlington, *The Ordination of a Tree: The Thai Buddhist Environmental Movement* (Albany: State University of New York Press, 2012). PBS has also produced a video featurette on this topic: "Forest Monks," PBS Religion & Ethics Newsweekly, last modified January 10, 2010, http://www.pbs.org/wnet/religionandethics/2010/01/15/january-15-2010-forest-monks/5472/

12. Thich Nhat Hanh, *The Heart of Understanding: Commentaries on the Prajnaparamita Heart Sutra*, ed. Peter Levitt (Berkeley: Parallax Press, 1988), 17.

13. This argument, which suggests a severe ideological clash between Theravada and Mahayana Buddhism, has recently been challenged in Buddhist Studies. For one such study, see: Jeffrey Samuels, "The Bodhisattva Ideal in Theravada Buddhist Theory and Practice: A Reevaluation of the Bodhisattva-Sravaka Opposition," *Philosophy East and West* 47.3 (1997).

14. For a classic treatment of nonduality in Zen thought, see: Shunryu Suzuki, *Zen Mind, Beginner's Mind: Informal talks on Zen Meditation and Practice*, ed. Trudy Dixon (Boston: Weatherhill, 2009).

15. Tonglen is a lojong, or "mind training," practice. For an introduction to lojong, see: Traleg Kyabgon, *The Practice of Lojong: Cultivating Compassion through Training the Mind* (Boston: Shambhala Publications, 2007). For a fascinating study on the use of lojong among Tibetan exiles, see: Sara E. Lewis, "Trauma and the Making of Flexible Minds in the Tibetan Exile Community," *Ethos: Journal of the Society for Psychological Anthropology* 41.3 (2013).

16. For a general study of Buddhism and violence, see: Michael K. Jerryson and Mark Juergensmeyer, *Buddhist Warfare* (Oxford: Oxford University Press, 2010). For a specific analysis of the conflict in Myanmar, see: Matthew J. Walton and Susan Hayward, *Contesting Buddhist Narratives: Democratization, Nationalism, and Communal Violence in Myanmar* (Honolulu: East-West Center, 2014).

17. For a concise history, see: Melvyn C. Goldstein, *The Snow Lion and the Dragon: China, Tibet, and the Dalai Lama* (Berkeley: University of California Press, 1999).

18. There are a number of traditional texts to draw on here, including the "goddess chapter" of the *Vimalakirti Sutra* (in which a goddess transforms the body of one of the Buddha's disciples from male to female to male again, in a demonstration of emptiness) and the oft-cited "tale of the dragon princess" from the *Lotus Sutra* (in which the dragon princess rapidly attains awakening in the presence of the Buddha and a gathered crowd, but only after attaining a male body). For a conference volume on the present-day debate regarding full ordination, see: Thea Mohr and Jampa Tsedroen, eds., *Dignity & Discipline: Reviving Full Ordination for Buddhist Nuns* (Boston: Wisdom Publications, 2010).

CHAPTER NINETEEN

Conscience and the Challenge of Civic Inclusion

MYNGA FUTRELL

Public schools are required not to privilege one religion over others, and not to favor religious beliefs over nonreligious beliefs. Legal decisions have made clear that educators who teach about religion should be *neutral*.[1] Consequently, educators are increasingly accepting responsibility for presenting a variety of religions with academic objectivity and factual empathy.

But what about that second aspect of neutrality?

Are we being even-handed between religion and nonreligion? More to the point, do we consider that to be part of the neutrality mandate at all?

- Is the "none" in the phrase "all faiths, or none" given its civic due?

- Is dissent from religion ever explored?

- Apart from growing religious diversity, is nonreligious diversity also acknowledged?

Doesn't consistently omitting the words "or none" create a bias toward religion in our educational programs?

When we fail to illuminate the full scope of the neutrality mandate, I do not think that we do justice to what makes religion and its various "none" counterparts so important in life education.

Whenever I encounter the curricular treatment of religion—whether the subject matter is focusing on a specified religion or on demographics or diversity—I look for evidence of a robust academic approach. I also look at the even-handedness criteria.

On that score, I frequently find myself regarding the overall presentation much as one might appraise a three-legged dog. Hey—Isn't something missing there?

We leave a gaping hole in student understanding unless we habitually address the concept of nonreligion when teaching about religion in the social studies. We owe it to our neutrality mandate—and to our students as future citizens—to direct some academic attention to filling in the aforesaid "missing limb."

Here are three compensating actions to pursue while teaching about religion(s):

- Model placing "faith" and "no faith" *on the same plateau*. For example, when you say one, just say the other. (Habitually using the words "religious and nonreligious diversity" shows linguistic savvy!)

- Concede some *unmerited* disadvantages that certain nonreligious citizens encounter, and prepare yourself to protect those who exercise their right to liberty of conscience.

- Teach directly toward wholesome *civic inclusiveness*, putting the words "faith or no faith" all together.

This chapter briefly engages that three-prong effort. The endnotes are a guide to some helpful resources on related topics.

THE CONTEXT FOR BRIDGING RELIGION AND NONRELIGION

Schools justify the study of religion because it makes so much of history, literature, and the arts, as well as contemporary life, more intelligible. But another objective is also significant: having our students exit their schooling *fully cherishing* "the first freedom" guaranteed in the Bill of Rights, *religious liberty*.

Despite its tagging, religious liberty is not just for the religious; it is freedom of belief for everyone. That's an important "crux of the matter" that we need students to understand. Luckily, with a neutral linguistic manner, we can advance even-handedness between religion and nonreligion. In using the phrase "liberty of conscience," we already have at hand objective terminology from which the word "religion" is notably absent.

Laying adequate groundwork in this concept is fundamental to our ensuring that students recognize and deeply empathize with a shared prerogative that, as citizens, we mutually want to protect. Teachers need to accentuate the American historical context from which this civic freedom arose.

FREE CONSCIENCE: A VENERATED RIGHT

My dictionary describes conscience as "a knowledge or sense of right and wrong, with a compulsion to do right." To my mind, an individual's conscience pretty much encompasses a person's moral sense. Hence, I hold to the position that human beings have a right to private and free conscience. It is an entitlement to live without a coercive or menacing pressure to believe or profess any specific thing. I would extend this right to the youngsters in our classrooms, too!

This interpretation seems to put me in good company. Many persons of historical note appear to have held human conscience in high regard. Long before Jefferson and Madison, John Milton ranked liberty of conscience high among all things that ought to be dearest and most valued. In *Areopagitica* (1644), he wrote: "Give me the liberty to know, to utter, and to argue freely according to conscience, above all other liberties."

By the late eighteenth century, educated persons absorbed in Lockean thinking were well acquainted with the doctrine of free conscience. For example, both Madison and Jefferson viewed a person's conscience as being at the core of the individual's moral knowledge and contemplation.

EVERYONE (RELIGIOUS AND NONRELIGIOUS) TOGETHER

At the time of the American Revolution, the Rhode Island colony that Roger Williams had founded existed as an important model of distinct religious, ethnic, and cultural groups coexisting as fellow citizens within the one governmental entity.[2] The colony's granting of "conscience freedom" to people of all faiths and none was an extraordinary break from the conventions of established churches in other colonies.

Williams' conscience doctrine, itself an idea with little precedent in human history, had by then evolved into a network of associated beliefs permeating other colonies. Activist ministers in the fast growing Baptist faith had become influential in advancing and intensifying the concepts of church/state separation. Even though most colonies had established churches, there was a greater acknowledgement of civic pluralism. The notion of protecting the right of conscience of all citizens appeared ingrained in a few of the other colonies' documents.

By the time that James Madison and other Framers amended the Constitution with a Bill of Rights, that tiny colony of Rhode Island had largely demonstrated *governmental responsibility* for conscience protection for *everyone*—not just Baptists, but atheists and Catholics, Quakers, Jews, and Muslims as well.

A FLOURISHING CIVIC IDEAL

It is probably fair to say that the right of conscience has become universalized as a principle of human rights. Following the 1948 U.N. adoption of the "Universal Declaration of Human Rights," the principle has been stated in numerous landmark documents.[3] Article 18 of the Universal Declaration takes care to note that the right of conscience extends beyond "having a religion" to "whatever belief of choice."

The ideal of people having liberty of conscience as an inalienable right is invaluable. Coercion may be a mainstay of civil authority, but governmental compulsion and intimidation to intrude and promote religious belief is unacceptable. I do not just mean a *particular* religious belief, but religious belief, period. And the same goes for compelling atheistic beliefs. Government neutrality is the ideal.

The United States has behind it over two centuries of being widely perceived as a bastion of this particular freedom. Today, the U.S. is far from alone in ostensibly guaranteeing to its citizens this grand ideal. Based on what can be read in founding statements or codes, over a hundred contemporary secular nations supposedly grant liberty of conscience to their citizenry.

Many Americans have reason to wonder, though, whether our nation's liberty of conscience is a "full-flowered" egalitarian version that embraces the *nonreligious* citizen equally with those citizens who hold (at least in verbal expression) to some–*any*–religion. I think they can rightfully question the degree to which ideals of free conscience are widely viewed as belonging equally to them.

In focusing curricular explorations on "faiths," educators need to be continuously bringing to light the concept of "or none"—the beliefs of people who do not have a religious faith. (See Table 1 on pages 168–169 for some prominent examples.) Only then will students recognize its relevance to (and likely presence within) any religion under study.

DEMOGRAPHICS (U.S.)
Among developed democratic nations today, the U.S. is generally considered a very religious country.[4] Religious affiliation is commonplace, and affirming it is widely considered as a positive in the popular vernacular.

Persons of "no faith" are distinctly less numerous, but there has been a recent flowering in the citizenry of persons unaffiliated with religion—the "Nones."[5] It is increasingly common to encounter open expressions of doubt and declarations of atheism in the public square. Nonetheless, it continues to be broadly more socially acceptable for an American to have and express a faith than to declare that he or she has none at all. Civic approbation of skeptical perspectives remains exceedingly rare. Widespread stigmatism of atheists persists.

While acknowledging these societal realities, fair-minded educators must counter faulty societal forces that would further disadvantage youngsters from nonreligious families because, in schools, stereotyping and stigmatizing are to be avoided for religious *and nonreligious* persons alike.

SPECIOUS ATTRIBUTIONS OF MORALITY
Much of present-day American society affixes a moral tinge of disfavor to the "none" segment of our "all faiths, or none" divide. This predisposition marginalizes skeptics from the cultural mainstream, and it especially denigrates atheists. (The everyday pejorative expression "*even* atheists..." is but one of numerous verbal examples of culturally commonplace moral disfavor.)

Whereas religious persons might base favorable moral conduct on specific teachings or texts, or ascribe it to following their religion (usually Christian), nonreligious persons may locate their basis for noble and selfless actions in other sources. (For example, scientific research shows that well before any delivery of parental lessons, pre-lingual infants show clear signs of built-in morality.)[6]

Teachers should make a *neutral* attribution of morality that recognizes that altruistic conduct can arise from humanitarianism, and should not necessarily be attributed to benevolent actions by those who are religious.

Table 1: Historically Influential Nonreligious Thinkers

The list below presents historically influential individuals who represented a variety of trends in nonreligious thought: Deism, Atheism, Agnosticism, Freethinking, naturalism, and skepticism. Several of these trends are not mutually exclusive: for example, a free thinker or skeptic can also be an atheist or an agnostic. However, these ways of thinking are conceptually distinct from each other, so I have presented them separately to clarify their individual characteristics.

DEISTS	NOTABLE DEISTS	SELECT QUOTATIONS
A deist accepts the existence of a creator on the basis of reason but rejects belief in a supernatural deity who interacts with humankind.	Ethan Allen Denis Diderot Benjamin Franklin Thomas Jefferson Thomas Paine Sir Walter Raleigh Jean-Jacques Rousseau Voltaire Mary Wollstonecraft	"Question with boldness even the existence of a God; because, if there be one, he must more approve of the homage of reason, than that of blind-folded fear." (Thomas Jefferson) "I do not believe in the creed professed by the Jewish Church, by the Roman Church, by the Greek Church, by the Turkish Church, by the Protestant Church, nor by any church that I know of. My own mind is my own church." (Thomas Paine)

ATHEISTS	NOTABLE ATHEISTS	SELECT QUOTATIONS
An atheist lacks belief in the existence of a deity or deities.	Charles Bradlaugh Richard Dawkins Emma Goldman Stephen Hawking Madalyn Murray O'Hair Ernestine Rose Bertrand Russell George Santayana	"We are all atheists about most of the gods that societies have ever believed in. Some of us just go one god further." (Richard Dawkins) "Whatever good you are willing to do for the sake of your God, I am full as willing to do for the sake of man." (Ernestine Rose) "An atheist believes that deed must be done instead of prayer said. An atheist strives for involvement in life and not escape into death." (Madalyn Murray O'Hair)

AGNOSTICS	NOTABLE AGNOSTICS	SELECT QUOTATIONS
An agnostic believes that nothing is known or can be known of the existence or nature of anything beyond material phenomena. An agnostic claims neither faith nor disbelief in a deity.	Susan B. Anthony Clarence Darrow W.E.B. Dubois Betty Friedan Matilda Joslyn Gage Thomas Huxley Robert G. Ingersoll Carl Sagan Elie Wiesel	"To be certain of the existence of God and to be certain of the nonexistence of God seem to me to be the confident extremes in a subject so riddled with doubt and uncertainty as to inspire very little confidence indeed." (Carl Sagan) "I do not consider it an insult, but rather a compliment to be called an agnostic. I do not pretend to know where many ignorant men are sure — that is all that agnosticism means." (Clarence Darrow)

Suggested resources for locating primary sources and quotations are: Gerald A. Larue, *Freethought across the Centuries* (New York: Humanist Press, 1996); Susan Jacoby, *Freethinkers: A History of American Secularism* (New York: Holt, 2005); and Mynga Futrell and Paul Geisert, *Different Drummers: Nonconforming Thinkers in History* (2002), a 400-page loose-leaf instructional module now available only via Amazon.com.

FREETHINKERS	NOTABLE FREETHINKERS	SELECT QUOTATIONS
A freethinker forms opinions on the basis of reason, independently of tradition, authority, or established belief.	Erasmus Molière Vashti McCollum Lucretia Mott Ayn Rand A. Philip Randolph Gene Roddenberry Margaret Sanger Elizabeth Cady Stanton Frances Wright	"It disturbs me no more to find men base, unjust, or selfish than to see apes mischievous, wolves savage, or the vulture ravenous for its prey." (Molière) "We must question the story logic of having an all-knowing all-powerful God, who creates faulty Humans, and then blames them for his own mistakes." (Gene Roddenberry) "No one knows any more of what lies beyond our sphere of action than thou and I, and we know nothing." (Lucretia Mott)

NATURALISTS	NOTABLE NATURALISTS	SELECT QUOTATIONS
A naturalist trusts that the world can be understood in terms of science.	Luther Burbank Marie Curie Copernicus Charles Darwin Leonardo Da Vinci Daniel C. Dennett Richard Feynman Galileo Ursula Goodenough	"Ignorance more frequently begets confidence than does knowledge: it is those who know little, and not those who know much, who so positively assert that this or that problem will never be solved by science." (Charles Darwin) "Scientific inquiry has provisioned us with a mind-boggling new core narrative — the epic of evolution, the epic of creation, the universe story, big history, everybody's story — where humans and human cultures are understood to be emergent from and, hence, a part of nature." (Ursula Goodenough)

SKEPTICS	NOTABLE SKEPTICS	SELECT QUOTATIONS
A skeptic maintains a doubting attitude with regard to the truth of a religion or its elements.	Isaac Asimov Lord Byron Robert Todd Carroll Rene Descartes Albert Einstein Martin Gardner Ruth Hermence Green Isaac Newton Michael Shermer Mark Twain	"Often, the less there is to justify a traditional custom, the harder it is to get rid of it." (Mark Twain) "'Tis much better to do a little with certainty, and leave the rest for others that come after you, than to explain all things by conjecture without making sure of any thing." (Isaac Newton) "I deny nothing, but doubt everything." (Lord Byron) "If you would be a real seeker after truth, it is necessary that at least once in your life you doubt, as far as possible, all things." (Rene Descartes) "The important thing is not to stop questioning. Curiosity has its own reason for existing." (Albert Einstein)

ASCENDANCY OF CEREMONIAL DEISM

Governmental mention of a generic God has, over time, become both legal and more permeating of social conventions (e.g., oaths for public office). Certain government-backed 1950s-era actions (e.g., the insertion in 1954 of "under God" in the Pledge of Allegiance, and the replacement in 1956 of the original "E Pluribus Unum" motto with "In God We Trust,") have disquieted many citizens who venerate the secular Constitution's separation of religion and government.

Although religious as well as nonreligious citizens have frowned on the creeping hegemony of ceremonial deism, its acceptance in the larger citizenry and manifestation in the public square is another factor in sidelining nonreligious persons who recognize and resist the speech and symbolism drawn from monotheistic religious contexts.

NONCONFORMITY AND THE NONTHEISTIC LANDSCAPE

Everyone seems to seek a personal understanding of the meaning and purpose of life and living. We all develop our own unique worldview.[7] In the interest of civic pluralism and inclusiveness, I would urge teachers to bring this important human commonality to the forefront.

Most of us derive answers to our inquiries about such matters from family and peers and from our cultural surroundings, particularly from the prevalent religion. In the United States, where the population is heavily Christian and ceremonial deism is ubiquitous, it is no surprise that the life understandings of most Americans generally conform to the surrounding monotheistic perspective. (Polytheistic and nontheistic worldviews may prevail in some locales.)

Wholly secular perspectives like atheism are plainly *nonconforming*. Nonetheless, they increased rather rapidly in the first decade of the 2000s, helped along by advances in Internet communications. More children are being reared in nontheistic homes than ever before, though they continue to swim upstream against the cultural flow.

NONRELIGIOUS THINKING

Throughout history, in the enduring human quest for meaning, many people have looked beyond their cultural surroundings to make their own determinations. For example, in the ancient days of western civilization, there were individuals whose worldviews conspicuously departed from the accepted religion of their day. Some examples were materialists like Archimedes, and some were rationalists like Socrates. Today's secularists and freethinkers follow in their footsteps. When people use their mental faculties and independent reasoning, they often reach conclusions that depart considerably from prevailing societal conceptions. When freedom to speak one's views exists, nonreligious views can thrive. Some who have reached autonomous conclusions firmly reject the prevalent "religious truths" of the time and place into which they were born. When prevailing custom or authority denies such freedom, the consequences for the candidly nonreligious can be harsh.

Leading nonconforming thinkers are worthy of study.[8] Table 1 on pages 168–169 lists the names of many nonconformists who had an influence on history.

Freethinkers of the past may be notable today because their unconventional thinking (not only about religion, but other matters as well) led to dramatic historical contributions to society. Social studies teachers may be surprised to learn how many human advances have been made by freethinkers. Thankfully, useful resources and instructional materials are available.

In today's context, a person who takes the pathway of autonomous freethought generally arrives at *secular explanations*. If the individual lives in an overbearing religious environment, departing from dominant explanations can be agonizing; the person might hide his or her views. If an openly nonconforming view is disparaged by family or peers, individuals may emerge distressed and isolated, or perhaps bitter from the mental struggle. Others, though, will surface with feelings of absolute freedom, having at last attained explanations that "finally make sense" to them.

Contemporary citizens who ardently identify as freethinkers may seek to organize and enjoy community with others under some self-chosen label that indicates their collective departure from the mainstream theism (e.g., nonbeliever, or nontheist).

COMPREHENDING NONTHEISTIC/NATURALISTIC WORLDVIEWS

What customarily sets most contemporary freethinkers apart from the broader religious public is their *naturalistic worldview*. There are just no supernatural or mystical elements in how they perceive life and living. This understanding of how the world works usually positions them not only as religious skeptics but also as general searchers for the empirical evidence behind claims.

There exist a number of resources for teachers exploring naturalistic and nontheistic worldviews. I myself have attempted to sketch out characteristics generally in evidence among individuals who have developed such perspectives.[9] If there is any one feature central to the outlook of such individuals, it is their expectation of having *only one life to live*. They give no credence to an afterlife in any form.

STRIVING FOR INCLUSIVE CIVIC PLURALISM

With awareness of nonconforming worldviews and comfort in modeling a neutral approach (inclusive of both religion and nonreligion), a teacher is well prepared to build similar capacities in students. Table 2 identifies direct teaching objectives that, if pursued, will bring all students closer to evidencing civic acceptance of persons across a wide range of human worldviews, *inclusive of nonreligion*.

The knowledge, skills, and attitudes in Table 2 on pages 172–173 work against stereotyping and the judgmental attitudes of others. Youngsters who understand liberty of conscience will know well that they do not have to be respectful of others' *beliefs*, only of their *right of conscience*. Conscience is something that they will all want to protect for themselves, and for everyone, religious and nonreligious alike.

NOTES

1. The Center for Public Education (CPE), an initiative of the National School Boards Association, provides a useful summary of the most crucial U.S. Supreme Court decisions that have shaped the legal landscape impacting teaching about religion and nonreligion in schools. The CPE web page points out that federal and U.S. Supreme Court decisions keep shifting the standards and expectations for public schools, and reminds readers that the Constitution ensures that every student who receives public schooling has the opportunity to express his or her sincerely held belief, or *to be free from the unwelcome pressure to believe at all.* (Emphasis added.) See http://www.centerforpubliceducation.org/Main-Menu/Public-education/The-law-and-its-influence-on-public-school-districts-An-overview/Religion-and-Public-Schools.html

2. The commitment of Williams to liberty of conscience for everyone happened to spring from deep religious convictions and a profound sense of obligation. He felt that true soul liberty was possible only when government does not control religion or enforce religious conformity. His colony had to protect the right of every citizen to "follow the dictates of conscience" in matters of faith. It did not have church establishment or religious tests for holding office. There were no religious taxes and there was no requirement to swear the oath "so help me God." (As Williams saw it, compulsion would render any such oath empty of meaning in God's sight.) "Freedom's Forgotten Hero," a video documentary about Roger Williams, is useful background for teachers and students alike. The video is available from the Center for Liberty of Conscience (CLC) at http://www.centerforliberty.org/media/rw-documentary. The CLC website also provides direct teacher or student access to the text of historical documents relevant to the protection of conscience: the U.S. Constitution, the Declaration of Independence, the Bill of Rights, the Memorial and Remonstrance against Religious Assessments, the Virginia Statute of Religious Freedom, and the Treaty of Tripoli. See http://www.centerforliberty.org/hial-documents/introduction/

3. Among further 20th century agreements affirming a right of conscience for all are the "International Covenant on Civil and Political Rights" (1966), the "U.N. Declaration on the Elimination of All Forms of Intolerance" (1981), and the "Vienna Concluding Document" (1989). In such international agreements, signatories agree to ensure the stated provisions, but these documents do not in reality carry force of law. It is up to the nation-states themselves to proceed to give the declared protections legal status. Consequently, we find varied degrees of implementation (and also many abuses of the documents' declared principles). Nevertheless, these agreements have helped shape both law and human rights expectations in many nations. See: http://www.un.org/documents/ga/res/36/a36r055.htm; https://berkleycenter.georgetown.edu/quotes/declaration-on-the-elimination-of-all-forms-of-intolerance-and-of-discrimination-based-on-religion-or-belief-article-1; and http://www.osce.org/mc/40881

4. The Pew Research Center has over the past decade looked closely at United States demographics by religious and nonreligious affiliation. Its more recent reports include "America's Changing Religious Landscape" (2015), available at http://www.pewforum.org/2015/05/12/americas-changing-religious-landscape/, and "If the U.S. had 100 People: Charting Americans' Religious Affiliations" (2016), available at http://www.pewresearch.org/fact-tank/2016/11/14/if-the-u-s-had-100-people-charting-americans-religious-affiliations/

5. A very broad spectrum of identities falls under the category of religiously unaffiliated that has been utilized by Pew Research Center and similar polling or survey agencies querying

Table 2: Some Key Concepts, Skills, and Attitudes

What do students need to know? Here are some examples of knowledge, skills, and attitudes that will help students to understand nonreligious as well as religious beliefs, and to advance civic pluralism.

KNOWLEDGE	OUR STUDENTS WILL RECOGNIZE THAT:
About liberty of conscience	• Liberty of conscience is not only for me and for those who think or believe like me; it is also for my fellow citizens who have different understandings. It is inclusive of all citizens, whether their beliefs are religious or not, supernatural or not, mystical or not. • In the civil law of this nation, everyone has the freedom of conscience, but not freedom of actions. • Liberty of conscience is something that has to be guarded even (perhaps, especially) for those whose thinking and traditions are unconventional or unfamiliar.

KNOWLEDGE	OUR STUDENTS WILL RECOGNIZE THAT:
About religious narratives and traditions	• No religion is monolithic. There is great diversity in the way a religion is expressed across cultures (e.g., Islam in India is not Islam in the United States), and there may be thousands of sects and variants. • Religions have a broad range of adherence and observance. There are devotees who take veneration so seriously that they are known as "fundamentalists," whereas others in the same religion are so casual about it that there may be no observable religious conduct. • Humans have a strong tendency to form "us/them" groupings, and good citizens must avoid the stereotyping of beliefs and typecasting of persons or populations. It is important to avoid simplistic and small-minded thinking that ignores the intricacies of reality and breeds dissension.

demographics. Although "no religious preference" is the broad conceptual umbrella, and surveys sometimes classify people as "atheist" or "agnostic," there are many specific identities that fall in the category of "no religious preference," such as: Nonreligious, Nontheistic, Freethinker, Nonbeliever, Secularist, Atheist, Agnostic, Humanist, Secular Humanist, Ethical Culturist, Bright, Naturalist, Humanistic Jew, and Skeptic. As with religions (Christian, Protestant, Methodist, etc.), these labels are not at all monolithic. There are definitional variants and a great amount of human diversity underneath almost any given label. Pew's somewhat closer examination of available data on the nonreligious are reported in these narrower studies: (1) "Nones on the Rise" (2012), accessible at http://www.pewforum.org/2012/10/09/nones-on-the-rise/; (2) "A Closer Look at America's Rapidly Growing Religious Nones" (2015), accessible at http://www.pewresearch.org/fact-tank/2015/05/13/a-closer-look-at-americas-rapidly-growing-religious-nones/; and (3) "Religious 'Nones' Are Not Only Growing, They're becoming More Secular" (2015), accessible at http://www.pewresearch.org/fact-tank/2015/11/11/religious-nones-are-not-only-growing-theyre-becoming-more-secular/

6. A useful science-based resource on human morality is the online "Morality Portal" at The Brights' Net. In this project, noted morality scientists summarize what is actually known about the origins of human morality. This removes such discussions from the speculative realm. An easy-to-read and sharable infographic with accompanying online explanations in 15 languages is readily accessible online. The bibliography (in English) lists recommended readings and provides a repository of published research studies supporting four scientific statements: (1) Morality is a product of evolution and human experience; (2) Morality is not exclusive to human beings: elements of it can be found in other animal relationships; (3) Because morality is acquired through evolution, it exists in all societies and cultures; (4) Infants exhibit signs of morality even before they have experienced much of the world. See http://the-brights.net/morality/

SKILLS	OUR STUDENTS:
These require practice!	• Are able to approach with skepticism broad generalizations asserted about a grouping ("them"). • Can stand up for an individual's right not to be coerced into conformity (i.e., to view the world differently from the conventional or majority view). • Will disentangle two types of actions: (1) taking notice of another's evident difference (in observable conduct, manners, apparel, etc.) vs. (2) attributing some nonspecific character trait (e.g., depraved, lazy, smarter, primitive, devious, insecure) to what one is noticing. • Consistently make the connection between "human rights" and "religious and nonreligious freedom." • Can state how families with very different beliefs can have common social goals. • Can identify "us versus them" instances and stereotyping.

ATTITUDES	THE STUDENT:
Demeanor	• Appreciates those aspects of our American heritage that safeguard individual freedom of conscience. • Can attribute "laudable actions/contributions" to individuals who have worldviews other than her or his own. • Stands up for others who are not being treated fairly. • Treats others as individuals (does not stereotype other youngsters based on labels or outward features of worldview identity). • Appreciates the fact that in a society that allows freedom of conscience, there is no necessity to "defend one's own tradition" or attack the traditions of others solely on the basis of their being different from one's own.

7. Succinct background information on worldviews specifically targeted to public school teachers exists on a single web page devoted to these topics: "What is a worldview?"; "Developing a worldview"; "Altering a worldview"; and "Perpetuating a worldview." In other pages on the same website, there is brief generic contrasting of religious worldviews with nonreligious worldviews. Exploring the available Worldview Sampler lets the reader view an interesting spectrum of human thinking about significant matters like mortality and afterlife, time, origins, nature and deity. See http://worldvieweducation. org/worldview.html; http://worldvieweducation.org/religiousworldview.html; http://worldvieweducation.org/nonreligiousworldview.html; and http:// worldvieweducation.org/worldviewsampler.html. For a deeper exploration, see also Nel Noddings, *Educating for Intelligent Belief or Unbelief: The John Dewey Lecture* (New York: Teachers College Press, 1993).

8. *Different Drummers: Nonconforming Thinkers in History* (2002), a 400-page loose-leaf instructional module now available only via Amazon.com, focuses on the topic of free and independent thought in historical context at middle school level. The Concept Lessons, Story Lessons, Activity Lessons, and Timeline of Independent Thought in History give attention to the nonconforming thoughts and actions of such notables as Thomas Paine, Socrates, Mary Wollstonecraft, Voltaire, Thomas Jefferson, Charles Darwin, Frederick Douglass, Galileo, Ernestine Rose, Mark Twain, and Frances Wright. The Buddha is presented as a nonconforming Hindu, Martin Luther as a nonconforming Catholic.

9. Related materials by the author of this chapter, written specifically for educators, are available for perusing online. They include the website, "Teaching about Religion: Focus on Freethought" (2002) at http://www.teachingaboutfreethought. org, and brief articles for the California 3Rs Project: "The Secular Side of the Coin" (2008) at http://ca3rsproject.org/ bulletins/Bulletin5-08Secularism.pdf, and "Broaching Borderlands beyond Religion, Parts 1 and 2" (2015) at http://ca3rsproject. org/bulletins/3RsBulletinJan2015.pdf and http://ca3rsproject.org/ bulletins/3RsBulletinApril2015.pdf. A focused exploration of freethought in the American context is to be found in the works of Susan Jacoby, in particular *Freethinkers: A History of American Secularism* (New York: Holt, 2005).

CHAPTER TWENTY

Teaching about Religion in the Elementary Classroom

KIMBERLY KEISERMAN

If you follow the news concerning religion and public schools, you will inevitably encounter headlines like these:

"School Prayer Debate Resumes in Federal Court"[1]

"North Carolina Elementary Schools Under Fire for Bible Classes: Unconstitutional?"[2]

"Religious Symbols in Classroom Stir Dispute in Peoria Schools"[3]

"New Textbooks Prompt Debate over Religion in Public Schools"[4]

"Schoolwork about Islam Triggers Backlash in Virginia County"[5]

Words like "dispute," "challenge," "debate," and "backlash" come up again and again. It seems that religion in public schools has become part of our nation's culture wars—and understandably, this has made many teachers reluctant to address religion as part of the curriculum. They may worry about inviting controversy and complaint, perhaps by misrepresenting a tradition, offending a student or parent, or even revealing their own religious beliefs. More than anything, they may be fearful of violating the separation of church and state.

At the Tanenbaum Center for Interreligious Understanding, we believe that it's crucial that educators overcome this reluctance. Not only is it constitutionally permissible to teach about religion from an academic perspective, but educators have a responsibility to do so, beginning at the elementary school level. This chapter will discuss:

■ Why it's important to teach about religion and religious diversity;

■ Guidelines for addressing religion and religious diversity in legal, inclusive, respectful, and age-appropriate ways;

■ and a Practical Strategy for teaching about religion and religious diversity at the elementary school level.

WHY IT'S IMPORTANT TO TEACH ABOUT RELIGION AND RELIGIOUS DIVERSITY

1. Our student body is diverse and will continue to become more diverse. In 1970, less than five percent of the United States population was foreign-born, and the vast majority of immigrants were Christian Europeans whose cultural and religious practices were familiar to native-born Americans.[6] By 2010, nearly 13 percent of the population was foreign-born, and the proportion from Latin America and Asia had greatly surpassed the proportion from Europe.[7] This means that today's public school students are the most diverse in our nation's history[8]—and their myriad religious beliefs, practices, and traditions are an important part of that diversity. Our children are growing up in an increasingly complex, multicultural, interconnected world, and this is the world in which we must prepare them to live and work. They must understand religion if they are to understand each other, now and in the future.

2. Religion plays a crucial role in current events. As children grow older, it is normal and desirable for them to become more aware of world events. In the post-9/11 age, it is impossible to shield them from information about the acts of violence, terrorism, and war that take place all over the world, often in the name of religion, or extremist religious ideologies. For many children—and adults for that matter—news and entertainment media are primary sources of information about less familiar religions, particularly Islam. If students don't learn about religion in school, they will have little context for understanding the violent, sensationalistic events covered by the media, and little capacity to differentiate between the mainstream followers of a religion and its extremists. The result can be a distorted view of a particular religion, contempt for the followers or perceived followers of that religion, or even antagonism against religion as a whole.

3. *Religion can be a key factor in prejudice, hate crimes, and bullying.* According to the U.S. Department of Justice's 2014 Hate Crimes Victimization report, the percentage of hate crimes motivated by religious bias was nearly three times higher in 2012 (28%) than in 2004 (10%).[9] More recently, the FBI's annual Hate Crimes Statistics report for 2015 found a six percent increase in the total number of hate crimes over 2014, with anti-Muslim attacks driving this surge. The 257 hate crimes recorded against Muslims in 2015 represent a 67 percent increase over the previous year, and are the highest number recorded since 2001, when attacks spiked in the aftermath of 9/11.[10] FBI reporting also reveals that a disturbing percentage of hate crime offenders are students in our nation's schools. Fifteen percent were under the age of 18 in 2015,[11] 19 percent in 2014,[12] and fully 32 percent in 2013.[13]

Although there are no comprehensive statistics on religious harassment in schools, there is increasing evidence that it is a serious and growing problem. There have been a number of high-profile cases of anti-Semitic bullying in recent years,[14] and Muslim, Sikh, and Hindu groups have documented a marked increase in acts of religious bullying since 9/11.[15] Reports of religious bullying surged once again in the wake of the terrorist attacks in Paris and San Bernardino,[16] and still more after the divisive 2016 presidential election.[17] In July 2016 the U.S. Department of Education announced a series of initiatives to gather data on religious harassment in schools and provide resources to combat the problem.[18]

These upward trends in hate crimes and bullying illustrate the cost of not teaching students about religion and religious diversity. Ignorance breeds bias and hate. Young people who understand different religious beliefs and traditions will be more likely to respect people of different religious backgrounds, in school and out.

All of these factors underscore the growing importance of religious literacy. If students are to function as globally competent citizens, they need to be religiously literate. The American Academy of Religion defines religious literacy as a basic understanding of the central texts, beliefs, and practices of the world's major religions; the role religion plays in history, politics, society and culture; and the great diversity that exists within religious traditions across time and place.[19] The importance of religious literacy is reflected by national and state standards, including those of the National Council for the Social Studies.

As with other forms of literacy, the development of religious literacy should begin during the early years of education. Elementary school students notice differences between themselves and others, and are interested in understanding them. Too often, however, students are not taught about different religious traditions until middle or high school, and by then they may already have developed the misconceptions and stereotypes that can lead to prejudice and bullying. Elementary school students may not be ready to delve into Buddhist history, Hindu texts, or religious aspects of the Arab-Israeli conflict, but they are ready to begin exploring their own identity and the identities of others in their learning community. Such elementary lessons about religious differences can cultivate attitudes of curiosity and respect—providing a foundation for engaging in more complex learning at the secondary level.

GUIDELINES FOR ADDRESSING RELIGION AND RELIGIOUS DIVERSITY

1. Teach from an academic perspective. In a series of landmark cases beginning in the early 1960s, the Supreme Court found state-sponsored school prayers and Bible readings to be unconstitutional. But the Court never found teaching about religion to be unconstitutional. Lessons about religion are perfectly legal as long as they are neutral, objective, and non-devotional. The key is neither to promote nor to denigrate religion, non-religion, or any particular religious practice.[20] Neutrality and objectivity may not always be easy to achieve and may be more difficult for some than others. The American Academy of Religion suggests that teachers "examine what assumptions they harbor about religion generally and religious traditions in particular."[21] Teachers who are aware of their own biases will be better able to overcome them and present facts and ideas in an objective manner.

2. Create a safe, respectful, inclusive classroom environment. When discussing any sensitive topic in the classroom, it's important that teachers are able to rely on a set of well-established ground rules for respectful communication so that all students feel comfortable participating. You can begin by asking students what respect looks like, sounds like, and feels like in order to help them translate an abstract concept into concrete and observable behaviors. Then allow students to come up with a list of rules that make them feel safe, respected, and included. Examples might include:

- Listen when others speak.

- Only one person speaks at a time.

- Speak for yourself, and let others speak for themselves.

- Speak to others as you would like to be spoken to; no name-calling.

- Try to learn from your classmates.

Make sure there is agreement to the ground rules before proceeding with sensitive discussions. Periodically remind students of the rules, referring back to them when confronted with disrespectful behavior. (Go to https://tanenbaum.org/wp-content/uploads/2015/10/IRU-Respecting-Each-Other.pdf to download "Respecting Each Other," a K-12 lesson plan that enables students to explore what respect looks like, sounds like, and feels like, and then generate a set of ground rules for their own classroom.)

3. Allow students to explore their own identities. Children will be better prepared to learn about and understand the identities of others if they learn about and express their own identities. To put it in elementary school terms, "The better I understand myself, the better I can understand you." For many students, religion is an important, even central, dimension of their personal or family identity. For others, religion is of little or no importance. For an increasing number, the role of religion is complicated. Their parents may come from different faiths, or they may be among the growing number of Americans who choose not to affiliate with any religion at all but may nonetheless hold religious beliefs and engage in spiritual practices.[22] Lessons that allow students to explore and share various aspects of their identities—including their complex and varying religious identities—will help them become cognizant of, and interested in, the similarities and differences that exist in their classroom and community. They will begin to recognize that difference is normal. This provides a foundation for the development of curiosity and respect.[23] (Go to https://tanenbaum.org/wp-content/uploads/2015/10/My-Traditions-3.4.2015-new-branding.pdf to download "My Traditions," an elementary level lesson plan that allows students to explore and share religious or secular traditions that are central to their identities.)

4. Capture the "diversity within diversity." It is important not only to address religion in the classroom, but to do so in a rich, multi-faceted way. Too often students study only the early development of the major world religions, not the way they have changed and adapted to contemporary life. In this approach the complex evolution of a religion gets reduced to its pre-modern history, and its diverse ideas and practices are boiled down to simple lists like "The Five Pillars of Islam" and "The Four

The Golden Rule in Religious Traditions All Over the World

Baha'i	"And if thine eyes be turned towards justice, choose thou for thy neighbor that which thou choosest for thyself." *Lawh'l 'Ibn'i Dhib, "Epistle to the Son of the Wolf" 30*
Buddhism	"Hurt not others in ways you yourself would find hurtful." *Udana-Varga, 5:18*
Christianity	"In everything do to others as you would have them do to you; for this is the law and the prophets." *Matthew 7:12*
Confucianism	"Do not unto others what you do not want them to do to you." *Analects 15:13*
Hinduism	"This is the sum of duty: do naught unto others which would cause you pain if done to you." *The Mahabharata, 5:1517*
Islam	"Not one of you is a believer until he loves for his brother what he loves for himself." *Fortieth Hadith of an-Nawawi, 13*
Jainism	"A man should wander about treating all creatures as he himself would be treated." *Surtrakritanga, 1:11:33*
Judaism	"What is hateful to you, do not do to your neighbor: that is the whole of the Torah; all the rest of it is commentary." *Talmud, Shabbat, 31a*
Native American	"Respect for all life is the foundation." *The Great Law of Peace*
Sikhism	"Don't create enmity with anyone as God is within everyone." *Guru Granth Sahib, page 259*
Taoism	"Regard your neighbor's gain as your own gain and your neighbor's loss as your own loss." *T'ai Shang Kan Ying P'ien*
Zoroastrianism	"That nature alone is good which refrains from doing unto another whatsoever is not good for itself." *Dadistan-I-Dinik, 94:5*

To download a poster of the Golden Rule from these twelve religious traditions, go to https://tanenbaum.org/wp-content/uploads/2014/02/The-Golden-Rule.pdf. At https://tanenbaum.org/wp-content/uploads/2015/04/RIMN-Exploring-Beliefs-about-Caring-and-Sharing.pdf you can download "Exploring Beliefs about Caring and Sharing," an elementary level lesson on the Golden Rule.

Noble Truths" of Buddhism. Not only is this approach inappropriate for younger students; it is often dry and dull for older students. Worse, it can foster a distorted impression of less familiar religions as primitive, foreign, and monolithic. To capture the diversity within religious diversity, it's important to expose students to the "lived religion" of real people by allowing them to read primary sources and personal stories, interact with guest speakers, interview members of their community, and take field trips to houses of worship. This approach will not only promote a deeper understanding of different religious traditions; it will also be more engaging, student-centered, and appropriate for elementary students.

5. *Explore the commonalities among belief systems.* Diverse belief systems often share similar ideas and practices. One example is the Golden Rule (see page 178), which can be found in religious traditions, and non-religious philosophies, all over the world. This simple principle is a great vehicle for discussing how common understandings can unite people with very different belief systems, because it is easily understood and discussed by elementary-aged students.

6. *When possible, incorporate teaching about religion into existing curricula.* Discussions of religion and religious diversity can be integrated into many areas of the elementary curriculum without requiring a great deal of additional time or resources. For example, a typical elementary lesson in which students use boxes and art supplies to create a model of a community can become a lesson in which they research different religions and create a model of an interreligious community. A lesson about the lunar cycle can become an opportunity to discuss religious festivals that have been influenced by lunar calendars. Lessons about religion will tend to have more depth and multidimensionality if they are integrated throughout the curricula, rather than being relegated to stand-alone activities related to

seasonal holidays or events. (Go to https://tanenbaum.org/wp-content/uploads/2016/01/RIMN-Exploring-Beliefs-about-Religious-Differences.pdf to download "Exploring Beliefs about Religious Differences," an elementary level lesson on creating an interreligious community. Go to https://tanenbaum.org/wp-content/uploads/2015/10/IRU-Lunar-Cycle.pdf to download an elementary level lesson on the Lunar Cycle.)

7. *Communicate with parents.* Given the controversy surrounding religion in public schools, it is advisable to communicate with parents about any plans to include religion and religious diversity in your curricula. Explain that their children will be provided with facts and information about different religions so that they can learn about religious differences, and that they are not being indoctrinated in a different religion. Emphasize that it is your responsibility to teach about religion from a neutral, objective, non-devotional perspective, and that you take that responsibility seriously. Be prepared to answer questions and allay concerns. If parents still object to their children learning about different religions, they have a legal right to excuse them from the lessons.

In communicating with parents, you may find that some family members are willing to speak to the class about their religious traditions and celebrations, and they may be able to share valuable primary resources such as photos, videos and letters. This kind of family participation can make the lesson more interesting, memorable and real for the students. Be sure that all family sharing is handled in a non-devotional manner and that all family members are asked to speak from their own experiences, not act as spokespersons for a whole religious group.

The Seven Principles for Inclusive Education

Tanenbaum's pedagogy, *The Seven Principles for Inclusive Education*, offers a strategic framework for integrating the topics of religion and religious diversity into classroom content in a way that emphasizes examining diverse identities, engaging in respectful conversations, and exploring a wide variety of primary sources. The principles are:

1. Teaching all Students	Educators should take several different approaches to teaching the same material so that information becomes more interesting and tangible to a greater number of students.
2. Exploring Multiple Identities	Students who are proud of themselves and excited by the world around them will be more compassionate and understanding people; the same is true for educators.
3. Preventing Prejudice	Educators should take a proactive approach to debunking preconceived stereotypes and preventing them from escalating into prejudices and negative biases.
4. Promoting Social Justice	Students are good judges of what is fair, especially when they are affirmatively challenged to consider issues of social justice. Educators should talk to them about issues of social justice and injustice in terms of fair versus unfair and respectful versus disrespectful.
5. Choosing Appropriate Materials	Inclusive classrooms use books and materials that reflect accurate images of diverse peoples and challenge stereotypes.
6. Teaching and Learning about Cultures and Religions	Educators should create curiosity and expand students' horizons by teaching about others in a positive manner. Students should have the opportunity to learn from their peers as well as other cultures.
7. Adapting and Integrating Lessons Appropriately	Educators should be flexible when using and adapting lessons. Many of the most teachable moments are unplanned and unscripted.

A comprehensive explanation of the pedagogy can be found at https://tanenbaum.org/programs/education/tanenbaums-pedagogy/

"A Garden of Questions and Answers about Beliefs"

A Practical Strategy for Teaching about Religion and Religious Diversity at the Elementary School Level

Based on *The Seven Principles for Inclusive Education*, this unit provides a conceptual framework for teaching about many different religious and non-religious beliefs and practices. It is adapted from "Big Questions with Many Answers," the second chapter of Tanenbaum's *Religions in My Neighborhood* (2012), a Common Core-aligned curriculum that is geared to grades K-4 but adaptable for older students. The citations for the books used are in the sidebar, "Books for Teaching about Religion in the Elementary Classroom," on page 183.

SETTING THE LESSON

Welcome your students into "a garden of questions and answers about beliefs." Ask them what they already know about gardens. Have they ever helped plant a garden or harvest a garden? What are some of the many purposes of gardens?

DAY 1

1. Introduce the unit by reading aloud *Grandma's Garden* by Mercer Mayer. Lead a discussion about the wide variety of plants that can grow in harmony and share the nutrients in Grandma's garden.

2. Facilitate an art activity in which your class creates a Community Garden Mural on long craft paper. Have them paint the sky and trees. Have each student use markers, crayons, paint, and construction paper to make at least one vegetable, plant, flower, or fruit. Ask each student to describe his or her plant to the class and then attach it to the mural.

3. Lead a discussion about the diversity of the garden. While all the plants share the same soil, sun, and water, each adds different colors, shapes, smells, and sizes to the garden.

DAY 2

1. Read aloud *The Three Questions* by John J. Muth (2002). In this book Nikolai asks three big questions, "When is the best time to do things? Who is the most important one? What is the right thing to do?" The book suggests some thought-provoking, humanistic answers, but the answers aren't the point. It is the questions

that are important; they provide a good starting point to get students thinking about their own big questions. This, in turn, provides a good starting point for discussing different religious and nonreligious beliefs and how they represent different answers to the big questions that many people share.

2. Point out that we all have big questions; we all wonder about things. You may wish to lead students in brainstorming their own big questions. They might come up with queries like, "How did life begin?" "Why are we here?" "How can I be a good person?" and "Why do bad things happen?" Emphasize that the class will not be answering the big questions. The purpose of the discussion is not to find answers but to demonstrate how the shared experience of wondering has given rise to many different beliefs.

DAY 3

1. Revisit the big questions from the previous day. Give each student a cartoon "word bubble" and invite them to write one of the big questions on it (or dictate it to an adult).

2. Next, turn students' attention to the Community Garden Mural. Use the metaphor of the garden to illustrate the big questions and the multitude of ways people have answered them through religion, philosophy, and science. In this garden, the seeds are the big questions; the environment consists of the factors that influence people's answers to the big questions; and the plants and flowers are the answers to the big questions. A garden grows from many seeds into many species

of plants and uses many different nutrients from the soil. This powerful metaphor allows students to picture a wide range of perspectives living in a great garden of human experience.

3. Ask the students to add their big question "word bubbles" as seeds beneath the surface of the garden. Lead the class in a discussion about the garden, highlighting factors that help the plants grow like the sun, water, and atmosphere. Guide the students in thinking about the many factors that help people answer questions. Point out that there may be some questions that are answered by religion, some by philosophy, some by science, some by a combination of the three, and some that go unanswered.

DAY 4

1. Read aloud *Faith* by Maya Ajmera, Magda Nakassis, and Cynthia Pon (2009). The book uses spare text and photographs to explore religious beliefs and practices throughout the world.

2. Lead a discussion of the book, using the Community Garden Mural. Discuss how the faiths represented are like plants in the garden. Have the students add flower and leaf shapes representing the faiths in the book.

DAYS 5 – 6

1. Read aloud *What is God?* by Etan Boritzer (1990), which provides a comparative introduction to Christianity, Islam, Judaism, Hinduism, and Buddhism as well as their holy books.

2. Lead a discussion of the many ways that different religions talk about the concept of a god or gods. Throughout the discussion, use chart paper to write down new vocabulary words related to religions and beliefs.

3. Revisit the garden mural and ask students to add the words to it. They can add leaf shapes and flowers representing different beliefs and belief systems, and raindrop shapes representing the people, holy books, and broad movements that have influenced people's beliefs.

DAY 7 AND BEYOND

1. This unit can be continued over a period of days, or even weeks, by exploring the different ways that people have answered their big questions. This can be done by reading a variety of storybooks representing a wide range of beliefs. You can find a list of suggested books in the sidebar on page 183.

2. As you read each book, discuss the beliefs represented in the story, introducing and reinforcing the vocabulary for describing and understanding beliefs. Revisit your garden mural and ask students how each story provides an answer to one or more of the big questions and represents a plant or flower in the garden. Children can continue to add leaf shapes and flowers representing different beliefs and belief systems (for example, monotheism, polytheism, atheism, humanism, Christianity, Buddhism, and so on). They can continue to add raindrop shapes representing the people, holy books, and broad movements that have influenced people's beliefs.

3. Conclude this unit with a discussion about how learning about different beliefs enriches our understanding of one another. Remind students that when we learn about other's beliefs, we are not learning that they are right or wrong, we are learning to understand and respect each other's perspectives.

The purpose of this unit is to explore the big questions rather than to arrive at "correct" answers to the big questions. Children will learn that people have asked many big questions and come up with a wide range of answers. They will see themselves and their beliefs affirmed in their classroom and depicted in the Community Garden Mural. Ultimately, this can help them develop a sense of empathy for others, responsibility for sharing and dialogue, and respectful curiosity about differences.

To download the original, unabridged version of this unit, go to https://tanenbaum.org/wp-content/uploads/2015/05/RIMN-A-Garden-of-Questions-and-Answers-about-Beliefs.pdf. For more information about the whole Religions in My Neighborhood curriculum, visit https://tanenbaum.org/programs/education/curricula_for_educators/. The curriculum is full of suggested resources and ideas for extension and assessment.

Books for Teaching About Religion in the Elementary Classroom

Books needed to teach the lesson in this chapter *All are appropriate for grades Kindergarten and up.*	Maya Ajmera, Magda Nakassis, and Cynthia Pon. *Faith.* Watertown, MA: Charlesbridge, 2009. Mercer Mayer. *Grandma's Garden.* New York: McGraw Hill, 2002. John J. Muth. *The Three Questions.* New York: Scholastic, 2002.
Other fiction and non-fiction books that enable elementary school students to explore a wide range of beliefs and perspectives *Grades Kindergarten and Up*	David A. Anderson. *The Origin of Life on Earth: An African Creation Myth.* Mount Airy, MD: Sights Production, 1991. Etan Boritzer. *What is God?* Ontario, Canada: Firefly Books, 1990. Hena Khan. *Night of the Moon: A Muslim Holiday Story.* San Francisco: Chronicle Books, 2008. Rafe Martin. *One Hand Clapping: Zen Stories for All Ages.* New York: Rizzoli Publications, 1995. Gerald McDermott. *Anansi the Spider: A Tale from the Ashanti.* New York: Henry Holt, 1972. Sheri Safran and Emma Damon. *All Kinds of Beliefs.* London, U.K.: Tango Books, 2000. Chief Seattle and Susan Jeffers. *Brother Eagle, Sister Sky.* New York: Dial Books, 1991. Rosemarie Somaiah and Ranjan Somaiah. *Indian Children's Favorite Stories.* North Clarendon, VT: Tuttle Publishing, 2006.
Grades 3 and Up	Helen Bennett. *Humanism, What's That?: A Book for Curious Kids.* Amherst, NY: Prometheus, 2005. Laura Buller. *A Faith Like Mine.* New York: DK Publishing, 2005. Sarah Conover. *Kindness: A Treasury of Buddhist Wisdom for Children and Parents.* Spokane, WA: Eastern Washington University Press, 2001. Carolyn Cinami DeCristofano. *Big Bang: The Tongue-Tickling Tale of a Speck that Became Spectacular.* Watertown, MA: Charlesbridge, 2005. Jennifer Glossop. *The Kids Book of World Religions.* Tonawanda, NY: Kids Can Press, 2003. Virginia Hamilton. *In the Beginning: Creation Stories from Around the World.* Orlando, FL: Harcourt, 1991. Anabel Kindersley and Barnabas Kindersley. *Children Just Like Me: Celebrations!* New York: DK Publishing, 1997. Mary Pope Osborne. *One World, Many Religions: The Ways We Worship.* New York: Knopf, 1996. Sanjay Patel. *The Little Book of Hindu Deities: From the Goddess of Wealth to the Sacred Cow.* New York: Penguin, 2006.

For more reading ideas, go to Tanenbaum's Recommended Reading for Preschool and Elementary Students at https://tanenbaum.org/wp-content/uploads/2016/01/Recommended-Reading-for-Preschool-and-Elementary-Students.pdf and Tanenbaum's K-6 Elementary Reading Lists at https://tanenbaum.org/programs/education/education-resources/k-6-elementary-reading-lists/#holidays.

NOTES

1. David Dykes, "School Prayer Debate Resumes in Federal Court," *Greenville Online*, November 15, 2014. Retrieved from http://www.greenvilleonline.com/story/news/local/2014/11/15/school-prayer-debate-resumes-federal-court/19121485/

2. "North Carolina Elementary Schools Under Fire for Bible Classes: Unconstitutional?" *Inquistr*, October 5, 2014. Retrieved from http://www.inquisitr.com/1521458/north-carolina-elementary-schools-under-fire-for-bible-classes-unconstitutional/

3. Mary Beth Faller, "Religious Symbols in Classroom Stir Dispute in Peoria Schools," *Arizona Republic*, October 6, 2014. Retrieved from http://www.azcentral.com/story/news/local/peoria/2014/10/03/religious-symbols-classroom-stir-dispute-peoria-schools/16691101/

4. Lauren McGaughy, "New Textbooks Prompt Debate over Religion in Public Schools," *Houston Chronicle*, September 17, 2014. Retrieved from http://www.houstonchronicle.com/news/politics/texas/article/New-textbooks-prompt-debate-over-religion-in-5760337.php

5. Moriah Balingit and Emma Brown, "Schoolwork about Islam Triggers Backlash in Virginia County," *Washington Post*, December 18, 2015. Retrieved from https://www.washingtonpost.com/news/education/wp/2015/12/17/furor-over-arabic-assignment-leads-virginia-school-district-to-close-friday/?utm_term=.2ba8861309a9

6. U.S. Census Bureau, *Historical Census Statistics on the Foreign-Born Population of the United States: 1850-1990* (Population Division Working Paper No. 29, 1999). Retrieved from https://www.census.gov/population/www/documentation/twps0029/twps0029.html

7. U.S. Census Bureau, *The Foreign-Born Population in the United States* (2010). Retrieved from http://www.census.gov/newsroom/pdf/cspan_fb_slides.pdf

8. National Center for Education Statistics. *Fast Facts* (2014). Retrieved from http://nces.ed.gov/fastfacts/display.asp?id=372

9. U.S. Department of Justice, *Hate Crime Victimization, 2004-2012 – Statistical Tables*. (NCJ 244409). Published in 2014. Retrieved from http://www.bjs.gov/content/pub/pdf/hcv0412st.pdf

10. Eric Lichtblau, "U.S. Hate Crimes Surge 6%, Fueled by Attacks on Muslims," *The New York Times*, November 14, 2016. Retrieved from https://www.nytimes.com/2016/11/15/us/politics/fbi-hate-crimes-muslims.html

11. Federal Bureau of Investigation, *Uniform Crime Reporting, 2015 Hate Crimes Statistics*. Published in 2015. Retrieved from https://ucr.fbi.gov/hate-crime/2015/topic-pages/offenders_final

12. Federal Bureau of Investigation, *Uniform Crime Reporting, 2014 Hate Crimes Statistics*. Published in 2014. Retrieved from https://ucr.fbi.gov/hate-crime/2014/topic-pages/offenders_final

13. Federal Bureau of Investigation, *Uniform Crime Reporting, 2013 Hate Crimes Statistics*. Published in 2013. Retrieved from https://ucr.fbi.gov/hate-crime/2013/topic-pages/offenders/offenders_final

14. See for example, Joseph Berger, "Settlement Over Anti-Semitic Bullying at Pine Bush Central Schools Is Approved," *The New York Times*, July 9, 2015. Retrieved from https://www.nytimes.com/2015/07/10/nyregion/settlement-over-anti-semitic-bullying-at-pine-bush-central-schools-is-approved.html. Other resources are: Noreen Ahmed-Ullah and Ron Grossman, "Chicago School Responds to Anti-Semitic Bullying," *Chicago Tribune*, June 4, 2014. Retrieved from http://www.chicagotribune.com/news/chi-chicago-school-bullying-20140603-story.html. Emily Sweeney, "Parent Suit Cites Attacks on Son," *Boston Globe* August 11, 2013. Retrieved from http://www.bostonglobe.com/metro/regionals/south/2013/08/10/parents-say-son-was-target-anti-semitic-attacks-carver-middle-high-school/vFIOVCjNHBMIPrLXjiuVJN/story.html

15. See, for example, Council on American-Islamic Relations, *Mislabeled: The Impact of School Bullying and Discrimination on California Muslim Students* (2015). Retrieved from https://ca.cair.com/sfba/wp-content/uploads/2015/10/CAIR-CA-2015-Bullying-Report-Web.pdf; Sikh Coalition. *Go Home, Terrorist: A Report on Bullying Against Sikh American Children* (2014). Retrieved from http://sikhcoalition.org/documents/pdf/go-home-terrorist.pdf; Hindu American Foundation, *Classroom Subjected: Bullying and Bias against Hindu Students in American Schools* (2016). Retrieved from https://www.hafsite.org/sites/default/files/HAFN_16_008-BullyingReport_final_RGB_r2.pdf

16. See, for example, Kirk Semple, "Young Muslim Americans Are Feeling the Strain of Suspicion," *The New York Times*, December 14, 2015. Retrieved from https://www.nytimes.com/2015/12/15/nyregion/young-muslim-americans-are-feeling-the-strain-of-suspicion.html; Kristina Rizga, "This Is What It's Like to Be a Muslim Schoolkid in America Right Now," *Mother Jones*, December 9, 2015. Retrieved from http://www.motherjones.com/politics/2015/12/muslim-kids-bullying-schools-teachers-islamophobia

17. Southern Poverty Law Center. *The Trump Effect: The Impact of the 2016 Election on Our Nation's Schools* (2016). Retrieved from https://www.splcenter.org/20161128/trump-effect-impact-2016-presidential-election-our-nations-schools

18. U.S. Department of Education, "U.S. Department of Education Takes Actions to Address Religious Discrimination" (Press Release, 2016). Retrieved from https://www.ed.gov/news/press-releases/us-department-education-takes-actions-address-religious-discrimination

19. The AAR Religion in the Schools Task Force, *Guidelines for Teaching About Religion in K-12 Public Schools in the United States* (2010). Retrieved from https://www.aarweb.org/sites/default/files/pdfs/Publications/epublications/AARK-12CurriculumGuidelines.pdf See Appendix 2 of this book for these guidelines.

20. The First Amendment Center, *A Teacher's Guide to Religion in the Public Schools* (2008). Retrieved from http://www.religiousfreedomcenter.org/wp-content/uploads/2014/08/teachersguide.pdf See Appendix 1 of this book for this Teacher's Guide.

21. The AAR Religion in the Schools Task Force, *Guidelines for Teaching About Religion in K-12 Public Schools in the United States* (2010), p.11. Retrieved from https://www.aarweb.org/sites/default/files/pdfs/Publications/epublications/AARK-12CurriculumGuidelines.pdf See Appendix 2 of this book for these guidelines.

22. Michael Lipka, "A Closer Look at America's Rapidly Growing Religious Nones," Pew Research Center. Retrieved from http://www.pewresearch.org/fact-tank/2015/05/13/a-closer-look-at-americas-rapidly-growing-religious-nones/

23. It should be noted here that it is perfectly legal for students to discuss their religious identities and beliefs. The Establishment Clause of the First Amendment limits a teacher's ability to discuss these matters, but it places no such limits on students' religious expression.

CHAPTER TWENTY ONE

Resources for Teaching about Religions in Public Schools

MARCIA BEAUCHAMP

This book includes insights from researchers, theorists, and practitioners in the field of teaching about religions in K-12 public schools. The following annotated list includes additional guidelines, opportunities for professional development for educators, and classroom resources for teaching about religions in ways that are constitutionally and educationally sound.

GUIDELINES AND INITIATIVES

Religious Freedom Center of the Freedom Forum

At the online home of the Religious Freedom Center of the Freedom Forum, teachers can find studies on the presence of religion in content standards for schools, model programs for teaching about religion, and guidelines on teaching about the Bible within a First Amendment framework, as well as professional development modules that are self-paced, interactive, and focused on the practical application of religious studies in the classroom.

▶ http://www.religiousfreedomcenter.org/programs/educators/professional-development/

Finding Common Ground: A First Amendment Guide to Religion and Public Schools by Charles C. Haynes and Oliver Thomas is a one-stop shop for advice and guidelines on legal issues and principles as well as practices regarding religion in the public school. Whether your question concerns developing a school district policy on religious holidays or the best approach to religion in school assignments, there is guidance in this volume. All of the guidelines are endorsed by a broad coalition of educational, religious, and civil liberties organizations and may be downloaded at:

▶ http://www.religiousfreedomcenter.org/wp-content/uploads/2014/08/rfc_publications_findingcommonground.pdf

The Georgia 3Rs Project

The Georgia 3Rs Project (which is described in Chapter 6 of this book) was launched by the Religious Freedom Center of the Freedom Forum in June 2016. This three-year initiative is designed to create demonstration models of religious literacy and religious liberty in three Georgia public school districts. The Georgia 3Rs Project will be guided by the national consensus guidelines on the role of religion in public schools collected in Finding Common Ground: A First Amendment Guide to Religion and Public Schools, mentioned above. The initiative will include graduate level courses for educators in three Georgia school districts as well as new educational resources that will sustain a commitment to religious literacy and religious liberty in the demonstration model school districts and in school districts across the state and nation.

▶ http://ga3rs.org/

American Academy of Religion (AAR) Guidelines for Teaching About Religion in K-12 Public Schools in the United States

These guidelines, published by the AAR in 2010, support a "constitutionally sound approach for teaching about religion in public schools" as a means to address religious illiteracy that can incite prejudice and intolerance. The guidelines were developed by the AAR's Religion in Schools Task Force under the leadership of Diane Moore, and are reproduced in Appendix 2 of this book.

Included in the guidelines are arguments for teaching about religion in schools, a discussion of Constitutional issues in the field, suggestions for pedagogical approaches to teaching about religion in K-12 education, and proposed directions in teacher education that develop the core competencies required to teach deeply and responsibly about religion. Of special note are the section on Frequently Asked Questions in the main document, which shares several examples applying an academic approach to questions about religions in the classroom, and the recommendations on teaching about religion through film, music, and creative arts in an Appendix of the guidelines.

▶ https://www.aarweb.org/sites/default/files/pdfs/Publications/epublications/AARK-12CurriculumGuidelines.pdf

The California Rights, Responsibility and Respect Project

The California 3Rs Project (CA 3R's) is a program for finding common ground on issues related to religious liberty and the First Amendment in public schools. The CA 3Rs' approach is based on the principles of American democracy and citizenship, reflected in the First Amendment of the Bill of Rights and applied in a public school setting.

For over a decade, the CA3Rs has provided online resources, professional development, and leadership training for teachers and education professionals in order to disseminate essential information about religious liberty and the history of religion in America.

▶ http://ca3rsproject.org

Religion and Public Education Project

Directed by Dr. Bruce Grelle, the Religion and Public Education Project (RPEP) at California State University, Chico, provides general information about the ethical, legal, and educational issues that arise in connection with the topic of religion and public education. RPEP consults with classroom teachers, school administrators, school board members, textbook publishers, academic researchers, journalists, members of the legal profession, and members of the general public in efforts to understand and support public education about religion in ways that are constitutionally permissible and academically sound. RPEP serves as a clearinghouse for resources on a wide range of issues arising in connection with the topic of religion and public education.

▶ https://www.csuchico.edu/rpep/

Religion & Education

Religion & Education is a journal of analysis and comment whose purpose is to advance public understanding and dialogue on issues at the intersections of religion and education. These issues emerge in various venues; manuscripts are invited from work in any such arena: public or private education at elementary, secondary, or higher education institutions; non-school or community organizations and settings; and formal or informal organizations or groups with religion or spirituality as an integral part of their work. Articles are invited from diverse methodological approaches and theoretical and ideological perspectives. Some articles are solicited, but unsolicited articles are encouraged. Unsolicited manuscripts are put through a peer review process. Michael D. Waggoner of the University of Northern Iowa edits *Religion & Education.*

▶ https://www.tandfonline.com/loi/urel20

CURRICULUM RESOURCES

Generation Global

Generation Global, a secondary schools program of the Tony Blair Faith Foundation endorsed by NCSS, has developed teaching modules on dialogue skills (Essentials of Dialogue) and on global issues considered from a variety of perspectives. (The program is described in Chapter 10 of this book.) Students learn and practice the skills of dialogue in the classroom before engaging in dialogue with their global peers through videoconferences or online blogging. Fully facilitated videoconferences immerse students in connections with classrooms across the world, allowing students to explore, articulate, develop and challenge their own views, while encountering and considering the views of others. The program includes a safe, secure, and monitored online community which allows students to develop their digital literacy and dialogue skills through written communication with their global peers. Each module is composed of a set of flexible lessons, which can be incorporated into existing courses and curricula. The modules are designed to suit a wide range of different educational systems and cultures. The program is offered free of charge to schools.

▶ http://generation.global/

Harvard Divinity School Religious Literacy Project

The Religious Literacy Project at Harvard Divinity School (HDS) is dedicated to enhancing and promoting the public understanding of religion. It provides resources and special training opportunities for educators, journalists, public health workers, foreign service officers, interfaith/multifaith groups, students, and others wishing to better understand the complex roles that religions play in contemporary global, national, and local contexts. In 2011, Diane L. Moore proposed the creation of the Religious Literacy Project as a way to sustain Harvard Divinity School's legacy of enhancing the public understanding of religion through education. HDS is uniquely situated to enhance the public understanding of religion because of its longstanding expertise in all of the world's religious traditions coupled with its history of more than forty years of focusing on education

about religion through various iterations of its teacher education program. The Religious Literacy Project is a new initiative that builds upon both of these legacies and focuses on how to understand the roles that religions play in human experience across political, economic, and cultural spheres with a special focus on contemporary issues related to conflict and peace.

This site offers teaching resources, including overviews of Buddhism, Christianity, Hinduism, Humanism, Islam, and Judaism. In these religion profiles, the focus is on particular religious traditions with an emphasis on their internal diversity, and the ways that the traditions are always evolving and changing.

▶ http://rlp.hds.harvard.edu/about

Of particular interest on this site is a section on teaching methodology for addressing study about religions. The program takes the "cultural studies" approach, which is outlined here.

▶ http://rlp.hds.harvard.edu/methodology

Harvard University Online Learning

Through Harvard University's Online Learning portal, students and teachers can access full online courses in many of the world's major religious traditions. By visiting the link below, interested learners can access free courses developed by some of the finest religious studies scholars in the world.

▶ http://online-learning.harvard.edu/courses?keywords=World+religions

Harvard University Pluralism Project

On Common Ground: World Religions in America is an interactive web resource based on the research of Harvard's Pluralism Project and its affiliates. For more than twenty years, under the direction of Diana L. Eck, the Pluralism Project has studied the emergence of an increasingly multi-religious America. The resources include historical documents, written background pieces, photos, videos, and sound files that bring to life the reality of religious communities across the United States. On Common Ground gives teachers and students opportunities to explore the historical dimensions and current realities of a multi-religious America.

▶ http://www.pluralism.org/ocg/

Hindu American Foundation

Hinduism 101: Teacher Training is an initiative established by the Hindu American Foundation to help school teachers across the country better teach about Hinduism. The initiative began as a result of conversations with educators nationwide on what could be done to provide them with more resources to teach about a religion that is over 5,000 years old, has 1 billion followers, and yet continues to be misunderstood in the United States. Moreover, with more Hindu American children in schools, teachers should have a better understanding of a rapidly growing demographic. Through free trainings, supplementary materials, and recommended readings, Hinduism 101: Teacher Training is a one-stop resource for educators seeking to have more up-to-date and comprehensive information for their students.

▶ http://www.hafsite.org/hinduism-101/hinduism-101-teachers-resource-teaching-about-hinduism

Elsewhere on its website, The Hindu American Foundation offers a range of reading materials on the basics of Hinduism for adults.

▶ http://www.hafsite.org/hinduism-101/hinduism-basics

Islamic Networks Group (ING)

ING's online curriculum, which is available free to classroom teachers just by registering at the site, includes three popular digital presentations related to teaching about Muslims and their faith: Getting to Know American Muslims and Their Faith, A History of Muslims in America, and Muslim Contributions to Civilization.

These curricula were designed to supplement content standards in social studies and world history and address many of the themes created by the National Council for the Social Studies Curriculum Standards and the National Center for History in the Schools at UCLA. Many of these themes are also addressed in state social studies content standards of states such as California, Texas, and New York.

Each curriculum includes the digital presentation, as well as lessons which accompany the presentation. Each lesson includes notes that describe each slide in the presentation. In addition to the presentation notes, each lesson also includes discussion questions and other activities. The lessons also include links to films, as well as discussion questions about the films. Each lesson concludes with references and suggested resources.

These curricula were designed to be used either jointly or independently, depending on the time available and your desired focus.

▶ https://www.ing.org/7-12

Kaur Foundation

The Kaur Foundation is a national non-profit organization that promotes cultural diversity and creates awareness of the Sikh identity and heritage. The Foundation believes that educators and administrators are in a unique leadership position to plant the seeds of cultural literacy and understanding, and help raise a new generation of more accepting Americans who participate in the global community. In their education package, the Kaur Foundation presents an engaging, learning tool to help teachers achieve the goal of cultivating awareness in classrooms and schools to ensure a safe and nurturing environment for all within the school system.

Included in the package are the Cultural Safari DVD and Teacher Resource Guide. The DVD is an educational vehicle celebrating American diversity. This 17-minute DVD was made after conducting extensive research of the educators and administrators at the national level. The DVD is scripted to answer questions raised by teachers about Sikh Americans. The teacher's resource guide accompanying the DVD includes activities and exercises that facilitate the teaching of the material.

▶ http://kaurfoundation.org/content/our-programs-public-schools-0

The Religion in American Life Series by Oxford University Press

Religion in American Life explores the evolution, character, and dynamic of organized religion in America from 1500 to the present day and is written for advanced middle to high school students. The authors are distinguished historians of religion, and their books weave together the varying stories that compose the religious fabric of the United States, from Puritanism to alternative religious practices. Primary source materials coupled with handsome illustrations and lucid text make these books essential in any exploration of America's diverse nature. Each book includes a chronology, suggestions for further reading, and an index.

▶ https://global.oup.com/academic/content/series/r/religion-in-american-life-rial/?cc=us&lang=en&

Society of Biblical Literature: The Bible in Secondary Schools

In 2007, the Society of Biblical Literature (SBL) initiated a taskforce on the Bible in secondary schools—in part a response to increased interest in Bible electives in public schools. SBL now offers "Teaching the Bible," a newsletter to support teachers of secondary school Bible electives and teachers interested in reliable resources for teaching about the Bible in history and literature.

The Bible in Secondary Schools section of the SBL website offers links to state Bible teaching standards for Georgia, Tennessee, and Florida courses; textbook reviews and teacher resources, including guidelines; relevant court cases and news articles; and links to organizations involved in addressing Bible courses in schools.

▶ http://www.sbl-site.org/educational/thebibleinpublicschools.aspx

The Bible Literacy Project

The Bible Literacy Project, Inc., is a non-partisan, non-profit endeavor to encourage and facilitate the academic study of the Bible in public schools. In 2005, the Bible Literacy Project published *The Bible and Its Influence*, a student textbook for academic study of the Bible in public high schools. Designed for high school students in grades 9-12, but also used by college students and adult learners, *The Bible and Its Influence* can be taught as an English, social studies, or humanities elective.

▶ http://www.bibleliteracy.org/

Tanenbaum

For more than 15 years, Tanenbaum has expanded multicultural education to include religious diversity. Whether used by an educator, parent, or student, Tanenbaum's practical tools are designed to stamp out bullying and malice in the classroom and beyond. Many Tanenbaum resources address or are aligned with Common Core Standards.

Lively, activity-filled lessons teach students about different religions and about respect and understanding. Tanenbaum's curricula offer educators the guidance they seek. Chapter 20 of this book presents some Tanenbaum resources that can be used in the elementary classroom.

▶ https://tanenbaum.org/programs/education/

Teaching About Religion in Support of Civic Pluralism

This website focuses attention on both religious and non-religious worldviews in its approach to teaching about religions. The site offers educational information in the form of a worldview sampler, background information on a broad range of critical concepts (e.g. religious liberty, teaching about religion and the nonreligious worldview, civic responsibilities), links to teaching materials such as free lesson plans, position statements, historical information and source material, and resources of additional interest to public school educators, especially in the areas of social science and history.

▶ http://teachingaboutreligion.org/

▶ http://www.pluralism.org/

Teaching Tolerance

The Teaching Tolerance project was founded in 1991 by the Southern Poverty Law Center. Teaching Tolerance is dedicated to reducing prejudice, improving intergroup relations, and supporting equitable school experiences for our nation's children. The Teaching Tolerance website provides free educational materials to teachers and other school practitioners in the U.S. and Canada. The self-titled magazine, *Teaching Tolerance*, is sent to 450,000 educators twice annually, and tens of thousands of educators use their free curricular kits. More than 5,000 schools participate in their annual Mix It Up at Lunch Day program. Teaching Tolerance's teaching materials have won two Oscars, an Emmy, and more than 20 honors from the Association of Educational Publishers (now part of the Association of American Publishers), including two Golden Lamp Awards, the industry's highest honor. Scientific surveys demonstrate that the Teaching Tolerance programs help students learn respect for differences and bolster teacher practice. Among the many fine teaching resources is a range of materials that address religious diversity in particular. The following link connects to that area of the site.

▶ http://www.tolerance.org/classroom-resources?keys= &type=All&topic=156&grade=All&domain=All&subject=15

Wisdom Stories

Stories to Light Our Way is an award-winning, entertaining educational Audio CD with music and sound effects, and an accompanying Study Guide that introduces and celebrates diverse cultures and traditions from around the world. Each of the eleven stories, narrated by renowned storyteller Ralph Singh, features a child or an animal as the protagonist, and teaches a particular value or reinforces a certain character trait. The study guide includes the essential and other thought-provoking questions to improve deep listening and critical thinking skills. Ideal for both educators and families, the stories provide the perfect opportunity to engage children in conversations that support making wise choices, nurturing compassion, building character, and creating a sense of social responsibility.

▶ http://www.wisdomthinkers.org/character-education/ storiestolightourway/

A Teacher's Guide to Religion in the Public Schools

"Congress shall make no law respecting an establishment of religion, or prohibiting the free exercise thereof; or abridging the freedom of speech, or of the press; or the right of the people peaceably to assemble, and to petition the Government for a redress of grievances."
— FIRST AMENDMENT TO THE U.S. CONSTITUTION

Each day millions of parents from diverse religious backgrounds entrust the education of their children to the teachers in our nation's public schools. For this reason, teachers need to be fully informed about the constitutional and educational principles for understanding the role of religion in public education.

This teacher's guide is intended to move beyond the confusion and conflict that has surrounded religion in public schools since the early days of the common school movement. For most of our history, extremes have shaped much of the debate. On one end of the spectrum are those who advocate promotion of religion (usually their own) in school practices and policies. On the other end are those who view public schools as religion-free zones. Neither of these approaches is consistent with the guiding principles of the Religion Clauses of the First Amendment.

Fortunately, however, there is another alternative that is consistent with the First Amendment and broadly supported by many educational and religious groups. The core of this alternative has been best articulated in "Religious Liberty, Public Education, and the Future of American Democracy," a statement of principles issued by 24 national organizations. Principle IV states:

> Public schools may not inculcate nor inhibit religion. They must be places where religion and religious conviction are treated with fairness and respect. Public schools uphold the First

A *Teacher's Guide to Religion in the Public Schools* is published by the First Amendment Center. The guide has been endorsed by the following organizations:

- American Association of School Administrators
- American Federation of Teachers
- American Jewish Committee
- American Jewish Congress
- Association for Supervision and Curriculum Development
- Baptist Joint Committee on Public Affairs
- Christian Educators Association
- International Christian Legal Society
- Council on Islamic Education
- National Association of Elementary School Principals
- National Association of Evangelicals
- National Association of Secondary School Principals
- National Council of Churches of Christ in the U.S.A.
- National Council for the Social Studies
- National Education Association
- National PTA
- National School Boards Association
- Union of American Hebrew Congregations
- Union of Orthodox Jewish Congregations of America

Written by: Charles C. Haynes
Editor: Natilee Duning

©2008 First Amendment Center
1207 18th Ave. S.
Nashville, TN 37212
615-727-1600
http://firstamendmentcenter.org

Publication No. 085.10-FAC
Revised September 2004, Reprinted March 2010

Amendment when they protect the religious liberty rights of students of all faiths or none. Schools demonstrate fairness when they ensure that the curriculum includes study about religion, where appropriate, as an important part of a complete education.[1]

The questions and answers that follow build on this shared vision of religious liberty in public education to provide teachers with a basic understanding of the issues concerning religion in their classrooms. The advice offered is based on First Amendment principles as currently interpreted by the courts and agreed to by a wide range of religious and educational organizations. For a more in-depth examination of the issues, teachers should consult *Finding Common Ground: A Guide to Religious Liberty in Public Schools*.[2] This guide is not intended to render legal advice on specific legal questions; it is designed to provide general information on the subject of religion and public schools.

Keep in mind, however, that the law alone cannot answer every question. Teachers and administrators, working with parents and others in the community, must work to apply the First Amendment fairly and justly for all students in our public schools.

TEACHING ABOUT RELIGION IN PUBLIC SCHOOLS

1. **Is it constitutional to teach about religion?**
Yes. In the 1960s' school prayer cases (that prompted rulings against state-sponsored school prayer and Bible reading), the U.S. Supreme Court indicated that public school education may include teaching about religion. In *Abington v Schempp*, Associate Justice Tom Clark wrote for the court:

> [I]t might well be said that one's education is not complete without a study of comparative religion or the history of religion and its relationship to the advancement of civilization. It certainly may be said that the Bible is worthy of study for its literary and historic qualities. Nothing we have said here indicates that such study of the Bible or of religion, when presented objectively as part of a secular program of education, may not be effected consistently with the First Amendment.

2. **Why should study about religion be included in the curriculum?**
Growing numbers of educators throughout the United States recognize that study about religion in social studies, literature, art, and music is an important part of a well-rounded education. "Religion in the Public School Curriculum: Questions and Answers," issued by a coalition of 17 major religious and educational organizations— including the Christian Legal Society, the American Jewish Congress, the National Education Association, the American Federation of Teachers, the American Association of School Administrators, the Islamic Society of North America, the National Council for the Social Studies, the Association for Supervision and Curriculum Development, the Baptist Joint Committee on Public Affairs, the National Association of Evangelicals, and the National School Boards Association—describes the importance of religion in the curriculum thus:

> Because religion plays a significant role in history and society, study about religion is essential to understanding both the nation and the world. Omission of facts about religion can give students the false impression that the religious life of humankind is insignificant or unimportant. Failure to understand even the basic symbols, practices, and concepts of the various religions makes much of history, literature, art, and contemporary life unintelligible.

> Study about religion is also important if students are to value religious liberty, the first freedom guaranteed in the Bill of Rights. Moreover, knowledge of the roles of religion in the past and present promotes cross-cultural understanding essential to democracy and world peace.

A number of leading educational groups have issued their own statements decrying the lack of discussion about religion in the curriculum and calling for inclusion of such information in curricular materials and in teacher education.

Three major principles form the foundation of this consensus on teaching about religion in public schools:

1. As the Supreme Court has made clear, study *about* religion in public schools is constitutional.

2. Inclusion of study about religion is important in order for students to be properly educated about history and cultures.

3. Religion must be taught objectively and neutrally. The purpose of public schools is to educate students about a variety of religious traditions, not to indoctrinate them into any tradition.

3. Is study about religion included in textbooks and standards?

"Knowledge about religions is not only characteristic of an educated person, but is also absolutely necessary for understanding and living in a world of diversity."

NATIONAL COUNCIL FOR THE SOCIAL STUDIES

Agreement on the importance of teaching about religion has begun to influence the treatment of religion in textbooks widely used in public schools, as well as state frameworks and standards for the social studies. The current generation of history textbooks mention religion more often than their predecessors, and, in world history, sometimes offer substantive discussions of religious ideas and events.

State frameworks and standards are also beginning to treat religion more seriously. Most state standards in the social studies require or recommend teaching about religion through specific content references and general mandates, and many also include such references in fine arts and literature standards. In California, for example, the History-Social Science Framework and the new History-Social Science Content Standards require considerable study of religion. Students studying U.S. History in California are expected to learn about the role of religion in the American story, from the influence of religious groups on social reform movements to the religious revivals, from the rise of Christian fundamentalism to the expanding religious pluralism of the 20th century.

Teaching about religion is also encouraged in the *National Standards for History*, published by the National Center for History in the Schools. The elaborated standards in world history are particularly rich in religious references, examining the basic beliefs and practices of the major religions as well as how these faiths influenced the development of civilization in successive historical periods. While the U.S. history standards include religion less frequently, many historical developments and contributions that were influenced by religion are nevertheless represented.

Geography for Life: The National Geography Standards, published by the Geography Standards Project, and the *National Standards for Civics and Government*, published by the Center for Civic Education, include many references to teaching about religious belief and practice as historical and contemporary phenomena. Study of religion in the social studies would be expanded considerably if curriculum developers and textbooks writers were guided by these standards.

4. How should I teach about religion?

Encouraged by the new consensus, public schools are now beginning to include more teaching about religion in the curriculum. In the social studies especially, the question is no longer "Should I teach about religion?" but rather "How should I do it?"

The answer to the "how" question begins with a clear understanding of the crucial difference between the teaching *of* religion (religious education or indoctrination) and teaching *about* religion. "Religion in the Public School Curriculum," the guidelines issued by 17 religious and educational organizations, summarizes the distinction this way:

■ The school's approach to religion is *academic*, not *devotional*.

■ The school strives for student *awareness* of religions, but does not press for student *acceptance* of any religion.

■ The school sponsors *study* about religion, not the *practice* of religion.

■ The school may *expose* students to a diversity of religious views, but may not *impose* any particular view.

- The school *educates* about all religions; it does not *promote* or *denigrate* religion.

- The school *informs* students about various beliefs; it does not seek to *conform* students to any particular belief.[3]

Classroom discussions concerning religion must be conducted in an environment that is free of advocacy on the part of the teacher. Students may, of course, express their own religious views, as long as such expression is germane to the discussion. But public-school teachers are required by the First Amendment to teach about religion fairly and objectively, neither promoting nor denigrating religion in general or specific religious groups in particular. When discussing religion, many teachers guard against injecting personal religious beliefs by teaching through attribution (e.g., by using such phrases as "most Buddhists believe ..." or "according to the Hebrew scriptures ...").

5. Which religions should be taught and how much should be said?

Decisions about which religions to include and how much to discuss about religion are determined by the grade level of the students and the academic requirements of the course being taught.

In the elementary grades, the study of family, community, various cultures, the nation, and other themes and topics may involve some discussion of religion. Elementary students are introduced to the basic ideas and practices of the world's major religions by focusing on the generally agreed-upon meanings of religious faiths—the core beliefs and symbols as well as important figures and events. Stories drawn from various faiths may be included among the wide variety of stories read by students, but the material selected must always be presented in the context of learning about religion.

On the secondary level, the social studies, literature, and the arts offer opportunities for the inclusion of study about religions—their ideas and practices. The academic needs of the course determine which religions are studied. In a U.S. history curriculum, for example, some faith communities may be given more time than others but only because of their predominant influence on the development of the American nation. In world history, a variety of faiths are studied in each region of the world in order to understand the various civilizations and cultures that have shaped history and society. The overall curriculum should include all of the major voices and some of the minor ones in an effort to provide the best possible education.

Fair and balanced study about religion on the secondary level includes critical thinking about historical events involving religious traditions. Religious beliefs have been at the heart of some of the best and some of the worst developments in human history. The full historical record (and various interpretations of it) should be available for analysis and discussion. Using primary sources whenever possible allows students to work directly with the historical record.

Of course, fairness and balance in U.S. or world history and literature are difficult to achieve, given the brief treatment of religious ideas and events in most textbooks and the limited time available in the course syllabus. Teachers will need scholarly supplemental resources that enable them to cover the required material within the allotted time, while simultaneously enriching the discussion with study of religion. Some schools now offer electives in religious studies in order to provide additional opportunities for students to study about the major faith communities in greater depth.

6. May I invite guest speakers to help with study about religion?

When teaching about religions in history, some teachers may find it helpful to invite a guest speaker for a more comprehensive presentation of the religious tradition under study. Teachers should consult their school district policy concerning guest speakers in the classroom.

If a guest speaker is invited, care should be taken to find someone with the academic background necessary for an objective and scholarly discussion of the historical period and the religion being considered. Faculty from local colleges and universities often make excellent guest speakers or can make recommendations of others who might be appropriate for working with students in a public-school setting. Religious leaders in the community may also be a resource. Remember, however, that they have commitments to their own faith. Be certain that any guest speaker understands the First

Amendment guidelines for teaching *about* religion in public education and is clear about the academic nature of the assignment.

7. How should I treat religious holidays in the classroom?

Teachers must be alert to the distinction between teaching about religious holidays, which is permissible, and celebrating religious holidays, which is not. Recognition of and information about holidays may focus on how and when they are celebrated, their origins, histories and generally agreed-upon meanings. If the approach is objective and sensitive, neither promoting nor inhibiting religion, this study can foster understanding and mutual respect for differences in belief. Teachers may not use the study of religious holidays as an opportunity to proselytize or otherwise inject personal religious beliefs into the discussion.

The use of religious symbols, provided they are used only as examples of cultural or religious heritage, is permissible as a teaching aid or resource. Religious symbols may be displayed only on a temporary basis as part of the academic lesson being studied. Students may choose to create artwork with religious symbols, but teachers should not assign or suggest such creations.

The use of art, drama, music or literature with religious themes is permissible if it serves a sound educational goal in the curriculum. Such themes should be included on the basis of their academic or aesthetic value, not as a vehicle for promoting religious belief. For example, sacred music may be sung or played as part of the academic study of music. School concerts that present a variety of selections may include religious music. Concerts should avoid programs dominated by religious music, especially when these coincide with a particular religious holiday.

This advice about religious holidays in public schools is based on consensus guidelines adopted by 18 educational and religious organizations.[4]

8. Are there opportunities for teacher education in study about religion?

Teacher preparation and good academic resources are needed in order for study about religion in public schools to be constitutionally permissible and educationally sound.

The First Amendment Center supports initiatives in several regions of the country designed to prepare public-school teachers to teach about religion. The most extensive of these programs is the California 3Rs Project (Rights, Responsibilities, and Respect). Co-sponsored by the California County Superintendents Educational Services Association, the project has created a network of resource leaders and scholars throughout the state providing support for classroom teachers. Teachers trained by the project give workshops for their colleagues on the constitutional and educational guidelines for teaching about religion. Religious studies scholars from local colleges and universities are linked with school districts to provide ongoing expertise and periodic seminars on the religious traditions that teachers are discussing in the curriculum.

The Utah State Office of Education co-sponsors a Utah 3Rs Project that is currently building a network of resource leaders in all of the state's school districts. Other states and districts have similar programs in various stages of development.[5]

Harvard University and the University of Pennsylvania offer master's level programs that are excellent opportunities for both current and prospective public- and private-school teachers interested in learning more about the study of religion and religious-liberty issues in American public life.[6]

Other colleges and universities offer assistance to teachers, including in-service programs focused on teaching about religion. A notable example is the Religion and Public Education Resource Center at California State University—Chico. This center provides resources, including curriculum guides and sample lessons in several subject areas.[7] Other organizations, such as the Council on Islamic Education, offer academic resources and workshops on teaching about specific religious traditions.[8]

9. What are good classroom resources for teaching about religion?

Teaching about religion in the public schools requires that sound academic resources be made readily available to classroom teachers. Fortunately, good classroom resources, especially in the social studies, are now available for helping teachers integrate appropriate study about religion.

Finding Common Ground: A Guide to Religious Liberty in Public Schools, published by the First Amendment Center, provides an extensive list of organizations and publishers that offer classroom resources for teaching about religion in public schools.

Two recent publications are examples of what is now available for study about religion in a secondary school classroom:

Religion in American Life is a 17-volume series written by leading scholars for young readers. Published by Oxford University Press, the series includes three chronological volumes on the religious history of the U.S., nine volumes covering significant religious groups (Protestants, Catholics, Jews, Orthodox Christians, Mormons, Muslims, Hindus, Buddhists, Native Americans, and others), and four volumes addressing specific topics of special importance for understanding the role of religion in American life (women and religion, church-state issues, African American religion, and immigration).[9]

Columbia University Press has published a CD-ROM titled *On Common Ground: World Religions in America*. This multimedia resource uses text, primary sources, photographs, music, film, and the spoken word to bring alive the extraordinary religious diversity in the United States. Fifteen different religions in various regions of America are represented, from the long-established Christian, Jewish, and Native American traditions to the more recent arrivals such as Hinduism and Buddhism.[10]

10. What is the relationship between religion and character education?

As discussed previously, the First Amendment prohibits public-school teachers from either inculcating or inhibiting religion. Teachers must remain neutral concerning religion, neutral among religions, and neutral between religion and non-religion. But this does not mean that teachers should be neutral concerning civic virtue or moral character.

Teachers should teach the personal and civic virtues widely held in our society, such as honesty, caring, fairness, and integrity. They must do so without either invoking religious authority or denigrating the religious or philosophical commitments of students and parents.

When school districts develop a plan for comprehensive character education, they should keep in mind that the moral life of a great many Americans is shaped by deep religious conviction. Both the approach to character education and the classroom materials used should be selected in close consultation with parents and other community members representing a broad range of perspectives. When care is taken to find consensus, communities are able to agree on the core character traits they wish taught in the schools and how they wish character education to be done.

For guidance on how to develop and implement a quality character education program, contact the Character Education Partnership in Washington, D.C.[11]

THE PERSONAL BELIEFS OF TEACHERS

11. May I pray or otherwise practice my faith while at school?

As employees of the government, public-school teachers are subject to the Establishment Clause of the First Amendment and thus required to be neutral concerning religion while carrying out their duties as teachers. That means, for example, that teachers do not have the right to pray with or in the presence of students during the school day.

Outside of their school responsibilities, public-school teachers are free like other citizens to teach or otherwise participate in their local religious community. But teachers must refrain from using their position in the public school to promote their outside religious activities.

Teachers, of course, bring their faith with them through the schoolhouse door each morning. Because of the First Amendment, however, teachers who wish to pray or engage in other religious activities—unless they are silent—should do so outside the presence of students. If a group of teachers wishes to meet for prayer or scriptural study in the faculty lounge during their free time in the school day, we see no constitutional reason why they may not be permitted to do so as long as the activity is outside the presence of students and does not interfere with their duties or the rights of other teachers.

Teachers are permitted to wear non-obtrusive jewelry, such as a cross or Star of David. But teachers should not wear clothing with a proselytizing message (e.g., a "Jesus Saves" T-shirt).

12. How do I respond if students ask about my religious beliefs?

Some teachers prefer not to answer the question, stating that it is inappropriate for a teacher to inject personal beliefs into the discussion. Other teachers may choose to answer the question straightforwardly and succinctly in the interest of an open and honest classroom environment.

Before answering the question, however, teachers should consider the age of the students. Middle and high school students may be able to distinguish between a personal view and the official position of the school; very young

children may not. In any case, the teacher may answer at most with a brief statement of personal belief—but may not turn the question into an opportunity to proselytize for or against religion. Teachers may neither reward nor punish students because they agree or disagree with the religious views of the teacher.

RELIGIOUS EXPRESSION OF STUDENTS

13. May students express religious views in public schools?

In "Religion in the Public Schools: A Joint Statement of Current Law," 35 religious and civil liberties organizations give the following summary of the rights of students to express their faith in a public school:

> Students have the right to pray individually or in groups or to discuss their religious views with their peers so long as they are not disruptive. Because the Establishment Clause does not apply to purely private speech, students enjoy the right to read their Bibles or other scriptures, say grace before meals, pray before tests, and discuss religion with other willing student listeners. In the classroom, students have the right to pray quietly except when required to be actively engaged in school activities (e.g., students may not decide to pray just as a teacher calls on them). In informal settings, such as the cafeteria or in the halls, students may pray either audibly or silently, subject to the same rules of order as apply to other speech in these locations. However, the right to engage in voluntary prayer does not include, for example, the right to have a captive audience listen or to compel other students to participate.[12]

14. May students express religious views in their assignments?

"Religious Expression in Public Schools," guidelines published by the U.S. Department of Education, offers the following guidance about religious expression in student assignments:

> Students may express their beliefs about religion in the form of homework, artwork, and other written and oral assignments free of discrimination based on the religious content of their submissions. Such home and classroom

work should be judged by ordinary academic standards of substance and relevance, and against other legitimate pedagogical concerns identified by the school.[13]

15. How should public schools respond to excusal requests from parents?

In "A Parent's Guide to Religion in the Public Schools," the National PTA and the First Amendment Center give the following advice concerning excusal requests:

Whenever possible, school officials should try to accommodate the requests of parents and students for excusal from classroom discussions or activities for religious reasons. If focused on a specific discussion, assignment, or activity, such requests should be routinely granted in order to strike a balance between the student's religious freedom and the school's interest in providing a well-rounded education.

If it is proved that particular lessons substantially burden a student's free exercise of religion and if the school cannot prove a compelling interest in requiring attendance, some courts may require the school to excuse the students.[14]

16. May public schools accommodate students with special religious needs?

Public schools are sometimes asked to accommodate students with special religious needs or practices. Sensitive and thoughtful school officials may easily grant many of these requests without raising constitutional questions. Muslim students, for example, may need a quiet place at lunch or during breaks to fulfill their prayer obligation during the school day. Jehovah's Witnesses ask for their children to be excused from birthday celebrations. As long as honoring these requests is feasible, school officials should do so in the spirit of the First Amendment.

Administrators and teachers should not, however, be placed in the position of monitoring a child's compliance with a particular religious requirement. Enforcing religious obligations such as prayer, dietary restrictions, or wearing a head covering is the responsibility of parents, not teachers.[15]

17. May students form extracurricular religious clubs?

The Equal Access Act passed by Congress in 1984 ensures that students in secondary public schools may form religious clubs, including Bible clubs, if the school allows other "noncurriculum-related groups." The Act is intended to protect *student-initiated* and *student-led* meetings in secondary schools. According to the Act, outsiders may not "direct, conduct, control, or regularly attend" student religious clubs, and teachers acting as monitors may be present at religious meetings in a non-participatory capacity only.[16]

The U.S. Department of Education in "Religious Expression in Public Schools" gives the following guidance for interpreting the Equal Access Act:

The Equal Access Act is designed to ensure that, consistent with the First Amendment, student religious activities are accorded the same access to public school facilities as are student secular activities. Based on decisions of the Federal courts, as well as its interpretations of the Act, the Department of Justice has advised that the Act should be interpreted as providing, among other things, that:

- Student religious groups at public secondary schools have the same right of access to school facilities as is enjoyed by other comparable student groups. Under the Equal Access Act, a school receiving Federal funds that allows one or more student noncurriculum-related clubs to meet on its premises during noninstructional time may not refuse access to student religious groups.

- A meeting, as defined and protected by the Equal Access Act, may include a prayer service, Bible reading, or other worship exercise.

- A school receiving Federal funds must allow student groups meeting under the Act to use the school media—including the public address system, the school newspaper, and the school bulletin board—to announce their meetings on the same terms as other noncurriculum-related student groups are allowed to use the school media. Any policy concerning the use of school media must be applied to all noncurriculum-related student groups in a nondiscriminatory manner. Schools, however, may inform students that certain groups are not school-sponsored.

- A school creates a limited open forum under the Equal Access Act, triggering equal access rights for religious groups, when it allows students to meet during their lunch periods or other noninstructional time during the school day, as well as when it allows students to meet before and after the school day.

18. May students distribute religious literature in school?

An increasing number of students are requesting permission to distribute religious literature on public-school campuses. According to the guidelines issued by the U.S. Department of Education:

Students have a right to distribute religious literature to their schoolmates on the same terms as they are permitted to distribute other literature that is unrelated to school curriculum or activities. Schools may impose the same reasonable time, place, and manner or other constitutional restrictions on distribution of religious literature as they do on nonschool literature generally, but they may not single out religious literature for special regulation.

NOTES

1. This shared vision of religious liberty in public education is remarkable both for who says it and for what it says. The National Education Association, the American Federation of Teachers, the National School Boards Association, the Association for Supervision and Curriculum Development, the National PTA, and the American Association of School Administrators join with the Christian Legal Society, the American Center for Law and Justice, and Citizens for Excellence in Education in asserting these principles. People for the American Way, the Anti-Defamation League, and the Union of American Hebrew Congregations are on the list, as are the Council on Islamic Education, the Christian Educators Association International, and the Christian Coalition. Free copies are available through the First Amendment Center.

2. *Finding Common Ground* by Charles C. Haynes and Oliver Thomas is available at www.amazon.com. A discount is available through the First Amendment Center for orders of 10 books or more. For the discount, call 202-292-6288.

3. Based on guidelines originally published by the Public Education Religion Studies Center at Wright State University.

4. "Religious Holidays and Public Schools: Questions and Answers" may be found in *Finding Common Ground*.

5. For details about the 3Rs (Rights, Responsibilities, & Respect) programs, contact Charles Haynes, chaynes@freedomforum.org.

6. For more information about the Program in Religion and Secondary Education at Harvard University, contact The Divinity School, 45 Francis Ave., Cambridge, MA 02138, 617-384-8047. Attention: Diane Moore, Director. Inquiries about the Religion in Public Life Certificate Program at the University of Pennsylvania should be addressed to Christopher Pastore, Director, Master of Liberal Arts Program, College of General Studies, University of Pennsylvania, 3440 Market St., Suite 100, Philadelphia, PA 19104-3335, 215-898-7326.

7. Direct questions about the Religion and Public Education Resource Center to Dr. Bruce Grelle, Dept. of Religious Studies, California State University—Chico, CA 95929-0740, bgrelle@csuchico.edu, 530-898-4739, or visit www.csuchico.edu/rs/rperc/

8. The Council on Islamic Education may be reached by calling 714/839-2929, writing to P.O. Box 20186, Fountain Valley, CA 92728-0186, e-mailing info@cie.org, or visiting www.cie.org

9. For more information about the Oxford University Press series *Religion in American Life*, call 800-445-9714, e-mail custserv.us@oup.com, or visit http://www.oup.com/us/catalog/general/series/ReligioninAmericanLife/

10. For more information about the CD-ROM *On Common Ground: World Religions in America,* call 800-944-8648.

11. The Character Education Partnership is located at 1025 Connecticut Ave., NW, Suite 1011, Washington, DC 20036. Call 800-988-8081 or visit www.character.org

12. "Religion in the Public Schools: A Joint Statement of Current Law" may be obtained by writing: "Religion in the Public Schools," 15 East 84th St., Suite 501, New York, NY 10028, or visiting http://www.ed.gov/Speeches/04-1995/prayer.html

13. The full text of the 1998 U.S. Department of Education guidelines may be found in *Finding Common Ground*.

14. Copies of "A Parent's Guide to Religion in the Public Schools," published by the National PTA and the First Amendment Center, are available free from the First Amendment Center.

15. A good resource for understanding the religious needs and practices of students is *America's Religions: An Educator's Guide to Beliefs and Practices* by Benjamin J. Hubbard, John T. Hatfield, and James A Santucci. It is available by contacting Teacher Ideas Press at 800-225-5800, P.O. Box 6926, Portsmouth, NH 03802-6926, custserv@teacherideaspress.com or www.teacherideaspress.com

16. The requirements of the Equal Access Act are described in detail in "Equal Access and the Public Schools: Questions and Answers," a pamphlet sponsored by 21 religious and educational groups. The full text is contained in *Finding Common Ground*.

Guidelines for Teaching About Religion in K–12 Public Schools in the United States

PRODUCED BY THE AAR RELIGION IN THE SCHOOLS TASK FORCE;
DIANE L. MOORE, CHAIR

EXECUTIVE SUMMARY

The United States Department of Education requires states to develop content standards and academic assessments for each subject taught in public schools from kindergarten through twelfth grade (K-12). State departments of education are guided in this task by national educational associations that have crafted their own standards and guidelines using the collective wisdom of scholars and educators in each subject. Though religion is not a separate, required subject in public K–12 schools, religion is embedded in curriculum standards across disciplines, especially in social studies and English, and there are a growing number of elective courses that focus on religious themes or topics explicitly.

Because (1) the study of religion is already present in public schools, (2) there are no content and skill guidelines for educators about religion itself that are constructed by religious studies scholars, and (3) educators and school boards are often confused about how to teach about religion in constitutionally sound and intellectually responsible ways, the American Academy of Religion (the world's largest association of religion scholars) has published these Guidelines as a resource for educators and interested citizens.

Three premises inform this project: illiteracy regarding religion (1) is widespread, (2) fuels prejudice and antagonism, and (3) can be diminished by teaching about religion in public schools using a non-devotional, academic perspective, called religious studies.

There are important differences between this approach and a faith-based approach to teaching and learning about religion. These Guidelines support the former, constitutionally sound approach for teaching about religion in public schools—encouraging student awareness of religions, but not acceptance of a particular religion; studying about religion, but not practicing religion; exposing students to a diversity of religious views, but not imposing any particular view; and educating students about all religions, but not promoting or denigrating religion.[1]

In teaching about religion, public school teachers draw on the following methodological approaches: historical, literary, traditions based, and cultural studies. Regardless of the approach(es) used, however, teaching about religion needs to convey three central premises of academic learning about religion: religions are internally diverse; religions are dynamic; and religions are embedded in culture.

Given that few educators have taken religious studies courses, the AAR encourages using these Guidelines in substantial teacher pre-service and professional training that imparts content, pedagogy, and academically and constitutionally sound approaches for teaching about religion in K-12 public schools.

INTRODUCTION

The United States Department of Education requires states to develop content standards and academic assessments for each discipline taught in public schools from kindergarten through twelfth grade (K-12). State departments of education are guided in this task by national educational associations that have crafted their own standards and guidelines representing the collective wisdom of scholars and educators in each relevant educational field. For example, the National Council for the Social Studies (NCSS) comprises elementary, secondary, and college level teachers and other educational personnel who work in the broad areas that encompass the social studies: history, geography, economics, political science, sociology, psychology, anthropology, and law. Similarly, the National Council of Teachers of English (NCTE) is made up of teachers and supervisors of English programs in elementary, middle, and secondary schools, faculty in college and university English departments, teacher educators, local and state agency English specialists, and professionals in related fields. There are similar organizations formed for the sciences, the arts, physical education, English as a second language, and technology, among others. The primary aims of these associations are to promote responsible education about their fields and to provide leadership, support, and service to their educators.

Though religious studies is not a required subject in public K-12 schools, religion is embedded in curriculum standards across disciplines, and it is especially prominent in social studies and English at the state and national association levels. Given the rising interest in the study of religion due to national and global affairs, there are also a growing number of elective courses offered in schools that focus on religious themes or topics explicitly, such as "The Bible as Literature" and "Introduction to World Religions." Given that (1) the study of religion is already present in public schools, (2) there are no content and skill guidelines for educators about religion itself that are constructed by religious studies scholars, and (3) educators and school boards are often confused about how to teach about religion in constitutionally sound and intellectually responsible ways, there is a strong consensus that a set of guidelines for teaching about religion is needed.[2]

THE AMERICAN ACADEMY OF RELIGION

There is not a similar national educational association like NCSS or NCTE that focuses on religious studies per se,[3] but the American Academy of Religion (AAR) is the professional organization best suited to construct scholarly guidelines for teaching about religion in K-12 schools. It is the world's largest association of scholars who research or teach topics related to religion. There are some 10,000 members comprised largely of faculty at colleges, universities, and theological schools in North America with a growing number from institutions of higher education in Asia, Africa, and Europe.

The AAR has been involved in addressing issues related to teaching about religion in public schools since the 1970s. These efforts have included producing publications in the 1970s and early 1980s addressing the legal, curricular, moral, and pedagogical dimensions of teaching about religion in public K-12 schools;[4] helping to establish a number of programs and resource centers at various universities throughout the U.S.;[5] and identifying opportunities for religious studies faculty at colleges to help educate K-12 teachers about religion. Given the absence of authoritative standards penned by religious studies scholars for teaching about religion in K-12 schools, in 2007 the AAR decided to develop a set of standards and guidelines as a resource for educators, parents and school boards, who are faced with an increasingly complex array of challenges regarding how to teach about religion responsibly in public school contexts. The AAR's Religion in the Schools Task Force guided this initiative.[6]

OVERVIEW OF GUIDELINES

Part One addresses why it is important to teach about religion, and Part Two outlines ways to teach about religion in constitutionally sound ways. Part Three is an overview of approaches to teaching about religion and includes grade-specific examples based on both the *National Curriculum Standards for Social Studies*[7] (produced by the National Council for the Social Studies) and *Standards for the English Language Arts*[8] (produced by the National Council of Teachers of English). Given that (1) religion is already present throughout both of these documents and (2) these standards are highly influential in the creation of state and local curricula frameworks, it is appropriate to utilize them to construct guidelines for religious studies.

Finally, Part Four makes recommendations for teacher educators regarding skill and content competencies required for teachers to have sufficient knowledge to teach about religion responsibly.

PART ONE

WHY TEACH ABOUT RELIGION?[9]

Three fundamental premises inform this project. First, there exists a widespread illiteracy about religion in the U.S.; second, there are several consequences that stem from this illiteracy, including the ways that it fuels prejudice and antagonism, thereby hindering efforts aimed at promoting respect for diversity, peaceful coexistence, and cooperative endeavors in local, national, and global arenas; and third, it is possible to diminish religious illiteracy by teaching about religion from an academic, non-devotional perspective in primary, middle, and secondary schools.

Religious illiteracy is defined in this document as a lack of understanding about the following:

- the basic tenets of the world's religious traditions and other religious expressions not categorized by tradition;

- the diversity of expressions and beliefs within traditions and representations; and

- the profound role that religion plays in human social, cultural, and political life historically and today.

Conversely, religious literacy is defined in the following way: the ability to discern and analyze the intersections of religion with social, political, and cultural life. Specifically, a religiously literate person will possess:

- a basic understanding of the history, central texts (where applicable), beliefs, practices and contemporary manifestations of several of the world's religious traditions and religious expressions as they arose out of and continue to shape and be shaped by particular social, historical and cultural contexts; and

- the ability to discern and explore the religious dimensions of political, social and cultural expressions across time and place.[10]

These definitions assume that religion is a social/cultural phenomenon that is embedded in human political, social and cultural life. They also assume that religion shapes and is shaped by the social/historical contexts out of which particular religious expressions and influences emerge. Finally, these definitions assume that there is a difference between devotional beliefs and practices and the study of religion from an academic, secular frame of reference. In this context, secular means a constitutionally defined approach to the teaching of religion that neither privileges nor rejects any particular religious tradition or expression.

One way to characterize this distinction is to recognize the difference between religious education that promotes a particular faith perspective (often but not exclusively associated with religious communities or schools) and learning about religion through a religious studies framework that is non-devotional, inclusive, and comparative in both form and function. Faith-based explorations are intended to promote a particular theological worldview and to encourage practitioners to articulate values and adopt practices that are consonant with that set of beliefs. A religious studies approach to teaching about religion is intended to introduce students to the vast array of faith-based expressions that exist within and between traditions with the aim of deepening understanding about religious diversity and the roles that religion plays in political, economic, and cultural life across time. Both approaches are legitimate ways to think about religion that can serve complementary but distinctive ends. It is important to note, however, that the non-devotional religious studies approach is the constitutionally appropriate one to employ for teaching about religion in public schools. These *Guidelines* represent a religious studies perspective.

Premise Number One: There exists a widespread illiteracy about religion in the U.S.

The following are examples of some of the ways that religious illiteracy manifests itself among a diverse array of U.S. citizens:

1. Religious traditions and expressions are often represented inaccurately by those outside of and within religious traditions and communities.

2. Religious leaders and believers of a given religious tradition or expression are assumed to be the best sources of information about the tradition or expression and are often looked to formally or informally as "experts."[11]

3. The distinction between the study of religion and religious devotional expression is rarely understood.

4. Religious traditions and expressions are often represented as internally uniform and static as opposed to diverse and evolving.

5. In some contexts, religion is interpreted as a "private" affair distinct from the secular "public" sphere of political, economic, and cultural life.

These common manifestations of religious illiteracy are widespread and should not be interpreted as evidence of a lack of intellectual capability or awareness on the part of those who harbor these and similar assumptions. Given that the main sources of information about religion come from training in or about one's own religious tradition (or none) and the media, it should come as no surprise that these and other forms of religious illiteracy are prevalent. Appropriately, individuals who are raised in or convert to a certain faith tradition or expression will learn about that tradition or expression within their faith communities or through devotionally based forms of education in the schools aimed at promoting a particular religious worldview and values that are consonant with it. Individuals who are not religious also learn particular worldviews and associated values from family and/or community members. In relationship to religion, these values are often a-religious or anti-religious. The other main source of information about religion is the media where coverage about religion is often inaccurate or focused on "newsworthy" events that present a distorted view of the role of religion in contemporary life.[12] Neither source (one's own faith tradition/worldview and the media) expose individuals to a comprehensive study of religion because they

1. Do not knowledgeably and even-handedly represent the diversity within a given tradition or expression, and

2. Do not explore and analyze religion as a social/cultural phenomenon.[13]

Such an understanding requires a non-devotional, academic approach to the study of religion and although there are some schools that offer instruction representing this approach in primary, middle, and secondary education, relatively few citizens have the opportunity to engage in this type of inquiry.

Premise Number Two: One of the most troubling and urgent consequences of religious illiteracy is that it often fuels prejudice and antagonism, thereby hindering efforts aimed at promoting respect for diversity, peaceful coexistence, and cooperative endeavors in local, national, and global arenas. [14]

Religious illiteracy is certainly not the sole or even primary cause of the heartbreaking violence that dominates local and global news stories. It is, however, often a contributing factor in fostering a climate whereby certain forms of bigotry and misrepresentation can emerge unchallenged and thus serve as one form of justification for violence and marginalization. Many others share this concern as evidenced by a consultation focusing on this topic in 2006 that was sponsored by the United Nations,[15] and numerous initiatives in Europe.[16] One example of the negative consequences of religious illiteracy is that it has contributed to Christian forms of anti-Semitism. Another example in countries where Muslims are in the minority is the widespread association of Islam with terrorism and the consequent justification of individual hate crimes against those perceived to be Muslim. A third example is the antagonisms that are fueled between different expressions of the same tradition (e.g. between Protestant and Roman Catholic Christians and between Sunni and Shi'a Muslims). A fourth and final example is when some dismiss religion altogether as obsolete, irrational, or inherently oppressive, thereby offending the dignity and sensibilities of people of faith everywhere. Enhancing literacy about religion can foster better understanding among people of different faiths and worldviews. Such knowledge can enrich civic dimensions of education and better prepare students for participation in democratic processes in our multi-religious nation.

Premise Number Three: It is possible to diminish religious illiteracy by teaching about religion from a non-devotional perspective in primary, middle, and secondary schools.

Training in religious literacy provides citizens with the tools to better understand religion as a complex and sophisticated social/cultural phenomenon and individual religious traditions or expressions themselves as internally diverse and constantly evolving as opposed to uniform, absolute, and ahistorical. Learning about religion as a social/cultural phenomenon also helps people recognize, understand, and critically analyze how religion has been and will continue to be used to inspire and sometimes justify the full range of human agency from the heinous to the heroic. Finally, those trained in religious studies learn to question the accuracy of absolutist claims such as "Islam is a religion of peace" or "Judaism and Islam are incompatible" or "All religions are fundamentally the same," thereby helping to deepen discourse about religion in the public sphere. Learning about religion is no guarantee that religious bigotry and chauvinism will cease, but it will make it more difficult for such bigotry and chauvinism to be unwittingly reproduced and promoted.

As was noted in the introduction, religion is already deeply embedded in curricula across the K–12 spectrum. Our aim is to help equip educators with the tools to teach about religion in intellectually responsible, constitutionally sound, and educationally meaningful ways. The following section focuses on the legal issues related to teaching about religion and Part Three will offer examples of how to integrate the study of religion into existing curricula and department structures.

PART TWO

RELIGION, EDUCATION, AND THE CONSTITUTION

Congress shall make no law respecting an establishment of religion, or prohibiting the free exercise thereof. [17]

There were two important and related Supreme Court rulings in the 1960s that were pivotal in defining the role of religion in public education. In *Engel v. Vitale* (1962) it was decided that government should not sponsor prayers in public schools. In *Abington v. Schempp* (1963) the Supreme Court ruled that the government should not sponsor Bible reading for devotional purposes and recitation of the Lord's Prayer in public schools. While many hailed these rulings as a strong endorsement of the separation of church and state and thus an affirmation of pluralism, others felt that they signaled the demise of a common moral foundation that served to unite all Americans amidst our diversity. These same tensions persist today, and many trace the roots of contemporary conflicts regarding religion in the public sphere to these rulings.[18]

Though the heart of these decisions addressed what was not permissible in public education, there was an important affirmation in *Abington v. Schempp* regarding what was allowed in the intersection of religion and the schools. As Justice Thomas C. Clark wrote:

> It might well be said that one's education is not complete without a study of comparative religion or the history of religion and its relationship to the advancement of civilization. It certainly may be said that the Bible is worthy of study for its literary and historic qualities. Nothing we have said here indicates that such study of the Bible or of religion, when presented objectively as part of a secular program of education, may not be effected consistently with the First Amendment.[19]

This important articulation has often been overlooked in the history of how the separation of church and state in the schools has been interpreted. Though there has been a slight shift over the past decade, most Americans since the 1960s believe that the separation of church and state that is affirmed in the rulings cited above meant that religion in all forms was banned. As Justice Clark's comments above clearly indicate, this is not at all the case. Indeed, some have argued that it may be a violation of the First Amendment when the study of religion is not included in public school curricula. Though it is clear that teaching about religion is acceptable, how to do so in a constitutionally sound and intellectually responsibly manner is a more complex undertaking.

GUIDELINES FOR TEACHING ABOUT RELIGION

In 1974, religious studies scholar James V. Panoch developed a set of guidelines for distinguishing between teaching religion in a way that promotes a particular faith and teaching about religion from a religious studies perspective.[20] A version of these guidelines was adopted by the First Amendment Center and is featured prominently in several of its publications, including one entitled *A Teacher's Guide to Religion in the Public Schools*:[21]

- The school's approach to religion is *academic*, not *devotional*.

- The school strives for student *awareness* of religions, but does not press for student *acceptance* of any religion.

- The school sponsors *study* about religion, not the *practice* of religion.

- The school may *expose* students to a diversity of religious views, but may not *impose* any particular view.

- The school *educates* about all religions, it does not *promote* or *denigrate* religion.

- The school *informs* students about various beliefs; it does not seek to *conform* students to any particular belief.[22]

These guidelines appropriately assume the distinction between teaching about religion from a non-devotional, academic perspective versus teaching religion through a devotional lens. As such, they provide a useful thumbnail sketch to guide educators in the public school context. Indeed, they have been very helpful in alerting teachers and administrators to the fact that there is a distinction between a secular and devotional approach. As noted above, one of the manifestations of widespread religious illiteracy is the equation of religious studies with devotional practice.

It is important to note here that teaching about religion from a non-devotional, religious studies approach is not without controversy. For example, teaching about religion gives credibility to religion itself as a valid field of inquiry and assumes the legitimacy of multiple religious perspectives. Some who believe that their convictions represent an exclusive truth may find these assumptions challenging. Many other citizens recognize the value of increasing literacy about religion and believe that the public schools are the appropriate venue for this type of learning to occur. *The AAR Guidelines for Teaching About Religion in K-12 Public Schools* represent this latter perspective and are based on the assumption that public schools are appropriately governed by secular laws and values that support the inclusion of the non-devotional study of religion from an academic perspective across the curriculum. The next section will focus on how to achieve this inclusion by outlining different approaches to the study of religion (historical, literary, tradition based, and cultural studies) and offering grade-specific examples of how to integrate theory with practice.

PART THREE

HOW TO TEACH ABOUT RELIGION
INTRODUCTION

This chapter provides an overview of various approaches for how religion gets taught in schools along with an assessment of the strengths and weaknesses associated with these methods. Discussion about religion presents unique challenges to classroom teachers, and this section presents ways for educators to introduce religion as a topic as well as ways they can help students develop a more nuanced understanding of religion beyond stereotyped or simplistic representations. In order to ground these ideas in practice, we have provided some snapshots of classroom practices across disciplines and grade levels as examples of what is possible.[23] This chapter ends with answers to frequently asked questions posed by students about religion.

APPROACHES TO TEACHING ABOUT RELIGION

Teachers are expected to teach about religion in a variety of ways in their classrooms. The three most common occur when

1. The curriculum demands coverage of the historical origins of religious traditions or their contemporary relevance;

2. The novels or stories they teach have explicit religious themes or allusions; and

3. Their students raise questions based on their own experiences and knowledge.

How teachers respond to these expectations differs greatly, and the choice of approaches used by teachers is influenced by their subject area, their training, and their own personal views. Three approaches to religion commonly taught in public schools are the historical, literary, and traditions-based methods. A fourth method, a cultural studies approach, incorporates dimensions of all these approaches and is promoted by religious studies and education scholars. These four approaches are outlined below and analyzed regarding their strengths and weaknesses for classroom use.

The Historical Approach

This approach is very commonly used in social studies classes where religion occurs within courses or lessons focused on history. The strengths of the historical approach are clear: the origins of a religion and its development are presented in historical context with the political and cultural influences represented as central to understanding how that religion emerged, gained followers, and spread. Religions do not evolve in a vacuum, and looking at the historical circumstances that shaped the development of a tradition or worldview can help students see that religions are complex webs of practices and values with a variety of expressions rather than monolithic, fully formed sets of ideas and beliefs. There is no inherent weakness in this approach, but in practice teachers report[24] that they lack the knowledge base in religious studies required to address the historical complexities of religion adequately. Furthermore, religions are often only explored in their pre-modern contexts in ways that can leave students with the impression that (1) religion became (and continues to be) obsolete in the modern era; or (2) that religious beliefs formed and then solidified into unchanging systems. Students rarely learn how religions continually evolve and change beyond the eighteenth century, nor are they given the necessary tools to knowledgeably consider and evaluate the roles religions play in modern cultures.

The Literary Approach

This is common in English language arts classes in which students read religious texts themselves or novels, stories, and poetry with religious themes and/or imagery. Using this approach, teachers help students gain an appreciation of the way that religion infuses all aspects of culture by seeing how religious allusion and metaphor can become a common language that is shared by a people. Looking at a particular story where religious expression is a theme helps students see the very specific ways that individuals experience their religion and helps to reinforce the idea that generalizations about religion are often flawed. When the focus is on religious texts themselves, students learn to appreciate their literary value and how religious texts influence literary styles. Similar to the historical approach, there is no inherent weakness in the literary method itself. The challenge is that most educators lack the training in religious studies that is required to provide the appropriate information about religion relevant to the texts that are studied. In the absence of such training, teachers often rely on their own devotional experiences of a tradition or reference other devotional interpretations as adequate sources of information. This often leads to partial or otherwise problematic interpretations as well as a limitation on the types of texts assigned. Teachers will understandably shy away from texts representing or informed by traditions or expressions that are unfamiliar.

The Traditions-Based Approach

This approach is often represented in world history textbooks, used in electives or stand-alone courses in higher grades, or used as the basis for comparative religion studies in lower grades. The focus is often on certain categories that apply to many religious traditions, such as beliefs, texts, rituals, origins, and holidays, or on essential questions that religions address related to the purpose of life, how one should live, and various interpretations of identity. This approach can help students see common themes in religious traditions and can provide a useful framework for understanding the varieties of religious expression. In looking at religious art or rituals, students can gain an appreciation for the ways all religions shape and are shaped by the culture around them. The main weaknesses of this approach are that (1) it often fails to adequately represent the internal diversity of religious traditions; and (2) it can exaggerate the commonalities among traditions. Additionally, the categories for comparison are themselves often shaped by particular religious assumptions (e.g. by including categories such as "founder" and "sacred text") that are not universally relevant and which therefore promote a biased and limited framework for analysis.

The Cultural Studies Approach

This approach is often used by those trained in religious studies programs and is well suited for area studies classes or classes that incorporate a multicultural lens of analysis. It serves as a tool to build upon and enhance the other three approaches in its emphasis on recognizing the ways that religion is embedded in culture and cannot be understood in isolation from its particular social/historical expressions. Additionally, this approach includes a consideration of social power and the ways that race, class, and gender (among other factors) provide important categories of analysis when investigating differing religious expressions and their cultural/political influences. Finally, a cultural studies approach recognizes that teachers and students (along with the authors and artists being studied) are interpreters of meaning and that conscious and unconscious assumptions about religion profoundly shape the ways that individuals express what they know and interpret what they learn about religion. The strengths of the cultural studies approach are that (1) it helps students recognize that religion is a part of the fabric of human experience and that in order to understand it one must consider religious beliefs and practices as they shape and are shaped by all elements of culture; (2) it provides tools to understand how some religious beliefs and expressions become culturally and politically prominent, while others become culturally and politically marginalized; and (3) it provides tools to recognize and analyze the interpretive dimensions of all knowledge claims. The main challenges related to this approach are that (1) it requires training in religious studies; and (2) it requires teachers to slow down and cover less content with more depth.

A NOTE ABOUT TEXTBOOKS

Most social studies teachers rely on textbooks as the main source of information for their students, and the strengths and weaknesses of this primary resource type are well known. Textbook authors are burdened by the need to cover vast amounts of material in ways that are easily accessible, and thus they are forced to simplify complex topics. This is especially pronounced in regard to coverage of religion. Most textbook authors employ a combination of the historical and traditions-based approaches in their coverage of religion, the latter typified by the ubiquitous chart in world history textbooks depicting several of the world's religious traditions outlined and compared by categories.[25] Minimally, teachers are encouraged to supplement such charts with culturally diverse and historically situated examples of religious practices that will help challenge the static and ahistorical depiction of religion that this common resource promotes.

A NOTE ABOUT MEDIA LITERACY AND RELIGION

Media literacy is a growing field in critical education studies and with good reason. Children of all ages are bombarded with media images and information from a variety of sources, and their ability to analyze and evaluate the credibility of information received is an important dimension of critical thinking in the modern age. As noted in Part One of these guidelines, the media is one of the two main sources for information about religion that citizens receive, so media literacy is especially relevant to efforts aimed at strengthening literacy about religion generally. Though a more detailed exploration goes beyond the scope of this project, we encourage educators to (1) explicitly address with their students the problems associated with relying on the media for information about religion and its role in human affairs; and (2) refrain from utilizing popular sites such as Wikipedia and YouTube as sole authoritative sources of information about religion.

SETTING THE CONTEXT

As outlined in Part One, the distinction between the study of religion and religious devotional expression is rarely understood by those who have never been exposed to religious studies. Making this distinction clear to students before embarking on any lessons that relate to religion will:

1. Help them realize that learning about religion is a legal and appropriate undertaking for public schools, and

2. Help them realize that the aim of teaching about religion is to better understand the religious dimensions of human experience, not to promote religion or a particular religious perspective.

Articulating the distinction between religious studies and a devotional approach to religion at the outset of a lesson or unit will clarify educational goals and minimize confusion and anxiety.

INITIAL STEPS

Teaching about religion in public schools brings with it particular challenges that teachers seldom face when addressing other subject areas. Students in a physics course rarely come to class with a sense that they have particular insights that will be relevant and helpful to a class discussion of vectors, but when the subject is religion, students can feel that their own personal experiences give them special knowledge and authority. Often students will have strongly held ideas about the positive or negative role of religion in the world, ideas about religious and non-religious people, and ideas about particular faiths. Teachers also may feel that their own background in a particular religious tradition prepares them sufficiently to teach that tradition, or may have views about religion and its relevance in their classroom that shape how they teach religious topics.

Thus one of the first challenges for teachers and students alike is to examine what assumptions they harbor about religion generally and religious traditions in particular.

Having students explore their assumptions is an essential first step in helping them look at religion clearly. Students can reflect in writing about some key words or concepts like religion, belief, or any tradition (such as Judaism, Islam, or Buddhism). Brainstorming quickly can help students identify their most basic associations, those rooted in long experience and snap judgment. It is important to be explicit with students about why an examination of their assumptions is a critical first step in their learning. By explaining how biases and assumptions can act as a filter on new knowledge, they gain an important tool that they can return to again and again throughout their explorations about religion specifically and other topics more generally. In addition, by reflecting on their own preconceived ideas about religion, students can also think about how their ideas may stereotype and misjudge the beliefs and practices of others, including those of their own peers in the classroom or school.

Talking about religion can touch the depth of someone's identity, causing some discussions to feel like an attack, especially when based on misinformation and stereotypes. Therefore, it is imperative to foster a climate of tolerance, respect, and honesty by encouraging students to

- Move away from making generalizations toward more qualified statements—from, for example, "All Christians are intolerant" to "I have heard that Christians are intolerant—is this true?" Or to "Some Christians are intolerant";

- Examine how their judgments may impact others; and

- Explore ideas and ask questions without fear.

Not everyone in the class is expected to agree. But students should understand that

- The goal is developing awareness and understanding; and

- Accurate representations of traditions reduce the misunderstandings arising from false generalizations, bigotry, or valorization of a particular religious or non-religious worldview.

Once students have had a chance to think about their preconceptions of religion, and educators have established a classroom culture of respect, teachers need to decide how to approach content. With limited time and resources, teachers are often faced with the challenge of selecting the most basic, central ideas of any religion to cover. A study of Buddhism becomes a look at the Four Noble Truths, for example, or reading an excerpt from Hesse's *Siddhartha*. While teachers will always be constrained by the concerns of coverage, time, and materials, introducing students to the following fundamental premises of religious studies will help challenge common misunderstandings and give students a good foundation for further study. The premises outlined below are that (1) religions are internally diverse; (2) religions are dynamic; and (3) religions are embedded in culture. There are three "snapshots" of practice that follow a description of each premise representing primary, middle, and secondary school age groups with examples focusing on either English language arts or social studies. There are several more snapshots included in Appendix D [pages 218–223].

PREMISES OF RELIGIOUS STUDIES

Religions are Internally Diverse

A basic premise of religious studies is that religions are not internally homogeneous but diverse. In schools and in popular culture, faith traditions are often presented as a single set of beliefs, practices, and representations without internal variation. While the major differences within a tradition may be introduced ("the majority of Muslims are Sunnis, while others are Shi'a"), less dramatic or clearly defined distinctions are often overlooked or presumed not to exist. It is important for students to learn, for example, that Muslims in Indonesia will practice their faith differently than Muslims in Nigeria. In a similar vein, wealthy Muslims in Jakarta may practice an Islam that looks somewhat different than poor Muslims in rural Java. Helping students see that there are many "Islams" (or Judaisms or Hinduisms) in the world enables them to consider carefully both what it means to study Islam and the complexity of answering the question, "What do Muslims believe?"

One general classroom strategy is to begin with an example of the diversities represented in a tradition that students are familiar with, such as Christianity, and then help them apply that understanding to other less familiar traditions and worldviews.

Snapshots of Practice

Elementary School English Language Arts

Ms. X. decides to do an oral storytelling unit with her first-grade classroom. Each day she reads aloud a Native American story from different tribes to her class.[26] Afterwards, she asks them to return to their desks and draw what they remember of the story. After several stories have been shared, each student chooses her or his favorite and is assigned to learn it and retell it to a friend or family member. Throughout the unit, Ms. X. discusses differences between oral, written, and visual representations and encourages her students to practice all three skillsets. Her students are exposed to both variety in the beliefs, subjects, and settings of Native American religions and many different forms of literacy.

Middle School Social Studies

Ms. Q. is teaching an eighth-grade world history course that covers the fall of Rome to the beginnings of the European Renaissance. As part of their study of the "Golden Age" she has them act as explorers of the diverse cultures that came under the rule of expanding Islamic empires. After reading excerpts from the logs of medieval Muslim travelers such as Ibn Jubayr, Ibn Batuta, and Naser-e Kosraw,[27] Ms. Q. has students watch clips from the documentary "Islam: Empire of Faith"[28] and conduct outside research on medieval cities from Central Asia, North and West Africa, the Iberian Peninsula, and Arabia that includes an investigation into mosques that were built in these locations during this time period.[29] Students conclude by creating their own "Explorer's Journals" in which they describe, through writing and illustration, the similarities and differences they saw between expressions of Islamic life and practice as Muslims moved into these culturally diverse regions.

Secondary School English Language Arts
  Before reading Hermann Hesse's *Siddhartha*, Ms. R. has her eleventh-grade students research the life of Hesse to introduce them to his cultural context and the influences that led him to write his most popular novel. While studying the text, she introduces students to readings from John Strong's *The Buddha: A Short Biography*[30] and Strong, ed., *The Experience of Buddhism: Sources and Interpretations*[31] to give her students tools to compare Hesse's interpretation of South Asian Buddhism with scholarly accounts representing a variety of different perspectives. She helps them explore these diverse interpretations and how different genres shape perception.

Religions are Dynamic

A second premise of religious studies is the recognition that religions are dynamic and changing as opposed to static and fixed. When religious practices or texts are taught without historical context, it is easy for students to view the rituals or stories as having one meaning that persists for all times and places. Religions, however, exist in time and space and are constantly interpreted and reinterpreted by believers. For example, the Confucian concept of the "mandate from heaven" evolved within dynasties, geopolitical regions, and historical eras and continues to evolve today. Seeing examples of the way that religious beliefs, practices and imagery change over time and place helps students recognize that, from a religious studies perspective, there is no such thing as "a single meaning" of a given tradition, practice, or belief system.

Snapshots of Practice
Elementary School Social Studies
  Mr. Y.'s fourth-grade social studies curriculum focuses on North American geography and peoples. His students learn about the lives of native communities in the U.S. and Canada before and during the time that European explorers and colonists began to make contact with the continent. He is also eager to include contemporary representations of the communities he is exploring and selects a few for students to research in groups and to present reflections regarding how the traditions have evolved and changed over the years and how core values have been interpreted and preserved.[32]

Middle School English Language Arts
  Ms. M.'s sixth-grade class is exploring the art of storytelling. She has students write a series of their own stories interspersed with selections of stories from a diverse array of cultures and traditions. In one section, she focuses on how ancient stories are often retold with contemporary significance and chooses selections from *Because God Loves Stories: An Anthology of Jewish Storytelling*[33] as one example of this common literary practice.

Secondary School Social Studies
  Mr. W. is in the midst of a unit on the Roman Empire with his tenth-grade world history students and wants to include a section on the origins of Christianity. He has students read the portion in their textbook about Jesus and his message, but supplements this lesson with additional resources to show (1) how there were many different and often competing interpretations of who Jesus was and what he promoted in the early years following his death, and (2) how those interpretations changed and evolved over time. He gathers a series of resources from the PBS series "From Jesus to Christ"[34] depicting these tensions and evolutions and engages his students in a series of inquiries regarding the significance of these insights.

Religions are Embedded in Culture

A third premise of religious studies is the recognition that religions are collections of ideas, practices, values, and stories that are all embedded in cultures and not isolated from them. Just as religion cannot be understood in isolation from its cultural manifestations, it is impossible to understand culture without considering its religious dimensions. In the same way that race, ethnicity, gender, and sexuality are always factors in cultural interpretation and understanding, so too is religion. Whether explicit or implicit, religious influences can virtually always be found when one asks "the religion question" of any given social/historical experience. For example, rather than assuming in an American history class that a focus on religion is only relevant when studying the Puritans, the Great Awakenings, or the rise of the "Moral Majority," this approach assumes that there are rich avenues of inquiry that open when one considers the religious influences that shaped the Constitutional Convention, the institution of slavery, women's suffrage, the Industrial Revolution, and the U.S. involvement in World War II. Finally, it is important to underscore (again) that religions are *influenced* by cultures while also *influencing* cultures.

Snapshots of Practice

Elementary School English Language Arts

Mr. B. and his third-grade class read *In the Heart of the Village: The World of the Indian Banyan Tree*[35] by Barbara Bash. They discuss how the tree functions as a central location of the community and compare the different people who meet there—kids at school, merchants trading goods, villagers gathering to talk. He then shows them images of Banyan trees around the world, including the oldest such tree in America in Fort Myers, Florida.[36] Several of these are artistic representations of the Hindu God Shiva in his aspect as Jnana Dakshinamurti, teacher of wisdom, always shown seated at the foot of a Banyan tree; others are of the Buddha under the Bodhi Tree, a Banyan species under which (according to legend) the Buddha gained enlightenment. Mr. B. and his class then discuss various places and objects that are central points in their own lives (school playground, churches, grocery stores, temples) and then write their own stories about all the different types of people who come there every day.

Middle School Social Studies

A consistent theme of Mr. H.'s seventh-grade geography class is the relationship between the inhabitants of each region his class studies and the major features of its natural landscape. Several times throughout the year he has asked his students to research and prepare short debates about use and protection of various natural resources, and each time he has his students consider the ways in which religious worldview may influence the assumptions of the perspectives they are representing. While his students are familiar with well-known natural sites of veneration such as the Ganges River in India, he also introduces them to less frequently considered contexts. Using Diana Eck's *A New Religious America*[37] as a resource, he provides examples such as the spot in Pittsburgh at which the Allegheny, Ohio, and Monongahela rivers converge. Known as a "sangam" in the Hindu tradition, students learn that this confluence has been recognized by many Hindu immigrants to Pennsylvania as a particularly auspicious location, holding much symbolic importance. Mr. H. uses such examples both to explore the ways immigration continues to transform the cultural geography of the modern world, and to encourage students to consider multiple, and perhaps overlooked, religious perspectives on the natural landscape of any geographic context.

Secondary School English Language Arts

Mr. J. always starts his tenth-grade English class with a unit on biblical stories in order to prepare his students for the Western classics they will read that year. First, he gives his students a selection of biblical-themed cartoons from *The New Yorker*[38] and asks them to identify in writing as many of the characters and stories as they can in five minutes. As most students discover they know only a few of the "big ones" (Adam and Eve, Noah, Moses), Mr. J. shows them "He forgot – and I – remembered" by Emily Dickinson and points out the various biblical allusions that they would need to know for an in-depth exploration of the poem. He then hands out a list of several popular biblical allusions to know[39] and students choose which story they will research and present. As part of a five-minute Powerpoint presentation, students must provide both of the following elements: a short synopsis of the story as it appears in the King James Bible (Mr. J. chooses this translation since it is the one the majority of English authors they are studying would have known and used) and a representation of this story in an art form other than literature. For an assessment at the end of the week's unit, Mr. J. gives his class the lyrics to Bob Dylan's "Angelina" and asks them to write a one-page essay on the use of biblical allusion.

See Appendix D [pages 218-223] for additional snapshots representing the three premises of religious studies.

FREQUENTLY ASKED QUESTIONS

Even the most carefully prepared lesson can be derailed by a difficult question, and lessons that involve the study of religion are especially challenging in this regard. Because of the level of sensitivity about religion, teachers may try to avoid addressing these questions for fear of offending or giving wrong information. Teachers may also fear that they will cross the line of what is constitutionally acceptable. When addressing difficult questions, teachers should help students remember that the goal of the academic study of religion is understanding, not agreement, and that different religious views may and often will conflict with one another. Nor is the academic study of religion designed to answer the same types of questions that religious communities answer for believers. Questions about what is the "right" or "true" belief are theological questions and not ones that teachers can answer for students in a class focused on the study of religion. It is also important to know that many common questions about religion frequently represent a host of problematic assumptions that are often too involved to address in the moment but which can be "flagged" for later follow up in a class discussion or incorporation into a lesson. The answers we offer here are not comprehensive, but we hope they will serve as helpful initial guides. With these general parameters in mind, here are a few commonly asked questions and possible answers or suggestions for how teachers can respond.

Why do people still believe in religion?

Some believe that religion is a product of the ancient world and that advances in science and philosophy have rendered religious belief obsolete. Religions, however, address more than answers to questions about the natural world; they address fundamental questions of meaning and provide frameworks for ethical reflection and structures of social formation. The assumption that religion is obsolete often rests upon a rigid and extremely narrow understanding of religion, history, and science. Therefore, helping students identify the assumptions that inform the question itself can be a useful exercise in its own right.

Are religion and science incompatible?

No, not categorically. Most religious traditions and worldviews can function in concert with scientific worldviews and are, indeed, complementary with them. Furthermore, there are many scientists who are people of faith and many people of faith who are devoted scientists. Within traditions, however, there are some theological beliefs that are in tension with certain scientific assertions. The most publicized example of these tensions in the US is between some Christian communities and the biological theory of evolution. Though these tensions are real for the communities involved, it is wrong to assume, for example, that all Christians experience a contradiction between their theological beliefs and evolutionary theory or, by extension, that religious and scientific worldviews are fundamentally incompatible.

Can creation science or intelligent design be taught in schools?

Yes, but **not** in science classes. Creation science and intelligent design represent worldviews that fall outside of the realm of science that is defined as (and limited to) a method of inquiry based on gathering observable and measurable evidence subject to specific principles of reasoning. Creation science, intelligent design, and other worldviews that focus on speculation regarding the origins of life represent another important and relevant form of human inquiry that is appropriately studied in literature or social sciences courses. Such study, however, must include a diversity of worldviews representing a variety of religious and philosophical perspectives and must avoid privileging one view as more legitimate than others.

Does the Bible say that homosexuality is wrong?

Some Jews and Christians believe that same-sex relationships of all kinds are sinful and often cite passages in the Torah and the Christian Bible to support this view. Others argue that passages referencing same-sex sexual encounters vary considerably in their details, offer different possibilities of interpretation, and as the product of ancient cultures they are of little relevance for understanding homosexuality in its contemporary forms. While some Jewish and Christian communities oppose same-sex marriages, others have endorsed their legality and support the ritualized blessing of such unions. The range of views found on this issue illustrates the internal diversity of these two traditions (among others) and the different ways in which sacred texts are given meaning through interpretation.

Do Jews believe in heaven?

Much of Jewish tradition and teaching is focused on human agency in this world with the assumption that what happens following death is unknowable and in the realm of the Holy. Still, there is also much speculation within Jewish tradition about the afterlife and most religious Jews believe that humans possess a soul that does not die when one's physical being dies. Though there are many and diverse views of the afterlife within Jewish tradition, it is important to note that Jewish perspectives tend to differ from Christian ones, and that common images of and associations with "heaven" are most likely informed by Christian viewpoints.

Did the Jews kill Jesus?

It is important to realize at the outset that our primary historical evidence for the existence of Jesus is limited to just four books, the New Testament Gospels, which present differing interpretations of Jesus and which themselves are subject to differing interpretations. What is known is that Jesus lived and died under the authority of the Roman Empire, the political power in Judea during his lifetime. He was, himself, a Jew who gained followers and most likely came to be seen as a threat to the peace and stability of the region by Roman officials and some members of the Jewish community who may have been troubled by his interpretation of Judaism. Most historians agree that it was the Roman authorities that sentenced Jesus to death by crucifixion, which was a common Roman form of execution at the time. The Jewish community was itself very divided on how it viewed Jesus, and those Jews who were his followers and took up his message had a vested interest in distinguishing themselves from those Jews who did not. There were also non-Jewish followers of Jesus, some of whom experienced tensions with factions of the Jewish community. Thus some early Christians began placing the blame for the death of Jesus on "the Jews," and this perspective (sometimes referred to as "blood guilt") became deeply intertwined with influential strands of early Christian beliefs and practices.

Is the Buddha a god?

The Buddha was a fifth-century BCE Indian prince named Siddhartha Gautama who, as legend has it, gained enlightenment and became known as the Buddha ("the one who woke up, enlightened one"). Some strands of the tradition represent the Buddha as human and challenge the legitimacy of any association of Buddha with cosmological significance. Other strands venerate him as a saint or as someone with special spiritual power. There is tremendous diversity of beliefs and practices among Buddhists in this regard. Exploring what the questioner means by "god" would be important in formulating a relevant response.

Do you have to follow all the rules of a religion to be religious?

Religious identification is both a deeply personal and broadly cultural feature of human society. Because religion is intertwined with ethnicity and culture, many people identify themselves as members of a religious community even if they infrequently participate in that religion's rituals or only partially adopt that religion's beliefs. Others can be deeply committed to their religious practice and yet see themselves as on the periphery of their religious community. What it means to be "really religious" within one tradition can also vary dramatically from place to place.

Is God real?

This is a theological question and one that is appropriate to address within the context of one's family and/or faith community. In the public school classroom, however, an appropriate response would be to turn the student's attention toward examining the diversity of beliefs regarding the existence of God.

Is Islam a violent religion?

Islam (like Christianity, Buddhism, Paganism, etc.) is neither violent nor nonviolent. In the hands of believers, all religious expressions are capable of being interpreted in ways that can inspire the full range of human agency from the heinous to the heroic. It is one of the clearest manifestations of religious illiteracy when any tradition is classified with a singular characterization. The widespread association in non-Muslim communities of Islam with violence is due to a host of factors, including media coverage of violent activities perpetrated by a minority of Muslims. In the absence of opportunities to study Islam in its rich and full diversity, these depictions are often wrongly interpreted as comprehensively representative of the tradition itself.

I'm Hindu (or Muslim, Christian, Buddhist) and my religion is really different from the Hinduism (or Islam, Christianity, Buddhism) we are studying. Why?

It can be disorienting for students to see their own tradition presented in unfamiliar ways, and teachers can help students by reminding them of the vast diversity of religious expressions within as well as between religious traditions. It is best to frame any unit or lesson on religion with this reminder at the outset so that when questions such as this one arise teachers can reference back to this framework and help the student situate his or her own practice within the wider tradition being studied. A good rule of thumb for teachers is that particular theological expressions of a tradition should be represented accurately and respectfully, but never exclusively.

Why do we need to study religion anyway? We're in school, not church!

There is a difference between the secular study of religion and the practice of religion as devotional expression. Unfortunately, many in the United States do not understand this distinction, and this has led to a belief that it is inappropriate to learn about religion in schools. However, the courts have made clear that, under the Constitution, learning about religion is both legal and an important dimension of a comprehensive education. It is impossible to understand human history and culture without understanding its religious dimensions. Furthermore, illiteracy about religion fuels prejudice and bigotry between and among communities. Learning about religion in schools deepens our understanding of human experience and promotes appreciation of diversity.

CONCLUSION

Teachers often feel ill prepared and anxious about the mistakes they might make when faced with the challenges associated with teaching about religion in their classes. The temptation can be to avoid religion altogether or to present only elements that seem the most "objective": the Ten Commandments, the Five Pillars, the Four Noble Truths, etc. Our goal here is not to make

teachers feel more overwhelmed or to place greater demands on them. Our goal is to help empower teachers to expand their repertoire of approaches to the study of religion, and to have good justifications for why this element of their curriculum deserves time and space.

PART FOUR

TEACHER EDUCATION

In order to effectively include the study of religion in K-12 curricula, teachers must be prepared to do so. If religion is left out of pre-service and in-service teacher education, it is likely either that religion will be left out of the classroom because teachers feel uncomfortable with content they feel unqualified to teach or, if included, that the treatment of religion by unprepared teachers may fall short of constitutional guidelines in approach or accuracy in regard to content.

The following brief recommendations regarding teacher education for the teaching of religion in public K-12 schools take a learning outcomes approach, rather than stipulate particular courses or require minimal credit hours of college or university work in religion.

The American Academy of Religion recommends that teacher education, especially in social studies and English, be driven by the following set of educational outcomes or competencies in teacher pre-service and in-service education.

CONTENT COMPETENCIES

All teachers should have some contact with the history and cultural context of the discipline of religious studies, including the awareness that "religion" itself is a Western construct.[40]

For those who teach world history, as well as world cultures, societies, religions, and arts

1. Familiarity with the basic outlooks, experiences, and practices of the widespread living religious traditions—Hinduism, Buddhism, Confucianism, Taoism, Judaism, Christianity, and Islam—and of indigenous regional religions (religions of the Americas, Africa, Asia and the Pacific), with special attention to the diversity of expressions and practices within as well as between religions and regions.

2. An understanding of how specific religions function in particular social/historical contexts.

3. An understanding of how religions affect and are affected by their cultural contexts and thus how religions are internally diverse and dynamic.

(This is the content often covered in university-level world religions courses.)

For those who teach U.S. history

1. Familiarity with the basic beliefs and practices of Native North American (and Hawaiian) religions, as well as the religions of important/sizable immigrant communities.

2. An understanding of the place of religion in the founding documents of the U.S., especially in the First Amendment, and how the religion clauses have been interpreted in the courts over the history of the nation.

3. An understanding of some of the ways in which religious belief, practice, and affiliation have affected the course of the nation—whether on an individual, group, or societal level—and including political, economic, and social behavior.

(This is the content often covered in university-level courses on U.S. religion.)

For those who teach the Bible as literature

1. An understanding of the ancient religious communities that produced various biblical texts.

2. An understanding that different faith communities have different Bibles (e.g., Jewish, Roman Catholic, Eastern Orthodox, Protestant) and that there are many different translations of the Bible that often reflect significant theological differences (e.g., the New Jewish Publication Society, the Living Torah, the New Standard Revised Version, the King James Version, the New International Version).

3. Familiarity with the most important narratives, characters, and teachings contained in the Bible from the perspective of differing traditions.

4. Understanding and working knowledge of the historical critical method for the study of the Bible (and other ancient texts).

(The above content is often covered in single university-level introductory courses on the Bible, or in introductory two-course sequences on the Hebrew Bible (or the Christian Old Testament) and the New Testament.)

5. Knowledge of how biblical narratives, characters, figures of speech, images, and teachings occur throughout the literary culture of the West.

PEDAGOGICAL COMPETENCIES

1. Be aware of examples of best practices in teaching about religion.

2. Be able to address in a constructive way religious disagreements and conflicts that arise in the classroom.

3. Be able to find and recognize appropriate resources about religion when needed, on the Internet or in more traditional media.

4. Be aware of, and manage effectively, religious diversity in the classroom.

5. Develop the ability to present multiple religious perspectives in a fair or neutral way.

6. Become familiar with the religious make-up of the larger community.

7. Understand the difference between the secular academic and devotional approaches to religion, and consistently use the secular academic approach.

8. Develop skills in leading students in discussion regarding their religious beliefs and practices, as well as the beliefs and practices of others.

9. Create an environment of respect and tolerance—a safe environment in which students feel free to talk about religion.[41]

APPROPRIATE ATTITUDES/POSTURES

1. Teachers should never try to coerce students to accept or reject any particular religious tradition, belief, or practice, as well as non-belief or atheism.

2. Teachers should not give any particular religious belief, practice, or tradition inappropriate (or unfair) emphasis.

3. Teachers should not discourage students' free expression of their religious beliefs or ideas.

4. Teachers should present religion content in the context of the approved curriculum.

5. The personal religious beliefs or practices of the teacher do not qualify or disqualify the teacher from teaching about religions in his or her classroom. Rather, academic training in religion content and pedagogy are the qualification for teaching religion in the schools, regardless of the personal religion, or lack thereof, of the teacher.[42]

EXAMPLES OF OPPORTUNITIES FOR TEACHERS TO LEARN ABOUT CONTENT

Many religious studies scholars in the American Academy of Religion have had the opportunity to work with professional educators who teach students across the kindergarten through twelfth grade spectrum. Most often, these opportunities take the form of workshops or seminars for in-service teachers who are hoping to strengthen their literacy about religion.[43] In some contexts, there are pre-service opportunities for would-be teachers to take religious studies courses at their college or university as part of their content area preparation.[44]

We in the American Academy of Religion urge programs that train pre-service educators to include at least one religious studies course in their requirements. We also encourage educators to avail themselves of opportunities to strengthen their literacy about religion by enrolling in religious studies courses at their local college or university. Obviously, the more exposure teachers have to the academic study of religion, the better equipped they will be to teach about the rich complexities of religion as it manifests itself in human political and cultural life. However, due to the widespread illiteracy about religion in the general population, exposure to even a single well-taught course in religious studies can dramatically enhance one's understanding of, and appreciation for, the important role of religion in human experience.

NOTES ABOUT LEGALITY, METHOD AND PEDAGOGY

In addition to learning about religion to enhance content knowledge, it is also important for educators to learn about the legal and pedagogical dimensions of teaching about religion in the schools. As we have highlighted throughout this document, educators are constantly confronted with challenges and opportunities related to religion in their classrooms and schools through content-related issues as well as through the religious diversity of the students they serve. There are helpful guidelines and manuscripts published to give educators important foundational information,[45] but whenever possible we also urge teachers to enroll in workshops and/or courses that explore these issues in more depth. What seem like clear guidelines in abstraction often become quickly muddled in practice. Having opportunities to explore the nuances of public policy debates about religion in the schools and how to construct lesson plans that incorporate more accurate representations of religion will provide educators with helpful tools for their own practice while also helping them to serve as a resource for their colleagues in the school and larger district.

CONCLUSION

We in the American Academy of Religion hope these guidelines will be a useful tool for public school educators, members of school boards, and general citizens as they experience the opportunities and challenges that accompany issues related to teaching about religion in our schools. It has been our pleasure to work closely with educators to construct these guidelines and to learn more about the important role that public school teachers play in helping their students better understand the rich diversity of religious expression in human experience.

APPENDIX A

LIST OF RELIGION IN THE SCHOOLS TASK FORCE AND WORKING GROUP MEMBERS

Religion in the Schools Task Force

- Diane L. Moore, *Chair: Professor of the Practice of Religious Studies and Education, Harvard Divinity School*

- Ann Marie Bahr: *Professor in the Philosophy and Religion Department, South Dakota State University (Task Force member until November 2008)*

- Mark Chancey: *Associate Professor, Department of Religious Studies, Southern Methodist University*

- Betty DeBerg: *Professor of Religion, University of Northern Iowa*

- David Haberman: *Professor of Religious Studies, Indiana University*

- Bruce Lawrence: *Nancy and Jeffrey Marcus Humanities Professor of Religion, Duke University*

- Stephanie McAllister: *History and Social Science Teacher, Brookline High School, Brookline, MA*

- Steve Herrick, *AAR Staff Liaison (ex-officio)*

Members of the Working Group

- Ann Marie Bahr: *Professor in the Philosophy and Religion Department, South Dakota State University (Working Group member as of December 2008)*

- Wallace Best: *Professor of Religion and African American Studies, Princeton University*

- Elizabeth Bounds: *Associate Professor of Christian Ethics, Candler School of Theology, Emory University*

- Bruce Grelle: *Professor of Religious Studies (Ethics), California State University, Chico*

- Carlene Mandolfo: *Associate Professor of Religious Studies (Hebrew Bible), Colby College*

- Anne Monius: *Professor of South Asian Religions, Harvard Divinity School*

- Keith Naylor: *Professor of Religious Studies (Religion in America), Occidental College*

- Martha Newman: *Professor of Religious Studies, University of Texas at Austin*

- Sarah Pike: *Professor of Religious Studies, California State University, Chico*

- Marc Raphael: *Nathan Gumenick Chair of Judaic Studies, College of William and Mary*

APPENDIX B

A SAMPLING OF CONSENSUS DOCUMENTS ON TEACHING ABOUT RELIGION

- *Finding Common Ground: A Guide to Religious Liberty in Public Schools* by Charles C. Haynes and Oliver Thomas. http://www.firstamendmentcenter.org/PDF/FCGcomplete.PDF

- *Matters of Faith: Religion in American Public Life*, 2000. http://www.americanassembly.org

- *Toledo Guiding Principles on Teaching About Religions and Beliefs in Public Schools*, sponsored by the European Commission. http://www.redco.uni-hamburg.de/web/3480/3483/index.html

- *The Williamsburg Charter*, 1988. (Signed by Presidents Carter and Ford and Chief Justices Burger and Rehnquist, among many others.) http://www.freedomforum.org/publications/first/ findingcommonground/C02.WilliamsburgCharter.pdf

APPENDIX C

NOTES ON OTHER DIMENSIONS OF TEACHING ABOUT RELIGION IN SCHOOLS

Stand-Alone Electives

Some public schools offer elective courses in religious studies, usually at the secondary level. The most typical are *Introduction to World Religions* and *The Bible as Literature*.

For courses on the Bible, we highly recommend that teachers utilize the resources offered through the Society of Biblical Literature (SBL), the scholarly association of Biblical scholars. The SBL has produced a very helpful document entitled *Bible Electives in Public Schools: A Guide*,[46] which is geared toward educators, and the SBL supports an e-publication entitled *Teaching the Bible: An E-Publication for High School Teachers*, which provides a wealth of information about both content and pedagogical strategies.[47]

For courses on world religions, the same approaches to teaching about religion that are outlined in the main document apply to these and similar stand-alone electives. Specifically, teachers should help students understand that religions are (1) internally diverse, (2) dynamic, and (3) embedded in cultures. Typical survey courses that use popular texts such as Huston Smith's *The World's Religions*[48] rarely represent these elements of religious studies and we urge teachers to include them. One way to do so is to supplement whatever text is used with specific and contrasting case study examples to represent these elements within each tradition.

Guest Speakers

It is common for educators to invite religious leaders or practitioners into class to give a presentation about their tradition to students. Though we realize that this helps give "life" to the traditions studied, we discourage this practice for reasons outlined in the document regarding the different training that religious leaders and practitioners receive about their faith in comparison to the training one receives from a religious studies perspective. Instead, we recommend that teachers invite religious studies scholars (or religious leaders who are also trained in religious studies) as presenters because they will be able to represent the diversity within the tradition or traditions under consideration. (You may be able to find possible speakers by contacting the religious studies department of a local university.) Another option is to utilize films or personal written narratives to provide at least two differing representations of a given tradition or perspective to give students exposure to some dimension of diversity within a tradition. A good example of diverse representations of Islam is the PBS Frontline video "The Muslims."[49]

Field Trips to Places of Worship

Another common way that educators introduce students to religion is to plan field trips to places of worship such as a church, mosque, temple, or shrine. Typically, students will receive a tour of the facility by a member of the community or religious leader and an explanation of the ritual and communal activities that take place there. This practice can be problematic for the same reasons articulated above regarding having religious leaders or practitioners as guest speakers representing their traditions. If students are able to have only one field trip to a place of worship for their study of Christianity, for example, which community should they visit? A Quaker meeting house? A Methodist storefront church? An Evangelical mega-church? A makeshift Roman Catholic chapel in a homeless shelter? A Congregational church? An Orthodox Cathedral? And what if there is only one mosque or temple in the area? Though good teachers will always explain to students about the diversity of religious expressions within as well as among traditions, the pedagogical power of experiential encounters has to be taken seriously. One way to preserve experiential learning in ways that supports the aim of meaningful exposure to diverse expressions is to plan two field trips and visit different communities within the

same tradition. This can give students the power of experiential encounters and the dissonances of differing representations through a case study that can then be applied to other traditions.

Teaching About Religions through Music, Theater, Film and the Creative Arts

These genres provide rich opportunities for studying religion from a nonsectarian perspective. There is a vast and growing literature produced by scholars of religion that explores the intersections of religion and the arts, and though further elaboration is beyond the scope of this project we encourage teachers to explore some of those resources and to seek out professional development opportunities in these arenas.

APPENDIX D

SNAPSHOTS OF PRACTICE REPRESENTING THE THREE PREMISES OF RELIGIOUS STUDIES

Note: this appendix includes snapshots already introduced in Part Three and includes new ones as well.

Religions are Internally Diverse

A basic premise of religious studies is that religions are not internally homogeneous but diverse. In schools and in popular culture, faith traditions are often presented as a single set of beliefs, practices and representations without internal variation. While the major differences within a tradition may be introduced ("the majority of Muslims are Sunnis, while others are Shi'a") less dramatic or clearly defined distinctions are often overlooked or presumed not to exist. It is important for students to learn, for example, that Muslims in Indonesia will practice their faith differently than Muslims in Nigeria. In a similar vein, wealthy Muslims in Jakarta may practice an Islam that looks somewhat different than poor Muslims in rural Java. Helping students see that there are many "Islams" (or Christianities, Hinduisms) in the world enables them to consider carefully both what it means to study Islam and the complexity of answering the question, "What do Muslims believe?"

Snapshots of Practice
Elementary School English Language Arts
Ms. X. decides to do an oral storytelling unit with her first-grade classroom. Each day she reads

aloud a Native American story from different tribes to her class.[50] Afterwards, she asks them to return to their desks and draw what they remember of the story. After several stories have been shared, each student chooses her or his favorite and is assigned to learn it and retell it to a friend or family member. Throughout the unit, Ms. X. discusses differences between oral, written, and visual representations and encourages her students to practice all three skillsets. Her students are exposed to both variety in the beliefs, subjects, and settings of Native American religions and many different forms of literacy.

Elementary School Social Studies

Mr. N. is teaching a third-grade geography lesson and decides to focus on different expressions of Buddhism through an exploration of architecture. He shows them a selection of images that include temples from around the world and throughout different time periods.[51] An investigation of various architectural representations provides an opportunity to discuss migration, immigration, and differing expressions of faith and practice.

Middle School English Language Arts

Mr. P.'s eighth-grade class is focusing on voice and perspective in nonfiction and assigns excerpts from *Jerusalem Mosaic: Young Voices from the Holy City*[52] as an example of differing experiences expressed about a shared place and time through the voices of adolescents. Themes addressed include politics, family, love, religion, and war. Mr. P. helps his students recognize the similarities and differences voiced by this diverse group of teens representing Jewish, Christian, and Muslim perspectives from varying positions on the secular-orthodox spectrum.

Middle School Social Studies

Ms. Q. is teaching an eighth-grade world history course that covers the fall of Rome to the beginnings of the European Renaissance. As part of their study of the "Golden Age" she has them act as explorers of the diverse cultures that came under the rule of expanding Islamic empires. After reading excerpts from the logs of medieval Muslim travelers such as Ibn Jubayr, Ibn Batuta,

and Naser-e Kosraw,[53] Ms. Q. has students watch clips from the documentary "Islam: Empire of Faith"[54] and conduct outside research on medieval cities from Central Asia, North and West Africa, the Iberian Peninsula, and Arabia that includes an investigation into mosques that were built in these locations during this time period.[55] Students conclude by creating their own "Explorer's Journals" in which they describe, through writing and illustration, the similarities and differences they saw between expressions of Islamic life and practice as Muslims moved into these culturally diverse regions.

Secondary School English Language Arts

Before reading Hermann Hesse's *Siddhartha*, Ms. R. has her eleventh-grade students research the life of Hesse to introduce them to his cultural context and the influences that led him to write his most popular novel. While studying the text, she introduces students to readings from John Strong's *The Buddha: A Short Biography*[56] and Strong, ed., *The Experience of Buddhism: Sources and Interpretations*[57] to give her students tools to compare Hesse's interpretation of South Asian Buddhism with a scholarly account representing a variety of different perspectives. She helps them explore these diverse interpretations and how different genres shape perception.

Secondary School Social Studies

The essential question of Mr. T.'s twelfth-grade U.S. History II course is "What does it mean to be an American?" He has already included study of the complex ways in which early twentieth-century immigrants to the U.S. constructed their American identity. In a continuation of this theme, Mr. T. has his students read excerpts from Robert Orsi's *The Madonna of 115th Street*[58] and James Fisher's *Catholics in America*[59] to facilitate a conversation about the diverse practices of peoples within a singular tradition. As students later consider how some Americans feared that the Roman Catholic John F. Kennedy would be a mouthpiece for a papal agenda if elected President, Mr. T. draws on this earlier work to further discuss the intersections between national, cultural, and religious identity. He and his students explore the ways in which these intersections lead to a vast diversity of religious expression and belief even within a tradition with a centralized hierarchy.

Religions are Dynamic

A second premise of religious studies is the recognition that religions are dynamic and changing as opposed to static and fixed. When religious practices or texts are taught without historical context, it is easy for students to view the rituals or stories as having one meaning that persists for all times and places. Religions, however, exist in time and space and are constantly interpreted and reinterpreted by believers. For example, the Confucian concept of the "mandate from heaven" evolved within dynasties, geopolitical regions, and historical eras and continues to evolve today.

Seeing examples of the way that religious beliefs, practices and imagery change over time and place helps students recognize that from a religious studies perspective, there is no such thing as "a single meaning" of a given tradition, practice, or belief system.

Snapshots of Practice

Elementary School English Language Arts

Mr.D.'s second-grade class is reading Faith Ringgold's chapter book *Tar Beach*.[60] As the students read, Mr. D. supplements the text with selections from books such as *The People Could Fly: American Black Folk Tales*,[61] *All Night, All Day: A Child's First Book of African-American Spirituals*,[62] *Stitching Memories: African American Story Quilts*[63] and recordings of spirituals by the modern R&B singer John Legend to further explore the variety of genres reflected in Ringgold's text. In his discussion, Mr. D. helps students identify different forms of literacy and the many ways that stories are passed on. In his discussion of themes, he includes those related to religion and helps students identify similarities and differences in how African American forms of Christianity are represented through American history.

Elementary School Social Studies

Mr. Y.'s fourth-grade social studies curriculum focuses on North American geography and peoples. His students learn about the lives of native communities in the U.S. and Canada before and during the time that European explorers and colonists began to make contact with the continent. He is also eager to include contemporary representations of the communities he is exploring and selects a few for students to research in groups and to present reflections regarding how the traditions have evolved and changed over the years and how core values have been interpreted and preserved.[64]

Middle School English Language Arts

Ms. M.'s sixth-grade class is exploring the art of storytelling. She has students write a series of their own stories interspersed with selections of stories from a diverse array of cultures and traditions. In one section, she focuses on how ancient stories are often retold with contemporary significance and chooses selections from *Because God Loves Stories: An Anthology of Jewish Storytelling*[65] as one example of this common literary practice.

Middle School Social Studies

Ms. C. is teaching a seventh-grade geography unit on Africa and the Caribbean as part of a year-long world geography curriculum. During this unit students learn about the beliefs and practices of the Yoruba peoples of Western Africa. Ms. C. then has students chart the movement of West African peoples from the continent of Africa to Cuba, Haiti, Brazil, and the U.S., and identify the traditions of Santeria, Vodun, and Candomblé that develop as a result of cultural and religious syncretization in those regions. While watching clips from "This Far By Faith: African American Spiritual Journeys,"[66] and reading contemporary testimonials excerpted from *Mama Lola: A Vodou Priestess in Brooklyn* by Karen McCarthy Brown[67] and *The Altar of My Soul: The Living Traditions of Santeria* by Marta Moreno Vega,[68] students explore how the African diaspora continues to result in intertwining features of geographic, religious, cultural, economic and political change.[69]

Secondary School English Language Arts

Ms. E. chooses Amy Tan's *The Joy Luck Club*[70] for her twelfth-grade literature class. Students investigate the cultural as well as the political history of 20th century China as background to understand and appreciate themes they will encounter such as the cultural revolution, arranged marriages, the veneration of ancestors, and social class structures.[71] Cultural/religious themes are present throughout the text and a better understanding of these inferences and references will enhance student understanding of this widely read novel.

Secondary School Social Studies

Mr. W. is in the midst of a unit on the Roman Empire with his tenth-grade world history students, and wants to include a section on the origins of Christianity. He has students read the portion in their textbook about Jesus and his message, but supplements this lesson with additional resources to show (1) how there were many different and often competing interpretations of who Jesus was and what he promoted in the early years following his death, and (2) how those interpretations changed and evolved over time. He gathers a series of resources from the PBS series "From Jesus to Christ"[72] depicting these tensions and evolutions and engages his students in a series of inquiries regarding the significance of these insights.

Religions are Embedded in Culture

A third premise of religious studies is the recognition that religions are collections of ideas, practices, values, and stories that are all embedded in cultures and not isolated from them. Just as religion cannot be understood in isolation from its cultural manifestations, it is impossible to understand culture without considering its religious dimensions. In the same way that race, ethnicity, gender, and sexuality are always factors in cultural interpretation and understanding, so too is religion. Whether explicit or implicit, religious influences can always be found when one asks "the religion question" of any given social/historical experience. For example, rather than assuming in an American history class that a focus on religion is only relevant when studying the Puritans, the Great Awakenings, or the rise of the "Moral Majority," this approach assumes that there are rich avenues of inquiry that open when one considers the religious influences that shaped the Constitutional Convention, the institution of slavery, women's suffrage, the industrial revolution, and the U.S. involvement in World War II.

Snapshots of Practice

Elementary School English Language Arts

Mr. B. and his third-grade class read *In the Heart of the Village: The World of the Indian Banyan Tree* by Barbara Bash.[73] They discuss how the tree functions as a central location of the community and compare the different people who meet there—kids at school, merchants trading goods, villagers gathering to talk. He then shows them images of Banyan trees around the world, including the oldest such tree in America in Fort Myers, Florida.[74] Several of these are artistic representations of the Hindu God Shiva in his aspect as Jnana Dakshinamurti, teacher of wisdom, always shown seated at the foot of a Banyan tree; others are of the Buddha under the Bodhi Tree, a Banyan species under which (according to legend) the Buddha gained enlightenment. Mr. B. and his class then discuss various places and objects that are central points in their own lives (school playground, churches, grocery stores, temples) and then write their own stories about all the different types of people who come there every day.

Elementary School Social Studies

Ms. G.'s fifth-grade social studies class is working on a unit about ancient China. Toward the beginning of this unit she uses resources produced for an Art Institute of Chicago (AIC) exhibit entitled "Taoism and the Arts of China,"[75] to construct a "gallery" walk activity for her students. Touring the classroom, students look closely at paintings and sculptures produced from the Warring States period to the Qing dynasty while recording their observations on a graphic organizer with the headings "What I See," "What I Guess," and "What I Wonder." After the students share their reflections with the class, Ms. G. prompts them to think about patterns they see in their observations. Again using materials from the AIC, the class reads about some of the major themes of Taoism and their development from the tradition's early stages to its "renaissance," and concludes by reflecting on how these perspectives may have affected the style and content of the art they have just analyzed. Using these aesthetic themes as a touchstone, Ms. G.'s class continues to trace the ways in which religious traditions of China influenced perspectives on power, leadership, nature, and social relationships during the eras of their study.

Middle School English Language Arts

For a lesson in her unit on journalism with her seventh-grade students, Ms. V. decides to focus on the history of the local community through an investigation of its monuments and burial grounds. Students are assigned a specific monument or burial ground to investigate and the class brainstorms a series of questions that student journalists will pursue in their research. General questions should include relevant religious dimensions of the subject under investigation. (For example, are burial grounds divided by religious affiliation? What religions are represented? Are there historic or contemporary inhabitants of the community who are not represented in burial grounds or monuments? If so, why not?) In addition to these general questions, Ms. V. wants them to focus on three areas of English Language Arts competency: (1) symbolism (both visual symbols, such as angels or stars of David, and textual symbolism, such as biblical quotations); (2) ethnography of names (what cultures are represented? how can you tell? can you tell where someone will be buried or what kind of monument they will have based on their name?); and (3) orthographic development (are there words that are unfamiliar to you? words you know but spell differently? how does this relate to the age of the monument/memorial?).

Middle School Social Studies

A consistent theme of Mr. H.'s seventh-grade geography class is the relationship between the inhabitants of each region his class studies and the major features of its natural landscape. Several times throughout the year he has asked his students to research and prepare short debates about use and protection of various natural resources, and each time he has his students consider the ways in which religious worldview may influence the assumptions of the perspectives they are representing. While his students are familiar with well-known natural sites of veneration such as the Ganges River in India, he also introduces them to less frequently considered contexts. Using Diana Eck's *A New Religious America*[76] as a resource, he provides examples such as the spot in Pittsburgh at which the Allegheny, Ohio, and Monongahela rivers converge. Known as a "sangam" in the Hindu tradition, students learn that this confluence has been recognized by many Hindu immigrants to Pennsylvania as a particularly auspicious location, holding much symbolic importance. Mr. H. uses such examples both to explore the ways immigration continues to transform the cultural geography of the modern world, and to encourage students to consider multiple, and perhaps overlooked, religious perspectives on the natural landscape of any geographic context.

Secondary School English Language Arts

Mr. J. always starts his tenth-grade English class with a unit on biblical stories in order to prepare his students for the Western classics they will read that year. First, he gives his students a selection of biblically themed cartoons from *The New Yorker*[77] and asks them to identify in writing as many of the characters and stories as they can in five minutes. As most students discover they only know a few of the "big ones" (Adam and Eve, Noah, Moses), Mr. J. shows them "He forgot—and I—remembered" by Emily Dickinson and points out the various biblical allusions that they would need to know for an in-depth exploration of the poem. He then hands out a list of several popular biblical allusions to know[78] and students choose which story they will research and present. As part of a five-minute power point presentation, students must provide both of the following elements: a short synopsis of the story as it appears in the King James Bible (Mr. J. chooses this translation since it is the one the majority of English authors they are studying would have known and used) and a representation of this story in an art form other than literature. For an assessment at the end of the week's unit, Mr. J. gives his class the lyrics to Bob Dylan's "Angelina" and asks them to write a one-page essay on the use of biblical allusion.

Secondary School Social Studies

Ms. K.'s eleventh-grade modern U.S. history class is studying the social movements and upheaval that occurred during the 1960s. As part of this unit Ms. K. has her students work in groups to write and perform vignettes depicting people from various conflicting social perspectives engaging in dialogue over some of the major political and cultural topics they have studied, among them shifting gender roles and family structures. Wanting her students to consider the varied and complex forces that converge to form individual and societal assumptions about these topics, Ms. K. includes in her resource packet excerpts from Rosemary Radford Ruether's *Christianity and the Making of the Modern Family*. After reading background on Ruether's perspective as a feminist Christian, students read various passages discussing the ways in which Christianities of the Western world have shaped shifting conceptions of the family from classical to modern times. Students consider the ways in which both personal religious commitments, as well as life in a Christian culture, might shape the assumptions of the characters that will populate their vignettes.

NOTES

1. This description of a constitutionally sound approach was first articulated by AAR scholars in the 1970s and has been adapted by the First Amendment Center, and reproduced in their *A Teacher's Guide to Religion in the Public Schools* (Nashville: First Amendment Center, 1999).

2. There have been several "consensus documents" compiled by religious practitioners, legal scholars, and educators related to teaching about religion in public schools that have been created over the years by nonprofit organizations such as the First Amendment Center and ad hoc groups such as the one formed to construct the Toledo Guiding Principles. (See Appendix 2 for a list of these and related documents.) Though these and similar initiatives provide fair, respectful, and constitutionally sound ways to teach about religion, none of them provide substantial guidance on what to teach

about religion, nor do so from the authoritative perspective of religious studies scholars themselves. These guidelines are intended to fill that significant void.

3. Religious Studies in Secondary Schools (RSiSS) is the closest equivalent, but it is an all-volunteer, grassroots organization comprised (primarily) of independent school teachers who are not subject to the legal and regulatory mandates that shape public schools.

4. Anne Carr and Nicholas Piediscalzi, eds., *The Academic Study of Religion: 1975 Public Schools Religion Studies* (Missoula, MT: Scholars Press, 1975); Nicholas Piediscalzi and Barbara De Martino Swyhart, eds., *Distinguishing Moral Education, Values Clarification and Religion-Studies* (Missoula, MT: Scholars Press, 1976); and Paul J. Will, ed., *Public Education Religion Studies: An Overview* (Chico, CA: Scholars Press, 1981).

5. In the 1970s and 1980s academic programs were established at Harvard Divinity School, Western Michigan University, the University of Kansas, and Wright State University. The following resource centers were also established during that time period: The Public Education Religion Studies Center at Wright State University, the Kansas Center for Public Education Religion Studies, the Center for Public Education Religion Studies at San Diego State University, and the National Council on Religion and Public Education. Of these programs and initiatives, two are still functioning: the graduate school program at Harvard Divinity School, now known as the Program in Religious Studies and Education (http://www. hds.harvard.edu/prse), and the Religion and Public Education Resource Center at the University of California at Chico (http://www.csuchico. edu/rs/rperc), the home of materials formerly housed at the National Council on Religion and Public Education.

6. See Appendix A [pp 216–217] for a list of the AAR's Religion in the Schools Task Force members.

7. See National Council for the Social Studies Curriculum Standards at http://www.socialstudies.org/standards. These standards were first constructed and adopted in 1994 and subsequently revised in 2010.

8. See National Council of Teachers of English Curriculum Standards at http://www.ncte.org/store/books/standards/105977.htm. These standards were published in 1996.

9. This section draws heavily from a previously published essay by Diane L. Moore entitled "Overcoming Religious Illiteracy: A Cultural Studies Approach," *World History Connected*, November 2006. http://worldhistoryconnected.press.uiuc.edu/4.1/moore. html. Many thanks to *World History Connected* for permission to reproduce these sections. See also Diane L. Moore, *Overcoming Religious Illiteracy: A Cultural Studies Approach to the Study of Religion in Secondary Schools* (New York: Palgrave, 2007). Stephen Prothero has also published a widely read book on the issues of religious literacy entitled *Religious Literacy: What Every American Needs to Know—And Doesn't* (San Francisco: Harper, 2007).

10. Diane L. Moore, "Overcoming Religious Illiteracy," *op. cit.*

11. This is problematic for two reasons. First, religious leaders and believers are appropriately trained in and have allegiances to a particular set of beliefs about their tradition. Many are not trained in other representations, and those that are often learn about other interpretations as heretical or unorthodox in relationship to their own theological worldview. (Note the tensions between some Protestant and Roman Catholic Christians and between some Sunni and Shi'i Muslims, for example.) It is inappropriate to assume, for example, that a

local Protestant clergyperson or member of a congregation could accurately and sympathetically represent the many expressions of Christianity as equally valid and worthy of study. Though some religious leaders and believers may also be trained in religious studies, their training as religious leaders or believers will usually not equip them to accurately depict the diversity within their traditions. Second, religious leaders and believers approach and practice religion from a devotional perspective that is appropriate for their roles within their own faith communities but inappropriate as a lens to represent religion in the public schools.

12. For example, in three separate searches throughout the day on January 18, 2010, the top Google search result for the entry "Religion, Haiti" referenced a controversial comment made by Christian televangelist Pat Robertson on the recent earthquake. Less "newsworthy" but more representative were the efforts by religious organizations and individuals worldwide that mounted or contributed to relief efforts. The media is also the primary contemporary source for the widespread association of Islam with violence and terrorism. [See Edward Said, *Covering Islam: How the Media and the Experts Determine How We See the Rest of the World*, revised edition (New York: Vintage, 1997).]

13. It is important to note that it is not the role or responsibility of faith communities or the media to present a comprehensive understanding of religion. It is the responsibility of education and educators to provide citizens with the knowledge base required to understand this important dimension of pluralism.

14. There are many other consequences stemming from illiteracy about religions that concern scholars of religion, including a diminished intellectual understanding of the rich role that religion plays in human social and cultural life. We highlight the civic consequences of religious illiteracy here for it is the one most universally relevant for educators across the K-12 spectrum.

15. The consultation was sponsored by the "Alliance of Civilizations," a UN program formed at the initiative of the Secretary-General to counter terrorism through understanding. The consultation took place over the month of May 2006.

16. For example, the European Commission launched a three-year project in 2006 entitled *Religion in Education: A Contribution to Dialogue or a Factor of Conflict in Transforming Societies of European Countries (REDCo)*. See http://www.redco.uni-hamburg.de/web/3480/3483/index.html for a review of this comprehensive initiative.

17. The religious liberty clauses of the First Amendment to the United States Constitution.

18. For an excellent study on the controversy regarding these decisions and their role in the current tensions about religion in public life, see Joan DelFattore, *The Fourth R: Conflicts over Religion in America's Public Schools* (New Haven: Yale University Press, 2004). For an excellent historical overview of the relationship between religion and public education in the United States, see James Fraser, *Between Church and State: Religion and Public Education in a Multicultural America* (New York: St. Martin's Griffin, 1999).

19. *School District of Abington Township, Pennsylvania, et al. v. Schempp, et al.* 374 US 203 (1963).

20. Peter Bracher, et al., *PERSC Guidebook, Public Education Religion-Studies: Questions and Answers* (Dayton, Ohio: Public Education Religion Studies Center, 1974), 2.

21. First Amendment Center, *A Teacher's Guide to Religion in the Public Schools* (Nashville: First Amendment Center, 1999). Another useful general guidebook is Charles Haynes and Oliver Thomas, *Finding Common Ground: A Guide to Religious Liberty in Public Schools* (Nashville, TN: The First Amendment Center, 2001).

22. First Amendment Center, *A Teacher's Guide*, 3.

23. Special thanks to public school educators Lisbeth Liles and Anna Mudd for their formidable help in constructing and vetting the snapshots found throughout these guidelines.

24. Harvard Divinity School Study About Religion in the Schools (H-STARS), 2005–present.

25. See, for example, Roger B. Beck et al., *World History: Patterns of Interaction* (New York: Houghton Mifflin Harcourt, 2005), 296.

26. Michael J. Caduto and Joseph Bruchac, *Native American Stories: Myths and Legends* (Golden, CO: Fulcrum, 1991) and Joseph Bruchac, *Native American Animal Stories* (Golden, CO: Fulcrum, 1991).

27. See Michael Wolfe, ed., *One Thousand Roads to Mecca: Ten Centuries of Travelers Writing about the Muslim Pilgrimage* (New York: Grove, 1997), 11–67, for edited excerpts of their travel journals.

28. See http://www.pbs.org/empires/islam for information about the DVD. Note: we suggest using relevant selected excerpts vs. viewing the film in its entirety.

29. For mosque resources, see the ARCHNET site at http://www.archnet.org/lobby. This site provides an excellent set of historical and contemporary resources about Islamic architecture from around the world. The site is free but requires registration. For general resources, see Malise Ruthven and Azim Nanji, *Historical Atlas of Islam* (Cambridge: Harvard University Press, 2004) and Azim A. Nanji, ed., *The Muslim Almanac: A Reference Work on the History, Faith, Culture, and Peoples of Islam* (New York: Gale, 1996.)

30. John S. Strong, *The Buddha: A Short Biography* (Oxford: One World, 2001.)

31. John S. Strong, *The Experience of Buddhism: Sources and Interpretations*, 3rd edition (New York: Thompson Wadsworth, 2008.)

32. See Joel W. Martin, *Native American Religion* (New York: Oxford, 1999), a volume in John Butler and Harry S. Stout, eds., *Religion and American Life* series; Joy Hakim, *The First Americans: Prehistory-1600* (New York: Oxford, 2003), a volume in Joy Hakim, *A History of US* series; and Lois Crozier-Hogle et al., *Surviving in Two Worlds: Contemporary Native American Voices* (Austin: University of Texas, 1997).

33. Steve Zeitlin, ed., *Because God Loves Stories: An Anthology of Jewish Storytelling* (New York: Fireside, 1997), 25–56.

34. See http://www.pbs.org/wgbh/pages/frontline/shows/religion

35. Barbara Bash, *In the Heart of the Village: The World of the Indian Banyan Tree* (Layton Utah: Gibbs Smith, 2002).

36. See http://www.panoramas.dk/fullscreen7/f23-banyan-tree.html for a 360-degree view.

37. Diana L. Eck, *A New Religious America* (San Francisco: Harper Collins, 2001), 154.

38. Robert Mankoff, ed., *The Complete Cartoons of The New Yorker* (New York: Black Dog and Leventhal Publishers, 2004). This volume comes with a two-CD set that is searchable by key term (e.g., "bible" or "Noah" or "ark").

39. See Martin Manser and David Pickering, eds., *Facts on File Dictionary of Classical and Biblical Allusions* (New York: Facts on File, 2003).

40. See Wilfred Cantwell Smith, *The Meaning and End of Religion* for an explanation of how "religion" is a European construct of relatively recent origin.

41. See *Toledo Guiding Principles on Teaching About Religions and Beliefs in Public Schools* (Warsaw: Office for Democratic Institutions and Human Rights, 2007), p. 35; Charles C. Haynes and Oliver Thomas, *Finding Common Ground: A Guide to Religious Liberty in Public Schools* (Nashville: First Amendment Center, 2001), 188.

42. Ibid., and *The Society of Biblical Literature, Bible Electives in Public Schools: A Guide*, http://www.sbl-site.org/assets/pdfs/SchoolsGuide.pdf, 2008, 8–9.

43. See, for example, workshops run by religious studies scholars through non-profit educational organizations such as Facing History and Ourselves, Teachers as Scholars, and Primary Source; courses offered by religious studies scholars through summer institutes or the continuing education arm of their college or university; and courses offered through national foundations such as the National Endowment for the Humanities or the Social Science Research Council. Additionally, the Harvard Divinity School has also partnered with the Harvard Extension School to offer a Citation in Religious Studies and Education for in-service educators who wish to pursue training in religious studies that goes beyond a single workshop or seminar. See http://www.extension.harvard.edu/2009-10/courses/citations/crse.jsp

44. For example, at California State University, Chico some undergraduates who are enrolled in a teaching credential program can fulfill one of their content requirements by taking an Introduction to World Religions course offered by members of the Department of Religious Studies. There is also one graduate school education program in the United States at the Harvard Divinity School that specializes in training pre-service middle and secondary school educators to teach about religion as it manifests itself within the context of several licensure areas. See http://www.hds.harvard.edu/prse

45. For example, see Kent Greenawalt, *Does God Belong in Public Schools?* (Princeton: Princeton University Press, 2007) and Charles Haynes and Oliver Thomas, *Finding Common Ground: A Guide to Religious Liberty in Public Schools* (Nashville: First Amendment Center, 2007) or online at http://www.freedomforum.org/publications/first/findingcommonground/FCG-complete.pdf

46. This document can be downloaded at http://www.sbl-site.org/educational/thebibleinpublicschools.aspx

47. The e-publication can be accessed at http://www.sbl-site.org/assets/media/TBv2_i1.htm

48. Huston Smith, *The World's Religions* (New York: HarperOne, 2009). This is the fiftieth-year anniversary edition.

49. "Muslims", Frontline DVD, 2003. See http://www.pbs.org/wgbh/pages/frontline/shows/muslims for more information.

50. Michael J. Caduto and Joseph Bruchac, *Native American Stories: Myths and Legends* (Golden, CO: Fulcrum, 1991) and Joseph Bruchac, *Native American Animal Stories* (Golden, CO: Fulcrum, 1991).

51. Anne Geldart, *Buddhist Temples* (Chicago: Heinemann-Raintree, 2005). Recommended for ages 9–12.

52. I.E. Mozeson and Lois Stavsky, *Jerusalem Mosaic: Young Voices from the Holy City* (New York: Simon and Schuster, 1994). Recommended for grades 6–12.

53. See Michael Wolfe, ed., *One Thousand Roads to Mecca: Ten Centuries of Travelers Writing about the Muslim Pilgrimage* (New York: Grove, 1997), 11–67, for edited excerpts of their travel journals.

54. See http://www.pbs.org/empires/islam for information about the DVD. Note: we suggest using relevant selected excerpts vs. viewing the film in its entirety.

55. For mosque resources, see the ARCHNET site at http://www.archnet.org/lobby. This site provides an excellent set of historical and contemporary resources about Islamic architecture from around the world. The site is free but requires registration. For general resources, see Malise Ruthven and Azim Nanji, *Historical Atlas of Islam* (Cambridge: Harvard University Press, 2004) and Azim A. Nanji, ed., *The Muslim Almanac: A Reference Work on the History, Faith, Culture, and Peoples of Islam* (New York: Gale, 1996).

56. John S. Strong, *The Buddha: A Short Biography* (Oxford: One World, 2001).

57. John S. Strong, *The Experience of Buddhism: Sources and Interpretations*, 3rd edition (New York: Thompson Wadsworth, 2008).

58. Robert Orsi, *The Madonna of 115th Street* (New Haven: Yale University Press) 2002. This is an ethnographic study and excerpts can be used and appreciated by a secondary school audience.

59. James T. Fisher, *Catholics in America* (New York: Oxford, 2000), a volume in John Butler and Harry S. Stout, eds., *Religion and American Life* series. This resource is written for a younger audience but can serve as a supplement to the Orsi text.

60. Faith Ringgold, *Tar Beach* (Albuquerque: Dragon y Books, 1996). Recommended for ages 4–8.

61. Virginia Hamilton, *The People Could Fly* (New York: Knopf, 2009). Recommended for ages 4–8.

62. Ashley Bryan, *All Night, All Day: A Child's First Book of African-American Spirituals* (New York: Athenium, 2003). Recommended for ages 4–8.

63. Eva Ungar Grudin, *Stitching Memories: African American Story Quilts* (Williamstown, MA: Williams College Museum of Art, 1990).

64. See Joel W. Martin, *Native American Religion* (New York: Oxford, 1999, a volume in John Butler and Harry S. Stout, eds., *Religion and American Life* series); Joy Hakim, *The First Americans: Prehistory—1600* (New York: Oxford, 2003), a volume in Joy Hakim, *A History of US* series; and Lois Crozier-Hogle et al., *Surviving in Two Worlds: Contemporary Native American Voices* (Austin: University of Texas, 1997).

65. Steve Zeitlin, ed., *Because God Loves Stories: An Anthology of Jewish Storytelling* (New York: Fireside, 1997), 25–56.

66. http://www.pbs.org/thisfarbyfaith/

67. Karen McCarthy Brown, *Mama Lola: A Vodou Priestess in Brooklyn* (Berkeley: University of California Press, 2001). This is an ethnographic study and excerpts can be used and appreciated by a middle school audience.

68. Marta Moreno Vega, *The Altar of My Soul: The Living Traditions of Santeria* (Oxford: One World, 2001). This is an ethnographic study and excerpts can be used and appreciated by a middle school audience.

69. Another resource to consult is Albert J. Raboteau, *African-American Religion* (New York: Oxford, 1999), a volume in John Butler and Harry S. Stout, eds., *Religion and American Life* series.

70. Amy Tan, *The Joy Luck Club* (New York: Penguin, 2006).

71. A helpful resource is James Miller's edited volume entitled *Chinese Religions in Contemporary Societies* (Santa Barbara: ABC-CLIO, 2006).

72. See http://www.pbs.org/wgbh/pages/frontline/shows/religion

73. Barbara Bash, *In the Heart of the Village: The World of the Indian Banyan Tree* (Layton, Utah: Gibbs Smith, 2002).

74. See http://www.panoramas.dk/fullscreen7/f23-banyan-tree.html for a 360-degree view.

75. See http://www.artic.edu/taoism/introduction.php. There is also a book that was published out of the exhibit: Stephen Little, *Taoism and the Arts of China* (Berkeley: University of California Press, 2000).

76. Diana L. Eck, *A New Religious America* (San Francisco: Harper Collins, 2001) 154.

77. Robert Mankoff, ed., *The Complete Cartoons of The New Yorker* (New York: Black Dog and Leventhal Publishers, 2004). This volume comes with a two-CD set that is searchable by key term (e.g. "bible" or "Noah" or "ark").

78. See Martin Manser and David Pickering, eds., *Facts on File Dictionary of Classical and Biblical Allusions* (New York: Facts on File, 2003).

BIBLIOGRAPHY

American Assembly. Matters of Faith: Religion in American Public Life. New York: American Assembly, 2000.

Art Institute of Chicago. "Introduction to the Exhibition." *Taoism and the Arts of China*. Art Institute of Chicago, 2000. http://www.artic.edu/taoism/introduction.php

Bash, Barbara. *In the Heart of the Village: The World of the Indian Banyan Tree*. Layton Utah: Gibbs Smith, 2002.

Beck, Roger B., et al. *World History: Patterns of Interaction*. New York: Houghton Mifflin Harcourt, 2005.

Bracher, Peter, et al., *PERSC Guidebook, Public Education Religion-Studies: Questions and Answers*. Dayton, Ohio: Public Education Religion Studies Center, 1974.

Brown, Karen McCarthy. *Mama Lola: A Vodou Priestess in Brooklyn*. Berkeley: University of California Press, 2001.

Bruchac, Joseph. *Native American Animal Stories*. Golden, CO: Fulcrum, 1991.

Bryan, Ashley. *All Night, All Day: A Child's First Book of African-American Spirituals*. New York: Athenium, 2003.

Caduto, Michael J., and Joseph Bruchac. *Native American Stories: Myths and Legends*. Golden, CO: Fulcrum, 1991.

Carr, Anne, and Nicholas Piediscalzi, eds. *The Academic Study of Religion: 1975 Public Schools Religion Studies*. Missoula, MT: Scholars Press, 1975.

Crozier-Hogle, Lois, et al. *Surviving in Two Worlds: Contemporary Native American Voices*. Austin: University of Texas, 1997.

DelFattore, Joan. *The Fourth R: Conflicts over Religion in America's Public Schools*. New Haven: Yale University Press, 2004.

Eck, Diana L. *A New Religious America*. San Francisco: Harper Collins, 2001.

First Amendment Center. *A Teacher's Guide to Religion in the Public Schools*. Nashville: First Amendment Center, 1999.

Fisher, James T. *Catholics in America*. New York: Oxford, 2000. Religion and American Life, edited by John Butler and Harry S. Stout.

Fraser, James. *Between Church and State: Religion and Public Education in a Multicultural America*. New York: St. Martin's Griffin, 1999.

Geldart, Anne. *Buddhist Temples*. Chicago: Heinemann-Raintree, 2005.

Greenawalt, Kent. *Does God Belong in Public Schools?* Princeton: Princeton University Press, 2007.

Hakim, Joy. *The First Americans: Prehistory-1600*. A History of US, edited by Joy Hakim. New York: Oxford, 2003.

Hamilton, Virginia. *The People Could Fly*. New York: Knopf, 2009.

Harvard Divinity School. "Program in Religious Studies Education." http://www.hds.harvard.edu/prse/

_____. "Study on Teaching About Religion in the Schools (H-STARS)." http://www.hds.harvard.edu/prse/hstars

Harvard University Extension School. "Citation in Religious Studies and Education." http://www.extension.harvard.edu/2009-10/courses/citations/crse.jsp

Haynes, Charles, and Oliver Thomas. *Finding Common Ground: A Guide to Religious Liberty in Public Schools*. Nashville, TN: The First Amendment Center, 2001. http://www.freedomforum.org/publications/first/findingcommonground/FCG-complete.pdf

Little, Stephen. *Taoism and the Arts of China*. Berkeley: University of California Press, 2000.

Mankoff, Robert, ed. *The Complete Cartoons of The New Yorker*. New York: Black Dog and Leventhal Publishers, 2004.

Manser, Martin, and David Pickering, eds. *Facts on File Dictionary of Classical and Biblical Allusions*. New York: Facts on File, 2003.

Martin, Joel W. *Native American Religion*. Religion and American Life, edited by John Butler and Harry S. Stout. New York: Oxford, 1999.

Massachusetts Institute of Technology Design Lab in the School of Architecture and Planning. ArchNet. http://www.archnet.org/lobby

Miller, James. *Chinese Religions in Contemporary Societies*. Santa Barbara: ABC-CLIO, 2006.

Moore, Diane L. "Overcoming Religious Illiteracy: A Cultural Studies Approach." *World History Connected*, November 2006. http://worldhistoryconnected.press.uiuc.edu/4.1/moore.html

_____. *Overcoming Religious Illiteracy: A Cultural Studies Approach to the Study of Religion in Secondary Schools*. New York: Palgrave, 2007.

Moreno Vega, Marta. *The Altar of My Soul: The Living Traditions of Santeria*. Oxford: One World, 2001.

Mozeson, I.E., and Lois Stavsky. *Jerusalem Mosaic: Young Voices from the Holy City*. New York: Simon and Schuster, 1994.

Nanji, Azim A., ed. *The Muslim Almanac: A Reference Work on the History, Faith, Culture, and Peoples of Islam*. New York: Gale, 1996.

National Council of Teachers of English. *Standards for the English Language Arts*. International Reading Association and the National Council of Teachers of English, 1996. http://www1.ncte.org/library/files/Store/Books/Sample/StandardsDoc.pdf

National Council for the Social Studies National Task Force for Social Studies Standards. *Expectations of Excellence: Curriculum Standards for Social Studies*. National Council for the Social Studies, 1994. http://www.socialstudies.org/standards

Organization for Security and Cooperation in Europe. Office for Democratic Institutions and Human Rights Advisory Council of Experts on Freedom of Religion or Belief. *Toledo Guiding Principles on Teaching About Religions and Beliefs in Public Schools*. Warsaw: OSCE Office for Democratic Institutions and Human Rights, 2007.

Orsi, Robert. *The Madonna of 115th Street*. New Haven: Yale University Press, 2002.

PBS. "From Jesus to Christ: The First Christians." WGBH Educational Foundation, 1998. http://www.pbs.org/wgbh/pages/frontline/shows/religion

_____. "Islam: Empire of Faith." DVD. Gardner Films, 2001. http://www.pbs.org/empires/islam

_____. "Muslims." DVD. WGBH, 2003. http://www.pbs.org/wgbh/pages/frontline/shows/muslims

PBS. "This Far by Faith: African American Spiritual Journeys." The Faith Project, 2003. http://www.pbs.org/thisfarbyfaith

Piediscalzi, Nicholas, and Barbara De Martino Swyhart, eds. *Distinguishing Moral Education, Values Clarification and Religion-Studies*. Missoula, MT: Scholars Press, 1976.

Prothero, Stephen. *Religious Literacy: What Every American Needs to Know—And Doesn't*. San Francisco: Harper, 2007.

Raboteau, Albert J. *African-American Religion*. Religion and American Life, edited by John Butler and Harry S. Stout. New York: Oxford, 1999.

Ringgold, Faith. *Tar Beach*. Albuquerque: Dragonfly Books, 1996.

Ris, Rolf. "The Banyan Tree at Fort Myers." Panoramas.dk, edited by Hans Nyberg. http://www.panoramas.dk/fullscreen7/f23-banyan-tree.html

Ruthven, Malise, and Azim Nanji. *Historical Atlas of Islam*. Cambridge: Harvard University Press, 2004.

Said, Edward. *Covering Islam: How the Media and the Experts Determine How We See the Rest of the World*. Revised edition. New York: Vintage, 1997.

School District of Abington Township, Pennsylvania, et al. v. Schempp et al. 374 US 203 (1963).

Smith, Huston. *The World's Religions*. 50th-year anniversary edition. New York: HarperOne, 2009.

Smith, Wilfred Cantwell. *The Meaning and End of Religion*. Minneapolis: Fortress, 1991.

Society of Biblical Literature. *Bible Electives in Public Schools: A Guide. Society of Biblical Literature*, 2008. http://www.sbl-site.org/assets/pdfs/SchoolsGuide.pdf

_____. "The Bible in American Public Schools." http://www.sbl-site.org/educational/thebibleinpublicschools.aspx

_____. *Teaching the Bible*. http://www.sbl-site.org/assets/media/TBv2_i1.htm

Strong, John S. *The Buddha: A Short Biography*. Oxford: One World, 2001.

_____. *The Experience of Buddhism: Sources and Interpretation*. 3rd ed. New York: Thompson Wadsworth, 2008.

Tan, Amy. *The Joy Luck Club*. New York: Penguin, 2006.

Ungar Grudin, Eva. *Stitching Memories: African American Story Quilts*. Williamstown, MA: Williams College Museum of Art, 1990.

University of Hamburg. *Religion in Education: A Contribution to Dialogue or a Factor of Conflict in Transforming Societies of European Countries* (REDCo). European Commission, 2009. http://www.redco.uni-hamburg.de/web/3480/3483/index.html

U.S. Constitution. First Amendment. http://www.archives.gov/exhibits/charters/bill_of_rights_transcript.html

University of California at Chico. *Religion and Public Education Resource Center*. http://www.csuchico.edu/rs/rperc

Will, Paul J., ed. *Public Education Religion Studies: An Overview*. Chico, CA: Scholars Press, 1981.

Williamsburg Charter. http://www.freedomforum.org/publications/first/findingcommonground/C02.WilliamsburgCharter.pdf

Wolfe, Michael, ed. *One Thousand Roads to Mecca: Ten Centuries of Travelers Writing about the Muslim Pilgrimage*. New York: Grove, 1997.

Zeitlin, Steve, ed. *Because God Loves Stories: An Anthology of Jewish Storytelling*. New York: Fireside, 1997.

Study about Religions in the Social Studies Curriculum

A POSITION STATEMENT OF NATIONAL COUNCIL FOR THE SOCIAL STUDIES (NCSS)

Approved and published 2014

INTRODUCTION

National Council for the Social Studies re-affirms that study about religions should be an essential part of the social studies curriculum. Knowledge about religions is not only a characteristic of an educated person but is necessary for effective and engaged citizenship in a diverse nation and world. Religious literacy dispels stereotypes, promotes cross-cultural understanding, and encourages respect for the rights of others to religious liberty.

INTENDED AUDIENCE

This position statement is aimed at informing the general public, the K-12 community, and all educators, from pre-kindergarten through graduate school, about the importance of addressing study about religions in the social studies curriculum in ways that are constitutionally and academically sound.

BACKGROUND

In the early 1960s, the U.S. Supreme Court ruled state-sponsored devotional practices unconstitutional in public schools. At the same time, however, the Court made clear that study about religions—as distinguished from religious indoctrination—is an important part of a good education. In *Abington v. Schempp* (1963), Associate Justice Tom Clark wrote for the Court:

> [I]t might well be said that one's education is not complete without a study of comparative religions or the history of religion and its relationship to the advancement of civilization. It certainly may be said that the Bible is worthy of study for its literary and historical qualities. Nothing we have said here indicates that such study of the Bible or of religion, when presented objectively as part of a secular program of education, may not be effected consistent with the First Amendment.[1]

Despite this guidance from the Supreme Court, controversy and confusion over the role of religion in public schools led many textbook publishers and educators to avoid inclusion of study about religions in the curriculum. In the late 1980s, however, a new consensus emerged about the need to address religion in the social studies and other subjects. In 1988, NCSS joined with 16 leading educational, religious and civil liberties groups to publish a common ground statement that stated, in part:

> Because religion plays a significant role in history and society, study about religion is essential to understanding both the nation and the world. Omission of facts about religion can give students the false impression that the religious life of humankind is insignificant or unimportant. Failure to understand even the basic symbols, practices, and concepts of the various religions makes much of history, literature, art, and contemporary life unintelligible.[2]

Over the next two decades, state social studies standards began to include more study about religions and many history textbooks began to expand their treatment of religions.[3] In 2000, the U.S. Department of Education disseminated to every public school a packet of guidelines on the constitutional role of religion in public schools, including "A Teacher's Guide to Religion in Public Schools," endorsed by NCSS and 21 other national organizations. The guidelines underscore the critical difference between teaching of religion (religious education or indoctrination) and teaching about religion:

- The school's approach to religion is *academic*, not *devotional*.

- The school strives for student *awareness* of religions, but does not press for student acceptance of any religion.

- The school sponsors study *about* religion, not the *practice of* religion.

- The school may *expose* students to a diversity of religious views, but may not *impose* any particular view.

- The school *educates* about all religions; it does *not promote or denigrate* any religion.

- The school may *inform* the student about religious beliefs, but should not seek to *conform* him or her to any particular belief.[4]

Despite recent improvements in study about religions brought about by the new consensus, religious illiteracy remains widespread in the United States.[5] Public schools can and should do more to take religion seriously in a world where religion—for better and for worse—plays a critical role in shaping events at home and abroad.

To encourage more religious studies in public schools, the American Academy of Religion (AAR) published in 2010 "Guidelines for Teaching about Religion in K-12 public schools in the United States." Religious illiteracy that "fuels prejudice and antagonism," the AAR states, "can be diminished by teaching about religion in public schools using a non-devotional, academic perspective."[6]

RATIONALE FOR RECOMMENDATIONS AND RECOMMENDATIONS

National Council for the Social Studies strongly supports inclusion of study about religions as an essential part of the social studies curriculum.

In public schools, the First Amendment provides the civic framework for teaching about religions in ways that are constitutionally and academically sound. Schools demonstrate a commitment to fairness and neutrality under the First Amendment when they include study about religions, wherever appropriate, in the social studies curriculum. Preparation for citizenship in a

religiously diverse country and world requires religious literacy. Study about religions combats intolerance and prepares students to engage people of different religions and beliefs with civility and respect.

Knowledge of religions is also necessary for understanding much of history, politics, ethics, art, and literature. Study about religions in the social studies explores the religious dimension of human existence in its broader cultural context, including its relation to economic, political, and social institutions, as well as its relation to the arts, geography, language, and literature.

Study about religions may take place in special courses and units or wherever and whenever knowledge of the religious dimension of history and culture is needed for balanced and comprehensive understanding.

NCSS recommends that state departments of education work to ensure inclusion of study about religions, including the role of religion in history and society, in all social studies programs. NCSS also supports course offerings in religious studies as long as the teachers teaching such courses have appropriate academic training in study about religions.

In order to take religious studies seriously, NCSS recommends that every public school district adopt clear First Amendment policies and guidelines on teaching about religions developed with broad involvement and support of the community. Through in-service programs, administrators and teachers must be prepared to carry out these policies. Parents and students should be informed about why and how the school is teaching about religions.

NCSS recommends that teacher education institutions expose prospective teachers to the constitutional framework for addressing religion in the curriculum. In addition, prospective social studies teachers should be encouraged to take at least one course in religious studies as part of their certification.

NCSS further recommends that state departments of education review social studies frameworks, setting standards for religious studies courses and the inclusion of study about religions where appropriate.

Finally, NCSS recommends that if there are to be courses in religious studies, there must be teachers competent to teach them.

IMPLEMENTATION

NCSS urges state education leaders, textbook publishers, and teacher educators to strengthen study about religions in public schools by acting on the recommendations contained in this statement.

NCSS members are encouraged to use this position statement to urge state departments of education and local school districts to adopt policies and practices for study about religions consistent with high academic standards for religious studies and First Amendment principles.

CONCLUSION

In the 21st century, religious literacy is essential for understanding the role of religion in public life, negotiating differences in the public square, and forging public policies that serve the common good. That's why schools have a civic and educational responsibility to include robust study about religions in the social studies curriculum. Only through learning about religions and beliefs will young people be adequately prepared for citizenship in a religiously diverse society and world.

National Council for the Social Studies has long led the call for inclusion of study about religions in the curriculum in ways that are both constitutionally and academically sound. With this position statement, NCSS renews that call by reminding Americans that the strength of our lively experiment in building one nation of many peoples and faiths depends in no small measure on understanding one another across differences that are often deep and abiding.

NOTES

1. *Abington School District v. Schempp*, 374 U.S. 203 (1963).

2. "Religion in the Public School Curriculum: Questions and Answers" was first published in 1988 and disseminated widely by NCSS and other sponsoring organizations. The full document may be found at http://www.religiousfreedomcenter.org

3. Susan L. Douglass, *Teaching about Religion in National and State Standards* (Nashville, Tenn.: Council on Islamic Education and First Amendment Center, 2000).

4. Based on guidelines originally published by the Public Education Religion Studies Center at Wright State University. The complete text of "A Teacher's Guide to Religion in the Public Schools" may be found at http://www.religiousfreedomcenter. org. For all consensus guidelines on religion in public schools, see: Charles C. Haynes and Oliver Thomas, *Finding Common Ground: A First Amendment Guide to Religion and Public Schools* (Nashville, Tenn.: First Amendment Center, 2007).

5. "U.S. Religious Knowledge Survey," Pew Forum on Religion & Public Life (Washington, D.C.: Pew Research Center, 2010); See also, Stephen Prothero, *Religious Literacy: What Every American Needs to Know—And Doesn't* (San Francisco, Calif.: HarperOne, 2007).

6. For the full text of the American Academy of Religion's guidelines, see https://www.aarweb.org/ sites/default/files/pdfs/Publications/ epublications/AARK-12CurriculumGuidelines.pdf

BIBLIOGRAPHY

Eck, Diana L. *A New Religious America: How a "Christian Country" Has Now Become the World's Most Religiously Diverse Nation*. San Francisco, Calif.: Harper, 2001.

Biondo, Vincent F. III, and Andrew Fiala, eds., *Civility, Religious Pluralism, and Education*. New York: Routledge, 2014.

Haynes, Charles C. and Oliver Thomas. *Finding Common Ground: A First Amendment Guide to Religion and Public Schools*. Nashville, Tenn.: First Amendment Center, 2007.

Lester, Emile. *Teaching about Religions: A Democratic Approach for Public Schools*. Ann Arbor, Mich.: The University of Michigan Press, 2011.

Moore, Diane L. *Overcoming Religious Illiteracy: A Cultural Studies Approach to Teaching About Religion in Secondary School*. New York: Palgrave, 2007.

Nord, Warren. *Does God Make a Difference? Taking Religion Seriously in American Schools and Universities*. New York: Oxford University Press, 2011.

APPENDIX 4

Religious Studies Companion Document for the C3 Framework

COMMITMENTS AND CONTEXT

In 2014, the National Council for the Social Studies (NCSS) reaffirmed its longstanding position that study about religions should be an essential part of the social studies curriculum in ways that are constitutionally and academically sound. NCSS emphasized that knowledge about religions is not only a characteristic of an educated person but is necessary for effective and engaged citizenship in an interconnected and diverse nation and world. It recommended that state departments of education work to ensure inclusion of study about religions, including the role of religion in history and society, in all social studies programs. Teachers teaching such courses should have appropriate professional training in the academic study of religion in order to facilitate meaningful, constitutional classroom dialogue grounded in content knowledge. NCSS affirmed that the First Amendment to the U.S. Constitution provides the civic framework for achieving these goals.

In 1963, the U.S. Supreme Court ruled that state-sponsored devotional practices are unconstitutional in public schools. At the same time, the Court made clear that the study of religion—as distinguished from religious indoctrination—is an important part of a "complete education." Justice Tom Clark wrote for the Court: "[I]t might well be said that one's education is not complete without a study of comparative religions or the history of religion and its relationship to the advancement of civilization."[2] Building upon the Supreme Court's guidance, NCSS joined with sixteen leading educational, religious, and civil liberties groups in 1988 to reaffirm that the study of religion is essential to understanding both the nation and the world.[3]

Over the next two decades, NCSS and its affiliates contributed to the development of state social studies standards that included the study of religion.[4] In 2000, twenty-one national organizations joined with

Approved by American Academy of Religion[1]
825 Houston Mill Rd NE STE 300
Atlanta, GA 30329-4205

This Supplement was added to the C3 Framework in June 2017

the NCSS and the U.S. Department of Education to disseminate a document to every public school about the constitutionality of religion in public schools. Widely accepted guidelines for teaching about religion state:

- The school's approach to religion is *academic*, not *devotional*.

- The school strives for student *awareness* of religions, but does not press for student *acceptance* of any religion.

- The school sponsors *study* about religion, not the *practice* of religion.

- The school may *expose* students to a diversity of religious views, but may not *impose* any particular view.

- The school *educates* about all religions; it does not *promote* or *denigrate* religion.

- The school *informs* the students about various beliefs; it does not seek to *conform* students to any particular belief.[5]

In 2010, the American Academy of Religion (AAR) published *Guidelines for Teaching about Religion in K-12 Public Schools in the United States* to emphasize the importance of using a religious studies approach to teach about religion. NCSS affirmed the AAR guidelines in 2014, emphasizing that "schools have a civic and educational responsibility to include robust study about religions in the social studies curriculum." This Supplement equips state departments of education and school districts with student learning indicators and a framework for studying religion in ways that are constitutionally sound and consistent with the AAR's high academic standards.

INTRODUCTION TO THE DISCIPLINARY CONCEPTS AND SKILLS OF RELIGIOUS STUDIES

Religious studies analyzes the impact of religion on the structure and culture of societies, examining both historical and contemporary perspectives in order to understand how religious beliefs, practices, and communities are created, maintained, and transformed over time. Through a non-devotional approach, students gain the ability to understand religions as diverse and dynamic, to explain how religions change over time, and to analyze how culture affects religion and religion affects culture. Student inquiry into complex issues—including the dynamic relationships within a religion, between religions, and between religion and secularism—provides a unique environment to learn how to recognize and evaluate assumptions without undermining personal religious identity, to navigate diverse and shifting cultural values, to engage respectfully with diverse neighbors, and to resist common misunderstandings that have negative real-world consequences. These skills are invaluable in a society whose increasingly multicultural schools, workplaces, and local, national, and international public spheres all need informed, critical, and engaged citizens.

The study of religion from an academic, non-devotional perspective in primary, middle, and secondary school is critical for decreasing religious illiteracy and the bigotry and prejudice it fuels. The AAR has defined religious literacy as "the ability to discern and analyze the fundamental intersections of religion with social, political, and cultural life." Specifically, the AAR states, a religiously literate person will possess

> a basic understanding of the history, central texts (where applicable), beliefs, practices and contemporary manifestations of several of the world's religious traditions and religious expressions *as they arose out of and continue to shape and to be shaped by particular social, historical and cultural contexts*; and the ability to discern and explore the religious dimensions of political, social and cultural expressions across time and place."[6] [Emphasis added]

RELIGIOUS STUDIES PREMISES AND METHODS OF INQUIRY

Religious studies scholars articulate four basic assertions about religions and the study of religion that serve to counter problematic assumptions while creating a useful method for inquiry. First, there is a difference between the devotional study of religion to encourage religious commitment and the nonsectarian study that seeks to understand religion without promoting or discouraging adherence to it. This premise affirms the credibility of particular religious assertions without equating them with absolute truths about the traditions themselves. Second, religions are internally diverse and not uniform as is commonly represented. Scholars recognize that religious communities are living entities that function in different social/political contexts. Third, religions evolve and change through time and are not static or fixed. Religious expressions and beliefs must be studied in social and historical context as they are constantly interpreted and reinterpreted by adherents. Fourth, religious influences are embedded in cultures and not separable from other forms of human expression.

College, Career, and Civic ready students:

- **D2.Rel.1.9-12:** Explain and analyze the distinction between a devotional assertion of religious beliefs and behaviors and the academic study of diverse devotional assertions from a nonsectarian perspective in specific social and historical contexts.

- **D2.Rel.2.9-12:** Describe and analyze examples of how religions are internally diverse at both macro levels (sects and divisions within traditions) and micro levels (differences within specific religious communities).

- **D2.Rel.3.9-12:** Describe and analyze examples of how religions evolve and change over time in response to differing social, historical, and political contexts.

- **D2.Rel.4.9-12:** Describe and analyze examples of how religions are embedded in all aspects of culture and cannot only be isolated to the "private" sphere.

APPLICATIONS OF RELIGIOUS STUDIES PREMISES: BELIEF, BEHAVIOR, AND BELONGING

Religious studies scholars investigate how individuals and communities construct their religious identities. Describing religious identity requires recognition of the historical, political, geographic, and economic factors that shape the beliefs people hold, the behaviors they exhibit, and their membership within multiple intersecting communities. Beliefs, behaviors, and the experiences of belonging to communities–including but not restricted to religious communities–shape and are shaped by one another. Beliefs and values include theological, doctrinal, scriptural, and ethical evaluative claims about daily life as much as those about a transcendent reality or experiences of the divine. Behaviors include practices associated with rites, rituals, and life both inside and outside of strictly religious settings. Experiences of belonging include membership in religious communities and other social communities with intersecting racial, national, ethnic, familial, gender, class, and other identities.

College, Career, and Civic ready students:

- **D2.Rel.5.9-12:** Explain how religious identities shape and are shaped by the beliefs people hold, the behaviors they exhibit, and the ways people experience membership in intersecting communities.

- **D2.Rel.6.9-12:** Identify how internal diversity is evident in beliefs, behaviors, and experiences of belonging to various communities.

- **D2.Rel.7.9-12:** Analyze how beliefs, behaviors, and experiences of belonging to communities change over time.

- **D2.Rel.8.9-12:** Interpret how beliefs, behaviors, and experiences of belonging to various communities affect and are affected by other social, political, and cultural forces.

- **D2.Rel.9.9-12:** Give examples of how beliefs, behaviors, and community experiences shape and are shaped by one another in particular social and historical contexts.

CRITICAL INQUIRY: REPRESENTATION, SOURCES, AND EVIDENCE

Inquiry from a religious studies perspective does not evaluate the theological or devotional question of what is "right" or "true" for a tradition or individual. Instead, religious studies scholars utilize primary and secondary sources to analyze how religious values, interpretations, and expressions both shape and are shaped by individuals and communities. Teacher-guided critical inquiry will explore how and why some religious individuals and communities gain social and political prominence and influence while others become socially and politically marginalized. Religious studies scholars identify conscious and unconscious assumptions about religious identity and its influence on beliefs, behaviors, and communities of belonging in private and public life.

College, Career, and Civic ready students:

- **D2.Rel.10.9-12:** Identify assumptions about the definition of religion and the proper role of religion in private and public life.

- **D2.Rel.11.9-12:** Describe which expressions of orthodoxy ("right" believing) and orthopraxy ("right" behaving) are socially and politically prominent or marginalized in specific contexts.

- **D2.Rel.12.9-12:** Identify which religious individuals, communities, and institutions are represented in public discourse, and explain how some are obscured.

- **D2.Rel.13.9-12:** Collect and analyze the meaning and significance of primary and secondary religious sources in their particular social, historical, and political context, including statements of theology and doctrine, sacred texts, depictions of rites and rituals, biographies, histories, ethnography, art and architecture, and demographic data.

- **D2.Rel.14.9-12:** Evaluate how diverse religious sources articulate the relationship between a religion and its social and historical context.

BRIEF OVERVIEW OF THE CONNECTIONS BETWEEN RELIGIOUS STUDIES AND THE ENGLISH LANGUAGE ARTS/LITERACY COMMON CORE STANDARDS

Connections with the College and Career Readiness (CCR) Anchor Standards. Looking through a religious studies lens, students develop and use a wide range of skills that are central to the Common Core College and Career Readiness Anchor Standards. Utilizing the methodologies, academic frameworks, and practices that form the field of religious studies provides students with the knowledge and skills they need to think critically about the historical and contemporary world.

Religious studies as an interdisciplinary academic field requires students to develop the skills necessary to describe, interpret, compare, explain, and examine the beliefs, behaviors, attitudes, and institutions associated with religions. Taking a religious studies approach allows students to critically examine both primary and secondary source material to determine central ideas or themes across or within religions. Students analyze how source materials address similar themes or topics in order to build knowledge, recognize patterns, or compare ideas. By studying religion, students come to understand how religions are internally diverse, dynamic and changing, and embedded in specific cultural and historical contexts. They then use this understanding to develop compelling questions, engage in research, formulate evidence-based claims, consider how to communicate conclusions to an audience, and consider possibilities for appropriate civic action. The study of religion, when integrated into the study of civics, economics, geography, and history, helps students hone the skills outlined in the Anchor Standards in Reading, Writing, Speaking and Listening, and Language. As such, religious studies supports students' successful entry into the world of work or post-secondary education.

C3 FRAMEWORK DISCIPLINARY INQUIRY MATRIX: RELIGIOUS STUDIES

In Appendix A [of the C3 Framework], the Disciplinary Inquiry Matrix articulates how each of the four Dimensions of the C3 Framework build upon one another through the use of a content-specific example: *How bad was the Great Recession?* The Disciplinary Inquiry Matrix describes what experts think and do. It is a four-part target example to which students should aspire. The matrix develops through the construction of disciplinary compelling and supporting questions (Dimension 1); the data sources, key concepts, and key strategies specific to each discipline (Dimension 2); the development of evidence-based claims (Dimension 3); and the means of expression (Dimension 4). In the table, the Great Recession is examined through the disciplinary lens of religious studies. The examples in the boxes are illustrative rather than exhaustive.

REFERENCES

- American Academy of Religion. (2010). Guidelines for teaching about religion in K-12 public schools in the United States. Accessible at https://www.aarweb.org/sites/default/files/pdfs/Publications/epublications/AARK-12CurriculumGuidelines.pdf.

- Biondo, V. F., III, and Fiala, A. (Eds.). (2014). *Civility, Religious Pluralism, and Education.* New York: Routledge.

- Douglass, S. L. (2000). *Teaching About Religion in National and State Social Studies Standards.* Fountain Valley, CA: Council on Islamic Education, and Nashville, TN: First Amendment Center.

- Eck, D. L. (2001). *A New Religious America: How a "Christian Country" has Become the World's Most Religiously Diverse Nation.* San Francisco, CA: Harper.

- Greenawalt, K. (2007). *Does God Belong in Public Schools?* Princeton, NJ: Princeton University Press.

- Haynes, C. C. (2008). *A Teacher's Guide to Religion in the Public Schools.* Nashville, TN: First Amendment Center.

- Haynes, C. C. and Nord, W. (1998). *Taking Religion Seriously Across the Curriculum.* Nashville, TN: First Amendment Center.

Disciplinary Inquiry Matrix

WAYS OF KNOWING	RELIGIOUS STUDIES RELIGIOUS STUDIES SCHOLARS SAY...
	DIMENSION 1
POSSIBLE DISCIPLINARY COMPELLING AND SUPPORTING QUESTIONS	How did the Great Recession affect religious life in the United States and the world? How did religious beliefs and values shape a person's understanding of, and response to, the Great Recession? How does an individual's worldview affect the way in which economic conditions are experienced? In what ways did religious institutions and individuals respond to the effects of the Great Recession? To what extent did the Great Recession impact religious beliefs and practices? How did different religious communities interact with one another—and with non-religious communities—in responding to the Great Recession?
	DIMENSION 2
DATA SOURCES NEEDED TO ADDRESS QUESTIONS	Statistics, surveys, and other types of sources that depict attendance figures for religious institutions, charitable giving, and community actions to address the adverse economic effects of the Great Recession, inter-religious or intra-religious initiatives to support individuals and communities in need, and interviews and media articles about perceived causes of the Great Recession. Newsletters, religious community bulletins, sermons, newspaper and magazine articles, or television news broadcasts that occurred before, during, and after the Great Recession. Ethnographies of various religious communities before, during, and after the Great Recession.
KEY CONCEPTS AND CONCEPTUAL UNDERSTANDINGS NEEDED TO ADDRESS QUESTIONS (non-exclusive questions)	Theories (including historical, literary, psychological, sociological, and philosophical approaches) of religion and cultural contexts; cultural, social, political, geographic, economic, and psychological influences on religious identity and institutions; intersections between religious beliefs, behaviors, and belonging; understanding religions as dynamic, diverse, and influenced by and influencing a complex set of cultural factors.
KEY STRATEGIES AND SKILLS NEEDED TO ADDRESS QUESTIONS (non-exclusive examples)	Reading and interpreting statistics, critical thinking, and applying religious studies frameworks to issues faced by local communities to encourage civic engagement and protection of rights associated with religious freedom. Analysis of the religious sources and evidence used by the media. Consulting multiple accounts of a single event to corroborate evidence.
	DIMENSION 3
EVIDENCE-BASED CLAIMS	Analyses of source material (statistical, narrative, visual, auditory, digital, primary, and secondary) using the disciplinary framework and methods of religious studies should form the bases for substantiating and justifying claims.
	DIMENSION 4
FORMS OF COMMUNICATION AND ACTION (illustrative examples)	Books and scholarly articles in peer-reviewed journals; newspaper and online op-ed pieces for either a targeted community or general readership; appearances on television and/or radio; websites and/or webinars; policy statements and reports for government bodies; research briefs; professional presentations to colleagues or major trade associations.

■ Haynes, C. C. and Thomas, O. (2011). *Finding Common Ground: A First Amendment Guide to Religion and Public Schools*. Nashville, TN: First Amendment Center.

■ Lester, E. (2011). *Teaching About Religions: A Democratic Approach for Public Schools*. Ann Arbor, MI: University of Michigan Press.

■ Lester, E. and Roberts, P.S. (2006). *Learning About World Religions in Public Schools: The Impact on Student Attitudes and Community Acceptance in Modesto, Calif.* Nashville, TN: First Amendment Center.

■ Marcus, B. (Forthcoming, 2018). In C.C. Haynes (Ed.), *Teaching About Religion in the Social Studies Classroom*. Silver Spring, MD: National Council for the Social Studies.

■ Moore, Diane L. (2007). *Overcoming Religious Illiteracy: A Cultural Studies Approach to Teaching About Religion in Secondary Education*. New York: Palgrave, 2007.

■ National Council for the Social Studies. (2014). *Study About Religions in the Social Studies Classroom: A Position Statement of the National Council for the Social Studies*. Silver Spring, MD: Author. Accessible at https://www.socialstudies.org/positions/study_about_religions

■ Nord, Warren. (2011). *Does God Make a Difference? Taking Religion Seriously an American Schools and Universities*. New York: Oxford University Press.

■ Prothero, S. (2007). *Religious Literacy: What Every American Needs To Know–And Doesn't*. New York, NY: HarperOne.

■ Waggoner, M. D. and Walker, N.C. (Eds.). (Forthcoming, 2017). *The Oxford Handbook of Religion and American Education*. New York: Oxford University Press.

NOTES

1. The writing team was composed of the following individuals (in alphabetical order): Jessica Blitzer, West Hartford Public Schools (CT); Seth Brady, Naperville Central High School (IL); John Camardella, Prospect High School (IL); Niki Clements, Rice University (TX); Susan Douglass, Georgetown University (DC); Benjamin P. Marcus, Newseum Institute (DC); Diane L. Moore, Harvard Divinity School (MA); and Nathan C. Walker, Teachers College Columbia University (NY).

2. *Abington School District v. Schempp*, 374 U.S. 203 (1963).

3. "Religion in the Public School Curriculum: Questions and Answers" was first published in 1988 and disseminated widely by NCSS and other sponsoring organizations. Downloadable at http://www.religiousfreedomcenter.org.

4. Susan L. Douglass, *Teaching about Religion in National and State Standards* (Fountain Valley, CA and Nashville, TN: Council on Islamic Education and First Amendment Center, 2000). Downloadable at http://www.religiousfreedomcenter.org.

5. Based on guidelines originally developed by James V. Panoch and published in 1974 by the Public Education Religion Studies Center at Wright State University. The guidelines quoted here are from the First Amendment Center's "A Teacher's Guide to Religion in the Public Schools," which may be found at http://www.religiousfreedomcenter.org/wp-content/uploads/2014/08/teachersguide.pdf. For all consensus guidelines on religion in public schools, see: Charles C. Haynes and Oliver Thomas, *Finding Common Ground: A First Amendment Guide to Religion and Public Schools* (Nashville, TN: First Amendment Center, 2011).

6. *Guidelines for Teaching About Religion in K-12 Public Schools in the United States* (Atlanta: AAR, 2010) p. 4. https://www.aarweb.org/sites/default/ files/pdfs/Publications/epublications/AARK-12CurriculumGuidelines.pdf. Diane L. Moore was Chair of the Task Force that produced these guidelines.

Index

C

F

G

H

T